YOUR
SONS & DAUGHTERS
SHALL PROPHESY

Dedicated to
David E. Schoch,
a true prophet of God,
a great mentor and a close friend to our family.
His dynamic ministry and gracious manner
have been felt around the world.

CONTENTS

Contents

TABLES

FOREWORD

I AM CONVINCED that one of God's chief springboards for taking the Church into the twenty-first century is the rapid emergence and broad acceptance of the ministry of prophets and apostles. During the decade of the 1980s prophets began to gain a recognition they had not previously enjoyed. The same thing happened to apostles during the decade of the 1990s.

This is extremely important. Up until now most churches have been attempting to function with a government of evangelists, pastors and teachers. Many churches have done well, but biblically it is clear that they cannot be all God wants them to be without prophets and apostles. The reason I say this is that I take a literal interpretation of Ephesians 4:11, which says that "[Jesus] Himself gave some to be apostles, some prophets, some evangelists, and some pastors and teachers" (NKJV). I must confess that for years I felt comfortable somehow drawing an artificial exegetical line between the first two offices on the list and the last three.

Ernest Gentile agrees with me. In fact, Ernest understood and practiced the biblical ministry of prophet long before I began to tune in to the fact that prophecy did not cease with the early Church. Of all those I know who are involved in active prophetic ministry, he would be considered among the most mature and experienced. I know of no one more qualified to write what I would describe as the first literal textbook on the subject.

Let me hasten to say that there is other excellent literature in the field. The book that helped me most to tune in to contemporary prophetic ministry was Bill Hamon's *Prophets and Personal Prophecy* (Destiny Image). My choice for the best book on how prophecy functions on the personal level would be Cindy Jacobs' *The Voice of God* (Regal). I would also mention Jack Deere's *Surprised by the Voice of God* (Zondervan) as a convincing argument against the cessationist notion that the gift of prophecy ceased with the apostolic age.

But none of those would qualify as a textbook covering the whole field. *Your Sons and Daughters Shall Prophesy* is one of a kind—a book that anyone who wants to be thoroughly informed about prophetic ministry today should read and digest. It is loaded with excellent research on biblical foundations, prophecy through Church history and the prophetic movement today.

The New Apostolic Reformation will be immensely helped by Ernest Gentile's book. As we move into the twenty-first century, leaders of apostolic movements everywhere will join me in thanking Ernest for his diligence, his wisdom, his discernment and his passion for the advancement of the Kingdom of God.

C. Peter Wagner, Chancellor
Wagner Leadership Institute

INTRODUCTION

THIS BOOK PROVIDES a biblical, practical understanding of the gift of prophecy and how it can build up today's Church and individual Christians. I will explore the scriptural background of prophecy as well as share personal observations, research, suggestions and firsthand accounts of my fifty-year participation in this charismatic work of the Spirit.

I use the word *charismatic* advisedly, since it is a favorite word of the apostle Paul when describing spiritual gifts or manifestations of the Holy Spirit. The word in our day is again becoming standard in the vocabulary of church operation. *Charismatic* is a term for the whole Church, not only for a movement within the Church, just as it was in the days of the first-century believers. In these days of spiritual renewal the charismatic dimension—the "grace gifts" of the Holy Spirit—help us receive and enjoy a new realization of God's presence among us.

With today's emphasis on the importance of the miraculous, however, the possibility of prophecy is experiencing serious concern.

The promise of prophecy in the Church was dramatically introduced by the apostle Peter in his unforgettable sermon in Acts 2. Peter, inspired by the Holy Spirit, explained the dynamic happenings on the Day of Pentecost by quoting the prophet Joel. The Jews frequently quoted these same verses with nostalgic longing for the coming messianic age. But Peter declared boldly that the wait was over, the day had arrived. "This is what was spoken by the prophet Joel," he said.

The title of this book comes from the third line of his quotation: "Your sons and your daughters shall prophesy" (Acts 2:17, NKJV). These words hang like a great banner over the Church age, giving vision and purpose to our mission. The era of the prophetic people of God had been launched!

God speaks to His people today in various ways; one of these is prophecy. A historic continuity links prophecy in Old Testament times, prophecy in the New Testament churches and prophetic ministry in contemporary

Christianity. Paul's admonition is timely for all Christians, both in the early Church and today: "Therefore, brethren, desire earnestly to prophesy . . ." (1 Corinthians 14:39, NKJV). This book is an attempt to explain, emphasize and bring to fulfillment this challenging admonition.

My desire is to appeal to all Christians, not just those called to prophetic ministry, and share principles that will help and encourage each one to a more vibrant life in the Spirit—and, in particular, to inspire a new appreciation in this generation for God's voice. Every reader will be encouraged to follow Paul's advice to "eagerly desire" prophecy (1 Corinthians 14:1, NIV).

Many serious Christians are frustrated by the absence of spiritual gifts in the Church and want to understand and participate in the gift of prophecy. I hope this book will help. I use a precept-on-precept approach in explaining prophetic history and ministry. We will consider the dangers of undisciplined prophecy but with a healthy view to correction, not elimination. I will not advocate naïveté or gullibility among church members, but present biblical proof that prophecy is truth for today, and call for balance in areas where prophecy has been mishandled, misrepresented or exploited. Prophecy is one of the most valuable and necessary gifts for the edification of the Church.

The books available on prophecy seem to be grouped mainly at the two ends of the spectrum. On the one hand, some informative monographs, such as doctoral dissertations and journal articles, present excellent research, but most Christians do not know this information even exists. On the other hand, books written in a popular, personal, subjective and exciting manner appeal to the general reading public. The first group deals for the most part with the past and does not promote contemporary prophecy. The second group, highly circulated, consists of the lighter-weight charismatic pamphlets, booklets and books that lack the scholar's depth but extend a happy biblical invitation for all Christians to enjoy this gift of God. Both groups have an important contribution to make.

My approach is different. I would like to bridge the gap between a scholarly approach and a popular presentation, taking issues that are academically important and making them intelligible to a wider audience, and at the same time making the biblical material practical and usable in our churches. Thus I have interspersed footnotes of renowned biblical scholars with those of charismatic pastors. Since my driving desire is to see prophecy reactivated and prospering in the Church, I seek balance between theoretical concepts and practical expression. This book is designed to hold the interest of the general reader and scholar alike.

Early Christian prophecy is a topic of wide range, and it would be impossible to cover it all in a study like this. I will concentrate on several aspects:

- An overview of prophecy in the Old Testament
- An appraisal of prophecy in the New Testament
- A brief look at prophecy in early and modern Church history
- Practical suggestions for implementing prophecy in today's churches

Real-life illustrations will bring clarification and make clear that prophecy for today is within everyone's grasp.

You will notice a section called "Reflections" at the end of each chapter with appropriate (usually sympathetic) quotations from popular writers, pastoral leaders and academic authors. Those quoted on a given page will not necessarily agree with my thesis for that chapter, but all of these authors (nearly one hundred of them) have a serious interest in the subject and valuable insights. You will find an amazing assortment of writers with a lot in common.

In ancient Hebrew times, selected individuals spoke forth the words of God to His people. Called prophets, these inspired men and women were spokespersons and messengers—forerunners of a coming era when all God's people would experience the prophetic Holy Spirit. Jesus came as a dramatic fulfillment of many predictions declared by those early vanguard prophets. He embodied the finest characteristics of every prophet who preceded Him while demonstrating amazing qualities and actions never before seen. Jesus walked among men and women as the supreme example of all things prophetic—in a real sense *the* Prophet of God.

When Jesus completed His earthly ministry, He returned to heaven and threw open the spiritual floodgates that would allow all nations and peoples to experience a wonderful new outpouring of the Spirit. Prophecy moved into the era of the Holy Spirit.

The Church was birthed amid a spectacular display of prophetic activity. Peter announced boldly that the grand happening of Pentecost was the fulfillment of Joel's prophecy. Continuing unabated during the time of the apostles and the writing of the New Testament, the voice of God caused the Church to flourish.

The apostles never taught that New Testament prophecy was just for their own generation. They believed fervently that this awesome manifestation held key importance in the life of the Church. Their clear intent: that prophecy continue as a vital function in the ongoing generations of the Church. This is the thesis of my book.

A worldwide resurgence of interest in contemporary, biblical prophecy is now taking place. This encourages me, for the prophetic experience belongs perpetually in Church life and its presence is a sign of spiritual health. The prophecy of the New Testament churches is lost only when it is neglected.

15

PART 1

THE IMPORTANCE OF PROPHECY

1

GOD'S THOUGHTS
TOWARD US

"As the heavens are higher than the earth, so are My ways higher than your ways, and My thoughts than your thoughts."

Isaiah 55:9

I LOUNGED WITH MY FAMILY on the sunny beach at Pajaro Dunes, California. Shifting my position in the warm sand, I noticed that some granules had stuck to my moist hand. Lightheartedly I decided to count those few grains of sand. I realized quickly, however, that my plan was a profound impossibility. I glanced at the miles of sand stretched out in both directions, with Santa Cruz Beach shining in the far distance. My beach, I suddenly perceived, was just one of thousands of beaches worldwide, each with its own boundless amount of sand.

I stared at my hand, overwhelmed by the spiritual thought now dawning in my mind. It was the marvelous statement of Psalm 139:17–18 (NIV): "How precious to me are your thoughts, O God! How vast is the sum of them! Were I to count them, they would outnumber the grains of sand. When I awake, I am still with you" (or, "You are still thinking of me!" LB).

The King James Version says God's thoughts are "unto" me, implying laser-beam action in my direction. Day or night God thinks of me! And these thoughts toward me are as innumerable as the sands of the sea. Even when I am not feeling good or filled with faith, His thoughts are in motion toward me. The following references give strong confirmation:

- "Many, O LORD my God, are . . . Thy thoughts toward us" (Psalm 40:5).
- "'I know the thoughts that I think toward you,' says the LORD, 'thoughts of peace and not of evil, to give you a future and a hope'" (Jeremiah 29:11, NKJV).
- "The eyes of the LORD are upon the righteous, and His ears attend to their prayer" (1 Peter 3:12).

God has shared His thoughts with humankind throughout history. He communicated with Israel and the early Church—and still has thoughts for His people today. Sometimes the Lord spoke audibly, sent angelic messengers, gave dreams and visions, used prophets, utilized catastrophes, even whispered quietly to the inner spirit of the human being. In less dramatic but equally important ways today, we also have the clear teachings of the Bible, impressions received in serious prayer, the obvious directions given through everyday circumstances and the wise advice of godly counselors. All these wonderful vehicles are used by God to speak His thoughts into our lives.

This brings us to the main theme of this book: prophecy. Prophecy is a key way God has spoken to His people in both ancient and modern times. Hebrews 1:1, referring to the Hebrew period, says that God "at various times and in various ways spoke in time past to the fathers by the prophets . . ." (NKJV). In the Christian era Paul heartily endorsed prophecy to the churches: "Therefore, my brethren, desire earnestly to prophesy . . ." (1 Corinthians 14:39).

Prophecy, in simple terms, is the verbalized expression of God's thoughts through a Spirit-inspired person "to a particular person or group of persons, at a particular moment, for a particular purpose."[1] To some people *prophecy* evokes the mental picture of skin-clad, destitute, thundering Old Testament prophets who either "forth-tell" (proclaim the divine will) or "fore-tell" (predict future events). This depiction is partially true, but it tends to override the simple beauty of the New Testament prophetic experience that can be enjoyed by the people of a local church in our day.

This book will clearly present the similarities and differences between Old and New Testament prophets, as well as the prophetic possibilities now available to the entire family of Spirit-filled believers who make up today's local New Testament Church. I hope the teaching will establish the credibility of prophecy for many biblically orthodox Christians who are not presently enjoying this avenue of divine edification.

Refinements will be made later, but my introductory thought is simple and foundational: God is beaming His thoughts down on His people. Explained simply, prophecy occurs when a prophetically inspired person extends his or her faith like a spiritual antenna, receives some divine thoughts of God for that given moment and then speaks them forth by the power of the Holy Spirit to an individual or group for the glory of God.

Psalm 139, the chapter that tells us of God's thoughts toward us, could be titled "I Am Important to God." Three descriptive paragraphs state brilliantly how the greatness of God is focused on each individual life:

- *Omniscience* (He knows all), verses 1–6: God is constantly aware of everything I do.
- *Omnipresence* (He is everywhere), verses 7–12: God is wherever I go, so there is no possibility I will escape His scrutiny.
- *Omnipotence* (He has all power), verses 13–16: God created me (the psalmist uses seven descriptive words) and knows every detail of my biological construction and development.

Sharing His Thoughts

It was a hot Sunday morning and I was about to stand up and preach the morning message in a native church in Nigeria. The women and girls were seated on one side of the church and the men and boys on the other side. They all sang joyfully to the Lord. I was agonizing mentally over my prepared message, for I sensed that God wanted me to change the message to "The Lord's Prayer." Although I have spoken often on that famous prayer, this time there was an inner spiritual urging taking place.

I had observed the poverty of the people—the graceful, tired women balancing great stalks of bananas on their heads as they walked to market in the early morning; the men eking out a bare existence in various kinds of drudgeries. As I waited to preach, I felt an unusual prophetic insight of the Spirit. I became acutely aware, as is possible only through spiritual revelation, that even the most destitute and forsaken person can find God's care extending to him if he will believe.

As I began the message, I made the mistake of starting with my prepared thoughts. The almost total disinterest of the people was painfully obvious. So I shifted to the prophetic insight—the thoughts God had for the people. Their attention turned on immediately, and I could not help noticing that the ushers, with their long sticks to prod sleepers and talkers, were no longer busy. What was happening? God was sharing some of His thoughts through His servant and the people were hearing it joyfully.

21

I have never forgotten that prophetic preaching experience, for I felt lifted out of myself—enabled to blend with the thoughts of God and feel the needs of the people. I experienced both the joyful confidence of the Lord and the despairing souls of the people seeking help. I had an unction from God.

Many of us who minister have experienced this prophetic touch on our preaching, and from time to time we should expect it. Perhaps this is why some feel that preaching and prophecy are actually the same, as some of the modern translations portray it.

On the other hand, I contend (here and throughout the book) that we should also expect actual prophecy—that is, direct statements of God's immediate thoughts for a given situation and people, delivered under the impetus of the Holy Spirit. The prophetic anointing brings an electrifying, edifying effect not achievable with ordinary preaching and teaching.

Prophecy comes as a "now word," the present expression of a contemporary God who is truly present and concerned. The truths and principles of the Scripture suddenly focus on a specific audience at a specific place at a specific time. This was brought home to me when a teenage girl told me after a prophetic service in her Oklahoma City church, "Although I've gone to church, I never realized before that God was really that interested in me." The members of a large Sunday school class were also affected strongly by prophecy during a special retreat: "They realized God intimately knew them. It was redemptive, life-bringing and freeing. The details prayed were just what they needed to hear."[2]

Prophecy is not meant to replace or supersede the Bible, but when used properly it does make Bible truths more relatable by awakening people to realize God is interested in them, both now and in their future.

"Thou God Seest Me"

The following account recalls the story of a message of God delivered by an angel. During that patriarchal time God's message was usually delivered by heavenly messengers (that is, angels)[3] rather than by human prophets. The angels became the prototype for the prophets yet to come in the times of Moses and Samuel. The anecdote illustrates the impact of God's voice on people, and therefore serves to introduce the nature of prophecy, using the first appearance of the angel of the Lord in the Bible. Prophecy, the voice of God in a given situation, had the same effect in churches of Bible days—and still does today.

God dispatched a startling message to a distraught Bedouin woman. The Egyptian Hagar, servant to Abram's wife, Sarai, had been made the surrogate parent to supply the aging couple with an offspring. Now pregnant with Abram's child, "she became very proud and arrogant toward her mistress" (Genesis 16:4, LB). Harshly rejected, the frightened, beaten Hagar fled to the wilderness, where the angel of the Lord found her by a spring of water. To her the heavenly thoughts must have glistened like a string of prophetic pearls:

- She must return to Sarai.
- God will multiply her seed.
- She is bearing a man-child.
- She will call him Ishmael ("God hears").
- The boy will have the roving spirit of the Arab.
- He will maintain his independence while becoming a mighty nation.

Overwhelmed, Hagar burst forth in thankfulness to God, coining a name to match her inspired thoughts: "Thou God seest me" (verse 13, KJV) or "You-Are-the-God-Who-Sees" (NKJV). She also named the well "The well of the living one who sees me" (verse 14, marginal note).

Fourteen years after Ishmael was born, Sarah miraculously conceived and bore her own son, joyfully calling him Isaac ("Laughter"). Later, infuriated by Hagar's taunting teenager, Sarah had Hagar and the boy driven from the camp (Genesis 21:9–10). The helpless vagabonds wandered in the wilderness of Beersheba. This time Hagar found no water, and she and her son despaired of life—until the angel reappeared. As he spoke, Hagar's eyes fell on a well of refreshing water.

The narration ends abruptly at this point, but God's prophetic destiny for the woman and boy had only begun. Starting with only a bow and arrow and the promise of God, Ishmael grew and prospered in the wilderness under the blessing of the Lord. He died at the age of 137, having fathered twelve princes, each of whom had his own tribe (Genesis 25:12–18). The thoughts of God found dramatic fulfillment! In the voice of God were life and hope.

When the prophetic word came in ancient Israel or in the New Testament Church, it also produced life and hope. Ezekiel describes how Israel's boneyard was transformed by the prophetic word into a mighty army of living men (Ezekiel 37). And the prophetic activity within the Corinthian church provoked men to declare, "God is certainly among you" (1 Corinthians 14:25).

We, too, need to hear the inspired, living words of God declared in our congregational meetings. Such prophecy does not replace the Bible or any of the great historic doctrines of the Church. It is not meant to overwhelm the congregational life of a church. But prophecy must not be neglected, for it is itself a great pillar in the temple of God. Surely there can be no question that today's Church needs to hear God's present thoughts of comfort, edification and exhortation.

REFLECTIONS

When we remember that God thought upon us from old eternity, continues to think upon us every moment, and will think of us when time shall be no more, we may well exclaim, "How great is the sum!" Thoughts . . . are evermore flowing from the heart of the Lord. Thoughts of our pardon, renewal, upholding, supplying, educating, perfecting, and a thousand more kinds perpetually well up in the mind of the Most High.[4]

Charles H. Spurgeon

God has an intense desire to speak to his people. . . . If you do not believe that God is willing to speak to us, then you do not understand God.[5]

Bruce Yocum

When we prophesy, we are proclaiming the thoughts of God to a gathering of believers for the present moment. Prophecy is a forth-telling of the thoughts of God to you right now. . . . Through prophecy God articulates His feelings toward us, His plan for us, His comfort for present distress, and the changes that need to be implemented in order to align ourselves with His will.[6]

Dick Stark

Prophecy verbalizes God's good thoughts. . . . When the reality of this grips us in the depths of our souls, we experience a deep inner response of trust and openness to the Lord.[7]

Glenn Foster

How does God accomplish His prophetic word? It begins with just a thought. God thinks about something. . . . If you could have just a glimpse of what God thinks about you, you would become a new person. His esteem for you is greater than you have for yourself.[8]

Kim Clement

INCREASED INTEREST IN PROPHECY

A lion has roared! Who will not fear? The LORD GOD has spoken! Who can but prophesy?

Amos 3:8

A REMARKABLE COVER and lead story appeared in the January 14, 1991, issue of *Christianity Today*. Caricatured on the front cover in striking pose, an acclaimed modern prophet stands on a jagged rock overlooking a city. The wind whips his tie and flowing cape as he stretches forth his left hand dramatically while grasping a Moses-like walking staff firmly in the other. The caption proclaims, *Seers in the Heartland*.[1]

In his opening page announcement of the lead article, managing editor David Neff says: "If, in the 1960s, you had said someone had 'a prophetic ministry,' you would have probably meant that person offered a radical social critique—and had an abrasive personality, long hair, and love beads. Say 'prophetic ministry' today, and people will think you mean someone speaks a word from God."

We live in a time when people desire—and desperately need—to hear from God. It is natural, therefore, that Bible-believing Christians are looking seriously at the gift of prophecy and the ministry of prophets. Is this ministry available and valid? The inquiry is legitimate since prophetism runs throughout the Bible.

The underlying, basic question is this: *How does God speak to His people?* Christians hear God's voice through His written Word, the Bible. God also uses counselors, circumstances, impressions, answered prayer, even human conscience. Most Christians experience such guidance at one time or another. In Bible days prophecy stood as probably the most usual way of hearing God's voice. Prophets and prophecy were an important part of God's Old Testament agenda as well as of Christ's agenda for the early Church.

A refreshing contemporary realization of this ancient biblical practice is now taking place, with many churches discovering that prophecy can be a wonderful and meaningful enhancement of today's Church life.

In both New Testament times and in the contemporary Church, *prophecy* refers to an inspired spoken message that God brings to a person or a group of people through a Spirit-filled Christian. The spokesperson is empowered spiritually to declare to a given audience words that have been imparted by divine revelation. This is a supernatural or miraculous happening—a divine communiqué!

The fact that leading magazines and journals carry articles on this subject, and that popular writers devote time to the subject, indicates a continuing concern and curiosity by Christian readers.[2] As one religious analyst puts it, "Currently there is a fashionable interest in prophecy."[3] This new (or is it just updated?) attitude is reflected in the more than three dozen contemporary books on spiritual gifts in my library—a mere sampling of the total literature available.

Coming from a wide range of denominational backgrounds, many of these modern authors believe that the phenomenon called prophecy exists in today's Church. Well-written and thought-provoking books from unexpected sources and publishers challenge traditional assumptions about the need for and importance of prophecy in today's Church.[4] Some feel so strongly about the prophetic renewal that they declare the Church is in an authentic "prophetic movement" today.[5] F. F. Bruce summarizes the situation well: "The prophetic ministry probably receives greater recognition in today's Church than it has enjoyed for a long time."[6]

The academic community also has experienced a heightened interest in prophecy. Reputable scholars have produced more than a dozen significant books during the past twenty years.[7] In addition, a great deal of in-depth, specialized material on prophecy is found in the monographs of the rather exclusive journals produced by theological seminaries, Bible societies and publishing houses. More than one hundred of these scholarly articles contain insights of interest here.[8]

26

Charismatic circles also have generated a flurry of writings about the prophetic. More than two dozen of these books and pamphlets, some academic and others geared for popular reading, are currently available. All advocate the prophetic ministry in today's Church.

In past years the discussion of spiritual gifts has sparked controversy among Bible scholars and Church leaders, especially over *glossolalia* or speaking in tongues. The focus today has made a surprising shift from speaking in tongues to the gift of prophecy. Two general positions emerge: the *continuance* school, which affirms that prophecy and spiritual gifts continue today, and the *cessationist* school, which denies that prophecy and gifts continued beyond the early Church.

A climate of intense interest in prophetism now exists because of this confluence of mounting popular attention, spiritual activity, scholarly debate and increasing prominence of various books. Wise counsel is given by John W. Hilber: "The issue is not purely academic but is a matter of serious pastoral concern."[9]

Interest in prophecy is not new. Church leaders always have faced the challenge of reconciling the blessed and often unpredictable breath of the Holy Spirit with the Church's secure, nailed-down traditions and standards. In fact, all the movements within Christendom can be seen from the perspective of the spirit of prophecy versus institutional order.[10]

An unrestrained spirit of prophecy always poses a danger of fanaticism and exclusivism. In contrast, dead institutionalism poses the ever-present danger of stifling the breath of God's Spirit. Let us seek the balance that will join the strength of the institution (unity, order and stability) to the dynamic of the prophetic (freshness, spontaneity and life). These two forces become a workable team when the approach is changed from "prophecy versus order" to the positive idea of "prophecy *and* order."

A belief in continuing revelation (i.e., God does speak today as well as yesterday) and the validity of prophecy in today's Church need not frustrate us. A harmonious and healthful tension can exist between:

- Biblical teaching;
- Popular/contemporary need;
- Scholarly/academic insights;
- Pastoral/practical concerns.

The Church needs balance rather than polarization! It will prove detrimental to gravitate toward just emotional experience or intellectual ivory towers or programmed efficiency . . . or to an incomplete biblical position.

Differing Viewpoints

A statement of four modern-day approaches to prophecy will help our discussion. My abbreviated summaries naturally reflect my own opinion (#4), but I am grateful for the worthwhile contributions each view has made to the total picture of prophecy in the Church.

1. The Form Critical School and the "I Sayings" of Jesus

This approach, espoused by some form critics of the New Testament, is hardly known outside of scholarly circles, but it has made a significant impact on the discussion of prophecy and the training of ministers.

This theory proposes that Jesus is both the Jesus of history as well as the living Lord in heaven. As the historical Jesus who walked on earth, He did give teaching, some of which was remembered and recorded. As the Lord in heaven, He possibly spoke through Christian prophets present in the early Church *prior* to the writing of the gospels. These prophets received and uttered words from the risen Jesus to the congregations. These sayings were then recorded as authentic sayings of the risen Jesus and incorporated into the Church's written tradition of the recorded sayings of the historical Jesus—even though He actually did not say them while physically on earth.[11] Whether or not these prophetic words were really the words of Jesus (or considered to be) is of little consequence, so they say, because they at least reflected the ideas of the early Christians.

Even scholars promoting this viewpoint admit the lack of conclusive evidence, and a number of New Testament scholars remain unpersuaded.[12] I cannot imagine that the integrity of the early Church leaders would have allowed them to mix the actual remembered, recorded sayings of Jesus with spontaneous, prophetic utterances given in the Church, and then record them all as the true account of Jesus' earthly ministry! I appreciate the serious effort expended to explain the Bible and the mystery of prophecy, but take strong exception to any effort to force the Bible into an anti-supernatural mode.

Bultmann and other liberal German theologians carried this approach to the extreme as they "demythologized" the New Testament, while at the same time using this theory of prophecy to explain the creativity of early Church beliefs. Recorded miracles became merely symbolic stories, and the utterances of "inspired" prophets became statements by Jesus.[13] Unfortunately many ministers have been trained in this approach during seminary studies, which has affected their view of prophecy and how they present the subject to their people.

The task of the early Church prophets was not to create words on a par with the original historical sayings of Jesus, but rather to speak contemporary application of spiritual principles for current situations. I must conclude that insufficient evidence, unprovable theories and an unfortunate lack of understanding of the true nature of the gift of prophecy in the early Church render this a most implausible theory.[14]

2. The Cessationist Approach

This view holds that biblical prophecy in both Testaments became the written biblical record called the Bible. The gift of prophecy made the writing of Scripture an inerrant experience so that the words of the original copies were completely accurate. There may have been, they say, some prophecy for domestic situations for a short while, but it was without error, for the message came in unmistakable clarity.

F. David Farnell, a leading advocate, says: "Current novel attempts at defining prophecy impugn the miraculous nature of New Testament prophecy. . . . The gift of prophecy played a vital role in the foundational aspects of the Church. With the Church firmly established through the ministry of the first-century apostles and New Testament prophets, prophecy passed from the scene."[15]

Cessationists are to be commended for their fervency in protecting the integrity and inspiration of the Bible. God's Word is certainly clear that the Spirit of prophecy did inspire the giving of Scripture. Unfortunately, no acknowledgment is given by cessationists that prophecy could be used in any other way. They make no recognition of other operations of the prophetic anointing (non-Scripture prophecy) that occurred in both Old and New Testaments.[16]

This viewpoint also neglects a most significant reference, Revelation 19:10: "He said unto me, See thou do it not: I am thy fellow servant, and of thy brethren that have the testimony of Jesus: worship God: for the testimony of Jesus is the spirit of prophecy" (KJV). If prophecy was to cease after the scriptural canon was established, would this not mean the cessation of Jesus' voice (through the Spirit) in the Church?

Although the Greek text supports either "the witness *about* Jesus" or "the witness *by* Jesus,"[17] it seems likely that this text equates prophecy in the Church with Jesus' voice. Jesus' own testimony is maintained in and through His Spirit-filled, prophetic people. We could say, then, that Jesus speaks to the local church not only through the Bible but also through inspired prophecy. I agree with Rick Joyner's comment on this verse: "All true prophecy is His testimony. It comes from Him and draws us to Him. It is what He is saying to His church."[18]

Revelation 19:10 is complemented by Revelation 22:6, which shows clearly that God controls the inspiration of the prophets: "He said to me, 'These words are faithful and true'; and the Lord, the God of the spirits of the prophets, sent His angel to show to His bond-servants the things which must shortly take place. . . ."

The God who is to be worshiped initiates in the hearts of His people the desire to worship Him. As the Church worships, the Person of Jesus is testified to among them (Hebrews 2:12), and they in turn are imbued with the spirit of prophecy. The Church thereby preserves Jesus' own present salvation testimony, which brings current application to His recorded words.

3. A Mediated Approach

The viewpoint of Wayne Grudem gained widespread acclaim through the 1988 publication of his book, *The Gift of Prophecy in the New Testament and Today.*[19] Espoused by the Vineyard and other "Third Wave" groups, this approach attempts to mediate a middle-of-the-road position between the cessationist stand and an extreme charismatic position that accepts contemporary prophecy as fully authoritative. His critics say Grudem "has stirred up a hornets' nest of discussion on the gifts."[20] A Bible scholar with impeccable credentials and a heart for the Church, Grudem affirms that prophecy does continue, but he argues that two forms of New Testament prophecy coexisted: *congregational prophecy,* in which people shared the thoughts that God brought to their minds; and *apostolic prophecy,* as the words written in the New Testament. Grudem considers the first nonauthoritative and the second authoritative.

Some feel that the questions raised by this modified approach to prophecy "threaten to become, if they have not done so already, a major storm center in New Testament theology and church worship."[21] Grudem explains his modification: "I am asking that charismatics go on using the gift of prophecy, but that they stop calling it 'a word from the Lord'— simply because that label makes it sound exactly like the Bible in authority, and leads to much misunderstanding. . . . On the other side, I am asking those in the cessationist camp to give serious thought to the possibility that prophecy in ordinary New Testament churches was not equal to Scripture in authority, but was simply a very human—and sometimes partially mistaken—report of something the Holy Spirit brought to someone's mind."[22]

This, I think, is a significant insight. I do not fully agree but am truly grateful for this breakthrough book that has raised prophetic consciousness throughout the Church world. My problem lies in Grudem's continuing attempt to define the "authority" of the prophecy of that day (and the associated "authority" of women in the Church). The questions raised by those with strong "canonical consciousness"[23] seem to hold little or no interest for Paul and the early Church; they apparently operated from a different frame of reference, showing no concern for some of our present-day prophetic discussions. It is true that the contemporary Church has unique problems that must be addressed, but I still feel safer following Paul's unaffected leadership in this.

Paul refers to only two kinds of prophets: those whose oracles are part of the Bible, and the prophets in the Church. He and all the other writers of the New Testament treat the prophets of that day as though they are in historic continuity with the prophets of the Old Testament, even if they are not writing Scripture. Since the Scriptures are our authority in the matter, we must rely on Paul's attitude and approach, even if we moderns might wish for more apostolic explanation.

Gordon Fee, in his significant discussion of the Holy Spirit in the letters of Paul, gives this evaluation: "[Paul] undoubtedly saw the 'New Testament prophets' as in the succession of the 'legitimate' prophets of the Old Testament, which explains in part why all such prophecy must be 'discerned,' just as with those in the Old Testament. But the nature of the prophecy was also understood to be of a different kind, precisely because of their present eschatological existence. A prophet who speaks encouragement to the Church in its 'between the times' existence speaks a different kind of word from the predominant word of judgment on ancient Israel."[24]

I personally am reluctant to discontinue referring to authentic contemporary prophecy as "a word from God." My reason is simple: The Bible's straightforward teaching gives us no reason to discontinue the practice, and there have been too many accurate, proven prophecies in the contemporary Church. Perhaps the Church should use Bible terminology without shame—but also consistently (and publicly) evaluate prophetic words and people without fear. Why not contend for one hundred percent accuracy in our local church prophecies and still not consider such recognition demeaning or threatening to the universal Word of God?[25]

Grudem's description of nonauthoritative congregational prophecy is similar to Rick Joyner's "lowest level of prophetic revelation." Joyner writes: "Most of what is called 'prophecy' today is on the lowest level of prophetic revelation, which is the impression level. These are general revelations that *we* have to put words to. Personally, I do not add the addendum 'thus saith the Lord' to what is in fact an impression that I have expressed in my own words. The word of the Lord is precious, and the last thing I want to do is put my words in His mouth. . . . In fact, it is debatable whether we *ever* need to include such a statement in our prophecies today. . . . We might be trusted with far more authority and higher levels of revelation if we start calling impressions just what they are, and do not so freely misuse those precious words 'thus saith the Lord.'"[26]

4. The Historic Continuity Approach

Prophecy given by the Holy Spirit in Old Testament times continued into the early Church and now extends into the contemporary Church. The early Christians felt themselves to be a prophetic people in historic continuity with the prophecy and prophets of the Old Testament. There is not the slightest hint of disagreement with this thought in the New Testament. Also, the clear tenor of the New Testament is that this supernatural activity was meant to continue throughout the Church age. My term *historic continuity* refers to the conviction that the voice of God is heard among His people on a continuing basis.

Prophecy in biblical times existed on two levels, both of which I feel may be called "inspired." I would suggest that the Word of God came as:

- *God-breathed words, such as the prophecy that was inscripturated into the Bible.* When God spoke in this manner He bypassed human frailties. Sometimes the prophet himself did not understand the words he gave. Scripture words were inerrant in the original and are God-spoken without possibility of error or need of evaluation. A God-breathed word is literally God's unquestioned and eternal Word (see my chapter 5). Such prophecy no longer comes since the canon of Scripture is complete.

- *Spirit-quickened words, which may be one hundred percent accurate yet are not placed on a par with Scripture.* Such words are inspired by the Spirit and use human frailties, but they are not God-breathed words. This is the prophecy that was in the Corinthian church and is in numbers of churches today. It is indeed a word from the Lord for the encouragement of a given audience at a given place at a given time, but it must be tested and approved by the congregation. Paul considered the Spirit-quickened prophecies of the Tyrean believers, for instance, to be a word of God (Acts 21:4), and the unbelievers visiting the Corinthian church meetings accepted contemporary prophecy as authentically from God (1 Corinthians 14). Such prophecy is to be judged for reasonable accuracy (see chapters 20 and 21).

Prophets in both Old and New Testament times uttered prophecies to audiences about domestic issues that were authoritative for those given situations, yet were not put on a par with Scripture or deemed universally significant for inclusion in the Bible. Also note that provision was made in both Testaments to test prophecy, indicating that the possibility of one hundred percent accuracy has always been present—but so has the possibility of partial or total inaccuracy.[27] Prophecy for domestic situations is *not* considered competition with the prophecy that produced the Bible. Such common prophecy, this viewpoint advocates, can exist today and is an integral part of a church flowing in continuity with the historic past.

Common prophecy, called by some a "now word" or a "*rhema* word" or "a word from the Lord," is not considered to be on the same level with the esteemed, written, recorded *Logos* Word of God. Both the New Testament and historical evidence indicate that such commonplace, domestic, community prophecy among trained, spiritual churches can be, and usually is, highly accurate and most assuredly a "word from God."

This last approach to prophecy is the one I am pursuing in this book.

Key Questions

This study will address the following questions as we proceed:

- Where did prophecy originate? How did the ancient Hebrew prophets function?
- What does the New Testament teach about prophecy? Is it the same as Old Testament prophecy?
- Is New Testament prophecy similar to, or the same as, or different in kind to, contemporary prophecy? Can there be authentic prophecy today?
- Should today's local church expect the kind of prophecy in her services that was experienced by the New Testament churches of Bible days?
- How can such a ministry of the Holy Spirit be encouraged and safeguarded in our churches so that fanaticism will not occur?

This study of prophetism works with three periods that overlap somewhat: Hebrew prophecy, New Testament prophecy and modern-day prophecy. We will find that the essential substance of prophecy—God's voice to mankind—remains unchanged, even though the subject matter, the audience and other details change. In that sense there is historical continuity.

Hebrew prophecy need not be tightly confined to its own time zone, for prophetic activity spills over into the Church age. In chapter 9 we will carefully compare and clarify the differences between the use of prophecy in Old and New Testament times. But for now I want to emphasize that prophecy in Christian churches is part of a great, continuing biblical tradition.

It would be a gargantuan task to analyze prophecy and prophets throughout Church history—certainly beyond the scope of this present effort. Examples of authentic prophecy are scattered throughout the entire Church age. But, like other spiritual gifts, prophecy has not always been an important item on the agenda of the Church. Often the reporting of the exercise of this gift was biased; thus it is difficult to evaluate.[28] Some periods of Church history are like the four hundred silent years between the Old and New Testaments when the prophetic voice in Israel appears to have been stilled.

We will not take time here to compare Hebrew and Christian prophecy with that of the ancient Near Eastern religions or the Greco-Roman culture. This work is done very credibly elsewhere.[29] Prophecy during the post-apostolic period (A.D. 90–325) will be only referred to since it is covered so well by Ronald A. N. Kydd.[30] Part 5 will analyze some significant prophetic movements in modern Church history (A.D. 1830–1980), with which I have more personal acquaintance, and which supply us with valuable insights and cautions. I acknowledge regretfully that I am leaving many years in the Church age undiscussed but trust that enough will be said in the space available to establish my thesis: the reality of and need for prophecy in our day.

The next chapter will open Part 2, "A Profile of the Ancient Hebrew Prophet." It seems appropriate to commence our study with the beginnings of biblical prophecy, then proceed later into the New Testament and end the book with practical suggestions for prophecy in today's churches.

REFLECTIONS

We live in a time when prophecy is becoming more and more recognized throughout the Body of Christ. The argument that God does not speak outside of the Bible may well belong on some "endangered doctrine" list. The best I can calculate, the resurgence of biblical prophecy and the prophetic movement began around 1980 and has been picking up speed ever since.[31]

C. Peter Wagner

In both the church and the world, there is a new hunger for the prophetic. This hunger stems from an increasing desire for guidance in order to survive the rampant confusion of our times. . . . Another reason . . . is because prophetic ministries and gifts of true biblical stature are being restored to the church today.[32]

Rick Joyner

If we are to see the gift of prophecy functioning in our churches today, we must first believe that it is possible that God would give us such "revelations" from time to time, and, second, we must allow ourselves to be receptive to such influences from the Holy Spirit, especially at times of prayer and worship.[33]

Wayne Grudem

Throughout the last two years [written in 1992], many Christians have been exposed to prophetic ministry for the first time. Prophecy is part of the ministry of the end-time church. In fact, Paul says the gift of prophecy should be cherished in the body of Christ.[34]

Jamie Buckingham

PART 2

A PROFILE
OF THE ANCIENT
HEBREW PROPHET

MISSION: WHAT WAS
A PROPHET?

The LORD *sent a prophet to the sons of Israel, and he said to them,*
"Thus says the LORD, *the God of Israel. . . ."*

Judges 6:8

WONDERFUL STORIES ABOUT STRANGE and mystical people called "prophets" appear throughout the ancient Hebrew Scriptures. One amazing episode involves Ahab, king of Israel, and a rough-hewn prophet called simply Elijah the Tishbite. The account will prepare our minds for a definitive discussion of what a prophet in Israel was and did.

King Ahab and Jezebel, his queen, apparently had a summer palace in Jezreel—a favorite place of retreat. Today's landscape affords no adequate idea of the bountiful beauty of the area that existed in those ancient times. Alfred Edersheim, noted Bible historian, describes the scene:

> Then the mountains of Gilboa were richly wooded, and sweet springs brought freshness to the air and luxurious beauty to the vegetation of Jezreel, even as they carried fertility down into the great plain beneath, which in the summer light shimmered and trembled like a sea of golden corn. At the northern declivity of Gilboa, where it descends, steep and rocky, on a knoll

about 500 feet high, stood Jezreel. Protected from the fierce southern sun by the delicious shade of Gilboa, that rises up behind, it looked—as suited to a summer residence in the East—northwards, across the plain to the mountains of Galilee, to Tabor, and in the distance to snow-capped Hermon. The height descended into the valley of Jezreel, where a sweet spring rippled, and close by gathered into a pool. Eastwards, you would look down on Bethshan, and, across the deep depression of the Jordan valley, to the mountains on the other side, on which rested the blue and purple light. To the west you might sweep those fifteen miles to Mount Carmel, and perchance the westerly breeze might carry up the plain the fresh scent of the sea. Such was the Jezreel of Ahab and Jezebel—the nearest, the safest, the sweetest summer retreat from Samaria.[1]

Since the royal summer palace was somewhat cramped, an adjoining piece of property seemed an ideal acquisition for conversion into a restful terraced garden. But there was a problem. Naboth, the righteous man who owned the desired piece of land, stubbornly refused every overture of the king, maintaining that he must not desecrate his family's inheritance. Jezebel acted quickly, rescuing her brooding husband from his misery by having Naboth "legally" dispatched (a judicial murder). On hearing the good news, Ahab arose joyfully to take possession of the coveted vineyard.

On that ominous day the Lord God commissioned one of His messenger boys to deliver a dispatch of terrifying news to the unsuspecting king. As Ahab surveyed his new acquisition with great satisfaction, an awesome figure rose suddenly before him. These two had met before— once when the prophet had announced a three-year drought and, more recently, when fire fell from heaven on Mt. Carmel. Now, clothed in a rough cloak of black camel's hair and a leather girdle, Elijah stood with burning eyes before the weak-kneed king. Ahab asked, "Have you found me, O my enemy?" Elijah answered, "I have found you, because you have sold yourself to do evil in the sight of the LORD" (1 Kings 21:20).

Without hesitation or compromise the prophet delivered the message of doom to the king and his wife—a detailed prediction of how the evil two would meet their untimely deaths. The astounding prediction later came to pass in graphic detail, just as Elijah, the servant of God, said it would.

Elijah acted simply as a spokesman, a mouthpiece for the Lord, his God. He was an ambassador for heaven's great Court. Given a message, he delivered it. That was the bottom line of his job description as a prophet: He was one who spoke on behalf of God. As Cecil M. Robeck Jr. points out: "The one who prophesies is not the inventor . . . merely the conveyer of the message. . . . There is no confusion between the person who speaks the message and the person whose message is spoken."[2]

Two good examples from modern politics illustrate this concept. First, the press secretary of the President of the United States. This person conveys the President's opinions, reactions, intentions and, when necessary, his very words. Often the secretary will read the message of his superior so there is no danger of mistake. When the press secretary holds a news conference, everyone expects and believes that this spokesperson will never give his own opinions. He is to express only what the President wants him to speak. This is also true of God and His prophets.

Another clear illustration is found in any country's ambassadors to foreign nations. The ambassador has been appointed to convey the official decisions, reactions and opinions of his government to the government of the other nation. The agenda is not of his own making; he represents another, a power bigger than himself. "The prophet," says Charles A. Briggs, "is an officer of the Deity, with a commission from the God whom he serves."[3]

More than fifty years ago H. Wheeler Robinson wrote a journal article of particular insight. The prophet, he said, received his message from "the intimate council of the Lord." This thought is summarized in a later article. "The true prophets," Robinson wrote, "stood in the intimate council of the Lord where they received his word, his direction for the situation at hand. . . . Admission to the intimate council of the Lord meant special acquaintance with the will, purpose, and plans of the Eternal, which the prophet-observer, by virtue of his position, must declare to God's people. He was summoned by the Lord to announce the decisions of the council."[4]

Jeremiah castigated the false prophets because they had not stood in the intimate council (or *sod*) of the Lord and had not seen or heard His word. "If they had stood in my intimate council," he laments, "they would have heard my words and would have turned my people from their evil ways and from their evil deeds" (Jeremiah 23:22, Myers' and Freed's paraphrase).

Robinson's thought is developed by another scholar, who takes it to a remarkable conclusion. A. R. Johnson writes: "The true prophet, then, was the Messenger (mal'ak) of Yahweh; he was a member of His intimate council. Moreover . . . the prophet, in functioning, was held to be *more than Yahweh's 'representative'; for the time being he was an active 'Extension' of Yahweh's Personality and, as such, was Yahweh—'in Person'"* (emphasis added).[5]

Spokesman, Seer, Visionary

A prophet was clearly a spokesman for God, but is it possible to amplify this definition from the original Hebrew word itself? Unfortunately the word *prophet* has no neatly stated definition, either in the Bible or in the Hebrew lexicons.

Three key Hebrew terms describe the Hebrew "prophet"—*roeh, hozeh* and *nabi.* The first two words both mean "to see" and are usually translated as "seer" in the English Bible. Together they appear, in one form or another, fewer than thirty times, and neither term appears before the book of 1 Samuel. The noun *nabi,* by contrast, is translated "prophet" and is the basic and most common term, appearing more than three hundred times, and the related verb more than one hundred times.

Three Key Hebrew Terms for *Prophet*

Hebrew Words	*roeh*	*hozeh*	*nabi*
Usually translated	*seer*	*seer*	*prophet*
Number of appearances	3 men so called: Samuel, Zadok and Hanani	6 men so called (3 men are called both *hozeh* and *nabi*)	As a noun, 300+ times; as a verb, 100+
Basic meaning	A seer; one given insight into the past, present and future	A visionary or gazer; one who receives a message in a vision; a beholder	An authorized spokesperson (for God), a messenger
Distinction	Emphasized the subjective element—i.e., the mode of receiving divine revelation by "seeing"; receiving insight from God		Stressed the objective or active work of the messenger of the LORD
Emphasis	Relation to God		Relation to people
	Reception of the message		*Declaring the message*

Nine men are specifically called "seer" in our English Bibles. Only three have the term *roeh* applied to them in the Hebrew text: Samuel, Zadok and Hanani (references follow). The rest are given the term *hozeh.*

1. Amos (Amos 7:12)
2. Asaph (2 Chronicles 29:30)

3. Gad (2 Samuel 24:11; 1 Chronicles 21:9; 29:29; 2 Chronicles 29:25)
4. Hanani (2 Chronicles 16:7, 10; 19:2)
5. Heman (1 Chronicles 25:5)
6. Iddo (2 Chronicles 9:29; 12:15)
7. Jeduthun (2 Chronicles 35:15)
8. Samuel (1 Samuel 9:19; 1 Chronicles 9:22; 26:28; 29:29)
9. Zadok (2 Samuel 15:27)

Concerning the two words translated *seer,* Leon Wood suggests that "these terms refer to the revelational aspect of the prophets' work, when they heard from God and discerned His will."[6] D. P. Williams identifies the seer as "one that sees in a trance, endowed with the faculty of seeing in the Spirit by Divine intuition, and of looking through the darkness of the then present hour with illumination upon and toward the future."[7] The two Hebrew terms translated *seer* emphasize the subjective element— a personal reception of divine revelation by visionary seeing or insight. Walter Kaiser writes: "A *roeh* is one who is given insight into the past, present, and future [i.e., a 'seer']. A *hozeh* is one who is given his message in a vision [i.e., a 'visionary'[8]]."[9]

Since a few people were actually called by both terms, *nabi* and *hozeh,* it appears that the terms, when referring to a prophet, could be interchangeable. Three examples are Gad, Iddo and particularly Amos.[10] 1 Chronicles 29:29 (NIV) uses all three terms in one verse: "As for the events of King David's reign . . . they are written in the records of Samuel the seer *(roeh),* the records of Nathan the prophet *(nabi)* and the records of Gad the seer *(hozeh)*." 1 Samuel 9:9 (KJV) indicates that the ministries of prophet and seer were substantially identical: "Beforetime in Israel, when a man went to inquire of God, thus he spake, Come, and let us go to the seer: for he that is now called a Prophet [*nabi*] was beforetime called a Seer [*roeh*]."

The Scripture makes no clear distinction concerning these designations. It seems logical, therefore, that a prophet could be called by any of the three terms. Further proof that there is no major difference between the *roeh-hozeh* and the *nabi* is the fact that "seers" were also spokesmen for God, not just receivers of messages.[11] *Nabi* describes the prophet objectively as the spokesman for the message, whereas *roeh* and *hozeh* refer to that same person subjectively as a seer or visionary who receives the message in a pictorial mode of revelation.

Bible seers like Samuel (and Elijah and Elisha, who were not so designated) could "see" who was coming to visit and for what (1 Samuel 9:15–16), know when donkeys had been lost and found (1 Samuel 9:20), detect whispers in the king's bedchamber (2 Kings 6:12), discern the deceit

43

of a covetous servant (2 Kings 5:26) and accurately forecast the end of a long drought (1 Kings 18:41).[12]

The complexity of explaining the term *nabi* is illustrated by the fact that some eighty pages are devoted to the Hebrew term *nabi* and the Greek term *prophetes* in the prestigious *Theological Dictionary of the New Testament*. That book states: "The picture of the prophecy of Israel presented in the Old Testament is by no means uniform. It embraces such different phenomena that it seems well-nigh impossible to bring it under a single common denominator."[13] Robert D. Culver adds succinctly that "the derivation of *nabi* is a matter of controversy."[14]

Usually scholars attempt to ascertain the root meaning of a word on etymological grounds, but with *nabi* there is no common agreement. In fact, there are four views, provoking much scholarly debate.[15] The noun is from:

1. An Arabic root, *naba'a,* meaning "to proclaim or announce"; hence the meaning of *prophet* is literally a "spokesman" or "speaker."
2. A Hebrew root, *naba',* a softened form of the Hebrew verb meaning "to flow, boil up, bubble forth"; hence, "to pour forth words." Once popular, this definition is no longer given strong scholarly support.[16]
3. An Akkadian root, *nabu,* "to call"; hence, the idea is "one called by God" or "one who felt called of God."
4. An unknown Semitic root, which does not itself occur in the Old Testament, thereby necessitating that the term will be determined by usage alone.

The meaning of the original root is therefore lost to us, but at least the essential idea of "authorized spokesman" is clearly established by general usage. The more traditional description would resemble this running summary from *Gesenius' Lexicon:* "A prophet, who as actuated by a divine afflatus, or spirit, either rebuked the conduct of kings and nations, or predicted future events. . . . He spoke not his own words, but those which he had divinely received. . . . He was the divine messenger of God, and the declarer of his will. . . ."[17]

Usage of *Prophet* in the Old Testament

Since the etymology of the word *prophet* is buried in antiquity, we must rely on the contextual usage in the Bible. Most scholars would agree with this statement: "There is really no way of talking about what the term meant or means absolutely, but only about how it has been used (and how it can properly be used now)."[18] Fortunately three passages from the time of Moses provide us with a clear, functional meaning of the word *prophet* (Hebrew, *nabi*).

1. Exodus 6:28–7:2. When God declares Moses the designated spokesman to Israel and Pharaoh, Moses objects, "Behold, I am unskilled in speech; how then will Pharaoh listen to me?" (6:30). God responds, "See, I make you as God to Pharaoh, and your brother Aaron shall be your prophet. You shall speak all that I command you, and your brother Aaron shall speak to Pharaoh that he let the sons of Israel go out of his land" (7:1–2).

The same thought is registered in Exodus 4:12, 16: "I, even I, will be with your mouth, and teach you what you are to say. . . . Moreover, [Aaron] shall speak for you to the people; and it shall come about that he shall be as a mouth for you, and you shall be as God to him."

It is clear, then, that a *nabi* is "a person authorized to speak for another, for Aaron, speaking in Moses' place to Pharaoh, is Moses' *nabi*."[19]

Thus, the prophet is a speaker for God—a mouthpiece, announcer or spokesman for the Almighty. I like the way my old *Smith's Dictionary* defines it: "One *who announces or pours forth* the declarations of God."[20] Our English word *prophet,* a transliteration of the Greek word *prophetes,* carries the same meaning. When the translators of the Septuagint (the Greek Old Testament) sought a word to translate the Hebrew *nabi,* they consistently used the Greek *prophetes,* a noun derived from the preposition *pro,* "for, on behalf of," and the verb *phemi,* "to speak." We have another ancient precedent, therefore, to substantiate that a prophet is one who speaks for another.

2. Numbers 12:1–8. A genuine prophet can be authentic only if he has received an actual message from God. This qualification was given dramatically by God Himself when he addressed Moses, Aaron and Miriam: "Hear now My words: If there is a prophet among you, I the LORD shall make Myself known to him in a vision. I shall speak with him in a dream" (verse 6).

3. Deuteronomy 13:1–5; 18:15–22. Moses gives an insightful five-point summary for Israel. Since his departure was at hand, he of necessity included in his closing message (that is, Deuteronomy) a summary of characteristics that would identify the continuing authentic prophetic ministry among the people: The true prophet would:

- Be an Israelite—that is, one in covenant relationship with the LORD (18:15, 18).
- Speak in the name of the LORD (18:16, 19–20).

- Successfully predict the near and distant future (18:21–22).
- Sometimes perform miraculous signs—but not to lure others away to idolatry (13:1–2).
- Speak a message in conformity with previously accredited revelation (13:2–5).

The Setting of a Prophecy

Consider the basic framework of ancient prophecy:[21]

1. God has *an audience* to whom He wishes to direct His thoughts. This may be:
   - An individual (like Ahab);
   - The nation of Judah or Israel;
   - A foreign nation (like Nineveh).
2. A *situation* has arisen with that audience requiring divine action:
   - His people may be in trouble (military threat, religious compromise, social upheaval);
   - God's integrity may be at stake;
   - World powers may need addressing.
3. There is *a message* to be delivered to that audience. This may be:
   - Spoken;
   - Written;
   - Demonstrated.
4. A *messenger,* or spokesman, is selected and *a mode of delivery* chosen:
   - The messenger must be an "in-covenant" Israelite and devoted to the God of Scripture;
   - There is no stereotyped "messenger type" qualification;
   - A great variety of delivery styles is possible; as, warning of judgment, call to repentance, summons to change, call to holiness.
5. An *empowerment of the Spirit* is given to hear and deliver:
   - The prophet hears God's voice, sees a vision, dreams a dream;
   - Receives an inner compunction to speak ("fire in the bones");
   - Receives a tangible, mantle-like anointing.
6. A *time and place* are selected for delivery:
   - This can be for now or later, in public or in private;
   - The time and place may or may not have symbolic significance.

7. *A response by the audience* is expected:
- Acceptance, rejection, neglect will occur; or
- Repentance, commitment, reaffirmation will take place.

The Two Kinds of Prophecy

Webster's Dictionary clearly states the two English meanings of prophecy:

1. The inspired declaration of divine will and purpose; and
2. A prediction of something to come.

These two functions have been given the two terms *forthtelling* and *foretelling*.

Forthtelling

Usually the prophet was forthtelling—speaking forth God's voice in contemporary situations for immediate applications. Like the lawyer acting as a mouthpiece for his client, the prophet spoke for God and His interests. Sometimes the form of speech was that of a herald speaking forth the will or decree of the king. Invariably it meant bringing forth the mind of God through inspired speech. To think of prophecy as predictive foretelling alone gives just a partial view of what the prophetic ministry properly embraces.

This statement by C. Douglas Weaver summarizes forthtelling: "The prophet serves as God's mouthpiece, and his message functions as the word of God to and for particular constituencies. This word is a forthtelling of God's will, and a call of restoration to that will."[22]

Foretelling

Foretelling/predictive prophecy is supernatural and miraculous. This is the way the Bible presents the nature of prophecy. Some modern critics assume that prediction of the distant future is impossible and thus reduce the miraculous element to a minimum. They leave us with a Bible robbed of its own integrity and bereft of its glorious messianic prophecies. What an unfortunate approach to both Scripture and Christianity!

Prophecy and miracles still remain as two great pillars of Christian truth and evidence. The Bible itself points to the fulfillment of prophecy. Jesus claimed that He fulfilled the predictions of the prophets. The early

47

apostles, as they preached the gospel, argued the authority and deity of Christ based on the prophets.

Clarence E. Macartney capsulates the essence of foretelling: "The argument from prophecy is that if we have a series of predictions foretelling clearly and closely future events which no native shrewdness and no clever guess could have arrived at and the fulfillment of which could not have been contrived by an impostor, then the fulfillment of such predictions necessitates a supernatural power at work. In other words, the fulfillment of prophecy proves that Christianity is a divine revelation."[23]

Slightly more than one-fourth of the Bible text has to do with the future. This surprising information comes from a most amazing book, *Encyclopedia of Biblical Prophecy: The Complete Guide to Scriptural Predictions and Their Fulfillment.* The author, J. Barton Payne, has done massive research on Bible prophecies, extracting 1,817 entries covering all predictions in the Bible. His statistical evaluations of the prophecies are particularly enlightening. The predictive matter in the Bible, he says, amounts to 27 percent (that is, 8,352 verses out of its total of 31,124), with the Old Testament at 28.5 percent and the New Testament at 21.5 percent.[24]

God told Ezekiel that the people were whispering about him behind his back, making fun of his foretelling. They were saying, "Come on, let's have some fun! Let's go hear the prophet tell us what the LORD is saying!" (Ezekiel 33:30, NLT). God responded with this classic statement: "But when all these terrible things happen to them—as they certainly will—then they will know that a prophet has been among them" (verse 33).

Here are eight examples of predictive prophecy:

- Ezekiel describing the exodus of Zedekiah (Ezekiel 12:8–13).
- Ezekiel declaring the exact day the siege began (Ezekiel 24:2).
- Jeremiah pronouncing the death of Hananiah (Jeremiah 28:16–17).
- Amos proclaiming the fall of Israel (Amos 5:27).
- Micaiah announcing the death of Ahab (1 Kings 22).
- Isaiah confirming the deliverance of Jerusalem from Sennacherib (Isaiah 37:26–37).
- Jeremiah heralding the seventy-year captivity and return (Jeremiah 25:11–12).
- Micah predicting the birthplace of the Messiah (Micah 5:2).[25]

There is a continuity between the Old Testament prophets, the New Testament prophets and today's prophetic Church. The two Testaments are not opposing books with Church history simply tacked on. The Testaments are, rather, two parts of the same book, speaking the same language and dynamically linked to the Church today through the agency of the blessed Holy Spirit. An unprejudiced approach to biblical prophetism and Church history only confirms the importance of prophecy for today's Church.

That opening story of Elijah the Tishbite seems astounding, but allow me to conclude this chapter with a thought-provoking incident from the life of a modern-day prophet.

The Words of a Prophet

The door burst open and there stood the impeccably dressed Smith Wigglesworth, British evangelist, with a stern expression on his face. It was only about 6:30 A.M. on a beautiful morning in 1936 in Johannesburg. David du Plessis, the 31-year old general secretary of the Apostolic Faith Mission, looked up from his work in surprise and apprehension. His house guest had not even knocked, interrupting David's hurried efforts to clean up his desk so that his day would be free.

David described the encounter like this:

> He wore a fierce expression and offered no greeting. Instead he raised his right hand and pointed the forefinger at me. "Come out here!" his voice boomed. . . .
>
> He put his hands on my shoulders and pushed me against the wall—not roughly, but certainly firmly—and he held me there. . . . I was more than a bit uneasy at that moment.
>
> He looked straight into my eyes. . . . "I have been sent by the Lord to tell you what He has shown me this morning," he began. "Through the old-line denominations will come a revival that will eclipse anything we have known throughout history. No such things have happened in times past as will happen when this begins. . . . It will eclipse the present-day, twentieth-century Pentecostal revival that already is a marvel to the world, with its strong opposition from the established church. But this same blessing will become acceptable to the churches and they will go on with this message and this experience beyond what the Pentecostals have achieved. You will live to see this work grow to such dimensions that the Pentecostal movement itself will be a light thing in comparison with what God will do through the old churches. There will be tremendous gatherings of people, unlike anything we've seen, and great leaders will change their attitude and accept not only the message but also the blessing."
>
> Again, a slight hesitation. "One final word, the last word the Lord gave me for you: All He requires of you is that you be humble and faithful under

all circumstances. If you remain humble and faithful, you will live to see the whole fulfilled."[26]

Wigglesworth's message was contrary to everything the Pentecostals of the time taught and believed. Because they had been ostracized from the mainline churches, the idea that they, too, would receive the Spirit's outpouring was startling, to say the least!

The old prophet made a quick exit and the younger man slumped into his chair, overcome by the awesome message. About ten minutes passed, and he heard a gentle knock at his door.

A friendly, very subdued Wigglesworth now came into his office. He explained that he had burst in before because he had to deliver the message without interruption and had not greeted even David's wife. Now, on his second visit, he explained that the message had come to him in visions and that he himself had questioned it. He also informed his younger colleague that David would play a prominent role in the coming renewal.

"It will not begin during my lifetime," Wigglesworth added. "The day I pass away, then you can begin to think about it." Then he asked the startled du Plessis if he ever got airsick or seasick. David replied that he had never been in the air or on the sea. Smith told him, just before laying his hands on David, that he would "travel more than most men." He closed with prayer for David's health and safety.[27]

> As Wigglesworth foretold, there were no dramatic events overnight. However, one thing came "out of the blue". Within three weeks of Wigglesworth's prophecy an airmail letter arrived from America, asking du Plessis if he would be one of the preachers at the Assemblies of God General Council for the following year (a prestigious event for an unknown South African minister).
>
> David's own "pilgrimage of faith" was to follow, and it was no rose petal pathway: financial hardships, a nomadic way of life, sacrifices galore, and finally rejection by his Pentecostal colleagues. But had not Smith described his message from God as a "warning"? He also said that there were to be two essential elements, humility and faithfulness. In 1947 Wigglesworth died. David thought that was the end of the prophecy, forgetting that it signalled the beginning.[28]

The 1936 prophecy of Wigglesworth found dramatic fulfillment in the unbelievable adventure that followed in the life of David Johannes du Plessis. Some idea is gained by reading the more than three and a half pages assigned to his life story in *Dictionary of Pentecostal and Charismatic Movements*.

John Mackay, president of Princeton Seminary, became the door for du Plessis to enter organized ecumenism. Du Plessis spoke at the 1952 meeting of the International Missionary Council, where he earned the title "Mr. Pentecost." He spoke to the 1954 World Council Assembly, and by 1959 was giving lectures at major theological centers—Princeton, Yale, Union, Colgate, Bossey and others. He was received by three Roman Catholic pontiffs—John XXIII, Paul VI and John Paul II. R. P. Spittler, author of the article in *Dictionary of Pentecostal and Charismatic Movements* and professor at Fuller Theological Seminary, says in closing his review:

> No one in the twentieth century so effectively linked three of the major movements of the time—the Pentecostal movement, the ecumenical movement, and the charismatic movement. *Time* magazine (September 9, 1974, 66) reported the choice of seven editors of religious publications for the leading "shapers and shakers" of Christianity. Du Plessis was among them, along with people like Billy Graham, Hans Kung, Jurgen Moltmann, and Rosemary Ruether. . . . Kilian McDonnell spoke of du Plessis as "a national treasure." In 1976 St. John's University in Collegeville, Minnesota, presented to him the prized Pax Christi award, clear evidence of his high repute in Roman Catholic circles. He was the first non-Roman Catholic ever to have received (in 1983) the distinguished Benemerenti award, presented on the pope's behalf by Jan Cardinal Willenbrands. In 1978 du Plessis received an honorary doctorate from Bethany Bible College (Santa Cruz, Calif.). His example, his wry and rabbinic teaching style—if not his consistent logic— inspired hundreds of younger Pentecostal leaders and subtly molded the emerging theology of a major force in Christendom. For the twentieth century at least, he was indeed "Mr. Pentecost."[29]

REFLECTIONS

In contrast to the heathen soothsayers and diviners the Hebrew prophets were men with the sense of a special call to the prophetic ministry. They were men of consecration and lofty character, courageous critics of the social, political, moral and religious wrongs of their day. Accuracy of prediction, confirmed by fulfillment on the historical plane, characterized their ministry.[30]

Hobart E. Freeman

The prophets are God's messengers. They are charged to proclaim to their contemporaries firstly God's decisions and, furthermore, his demands. Whereas divination in various forms occurs among all nations, the prophets with whom we are dealing here are a distinct Israelite phenomenon.[31]

Bernhard Duhm

The prophets of Israel stand in a class by themselves in ancient Near Eastern history. No countries other than Israel had persons who can truly be compared with them. In Israel their significance for the religious condition of the people can hardly be overstated. It is true that there was considerable defection from God's Law in spite of them, but apart from them this waywardness would have been far more extensive.[32]

Leon J. Wood

In all of the various periods of Israel's history in the Old Testament, there appears to be no greater or grander ministry than that of the prophets. The prophets were noble and holy men of God. They were the representatives of God to Israel, declaring His word, His mind and His will to the nation in times of prosperity or adversity.[33]

Kevin Conner

MAKEUP: TRAITS THAT CHARACTERIZED A PROPHET

". . . I sent to you through My servants the prophets."

2 Kings 17:13

DID YOU EVER watch your mother make cookies? After mixing the dough, she would roll it out flat so the cookie pieces could be cut out and arranged on the baking pan. I was fascinated as a boy by the cookie-cutter—a metal form with design-shaped edges that enabled my mother to cut out the dough so the cookies would all look alike and bake uniformly in size and shape.

Prophets in the Bible did not all come from the same spiritual "cookie-cutter"! That is, they did not share the same nature and personality. They did not speak and minister in the same style, nor were their prophecies consistently of the same type. They served different audiences in a variety of circumstances and places, and each seemed to have a very special form of the prophetic mantle for his or her calling.

Yet in spite of great diversity, certain traits did characterize the prophets, traits we will emphasize in this chapter. A common bond of devotion and dedication, similar to that of a military unit, caused their differences to fade in the light of their primary calling.

Some 65 named people prophesied in the Old Testament (see appendixes 1 and 2). This list can be enlarged with an additional 14 unnamed prophets and approximately 22 groups or bands of people who were used prophetically. Great differences existed among this host of people; they were not all star-shaped cookies! Yet with their obvious personal differences and modes of expression, the prophets possessed traits revealing a common denominator: In striking contrast to the heathen prophets of that day, these awesome men and women spoke for the true and only almighty God.

Israel was no religious or social island. By divine design this little country was (and still is) positioned where the great continents of Europe, Africa and Asia come together. Located at the crossroads of world trade caravans, Israel undoubtedly experienced cultural and religious pressures from the neighboring nations. This raises an important question: Was the prophetism of the Hebrew people borrowed from or heavily influenced by the prophetic activity among their heathen neighbors?

Fortunately the achievements of archaeology and textual studies during the past two centuries have shed considerable light on the Old Testament. An extensive knowledge of the world of Israel's day is now available. These new insights not only facilitate the interpretation of the prophetic messages but heighten our recognition of the uniqueness of the Hebrew prophetic institution. As Edward J. Young, scholar of Hebrew Scripture, says: "The mere comparison of these [alleged] 'prophecies' [from the ancient Near East] with those of the Old Testament will at once make it evident that they were separated by a wide gulf. They were different one from another as day is from night. And the reason for this difference is to be found in the fact that in Israel God spoke through His servants the prophets."[1]

Some critical scholars believe that all aspects of Israel's prophecy were borrowed from Canaan. Others suggest that Israel observed the phenomenon of prophecy simply because the rest of the world did. These approaches sometimes depict the early Hebrew prophets as unstable, crude, ecstatic types similar to the prophets of Baal encountered by Elijah on Mount Carmel.[2] The same traits that marked the heathen prophets, say these critics, would also have characterized the Hebrew prophets—traits like divination, self-torture, necromancy and casting spells.[3]

A careful study of the Scriptures, however (our only real source of information about the Hebrew prophets), shows that just the opposite was true. Israel actually possessed its prophetic institution *before* entering Palestine. The Law and the prophets were dead-set against the adoption of the priestly and prophetic practices of Canaan. The Hebrew prophets specialized in the denigration of idolatry, immorality and heathen divination. There is simply no objective evidence in the Hebrew Scripture to indicate that the prophets borrowed from the heathen.[4]

Many Bible references bear this out. My favorite is Isaiah 8:19–20, representative of Scripture's continuing emphasis that the Hebrew prophets did not borrow or learn their prophetic ministries from the heathen: "And when they say to you, 'Consult [for direction] the mediums and the wizards who whisper and mutter ["squeak and gibber," Phillips],' should not a people consult their God? Should they consult the dead on behalf of the living? To the law and to the testimony! If they do not speak according to this word, it is because they have no dawn."[5]

Another passage that points up the uniqueness of Hebrew prophecy is Jeremiah 23:28–29: "'The prophet who has a dream may relate his dream, but let him who has My word speak My word in truth. What does straw have in common with grain?' declares the LORD. 'Is not My word like fire?' declares the LORD, 'and like a hammer which shatters a rock?'"

Israel recognized that there were many idols but only one true God who spoke to His people through prophetic revelation. His uncompromising will would be made known by His prophets. The message did not result from the prophet's own reason or imagination; it was supernatural in origin.

The prophetic institution in Israel existed to establish the reality of the one true God before the nations, revealing His will to His people and safeguarding them from the divination and abominable practices of Canaan and the other Near Eastern cultures. Religion and prophecy in Israel were unquestionably unique. Notice Moses stressing in Deuteronomy 18 (*before* Israel entered the Promised Land) that the people of God were not "to imitate the detestable things of those nations" (verse 9). Moses then listed nine things abhorrent to God: februation (the custom of passing one's son and daughter through the fire),[6] divination, witchcraft, interpreting omens, sorcery, casting spells, channeling spirit messages, spiritism and necromancy.

Moses taught that God's people have no need to resort to these devices, for the prophetic voice in Israel would be God's gift of direction and protection against destructive heathen practices. In Deuteronomy 18:15, 18, Moses promised that "the LORD your God will raise up for you a prophet like me from among you . . . and I will put My words in his mouth, and he shall speak to them all that I command him." These statements find ultimate fulfillment in Jesus Christ (see Acts 3:22), but they may imply a double reference to Jesus and the prophetic institution,[7] for both Jesus and the prophets are to mediate between Israel and God.

Descriptive Terms

In the previous chapter we described the prophet as a spokesman for God *(nabi)* who often received his message by seeing visions (a "seer," *hozeh* and *roeh*). Six additional descriptions in Hebrew Scripture also apply to the prophets of the New Testament.

1. Friend of God. The first person in the Bible to be called a prophet was Abraham. The claim was made forcefully by God Himself, who told Abimelech in a dream that "[Abraham] is a prophet" (Genesis 20:7). The reasons for this title are not given, but Abraham's lifestyle—seven recorded encounters with God—bears it out.

Abraham is the only man in the Bible called "the friend of God" (2 Chronicles 20:7; Isaiah 41:8; James 2:23). This could well be the most important trait of the prophet. A friend is "one attached to another by affection or esteem; a favored companion." This, I believe, is why God would not destroy Sodom and Gomorrah without bringing it to Abraham's attention: "The LORD said, 'Shall I hide from Abraham what I am about to do . . .'?" (Genesis 18:17).

In Numbers 12:8 God says of Moses (from Edward Young's literal translation), "Mouth unto mouth will I speak with him, and plainly. . . ." The phrase *mouth to mouth* (only in this passage) and the expression *face to face* shows that God conversed with Moses as a friend, directly and without reserve. It was said of Moses after his death: "Since then no prophet has risen in Israel like Moses, whom the LORD knew face to face" (Deuteronomy 34:10; see Exodus 33:11). Moses was a friend of God.

Amos 3:7 declares, "Surely the LORD God does nothing unless He reveals His secret counsel to His servants the prophets." Natural friends walk closely together, sharing personal issues. Rick Joyner says, "The Lord does not *want* to do anything without sharing it with the prophets, because the prophets are His friends. . . . The essence of prophetic ministry is to be the special friend and confidant of the Lord."[8]

In our time we have this wonderful saying of Jesus to apply to our lives: "No longer do I call you slaves; for the slave does not know what his master is doing; but I have called you friends, for all things that I have heard from My Father I have made known to you" (John 15:15). This available friendship should apply in a particular way to God's New Testament prophets.

2. Man of God. This much-used term illustrates a basic trait of a true prophet: "He is in direct communication with Yahweh."[9] He belonged *to* God; his passions and objectives were subordinated to those *of* God as he declared, followed and upheld the ways of God. He knew God in a personal way; he was chosen and sent *by* God on a mission with a message *from* God. The term *man of God* indicates sole dedication, no compromise, and is used of various men. Three examples: Moses (Deuteronomy 33:1), Samuel (1 Samuel 9:6) and Shemaiah (1 Kings 12:22). This expression is used of Elisha 36 times.

3. Messenger of the LORD. This term goes to the heart of prophetic ministry. The prophet is a faithful messenger. He brings a message of great importance from the King of Heaven! The prophet chooses neither the message nor the receiver; his sole responsibility is to his Boss, the Lord, from whom he received the message. The prophets, like the angels, were merely delivery persons. Angels were spiritual messengers while prophets delivered the revealed words of God, so the same Hebrew word, *malak,* is used for both.

A messenger might be sent to nations, cities, tribes or individuals. The consciousness of being sent was common to all the prophets: "Go, and tell this people" (Isaiah 6:9; see Jeremiah 26:15). The message was often contemporary, but it could also interpret the past, predict future events or be messianic in nature. Haggai, among others, was called "the messenger of the LORD" (Haggai 1:13; see 2 Chronicles 36:15–16; Isaiah 44:26; Malachi 3:1).

On one frightening occasion the Lord, offended by King David's presumptuous sin of numbering Israel (putting trust in military power), sent the prophet-seer Gad to David with a choice of three options of how God would send His judgment on Judah. Gad delivered his message and then made this impatient statement to the humbled king: "Now, therefore, consider what answer I shall return to Him who sent me" (1 Chronicles 21:12).

Paul boldly picked up the designation of *messenger* for himself and other Christian ministers when he said, "We speak as messengers who have been approved by God to be entrusted with the Good News" (1 Thessalonians 2:4, NLT).

4. Servant of the LORD. The prophet was a slave of the Lord by choice and affection. Like the bondservant who willingly made himself a permanent slave of his benevolent master (see Deuteronomy 15:12–17), the prophet willingly accepted this humble role. The law required the bondservant to have his ear pierced (probably a ring was then inserted), thereby indicating that he lived to hear and obey his master—a perfect illustration of the prophet. He served only one master, whatever his will and desire might be. God refers lovingly to "My servants the prophets" (2 Kings 9:7; 17:13; Jeremiah 7:25; 35:15; Ezekiel 38:17; Zechariah 1:6). What a compliment for the Scripture to so record a prophet's name! For example, "According to the word of the LORD which He spoke through his servant Ahijah the prophet" (1 Kings 14:18).

5. Watchman. Ancient cities employed alert sentinels who stood on the city walls to warn when enemies approached or catastrophe was imminent. They manned their posts even at night while others slept. Like them, the prophet was to watch the events of his time from the high wall of spiritual dedication. Even when the people were lulled to sleep by their own indifference, the prophet was to remain alert! He or she represented a warning voice, a caretaker of God's inheritance, a guardian, one who awakened the people to action[10] (Psalm 127:1; Isaiah 21:6; 52:8; 62:6; Jeremiah 6:17; Ezekiel 3:17; 33:6–7; Hosea 9:8; Habakkuk 2:1).

Jeremiah's call to ministry began with the symbolic vision of a branch of the almond—the first of the fruit trees to blossom. In the Central Valley of California, many acres of these trees burst with white blossoms when it seems that all nature is still asleep. The almond is a harbinger of coming life. Matthew Henry called it "the hasty tree." John Skinner comments: "The almond, which blossoms in January, was poetically named by the Hebrews the *wakeful* tree, as the first of all the trees to wake up at the touch and promise of spring. Looking at it, the prophet is impelled to pronounce its name: *Shaked,* 'awake.' What does it signify? The answer comes unbidden: 'I am wakeful [*Shoked*] over My word to fulfil it.'"[11]

Before anyone else realizes what is happening, God is declaring through His prophets what will be! But the almond merely announces spring, whereas God is involved in both predicting *and* bringing His prophetic word to pass.

6. Interpreter. This rare term is found in Isaiah 43:27 (Interlinear Bible; Rotherham; NKJV and NASB margins). *Theological Wordbook of the Old Testament* says, "The interpreters in Isaiah 43:27 are the teachers of Israel, God's priests and prophets who have sinned by refusing to give out God's word as he first gave it."[12]

This insight from Hastings' *Dictionary of the Bible* is helpful: "The name . . . is descriptive of the position of the prophet in regard to history and God's providence. God speaks in events, and the prophet interprets Him to men. Prophecy arises out of history, keeps pace with it, and interprets it. God is the author of Israel's history, and His meaning in it, His disposition towards the people as expressed in it, reflects itself in the prophet's mind. . . . History is a moral current, and at whatever point the prophet stands he feels whence it has come and whither it is flowing."[13]

Women, Too

Women as well as men served as prophets in the Old Testament, and it is clear that they also prophesied in the New Testament churches. The study of prophetic ministry focuses on the male because of the number of male prophets mentioned in the Bible and because of the expression *man of God*. But the small number of women mentioned does not indicate that God was compelled to use them because no men were available; nor are they an exception to the rule or of lesser spirituality. Women prophets, like men, were called and chosen of God by His discretion and will. Apparently because of certain physical limitations—such as home duties, the mores or binding customs of that society and the physical abuse heaped on the prophets—the Lord did not call as many women as men at that time, but call and use them He did, and still does.

A female prophet is called a prophetess (Hebrew *nebiah;* Greek, *prophetis*). The first four women listed below from the Old Testament are so designated:

- Miriam (Exodus 15:20)
- Deborah (Judges 4:4)
- Huldah (2 Kings 22:14; 2 Chronicles 34:22)
- Isaiah's wife (Isaiah 8:3)
- Possibly the mother of King Lemuel (Proverbs 31:1)
- Noadiah (probably a false prophetess; Nehemiah 6:14)

In the New Testament:

- Anna (Luke 2:36)
- "Sons and daughters . . . men and women" (Acts 2:17–18)
- Philip's four daughters (Acts 21:9)
- Women in the Corinthian church (1 Corinthians 11:5)
- Jezebel (a false prophetess; Revelation 2:20)

We certainly have sufficient evidence that a woman can be a prophetess.

Prophetic Families

Is the prophetic gift inherited? Is a person born with the gift? There is no "cookie-cutter" answer to these questions and no one way God calls people to prophetic ministry. We will address the call of the prophet in the next chapter, but for this discussion on the makeup of a prophet, we can say that Scripture indicates a qualified yes to the above questions.

Some prophets were called from birth, such as Jeremiah (Jeremiah 1:4–5) and John the Baptist (Luke 1:15–16). Other prophets had unique personal experiences with God. Amos, for instance, made it clear that he was not the son of a prophet or of any professional group of prophets, but was called by God while tending his flocks (Amos 7:14–15).

Bible scholars generally feel that "the prophetic gift was not hereditary."[14] I concur with this conclusion in the sense that each prophet must know God and His voice in a personal and genuine way. Even so, we must not overlook the references strongly indicating that the prophetic anointing sometimes runs in and abides on families. Families are often involved in the same secular businesses, and children through exposure and inherited talents sometimes follow the same line of endeavor as their parents. So it is not strange to find the following fourteen families participating in prophecy:

- Abraham and his grandson Jacob (Genesis 20:7; 48:14–21; 49)
- Moses and his brother Aaron (Exodus 4:14–16; Deuteronomy 18:15; 34:10) and their sister Miriam (Exodus 15:20)
- David and his son Solomon (Proverbs 1:1; Song of Solomon; Acts 2:30)
- Samuel and his grandson Heman (1 Chronicles 25:1)
- Heman and his sons (1 Chronicles 25:1, 5)
- Asaph and his sons (1 Chronicles 25:2)
- Jeduthun and his sons (1 Chronicles 25:1–3)
- Oded and his son Azariah (2 Chronicles 15:8)
- Hanani and his son Jehu (2 Chronicles 16:7; 19:2)
- Iddo and his grandson Zechariah (Zechariah 1:1)
- Zechariah and his son Jahaziel, a great-grandson of Asaph (2 Chronicles 20:14)
- Isaiah and his sons (Isaiah 7:3; 8:3, 18)
- Zacharias and his son John the Baptist (Luke 1:67, 76)
- Philip and his four daughters (Acts 21)

If a son or daughter is spiritually sensitive to and has a high respect for a parent's prophetic gifting, that child will likely have the parent's gifting imparted to him or her. The above references enforce this concept. Philip's house in New Testament times was certainly blessed by the four daughters who prophesied. My observation of my own four children and other children I have observed in churches through the years bears this out.

Prophetic Categories and Periods

Generally someone who mentions the prophetic books of the Old Testament is referring to the sixteen books from Isaiah to Malachi. (Some would include Lamentations as well.) These books are further subdivided into the four major prophets (Isaiah, Jeremiah, Ezekiel and Daniel) and the twelve minor prophets. As H. L. Ellison explains, "The distinction between Major and Minor Prophets is first found in the Latin churches, and Augustine rightly explains that it means a difference in size, not in value."[15] The breakdown in the Hebrew Bible is different. It is divided into the *Torah* (Law), *Neviim* (Prophets) and *Ketuvim* (Writings). The second section, the Prophets, consists of eight books (books in two parts count as one book): Joshua, Judges, Samuel and Kings (the former Prophets); and Isaiah, Jeremiah, Ezekiel and "the Twelve" (the latter Prophets).[16] Daniel is not included, being considered more apocalyptic than prophetic. (Note, however, that in Matthew 24:15 Jesus calls Daniel a prophet.)

Usually the lists refer to the prophets whose written books appear in the Scripture as "canonical prophets," "classical prophets," "writing prophets" and "major and minor prophets." The prophets can also be categorized by actions, time periods, kings, objectives, miracles, themes and locations. My chart on page 62 identifies thirteen time periods and lists some of the key prophets in each period. Prophetic progression continues through these various periods, right up to the present day. A common conviction gripped them all: They believed they brought a word from God.

Sometimes prophetic roles are duplicated in different time periods, so we would be wrong to pigeonhole a certain kind of prophetic activity and hold it to just one time slot. Amos, for instance, is called the first of the writing prophets, yet we know that earlier seers also did writing. Daniel is not famous like Elijah for working miracles, yet his bout in the lions' den and prophetic statesmanship to four kingdoms can hardly be classified as nonmiraculous! Isaiah wrote history, predicted the future and was involved with miracles.

The best approach is to accept the prophets, each in his or her own time zone, as serving God faithfully in the discharge of the duty given and the needs of that particular time frame. Some were obscure and little

The Prophetic Periods

Time Period	Some Key Prophets	Prophetic Activity
1. Patriarchal period (4000–1500 B.C.)	• Enoch • Abraham	Genesis of prophecy
2. Mosaic period (1500–1000 B.C.)	• Moses • Aaron, Miriam, Deborah	Founding of Hebrew prophetism
3. Early monarchy (approx. 1000 B.C.)	• Samuel • "Sons of the prophets" • David • Nathan, Gad, Ahijah • Psalmic prophets	Institution of the prophetic office
4. Divided monarchy (931–722 B.C.)	• Elijah • Micaiah • Elisha	The early prophets
5. Ninth-century prophets	• Obadiah • Joel (837?)	Time of the prophetic writings
6. Eighth-century prophets	• Amos (760) • Jonah (760) • Hosea (755) • Isaiah (740) • Micah (735)	
7. Seventh-century prophets	• Nahum (660) • Zephaniah (630) • Habakkuk (607)	The later or writing Prophets
8. Exilic prophets (605–520 B.C.)	• Jeremiah (627) • Daniel (605) • Ezekiel (592)	
9. Post-exilic prophets	• Haggai (520) • Zechariah (520) • Malachi, last prophet (422)	
10. Intertestamental period (300–0 B.C.)	• No biblical prophets	Little or no activity
11. The early Church	• Agabus, Judas, Silas	Joel's fulfillment
12. The Church age	• Various sporadic activity	
13. Twentieth-century Church	• Pentecostal, Latter Rain, charismatic, Third Wave, restoration movements	

known; others became famous for their activities. Each, however, was true to the divine call. This is the bottom line of the prophet's makeup. If you keep my outline on "The Setting of a Prophecy" (chapter 3) in mind, the differences in people, times and historical settings will blend more easily so we can discover the basic calling of each prophet.

The Place of Moses

What was the place of Moses? Numbers 12 records the awesome story of God's dramatic solution to sibling rivalry when a jealous brother and sister challenged the prophetic authority of God's servant Moses. Using Moses' marriage to a Cushite woman as a pretext for criticism, Aaron and Miriam quickly came to the real issue: Moses' prophetic standing with God.

But while they were still uttering their complaint, the Lord suddenly spoke. The two brothers and sister were summoned to the Tent of Meeting, and "the LORD came down in a pillar of cloud and stood at the doorway of the tent" (Numbers 12:5). He called Aaron and Miriam forward, then made a classic statement that clearly established Moses in an entirely different category from other prophets:

"Hear now My words: If there is a prophet among you, I the LORD shall make Myself known to him in a vision. I shall speak with him in a dream. Not so, with My servant Moses, he is faithful in all My household; with him I speak mouth to mouth, even openly, and not in dark sayings, and he beholds the form of the LORD. Why then were you not afraid to speak against My servant, against Moses?" (verses 6–8).

Moses was not just an ideal kind of prophet. In fact, he is not even called a prophet in this text, nor is he set up as the first and greatest of the prophets. All other authentic prophets are not considered inferior; they belong to the same select group of true prophets. Moses, however, is in a class all his own—an entirely different category.

When God said, "Not so, with My servant Moses," He assigned Moses a position separate from all His other servants. God spoke clearly and distinctly to Moses with no ambiguities. Moses was faithful and trusted in God's "house" or "household." This refers not to a physical house but to the entire dispensation of the Old Testament (see Hebrews 3:5). It includes the Law and the covenant and the dealings of God with His people. Young comments, "Moses' commission . . . comprised the entire house of God, so that he might be regarded as an over-servant."[17]

Our conclusion: Moses was indeed a prophet, but his responsibility and position in God's program placed him in a unique position—and this position required a relationship with God not shared by other prophets.

The Sons of the Prophets

Were people trained for prophetic ministry during the Old Testament period? This question is usually raised because of the bands of prophets mentioned in 1 Samuel 10 and 19 and "the sons of the prophets" mentioned in 1 and 2 Kings.[18] Sometimes called "The School of the Prophets,"[19] these groups have led to much speculation about what was actually taking place. Did prospective prophets join themselves to these groups in order to qualify as prophets? Was there some kind of training program to produce prophets? Was education one of the prophetic traits?

Samuel, the first of the prophets in an institutional sense, was most likely the instigator of apprentice prophets and their personalized training (although the Scripture does not explicitly say so). Notice on our chart on p. 62 that this falls at the beginning of the third period or the early monarchy. Previously the gift of prophecy had been manifested in isolated cases through the patriarchal and Mosaic periods. Now Samuel emerged as the first of *the prophetic office*. As Fairbairn says: "Prophecy, in its formal character, comes into view only in the age of Samuel, with whom properly originates the prophetical order of the Old Testament."[20]

Israel had barely survived the hectic, sporadic time of the judges, and the spirituality of the nation was at an all-time low. The prophet Samuel, submitted to God and called from childhood, became the focal point for the spiritual renewal of the nation. This new prophetic era returned a conscience to the nation and its leadership, giving birth to a new sense of loyalty through the ministry of Samuel and his associates.

Prophets had existed previously, of course, starting with Abraham (Genesis 20:7). Living as he did two thousand years before Christ, he walked in faith and developed an intimate friendship with God, but this was just his personal experience. Moses, similarly, was considered a great prophet, but he was such because of an experience with God (unattainable by others) and a most uncommon commission from God (Numbers 11:25; Deuteronomy 34:10; Hosea 12:13). Miriam was called a prophetess (Exodus 15:20), and the days of the judges also had prophets (Judges 4:4; 6:8; 1 Samuel 2:27). Thus it was at the time of Samuel's birth that, according to 1 Samuel 3:1, "word from the LORD was rare in those days, visions were infrequent" (literally, prophetic "vision was not spread,"[21] or, "there was no vision breaking through"[22]).

We must assume, therefore, that groups of prophets did not exist at the time of Samuel's birth but somehow came into existence during his lifetime. The strongest evidence that they were founded by Samuel is 1 Samuel 19:20, where he is portrayed as "standing and presiding over them" at Ramah. Samuel probably gathered these prospective ministerial students together on occasion in order to:

- Build camaraderie among prophetically gifted ministerial students;
- Fashion a force that would help check the decline in religious life and maintain spirituality throughout the kingdom;
- Study and learn the Law of God, prayer and worship;
- Experience the power of the supernatural; and
- Write the canonical history of God's people.

While undergoing training, they must have had wonderful supernatural demonstrations among themselves! A prophetic aura surrounded their encampment so that even Saul and his followers came under the afflatus of the Spirit (1 Samuel 10:5, 10; 19:18, 20). Although some prophets did come from their ranks, God did not depend solely on these training groups for the calling of His prophets. This affirms once again the free will and choice of God.

The expression *sons of the prophets* is found only in 1 and 2 Kings during the time of Elijah and Elisha, during the divided monarchy, and seems to indicate a continuation of the program initiated by Samuel.[23] These "sons" were pupils or disciples of (not literal children of) a prophet. The instructor or leader was considered a spiritual or prophetic "father" (2 Kings 2:12).[24] The sons of the prophets were those disciples of the prophets who devoted themselves studiously to this ministry, sometimes acting as the messengers or ministers to carry out the direction of their leaders.

Samuel apparently realized quickly, like many religious leaders through the ages, that the importance of his prophetic gift and office must be perpetuated. What better way than to gather and train disciples to carry on his ministry? He realized he had launched a restoration or renewal movement, but that he must also take measures to make his work permanent. We know little of how Samuel did this, but we must remember that those were primitive times. Samuel was less interested in establishing an accredited university or seminary than he was in a practical, hands-on training program for serious and devoted followers.

Character Qualities

We have already discussed a number of traits of the prophet and looked at his or her external, perceptible work or ministry: as spokesman, seer, servant, messenger, watchman, almond branch or interpreter (whether alone or with a family or group). These designations are like the visible tip of an iceberg whose vast bulk floats unseen beneath the water. The most significant part of a prophet is the unseen, inner spirituality. Any visible prophetic attributes are supported by a foundation of solid character traits.

Micah 6:8, a challenge not only to Israel but to the prophet as well, capsulates in a few, well-chosen words the prophetic calling: "What does the LORD require of you but to do justice, to love kindness [loyalty], and to walk humbly [circumspectly] with your God?"

We could discuss many character qualities, but I will use five general categories, illustrated by biblical characters.

1. Devoted, Loyal. At times these men and women showed reckless disregard for safety or personal welfare. Like kamikaze pilots flying explosive-laden planes to crash enemy targets, the prophets were willing to die for their missions. Theirs was the marvelous combination of mental determination, deep religious conviction and spiritual enablement. They knew their cause was right.

- *Elijah* refused to compromise the worship of Israel, challenging King Ahab, Queen Jezebel and all the prophets of Baal and risking his own life (1 Kings 18; 19:1–2).
- *Micaiah* declared God's judgment on King Ahab's efforts, withstood the king's false prophets and was sent to prison for his efforts (2 Chronicles 18:6–27).
- *Zechariah* was stoned to death for his stand against King Joash (2 Chronicles 24:20–21).
- *A man of God* warned King Amaziah against recruiting Israelite soldiers for his army, although that was not the popular thing to do (2 Chronicles 25:7).
- *Uriah* was slain by sword by King Jehoiakim's order (Jeremiah 26:20–23).
- *Jeremiah* was thrown into a cistern by the city officials and his message was rejected; he sank into the mud yet maintained his devotion to God (Jeremiah 38:6).

- *Judas,* a prophet and faithful servant of God in the early Church (Acts 15:32), had risked his life for the name of our Lord Jesus Christ (Acts 15:25–27).

2. Committed, Obedient, Humble. Edersheim observes, "For the fundamental idea, the very law, of prophetism was absolute, unquestioning obedience to the command of God. . . . It explains how sometimes exceeding strange things were given them to do in public, so that in the absoluteness of their obedience they might exhibit the absoluteness of God's authority."[25]

- *Hannah's* remarkable prophetic ode of thanksgiving poured from a humble, thankful heart (1 Samuel 2:1–10).
- *Jahaziel,* one of the singing priest-prophets, obediently brought an astounding—seemingly impossible—word to Jehoshaphat and Judah when they faced annihilation by hostile armies (2 Chronicles 20:14–17).
- *Isaiah and his wife* gave strange names to their children by divine direction, thereby predicting the future, even though the names were humiliating to use (Isaiah 7:3; 8:3, 18).
- *Ezekiel* was commanded to show no personal grief over the upcoming death of his wife (Ezekiel 24:16–18).

3. Holy, Prayerful, Compassionate. Prayer allowed God to work marvelous things in the prophets' natures. They knew the impossibility of their tasks without His help. They felt the feelings of God, so we find passionate, spontaneous prayers scattered throughout the prophetic books (Jeremiah 18:19–23; Daniel 2:19–23; Jonah 2:1–9; Habakkuk 3:1–2). Ezekiel and others fulfilled the role of intercessors as they responded to the burning call of God: "I searched for a man among them who should build up the wall and stand in the gap before Me for the land, that I should not destroy it" (Ezekiel 22:30).

- *Joseph* saw the fulfillment of his prophetic dreams, yet humbly received his family back again (Genesis 45).
- *Moses* remained humble and dependent on God as hostile leaders sought to take over his leadership; and also when his own brother and sister rebelled against him (Numbers 12:1–2; 16:1–3). Prayer was his first recourse in every circumstance.
- *Daniel* defied the king's decree, continuing his daily custom of bowing in prayer three times a day (Daniel 6:10).

- *Zacharias,* father of John the Baptist, was a humble, poor, holy priest whose prayers were answered with the news delivered by an angel (Luke 1:11–17).

4. Daring, Bold, Faith-Filled. The prophets were people of conviction. A holy boldness seemed at times to grip them as they defied kings, nations, wild animals and natural calamities. They possessed confidence not only that their God existed but that He had commissioned them to do certain things. Their faith stood in stark contrast to the unbelief of those about them.

- *Deborah,* prophetess and mother in Israel, told the frightened Barak that the enemy general Sisera would be defeated and fall by the hand of a woman (Judges 4:9); she then sang a powerful prophetic ode (Judges 5).
- *Nathan* faced King David and boldly denounced the king's sin (2 Samuel 12:1–4).
- *Ahijah* confronted Jeroboam and announced that he would be king of the northern tribes (1 Kings 11:29–39). Later he pronounced judgment on Jeroboam's household and told the king's wife that her child would die when she reentered her home (1 Kings 14:1–18).
- *Isaiah* comforted his people and brought a scathing word of denunciation against the Assyrians who had surrounded Jerusalem (2 Kings 19).
- *Elijah* sent a letter of judgment to King Jehoram, knowing full well the possible consequences (2 Chronicles 21:12–15).
- *Amos,* a humble shepherd, pronounced death on Amaziah and judgment on his family (Amos 7:16–17).
- *Agabus,* the New Testament prophet, warned Paul of impending arrest (Acts 21:11).

5. Studious, Patriotic. In spite of their vigorous denunciation of sin and idolatry, the prophets evidenced a great love for Israel and Judah and especially Jerusalem. Even when things were bad, the prophetic voices declared restoration for God's people. They were among the most patriotic of the Israelites, even as they understood that God's people had more than national pride; they had an obligation to the living God. Also, unlike religious people who refuse to read the daily newspaper, the prophets showed a studious concern for the nations and events of their day.

- *Miriam* sang a song of victory for Israel, showing the highest of patriotic confidence in God's people (Exodus 15:20–21).

- *Shemaiah,* realizing that both Judah and Israel were covenant peoples, told King Rehoboam boldly to return and not fight against his brothers (1 Kings 12:22–24).

- *Jonah* predicted restoration of Israel's border (2 Kings 14:25) and then, under duress, was sent to the wicked city of Nineveh, of which he was well aware (Jonah 1:1–2).

- *Huldah* the prophetess brought a word of judgment concerning Jerusalem, yet encouraged King Josiah so much that a minor revival resulted (2 Chronicles 34:22–33).

- *Jeremiah* so believed in the restoration of Judah that he publicly bought land even when the oppressor occupied it (Jeremiah 32:14–15).

- *Ezekiel* brought lamentations over six nations for specific sins (Ezekiel 25–32).

- *Amos* spoke boldly and informedly about six foreign nations of his day, specifying certain cities for divine judgment (Amos 1, 2).

The Shakarian Story

I would like to close this chapter with a story of a modern-day prophet who reminds me of Samuel. The anecdote took place at the turn of the century in the country of Armenia. The similarity between Samuel and the old Russian cannot be missed, and the story clearly illustrates the continuity and unity of prophecy.

Demos Shakarian, founder and former president of the Full Gospel Business Men's Fellowship International, tells the story. Shakarian was a California dairyman who walked with God in an unusual way. His Fellowship reached more than a billion people each year with the life-changing message of Christ's love. His exposure to prophetic activity was part of the rich heritage connected with Spirit-filled Armenian churches. The following episode involves his grandfather (also named Demos) and is told by Demos in his personal story, *The Happiest People on Earth*—an amazing validation of prophecy at work today.

In the year 1900, when Isaac [Demos' father] was eight and his younger sister, Hamas, was four, the news arrived that a hundred Russian Christians were coming over the mountains in their covered wagons. Everyone was pleased. It was the custom in Kara Kala [in Armenia] to hold a feast for the visiting Christians whenever they arrived. In spite of the fact that he didn't agree with the "full Gospel" preached by the Russians, Grandfather considered their visits as times set apart for God, and insisted that the welcoming feast be held on the large level plot of ground in front of his own home.

Now, Grandfather was proud of his fine cattle. With the news that the Russians were on their way, he went out to his herd and looked them over. He would choose the very finest, fattest steer for this special meal.

Unfortunately, however, the fattest steer in the herd turned out, on inspection, to have a flaw. The animal was blind in one eye.

What should he do? Grandfather knew his Bible well: He *knew* he should not offer an imperfect animal to the Lord, for didn't it say in the twenty-second chapter of Leviticus, verse 20, "But whatsoever hath a blemish, that shall ye not offer: for it shall not be acceptable . . ."?

What a dilemma! No other animal in the herd was large enough to feed a hundred guests. Grandfather looked around. No one was watching. Suppose he slaughtered the big steer and simply hid the blemished head? Yes, that was what he would do! Grandfather led the half-blind steer into the barn, butchered it himself, and quickly placed the head in a sack which he hid beneath a pile of threshed wheat in a dark corner.

Grandfather was just in time, for as he finished dressing the beef, he heard the rumble of wagons coming into Kara Kala. What a welcome sight! Coming down the dusty road was the familiar caravan of wagons, each pulled by four perspiring horses. Beside the driver of the first team, erect and commanding as ever, sat the white-bearded patriarch who was leader and prophet of the group. Grandfather and little Isaac ran up the road to greet their guests.

All over town preparations for the feast were underway. Soon the big steer was roasting on a spit over a huge bed of charcoal. That evening everyone gathered, expectant and hungry, around the long plank tables. Before the meal could begin, however, the food must be blessed.

These old Russian Christians would not say any prayer—even grace over meals—until they had received what they called *the anointing*. They would wait before the Lord until, in their phrase, the Spirit fell upon them. They claimed (a little to Grandfather's amusement) that they could literally *feel* His Presence descend. When this occurred they would raise their arms and dance with joy.

On this occasion as always, the Russians waited for the anointing of the Spirit. Sure enough, as everyone watched, first one and then another began to dance in place. Everything was going as usual. Soon would come the blessing of the food, and the feast could begin.

But to Grandfather's dismay, the patriarch suddenly raised his hand—not in sign of blessing but as a signal that everything was to stop. Giving Grandfather a strange, penetrating look, the tall, white-haired man walked from the table without a word.

Grandfather's eyes followed the old man's every movement as the prophet strode across the yard and into the barn. After a moment he reappeared. In his hand he held the sack which Grandfather had hidden beneath the pile of wheat.

Grandfather began to shake. How could the man have known! No one had seen him. The Russians had not even reached the village when he had hidden that head. Now the patriarch placed the telltale sack before Grandfather and let it fall open, revealing to everyone the head with the milk-white eye.

"Have you anything to confess, Brother Demos?" the Russian asked.

"Yes, I have," said Grandfather, still shaking. "But how did you know?"

"God told me," the old man said simply. "You still do not believe that He speaks to His people today as in the past. The Spirit gave me this word of knowledge for a special reason: that you and your family might believe. You have been resisting the power of the Spirit. Today is the day you will resist no longer."

Before his neighbors and guests that evening Grandfather confessed the deception he had attempted. With tears rolling down his face into his bristly beard, he asked their forgiveness. "Show me," he said to the prophet, "how I, too, can receive the Spirit of God."

Grandfather knelt and the old Russian laid his work-gnarled hands on his head. Immediately Grandfather burst into joyous prayer in a language neither he nor anyone present could understand. The Russians called this kind of ecstatic utterance "tongues" and regarded it as a sign that the Holy Spirit was present with the speaker. That night Grandmother, too, received this "Baptism in the Spirit."[26]

What a story! This is just one of many accounts from around the world that illustrate the possibility of prophecy today with the same beneficial effects as recorded in the Bible.[27] Although this chapter has concentrated on the Old Testament prophets, I include this episode about the old Russian to keep before us the concept of prophecy today as in continuity with that of Bible times.

REFLECTIONS

Prophets had to be people of outstanding character, great minds, and courageous souls. They had to be this by nature and then, being dedicated to God, they became still greater because of the tasks and special provisions assigned them. Thus they became the towering giants of Israel, the formers of public opinion, the leaders through days of darkness, people distinguished from all those about them either in Israel or other nations of the day.[28]

Leon Wood

In Hebrew thought in general, and the prophetic writers in particular, one finds a uniqueness in the concept of history that differs from the secular philosophy of history. This difference lies in the prophetic awareness of the overruling divine providence directing all events of history toward one central purpose . . . that God, as the Lord of history and providence, was controlling the issues and movements of history for a purpose. With one voice the prophets declare that his purpose, toward which all history is being directed, is the establishment of the *kingdom of God*—the sovereign reign and rule of God upon earth.[29]

H. E. Freeman

The priests had authority to perform ritual, the scribes had authority to copy the law and even interpret it, but only the prophets had the authority to speak in the Name of God. . . . They were expected to declare what God was saying to the nation in the circumstances of the day.[30]

Clifford Hill

When the nation turned its sail to the wind of prosperity, and the masses were being borne away on the downward drift of indifference to God's Voice, reckoning popularity as an evidence of truth, the prophets of God still held their ground, although denied, deserted, misused, and isolated. The Word spoken through them made nations like Egypt, Syria, Assyria, Nineveh, Babylon, Persia, Canaan, Asia, Rome as boiling cauldrons; dethroned kings, and turned princes to dust.[31]

D. P. Williams

Through the Spirit, ancient prophets bemoaned with tears in the most sorrow-smitten anguish, the tragic failure and fall of God's people in their day. Are there no prophets to take up lamentation in the Spirit for the lapse of God's people today and seek again this deeper moving of His presence?[32]

Seeley D. Kinney

MIND: HOW DID PROPHECY COME TO A PROPHET?

"You will hear a message [word] from My mouth, and give them warning from Me."

Ezekiel 33:7

THE PROPHETS SEEMED to have a special awareness of God, familiarity with His ways and perception of His will. This prophetic consciousness is our focus in this chapter.[1] Our discussion will revolve around four important questions:

- How was a person called to be a prophet?
- How did he or she prophesy?
- Were the prophets ecstatics?
- How were the Scriptures "inspired"?

The sacred nature of our subject cautions against any hasty or absolute conclusions. At the same time, the Scripture does discuss prophecy in a way that encourages our interest and even participation. Bishop David Pytches, a leading Anglican charismatic, wisely suggests that "the secret of prophetic consciousness eludes scientific investigation and the process of spiritual inspiration resists exact definition."[2] Let's keep his good advice in mind.

More important than our ability to grasp and analyze the psychology of *how* it all worked is the simple faith to accept that it did happen—that is, to believe that God exists, that He does speak to people and that people were actually used in Bible times to be His mouthpiece to others. Little detail is offered about the way in which it happens, but the entire Bible records that a large, diverse group of people in a variety of circumstances did experience such a call and that they did prophesy.

Revelation: How Did It Come?

Both the call to be a prophet and the performance of that call required divine revelation. The prophet had to perceive the voice (that is, the word) of God, which somehow involved a supernatural happening—a divine impartation, an unveiling, a revealing—of God's thoughts to that prophet. This sacred communication came in one or all of four ways:

- An audible voice
- A mental picture (vision)
- An immediate unction
- An ecstatic experience

In each case of getting the message and giving it out to the people, there was an attendant or overriding "unction," or empowerment, of the Holy Spirit. On page 75 I have summarized in a chart the four ways in which God's thoughts came.

An Audible Voice

The expression *and the word of the LORD came to* appears some 135 times in Hebrew Scripture.[3] Twenty-three people are mentioned as having received such a word. On most of these occasions the prophet heard a clear, discernible voice (either internal or external), so clear it could be quoted. The expression appears with a regularity suggesting an experience that was accepted and appreciated among God's people.

The word of the Lord came to Ezekiel 49 times, Jeremiah 44 times and Isaiah three times, according to the actual biblical record. The voice of God spoke to eight of the minor prophets, as well as to Abraham, Samuel, Nathan, Gad, Solomon, Shemiah, an unnamed man of God, an old

Revelation and Communication

How God Communicated to and through the Prophet	How the Message Came to the Prophet	How the Prophet Communicated the Message	The Style of Expression
1. Audible Voice	• A spoken word, either internal or external • Given before or at the time of the prophecy's utterance	• Related in own words • Related verbatim • Repeated under divine unction	• Reading • Hymn or song • Exhortation • Prediction • Lamentation • Messianic prediction • Enacted prophecy • Denunciation
2. Mental Picture	• A vision or mental image that is true to life or apocalyptic • Coming while conscious or unconscious • With eyes open or in dream or trance	• Described in prophet's own words as it is being seen, or told after it is seen • A spontaneous prophetic word as the vision is in progress • Recorded and read later	• A simple, under-standable, descriptive account • An impassioned description and plea
3. Immediate Unction	• A bursting forth of words without premeditation • "as the Spirit gives utterance"	• Spoken with unction and enthusiasm	• Same as #1, except for reading
4. Ecstatic Experience	• In trance, dream or semi-conscious condition • An afflatus • A sudden over-powering while conscious	• Spoken during the experience • Spoken after • Recorded and read later • Deliberately retold • Given under im-mediate outburst	• All the above

prophet, Jehu, Elijah, Nathan and David. The word came to the major and minor prophets who wrote Scripture as well as to noncanonical prophets who did not write Scripture. About others who had the same experience, this particular expression is not used, such as when "the prophet Gad said to David, 'Do not stay in the stronghold; depart, and go into the land of Judah'" (1 Samuel 22:5).

When "the word of the LORD came," the prophet certainly knew it. The people of that time were not continuously filled with the Spirit, as in New Testament times, so the sudden voice was unexpected, startling, incontestable and undeniable. The message was crystal clear and absolute in authority, and it demanded a response.[4] Sometimes the Bible records that the word came to a certain individual at a specific time and place, such as, "On the fifth of the month in the fifth year of King Jehoiachin's exile, the word of the LORD came expressly to Ezekiel the priest, son of Buzi, in the land of the Chaldeans by the river Chebar" (Ezekiel 1:2–3). Or, "It came about in the same night that the word of the LORD came to Nathan, saying . . ." (2 Samuel 7:4). The word was obviously not premeditated or researched, but came as an immediate, profound, inspired, specific communication received clearly in the mind of the prophet with no doubt of what had been said.

A careful reading of all the references will demonstrate that the voice of God was sometimes external, in the sense that the prophet heard physically audible words, as the lad Samuel heard God calling him in 1 Samuel 3:2–8; and sometimes internal, in the sense that the prophet heard God's word spoken into his mind, yet it did not arrive on literal sound waves.[5]

The astounding story of the prophet Elijah hearing God's voice on Mount Horeb may be an example of this internal word.

His experience in sequence of the highest and lowest spiritual points of his illustrious career is strikingly illustrated in my home state of California, which has the highest and lowest geographical points in the lower 48 states. Mount Whitney, at 14,494 feet, reaches higher than any other mountain, and within fifty miles lies Death Valley at 282 feet below sea level. Within a short time the prophet Elijah plummeted from the pinnacle of ministerial success to the doldrums of rejection and despair.

Elijah had defied the prophets of Baal, called fire down from heaven, recalled rain to the drought-stricken land and outrun Ahab's chariot to Jezreel. A high peak indeed! Then, hearing that Queen Jezebel had sworn to take his life, he fled to Beersheba, the farthest southern boundary of the neighboring kingdom of Judah. In terrible depression, he slept under a juniper tree, then was awakened and fed by an angel. He pushed on another two hundred miles south to the mountain of God where Moses had received the Ten Commandments.

There, in the mouth of a cave,[6] God gave the prophet a spectacular display of tempest, earthquake and fire—but somehow Elijah knew that God was not in any of these things. Then came a voice, still and small, like a gentle rustling—a delicate, whispering voice that spoke to the depths of his soul. That undeniable voice, whether external or internal, grabbed Elijah's attention, restored his vision and recommissioned him to service (1 Kings 19:1–18). The voice changed the man!

Some prophets appear in the Scripture with no explanation about their calling or manner of prophecy, whereas others are described as hearing a voice, seeing a vision, gushing forth a prophecy or having an ecstatic experience. Here is a random sampling:

- *Ahijah* confronted Jeroboam on a country road, declaring that God would make him king over ten of the tribes (1 Kings 11:29–39). We know nothing of his call and only a few of his activities.
- *Amasai,* who is not specifically called a prophet, had "the Spirit come upon" him and gave a short prophetic ode to David (1 Chronicles 12:18).
- *Azariah* went out to bring prophetic guidance to King Asa (2 Chronicles 15:1–7) because "the Spirit of God came on" him.
- *Huldah* spoke forth a prophecy spontaneously to the king's delegation that had come to call on her (2 Chronicles 34:22–28). We know nothing of her beyond this, although it appears that she was well known.
- *Isaiah* had a profound calling in which he heard God's voice, saw His throne and experienced the touch of "a burning coal" (Isaiah 6:1–7).
- *Daniel* was thrust into prominence because he and his friends prayed to receive the king's forgotten vision with its interpretation. This came to Daniel "in a night vision" that he simply recounted (Daniel 2:19).
- *Amos* says that "the LORD took me from following the flock and the LORD said to me, 'Go prophesy to My people Israel'" (Amos 7:15).

All are gripped with a conviction that they have been handed an assignment by almighty God to deliver a message for Him. Who can answer the question of how a person hears the voice of God? It just happens—and when the word comes it cannot be denied. The Bible gives little detail about either the calling of His prophets or the prophetic process in their lives. But since nothing human or mechanical will produce it, the unknown details are not as essential as we might think. One simply waits for His voice.

Once as I was walking through the long underground tunnel at Los Angeles Airport that connects the arrival gates with the main terminal, I heard a voice boom out, "Reverend Gentile, please meet your party at the baggage claim area" at the very moment that I was walking beneath one of the overhead speakers. The impact of that voice calling my name directly overhead was electrifying! This, I believe, is the dramatic fashion in which God sometimes spoke to the prophets.

Some wonder, "Is the voice audible?" To the person who hears, this question is inconsequential, since the message is clear and undeniable. Prophets of old certainly had the capability to hear from God—but is this not possible for all of us? God speaks as easily to a person as we speak to one another. Each of us is capable of hearing from Him. Jesus said, "My sheep hear My voice" (John 10:27).

While in prayer at the church sanctuary one afternoon, I felt the Lord urge me to leave the church property. In the car I felt the Lord speak to me to go into the Purple Heart used clothing store. It was as though the steering wheel spun in my hands without my guidance! Nervously I entered the store (which I had never been in before), bought a candy bar and tried to look inconspicuous as I wandered around, trying to figure out why God would want me here. Suddenly, near the back of the store, I encountered a woman who attended our church. Her husband, who always ran out of his house when I came around, was with her. He asked me if we had made arrangements for getting the cement for our sidewalk. (At the time our church was new and small with a big sidewalk problem.) To make a long story short, he talked himself into bringing two other men to deliver and lay the cement for us, free of charge. Only God could have worked out such an answer to our need. Was I glad I listened!

We should not be consumed with *how* it happens, but rather spend our time positioning ourselves in prayer and attitude so that it *can* happen. God speaks; a man or woman hears and obeys. There you have it. It was so with the biblical prophets and it is still so today. I remember vividly when God spoke to me (a young pastor of 28 in Spokane, Washington) and said, "Go to San Jose and start a church." I understand this sort of leading is difficult for some people to accept, but I knew beyond a shadow of a doubt that God had spoken to me. And when this happens, no person or circumstance can talk you out of it.

I realize, of course, that God does not limit Himself to just an audible voice. He also uses natural means such as dreams, visions, trances, sentence fragments, single words, impressions and human messengers.[7] The audible voice here is our focus because it was used commonly in divine communication with the prophets.

Perhaps some of the mystery of such prophecy will be dispelled, and it will seem more possible for our own time, if we consider the most elementary form of prophecy as "two-way prayer." In fact many Christians, regardless of their view of the gifts, would affirm the idea that if we take time to wait for God to speak in our prayer times, He often does. This may take the form of an impression, a clear thought or a strong inclination. More than that, however, the voice of the Lord can be so clear and distinct at times that the words are actually quotable![8]

This can be an established part of Christian experience, just as it was with Old Testament prophets. Once we understand this, it does not seem impossible or even improbable to find the word of God expressed in the Church as well as on a personal level.

A Mental Picture

On occasion the Lord dramatized His word with attention-getting visual effects. A vision or mental image can sometimes make a clearer statement than words, and often human memory retains such an impression better. Jeremiah's call, for instance, involved the audible voice of God speaking to his mind, but the words were accompanied by two visions that dramatically pictured what would come to pass:

- A boiling pot pouring from the north, symbolizing coming invasion; and
- The branch of an almond tree, symbolizing Jeremiah's ministry as a harbinger.

Seventeen men in the Scripture are mentioned as having seen visions,[9] but others had the same experience even though the word *vision* does not appear. Zechariah, for instance, recounts a whole series of visions. He says things like, "I lifted up my eyes and looked, and behold, there was a man with a measuring line in his hand" (Zechariah 2:1). Ezekiel says, "The hand of the Lord GOD fell on me there. Then I looked, and behold, a likeness as the appearance of a man . . ." (Ezekiel 8:1–2).

A vision can be true to life, partially true to life (sometimes with an unusual twist) or apocalyptic. The five visions of judgment given to Amos were all taken from life experiences and carried easily applied spiritual meanings: the locust swarm, a consuming fire, a plumbline on a wall, a basket of summer fruit and the smitten doorposts (Amos 7:1–9:10). Daniel saw a vision of a two-horned ram and a one-horned goat locked in combat, but the victorious goat had his horn broken and replaced by four horns (chapter 8). (These animals and horns represented literal earthly kingdoms.) Sometimes a vision pictured a creature unlike anything on earth, such as Daniel's vision of the fourth beast with iron teeth (Daniel 7:7) or John's vision of a great red dragon (Revelation 12:3–4).

God's purpose is sometimes conveyed by ordinary events and creatures, and sometimes an apocalyptic twist adds special significance. An unnatural, exaggerated item in a vision can prove the most significant factor. An example is the sheaves of wheat, representing Joseph's family, bowing down to Joseph's sheaf of wheat (Genesis 37:5–7)—an unlikely scenario, to say the least. Later, of course, when famine overwhelmed that part of the world, Jacob's sons came to buy grain from Egypt and bowed before the prime minister (Genesis 42:6), who turned out to be their very own brother.

These visual impressions can come while a person is conscious or unconscious, dreaming or in a state of trance. God used a dream to warn the wise men not to return to King Herod (Matthew 2:12). Christians of diverse backgrounds testify of the impact of a spiritual dream; and whereas the recitation of it may seem insignificant to a listener, for the dreamer it is a life-changing experience.

Examples given in Scripture indicate that the prophet communicates his visionary message in several ways. In some instances he describes the vision as he sees it (1 Kings 22:17–23). Or, after seeing it, the prophet tells it publicly or records it and has it read (Habakkuk 2:2–3). The presentation can be a simple, descriptive narrative (Daniel 2:19–45), or a highly impassioned description and plea accompanied by exhortation and other prophetic emphases (Ezekiel 2:1–7), or a spontaneous burst of prophetic unction (2 Kings 5:25–27). These varied kinds of activity, I am persuaded, were meant to be part of New Testament Christianity as well as Hebrew religion (Acts 27:21–26).

When I was a young Christian I prayed fervently for a vision of Jesus, or an angel, or just any vision. Nothing happened for many years, but I learned to trust the Bible and stopped being so concerned about visions. Years later, while attending a prophetic meeting, sharp mental pictures suddenly started coming to my mind concerning various people. As the years have gone by, this form of vision has proven for me to be from God. While praying over a Christian young man I did not know, for instance, I saw him in a vision sloshing through jungle water and underbrush. Years later as a returned missionary he saw me and said, "It actually came to pass just as you said!"

An Immediate Unction

This kind of prophecy is unpremeditated. Like water gushing from a broken water main, so prophetic words burst forth from the prophet. What is happening is more than waxing eloquent; it is a welling up and rushing forth of "unctionized" words. They can come as a strong, calm current or more dramatically, but it is immediately obvious that God is doing it.

Unction is an archaic term, but I like it and use it in the same sense that Charles H. Spurgeon did. He called it "a dew from the Lord, a divine presence which you will recognise at once . . . 'an unction from the holy one.'"[10] Spurgeon emphasized the close connection between the prayer closet and this public anointing with the Spirit. Although well known for his preaching, Spurgeon reckoned that there were as many as a dozen cases in which, interrupting his sermon, he had suddenly pointed to someone in his audience and given a striking description without any knowledge of the person. These spontaneous descriptions had usually caused the conversion of the person addressed.

"While preaching in the hall on one occasion," he recounted, "I deliberately pointed to a man in the midst of the crowd and said, 'There is a man sitting there, who is a shoemaker. He keeps his shop open on Sundays. It was open last Sabbath morning, and he took ninepence—with fourpence profit from it. His soul is sold to Satan for fourpence!'" Later a city missionary happened to meet the shoemaker. As they discussed Spurgeon, the shoemaker explained that Spurgeon's word was exactly right and had caused his conversion. Fearful at first to return to the church and risk further exposure, the man finally concluded that it must have been God. From then on he shut up his shop on Sundays and went to God's house to hear the Baptist prophet preach.[11]

Second Chronicles 34 offers the remarkable account of Huldah the prophetess. King Josiah sent a delegation of five officials to inquire what they should do about the apostasy of Judah. Huldah did not know of their coming, but her bold, fervent, instantaneous reply exemplifies immediate unction. She predicted terrible judgment because of the idolatry but blessed the king for his humility. A brief revival swept through the nation as the king took her word to heart and the people repented.

This kind of prophecy is like glossolalia, or speaking in tongues. The Holy Spirit speaks forth words that are not known ahead of time. Sometimes the message flows quietly and evenly; at other times it is loud and animated. There are various degrees of intensity in Holy Spirit activity. Usually, however, the prophet has control over whether the speech comes forth.

An Ecstatic Experience

The word *ecstasy* has sometimes been used to describe the mental or emotional state of a person prophesying or receiving revelation. It is an awkward word to use since there are a variety of definitions and the word does not appear in the King James Version, the Revised Standard Version or the New English Bible. Robert L. Alden of Hebrew Union College says, "There is no adequate and accurate definition of 'ecstasy.' Hardly any two authors agree although many are of one mind that the prophets were ecstatic."[12]

One meaning, the first listed in my *Webster's Collegiate Dictionary,* Tenth Edition, tends to make religious people skittish: "A state of being beyond reason and self-control." Sometimes ecstasy is attached to hallucination, frenzy, mania, the unconscious, the subconscious, clairvoyance and many more such textbook terms. Actually there is no concrete example of a true prophet of the Lord going into an ecstatic state that would produce an irresponsible delirium or rage. Three frequent proof texts for abnormal prophetic actions concern Balaam (Numbers 23–24), Saul (1 Samuel 19:24) and the priests of Baal on Mount Carmel (1 Kings 18:26–29), but the arguments do not hold water. None of these people was called a prophet or functioned in a typical prophetic manner.[13]

One leading commentator described the Hebrew prophet's behavior in the following strange manner, even though there is no one clear biblical instance of a true prophet acting like this:

> We can now call before our minds a picture of the Prophet's activity in public. He might be mingling with the crowd, sometimes on ordinary days, sometimes on special occasions. Suddenly something would happen to him. His eye would become fixed, strange convulsions would seize upon his limbs, the form of his speech would change. Men would recognise that the Spirit had fallen upon him. The fit would pass, and he would tell to those who stood around the things which he had seen and heard. There might have been symbolic action, and this he would explain with a clear memory of all that had befallen him, and of all that he had done under the stress of the ecstasy. Such manifestations were common, and there were many who were subject to them.[14]

Evangelical scholars react against such interpretation, and rightly so, using the Pauline admonition of 1 Corinthians 14:32 that "the spirits of prophets are subject to prophets." The implication is that anyone prophesying should be rational and under control. I agree. But this approach taken to the extreme is not the answer either, for the prophets must not be stripped of human personality and emotion. They are not just cerebral spokesmen for God, especially when their message is dynamic and they are energized by the powerful Holy Spirit.

Who among us is the perfect conduit for God's revelation? Every person has a unique set of responses to a given situation, especially if it is extremely forceful. Consider a live electrical wire lying on the street. One man comes along and picks it up; he jerks and passes out. Another picks it up, screaming and yelling as he does so. Another has violent convulsions. And so it goes in the natural. So why should we think every reaction to the dynamic Spirit will be subdued, restrained and uninteresting?

This definition of *ecstasy* is given in *The International Standard Bible Encyclopedia*: "Defined in a distinctively religious sense, an abnormal state of consciousness in which revelatory communications (both visionary and auditory) are believed to be received from supernatural beings. . . . 'Ecstasy' is a transliteration of the Greek noun *ekstasis*, derived from the verb *existemi* (or *existano*), the root meaning of which is 'displace,' 'stand apart from,' or 'put out of place.'" The article finally settles on "the revelatory state of consciousness"[15] to describe in a positive way the prophetic consciousness.

The Greek Old Testament uses *ekstasis* thirty times to translate eleven different Hebrew words, the majority of which are synonyms for "fear" or "terror." There is no single Hebrew word that describes the revelatory state, so these eleven Hebrew words are funneled into the one word of the Greek Old Testament. My conclusion, then, is that a precise definition for *ecstasy* is not possible.

In the New Testament *ekstasis* is used seven times. In three of these passages it is appropriately translated "trance," and in the other four places the meaning is "amazement" or "astonishment." In a state of trance both Peter (Acts 10:10; 11:5) and Paul (Acts 22:17) "received direction and guidance from God. The experience included both visionary and auditory components. . . . Both of these instances . . . lend support to the term [trance] as a legitimate descriptor of a visionary activity within the New Testament."[16]

Were the prophets ecstatics? We know that supernatural activity is the process by which communication between God and mankind takes place. The prophets may or may not have been "ecstatic," but we do know they were used or possessed by the Holy Spirit. The following list of Old Testament expressions might be termed "ecstatic" in the sense that the prophecy came strongly and irresistibly to the prophet. (These expressions can also fit at times under my heading of "Immediate Unction," but this is arbitrary.)

- "The hand of the LORD" fell or was on someone (Ezekiel 3:14, 22; 8:1; 33:22; 37:1).
- "The Spirit of God came upon" a certain one (Numbers 24:2; 1 Samuel 10:10; 11:6; 19:20, 23; 2 Chronicles 15:1; see Isaiah 61:1).
- "The Spirit lifted me up" (Ezekiel 8:3; 11:1, 24; 43:5).
- "The Spirit entered me" (Ezekiel 2:2; 3:24).
- "The Spirit rested upon them" (Numbers 11:25–26).

- "The word of the LORD came" to a certain prophet (1 Samuel 15:10; 2 Samuel 24:11; 1 Kings 19:9; Jonah 1:1; Haggai 1:1; 2:1, 20; Zechariah 7:1, 8; 8:1).
- "The Spirit of the LORD clothed" [lit. Hebrew] people such as Gideon, Amasai and Zechariah (Judges 6:34; 1 Chronicles 12:18; 2 Chronicles 24:20).

This we know: When a person experienced the revelatory state, it was distinct from his or her natural state of consciousness. Certainly some compulsion of the Spirit occurred, an out-of-the-ordinary state of being overcome. Such an ecstatic condition was healthful and beneficial, not in the least destructive. We also know the prophets were especially called of God and given their messages by direct divine communication. If we accept the idea of supernatural intervention, we may take all the biblical passages at face value without manufacturing some farfetched idea of ecstatic frenzy or mad behavior.

The Prophetic Call

Two examples of prophetic calling are particularly important:

- The *first* man considered to hold the Old Testament prophetic office
- The *last* man to hold the Old Testament prophetic office

Approximately one thousand years separate Samuel and John the Baptist, yet they show similarity and continuity in ministry. Since the Bible focuses special attention on their introductions, and since they occupy significant positions, a brief review and comparison of their backgrounds seems appropriate. Neither man is considered a canonical prophet (no prophetic books were written by them) but their stories and many of their words appear in Scripture.

The Call of Samuel

Although prophets had already existed in Israel, Samuel is generally considered the first of the prophets who not only had a *gift* to prophesy but also held the *office or ministry* of prophet in an institutional sense. Before Samuel a few prophets on rare occasions were recorded, but there was no organized, recognized prophetic office. With Samuel it was not a case of isolated commissions; he assumed a regular office of prophet with "the word of the Lord" permanently with him. He instituted the training of prophets and originated a prophetic order and procedure that was the prototype for succeeding generations. For these reasons, although he was also a judge, he is often thought of as "the first of the prophets." Three verses from the New Testament seem to confirm this:

- "All the prophets from Samuel and those that follow after, as many as have spoken, have likewise foretold of these days" (Acts 3:24, KJV).
- "After that [God] gave unto them judges about the space of four hundred and fifty years, until Samuel the prophet" (Acts 13:20, KJV).
- "What shall I more say? for the time would fail me to tell of Gideon, and . . . Samuel, and of the prophets" (Hebrews 11:32, KJV).

Samuel was the last of the judges as well as the first of the prophets. His appearance also marks the beginning of the institution of the monarchy. The time of the judges with its sporadic leadership had been difficult for the new nation, and now the Philistines were growing more menacing and demanding. The people panicked like sheep without a shepherd, and a national cry, led by the elders, arose for a king with political and military might who could defend them. The history of the rise and fall of the Israelite monarchy, starting with the anointing of the first king, Saul, by the prophet Samuel, is recorded in the books of Samuel, Kings and Chronicles. In a sense this registry is an account of the interaction between kings and prophets.

The first three chapters of 1 Samuel tell the fascinating story of a desperate couple's desire for a child, the wife's sincere prayer that produced the miracle and the introduction of the boy Samuel to the prophetic realm. The national religious scene was deplorable. The priest Eli and his profligate sons had corrupted the priesthood and the worship of God's people. Yet into this hopeless situation the baby Samuel was born and, as a child, dedicated to begin his service in the house of God.

The account reminds me of a scene I saw more than thirty years ago on my first missionary trip to Brazil. In the dirtiest of *barrio* settings I spotted a solitary orchid blooming, obviously not planted by the hand of man. This beautiful flower seemed oblivious to the awful filth surrounding it. So, in similar fashion, the child Samuel was brought, newly weaned, to the aged priest Eli as the seed of a new ministry—to bloom in the worst of spiritual conditions.

An unnamed prophet (one of the few of that time) had previously come to Eli declaring impending judgment on the priest and his sons and predicting a restored priesthood and the voice of God in Israel. The old man, recognizing the validity of the charges, hid the ominous tidings in his heart, waiting to see how events would unfold.

It happened through Samuel. He was a boy of about twelve when he first heard the voice of God.[17] Previously the young man had had no sense of a personal revelation of God, no special knowledge of the Lord and His word. He simply walked as faithfully as he could, serving as a Levite, "ministering to the LORD before Eli" (1 Samuel 3:1). One night "the LORD called Samuel" (verse 4). Rising from his bed, the lad ran to Eli, thinking the priest had called him. After the second time the startled old man realized it must be God calling the boy. Once more the Lord called, and Samuel responded as Eli advised: "Speak, LORD, for Thy servant is listening" (verse 9). The awesome message of judgment reiterated exactly what had been given Eli by the unnamed prophet.

The next morning the anxious elder summoned young Samuel and insisted on hearing all that had been told him. The woeful message was painful to deliver, but the lad gave the full report carefully and truthfully. Thus Samuel passed the most basic test for prophetic ministry: the ability to receive God's message and the courage to deliver it regardless of content or circumstances. Trumpets did not blare or bells ring, but a new period in the history of the Kingdom of God had come quietly into being.

"Thus Samuel grew and the LORD was with him and let none of his words fail ["Left no word unfulfilled which He spoke through Samuel," *Keil and Delitzsh Commentary*]. And all Israel from Dan even to Beersheba knew that Samuel was confirmed ["was found trustworthy, or approved," *KD*] as a prophet of the LORD. And the LORD appeared again at Shiloh, because the LORD revealed Himself to Samuel at Shiloh by the word of the LORD. Thus the word of Samuel came to all Israel" (1 Samuel 3:19–21; 4:1).

The Call of John the Baptist

A millennium passed. The time arrived to close the old era and issue in the new. The last and greatest of the Old Testament prophets[18]—he who was to introduce the Messiah to Israel—was presented dramatically. Bypassing the high-and-mighty political and religious figures of the time, "the word of God came to John, the son of Zacharias, in the wilderness" (Luke 3:2). A most unlikely candidate by outward standards for such an important assignment, he was the son of poor, priestly parents who made their home in the hill country of Judea. He was a miracle child, born at a time when it was physically impossible for his parents to have a child. An angel made the announcement to Zacharias the father, who found the news so incredible that the angel had to impose a nine-month silence (an act of confirmation) on the bewildered old man. Finally, when John was born, the elderly priest gushed forth joyfully with one of Scripture's most powerful prophecies (Luke 1:67–79).

John "grew up and became strong in spirit. Then he lived out in the wilderness until he began his public ministry to Israel" (Luke 1:80, NLT). Possibly John knew from his parents about his calling, but this alone did not and could not make him a prophet; he needed the divine call. And it happened. "The word of God came to John . . . in the wilderness."

We moderns, like news reporters clamoring for a story, are impatient with such a simple explanation. What was John feeling? *Silence.* What did God say? *Silence.* What were the details of this calling? *Silence.* The record says simply that the word came.

Similarities between Samuel and John

The story of the boy Samuel is significant. It shows the bypassing of the old priest set in his ways and sins, indicating that a prophet must have a fresh heart for God and His ways. The boy Samuel was unencumbered with distractions. John the Baptist, living a simple, nomadic life, also had this trait. Both heard the voice of God. Probably audible to the natural ear, the "word" could just as easily have been a quiet, powerful voice speaking within the mind and spirit. The bottom line remains: They heard the call and wasted no time in responding.

Some other interesting similarities are evident in the lives of Samuel and John:

- Both had godly, dedicated parents.
- Both had parents who prayed for a child.
- An elderly priest and a godly woman were prominent in both stories.
- Eli confirmed the mother's prayer; an angel confirmed Zacharias'.
- Both men were "life Nazirites," dedicated to God and His will.
- Both were raised by a priest.
- Both of the priests were judged.
- Both prophets came from humble circumstances.
- Both heard and responded to the voice of the Lord.
- Both challenged the corrupt priesthood of their day.
- Both were used by God to open a new era of spiritual renewal.
- Samuel introduced the first (mortal) king of natural Israel; John the Baptist introduced the first (immortal) king of spiritual Israel.
- Samuel anointed David; John baptized Jesus.

- Both had disciples.
- Both were accepted by the whole nation.
- Both were noncanonical prophets, although their histories and words are given in Scripture.

Here are some lessons we can learn from Samuel and John about prophets:

- Dedicated parents play an important part in developing a spiritual ministry.
- A youth as well as an adult is capable of hearing the voice of God.
- Prophets should be as free as possible from worldly entanglements (both were Nazirites).
- Dedication and faithfulness, even unto death (as with John), are essential.
- A prophet should have the willingness to hear and faithfulness to deliver, regardless of surrounding circumstances.
- Length of ministry time may vary. John's ministry was short-lived and Samuel's lasted forty years, yet each man was true to the assignment given him.
- Both were considered by all to be prophets, yet their ministries were different: Samuel was a father to the nation, visiting towns and cities; John was the voice of a herald crying in the wilderness and beside the Jordan River.

Canonical and Noncanonical Prophets

The books included in our Bibles are "canonical" because they qualified to be included in the canon of Scripture. *Canon* comes from the Greek *kanon,* which refers to a reed used as a measuring rod or standard. Applied to Scripture, *canon* refers to the 66 books officially accepted into our Bible.[19]

Canonical prophets are those who wrote (or had written for them) the prophetic books worthy to be included in the Bible. These prophets did not simply rely on natural literary skills; they were inspired by the Holy Spirit to write these books or sections of the Bible. The Word of God that came to them was then both spoken to the people and transcribed for future generations.

The chart on page 89 lists the prophets named in Scripture. In the first column are the sixteen men (the major and minor prophets) who wrote the biblical books bearing their names. The second column lists seventeen other prophets who contributed a significant passage or passages in the Scripture. The 28 prophets in the third column (plus unnamed prophets) did not produce or write prophecy for Scripture, but their exploits are recorded there.

Not all the biblical prophets wrote books of the Bible or prophesied with the impressive ability of Isaiah. Michael Harper says that "prophecy

Chart of the Prophets

Canonical*	Noncanonical (some Scripture†)	Part of Narrative‡
Amos	Asaph	Aaron
Daniel	David	Abraham
Ezekiel	Deborah	Agabus
Habakkuk	Ethan	Ahijah
Haggai	Ezra	Amasai
Hosea	Heman	Anna
Isaiah	Jacob	Azariah
Jeremiah	Job	Eliezer
Job	John the Apostle	Elijah
Joel	John the Baptist	Elisha
Jonah	Joseph	Enoch
Malachai	Miriam	Gad
Micah	Moses	Hanani
Nahum	Samuel	Heman
Obadiah	Simeon	Huldah
Zechariah	Solomon	Iddo
	Zacharias	Jeduthun
		Jehu
		Judas
		Micaiah
		Nathan
		Oded
		Shemaiah
		Silas
		Solomon
		Unnamed prophets§
		Uriah
		Zadok
		Zechariah (son of Jehoiada)

* A major or minor prophet
† The prophet has an important passage in the Bible
‡ No Scripture written
§ In appendixes 1–3 I have given a complete record of all prophetic activity, including the unnamed prophets. I realize that usually *canonical* refers to the major and minor prophets of the eighth century on (usually beginning with Amos). However, Moses, David, Solomon, Samuel, the two Johns and others all supplied a large section of the Scripture, so I felt they should be included in my second column so their contributions are not overlooked.

in the Old Testament was not limited to the Canonical Prophets—nor was it in the New Testament. . . ."[20] Most of the prophetic activity in both testamental times was of a personal, domestic type that would not be given or appropriate for widespread public announcement or permanent record.

Canonical prophecy—prophecy worthy to be included in Scripture—was a high-level, extraordinary kind of prophecy given uniquely for that purpose. When such special revelation found incorporation in Scripture, it was considered *inscripturated*. (This academic word, not found in the average dictionary, describes a prophecy's transition from a spoken statement into an embodiment in Scripture.) Obviously inscripturating prophecy is in a class of its own, and such prophecy ceased with the book of Revelation given to the apostle John.[21]

Two well-known references substantiate the inherent revelation and nature of Scripture. The first from 2 Timothy 3:16 is called by Henry Swete "the *locus classicus* on this subject," and he correctly suggests that the second of the following two references gives the best comment on the first:[22]

"From childhood you have known the Holy Scriptures, which are able to make you wise for salvation through faith which is in Christ Jesus. All Scripture is given *by inspiration of God,* and is profitable for doctrine, for reproof, for correction, for instruction in righteousness" (2 Timothy 3:15–16, NKJV, emphasis added).

"Knowing this first, that no prophecy of Scripture is of any private interpretation, for prophecy never came by the will of man, but holy men of God spoke as they were *moved by the Holy Spirit*" (2 Peter 1:20–21, NKJV, emphasis added).

These are two superb statements of the highest purpose and realm of prophecy: the ministry of the canonical prophet-apostle who brought, through human language, the exact word of God to mankind, both in a contemporary and an eternal sense. Charles Hodge, the famous Princeton theologian, says: "On this subject the common doctrine of the Church is, and ever has been, that inspiration was an influence of the Holy Spirit on the minds of certain select men, which rendered them the organs of God for the infallible communication of his mind and will. They were in such a sense the organs of God, that what they said God said."[23]

Let's look at each of these key Scriptures.

The Meaning of "Inspiration" (Theopneustos)

Inspiration is the key word in 2 Timothy 3:16. This English word, meaning simply "to breathe in," is not adequate for the meaning Paul intended. Most translations of the Greek word *theopneustos* state that all

Scripture is "inspired by God" (TEV, JB, NASB, NLT, Phillips, RSV, Williams) or "is given by inspiration of God" (KJV, NKJV). Two somewhat misleading translations are: "Every scripture inspired of God" (ASV) or "every inspired scripture has its use" (NEB). The most literally accurate translation would make the Scriptures "God-breathed" (as in Amplified, Interlinear, Message, NIV, Rotherham).

The Expositors Bible Commentary says: "All Scripture is God-breathed. That is exactly what the Greek says. The adjective *theopneustos* (only here in the NT) is compounded of *theos*, 'God,' and the verb *pneo*, 'breathe.' This is one of the greatest texts in the NT on the inspiration of the Bible."[24]

Alan M. Stibbs, British theologian, adds this insight: "The word 'inspired,' . . . indicates rather *how* the writing came into being. It asserts that the writing is a product of the creative activity of the divine breath. . . . Scripture has in its origin this distinctive hallmark, that it owes its very existence to the direct creative activity of God himself."[25]

Harold Lindsell, noted biblical scholar and seminary professor, says: "God indeed is the author of Scripture, and Scripture is the product of His creative breath. The emphasis is not on inspired writers as much as it is on inspired Scripture. Scripture is 'breathed out.' This is not to suggest that the Holy Spirit did not move on the writers themselves, but that the writers produced a product, which, while it was their own, was also the Word of the Living God."[26]

Edward J. Young, noted professor and Hebrew linguist, says: "The true meaning is passive, 'that which is breathed out by God.' . . . Timothy . . . is being asked to place his confidence not in writings which merely express the hopes and aspirations of the best of men, but rather in writings which are themselves actually breathed out by God, and consequently of absolute authority."[27]

The Significance of Moved

The key word found in 2 Peter 1:21, our second important text, is *moved:* "Holy men of God spake as they were *moved* by the Holy Ghost" (KJV, emphasis added). This comment explains how God gave the prophets a "God-breathed word." The word translated "moved" comes from the Greek *phero*, which justifies a stronger translation: "to bear or carry." This "figure of speech is borrowed from the nautical vocabulary, in the sense that a sailboat is carried along by the wind."[28]

The NIV says: "Prophecy never had its origin in the will of man, but men spoke from God as they were carried along by the Holy Spirit." The Amplified gives additional insight: "For no prophecy ever originated

91

because some man willed it [to do so]—it never came by human impulse—but as men spoke from God who were borne along (moved and impelled) by the Holy Spirit."

Second Peter 1:20 clarifies the nature of this Holy Spirit moving: "No prophecy of the Scripture is of any private interpretation" (KJV). Human beings, acting independently and alone, are not the prime mover in either the production or interpretation of Scripture. Alan M. Stibbs says: "For true prophecy has never emerged, except when men have been taken up into an activity of the Spirit of God, and borne along to the place, or into the circumstances and the conditions, where they gave utterance to words of which God was the primary originating cause."[29]

A writing prophet was "carried along" (that is, sustained in a certain mental state or condition), held by the Spirit in a receptive mode that allowed divine impartation, keen memory retention and an unctionized delivery. Certainly if God could invade the mind of Nebuchadnezzar, the worldly king of Babylon, He could bring words and visions to His servants the prophets.

The Actual Words of God

No question existed in the minds of the New Testament writers that the Old Testament Scriptures were actually the Word of God. Old Testament quotations are introduced in the New Testament with this absolute conviction. In Romans and 1 and 2 Corinthians, the apostle declares with finality, "It is written," or, "As it is written," then gives a quotation. Sometimes the New Testament quotes an Old Testament prophet, then attributes the very words to God as the author ("He says"—referring to God).[30] The writer of Hebrews quotes the Old Testament prophets by stating that God or the Holy Spirit "says" or "has said" or "is saying" something.[31] The book of Acts attributes words from various prophets to the Holy Spirit.[32] In Matthew the Old Testament quotations are said to be "through" the prophet Isaiah[33] or Jeremiah[34] or Zechariah.[35]

Writers of the New Testament considered the sacred Scriptures of the Jewish canon to be the actual words of God. They believed God "breathed" these words into the prophets as He "carried them along."

The same inspiration is claimed for the apostles and writers of the New Testament. The Church includes these writings along with the Hebrew Scriptures to make up the aggregate of written Scripture. The inscripturated words of Paul and other New Testament writers are accorded the same status as that of the Old Testament prophets; their words are the very words of God.[36] These references are clear in this matter:

"We also constantly thank God that when you received from us the word of God's message, you accepted it not as the word of men, *but for what it really is, the word of God,* which also performs its work in you who believe" (1 Thessalonians 2:13, emphasis added).

"Remember the words spoken beforehand by the holy prophets and *the commandment of the Lord and Savior spoken by your apostles*" (2 Peter 3:2, emphasis added).

"Our beloved brother Paul, according to the wisdom given him, wrote to you, as also in all his letters, speaking in them of these things, in which are some things hard to understand, which the untaught and unstable distort, as they do also *the rest of the Scriptures,* to their own destruction" (2 Peter 3:15–16, emphasis added).

So the Scriptures of both Testaments come to the Church as the revelation of divine truth, the standard of orthodox teaching. The canon of the Bible stands as the eternal standard of measurement. Any statement purporting to be a word from God is judged by the golden rod of Scripture. Although recorded by human agents, the Bible is the highest example of God communicating His thoughts to mankind. It is the grandest expression of prophecy ever given to men.[37]

Prophetic Warning in Armenia

In the last chapter I gave the true story of an old Russian prophet and patriarch and the grandfather of Demos Shakarian, founder of the Full Gospel Business Men. Another astounding episode in that story proves once again the feasibility of authentic (but noncanonical) prophecy in today's Church:

> It was the beginning of great changes in our family's life, and one of the first was a change in attitude toward Kara Kala's most famous citizen. This person was known throughout the region as the "Boy Prophet" even though at the time of the incident with the steer's head the Boy Prophet was fifty-eight years old.
>
> The man's real name was Efim Gerasemovitch Klubniken, and he had a remarkable history. He was of Russian origin, his family being among the first Pentecostals to come across the border, settling permanently in Kara Kala. From earliest childhood Efim had shown a gift for prayer, frequently going on long fasts, praying around the clock.
>
> As everybody in Kara Kala knew, when Efim was eleven years old he had heard the Lord calling him again to one of his prayer vigils. This time he persisted for seven days and nights, and during this time received a vision.

This in itself was not extraordinary. Indeed, as Grandfather had been accustomed to grumble, anyone who went that long without eating or sleeping was bound to start seeing things. But what Efim was able to *do* during those seven days was not so easy to explain.

Efim could neither read nor write. Yet, as he sat in the little stone cottage in Kara Kala, he saw before him a vision of charts and a message in beautiful handwriting. Efim asked for pen and paper. And for seven days sitting at the rough plank-table where the family ate, he laboriously copied down the form and shape of letters and diagrams that passed before his eyes.

When he had finished, the manuscript was taken to people in the village who could read. It turned out that this illiterate child had written out in Russian characters a series of instructions and warnings. At some unspecified time in the future, the boy wrote, every Christian in Kara Kala would be in terrible danger. He foretold a time of unspeakable tragedy for the entire area, when hundreds of thousands of men, women, and children would be brutally murdered. The time would come, he warned, when everyone in the region must flee. They must go to a land across the sea. Although he had never seen a geography book, the Boy Prophet drew a map showing exactly where the fleeing Christians were to go. To the amazement of the adults, the body of water depicted so accurately in the drawing was not the nearby Black Sea, or the Caspian Sea, or even the farther-off Mediterranean, but the distant and unimaginable Atlantic Ocean! There was no doubt about it, nor about the identity of the land on the other side: the map plainly indicated the east coast of the United States of America.

But the refugees were not to settle down there, the prophecy continued. They were to continue traveling until they reached the west coast of the new land. There, the boy wrote, God would bless them and prosper them, and cause their seed to be a blessing to the nations. . . .

Well, many people in Kara Kala smiled at these romances of a little boy. Surely there must be some explanation of the "miraculous" writing. Perhaps he had secretly taught himself to read and write, just in order to play this trick on the village.

Others, however, took to calling Efim the Boy Prophet and were not at all convinced that the message was not genuine. Every time news of fresh political troubles reached the tranquil hills around Ararat, they would get out the now-yellowed pages and read them again. . . .

And then, a little after the turn of the century, Efim announced that the time was near for the fulfillment of the words he had written down nearly fifty years before. "We must flee to America. All who remain here will perish."

Here and there in Kara Kala Pentecostal families packed up and left the holdings that had been their ancestral possessions time out of mind. Efim and his family were among the first to go. As each group of Pentecostals left Armenia, they were jeered by those who remained behind. Skeptical and disbelieving folk—including many Christians—refused to believe that God could issue pinpoint instructions for modern people in a modern age.

But the instructions proved correct. In 1914 a period of unimaginable horror arrived for Armenia. With remorseless efficiency the Turks began the bloody business of driving two-thirds of the population out into the Mesopotamian desert. Over a million men, women and children died in these death marches, including every inhabitant of Kara Kala. Another half a million were massacred in their villages, in a program that was later to provide Hitler his blueprint for the extermination of the Jews. . . .

The few Armenians who managed to escape the besieged areas brought with them tales of great heroism. They reported that the Turks sometimes gave Christians an opportunity to deny their faith in exchange for their lives. The favorite procedure was to lock a group of Christians in a barn and set it afire: "If you are willing to accept Mohammed in place of Christ we'll open the doors." Time and again, the Christians chose to die, chanting hymns of praise as the flames engulfed them.

Those who had heeded the warning of the Boy Prophet and sought asylum in America heard the news with dismay.

Grandfather Demos was among these who had fled. After his experience with the Russian patriarch, Grandfather no longer discounted the validity of prophecy. In 1905 he sold the farm which had been in the family for generations . . . selected the possessions that his family would carry on their backs . . . and with his wife, his six daughters . . . and . . . thirteen-year-old Isaac, he set out for America.[38]

REFLECTIONS

It was by the agency of the Spirit of God that the prophets received the Divine communication. . . . But the means by which the Divine Spirit communicated with the human spirit under which the Divine communications were received, have not been clearly declared to us.[39]

William Smith

The responsible personhood of the prophet remains intact even though the whole man with his understanding and will stands under the operation of the Spirit.[40]

G. Friedrich

The prophetic ministry could be summed up as simply the ability to hear God. There are spiritual gifts involved, but the most important quality for anyone who is called by God to have is the ability to understand what God is saying. We will only be able to understand what He is saying if we know Him, and know His language.[41]

Paul Cain

95

The eagle of prophecy had its nest on the rock of accomplished fact; but to that rock it was not chained. It had a pinion strong enough to bear it up towards the sun, to an elevation from which it could descry things then distant, yea, and things yet to come.[42]

Joseph Bryant Rotherham

What, then, shall we think about the Bible? I will tell you very plainly what I think we ought to think. I hold that the Biblical writers, after having been prepared for their task by the providential ordering of their entire lives, received, in addition to all that, a blessed and wonderful and supernatural guidance and impulsion by the Spirit of God, so that they were preserved from the errors that appear in other books and thus the resulting book, the Bible, is in all its parts the very Word of God, completely true in what it says regarding matters of fact, and completely authoritative in its commands.[43]

J. Gresham Machen

MESSAGE: VARIOUS WAYS OF PROPHETIC EXPRESSION

"It is Your message I have given them, not my own."

Jeremiah 17:16b (NLT)

THE ABILITY TO COMMUNICATE is an awesome gift of God. Unlike whales and birds and chimpanzees, who can make known only some of their most basic wants and feelings, we humans have a vastly superior and highly sophisticated language ability. It is part of the image of God stamped in us. Adam quickly discovered his innate ability to speak, and humans have been talking ever since. After man's sin God particularly desired to communicate His concerned thoughts to the fallen creature made in His image.

From the divine standpoint, prophecy is God speaking His mind and sharing His words with mankind. From the human point of view the prophet is the conduit, channel or spokesman for those words, and in such use speech is elevated to the highest possible function. For the current of divine revelation to flow, there must be a live contact at both ends. The prophet-spokesman, obedient to God and sympathetic with man, was God's human contact.

In this chapter we will discuss the variety of ways prophecy was expressed. Since prophets are people (although God did speak once through a donkey!), there are of necessity quite an assortment and degrees of manifestations, for God puts His word in many different kinds of people, allowing the divine message to be clothed with the human characteristics and weaknesses of the prophet, so that he or she will be identifiable and compatible with the audience.

The main feature of the prophet's vocation and work was oral communication. Gene Tucker states it well: "Whatever else it entails, 'to prophesy' means to speak. Furthermore, even if there were . . . only prophetic words themselves, it would be clear from the form, style, and content of those words that the prophets were fundamentally speakers."[1] Numerous passages support this fact. For instance:

- "The Spirit of the LORD spoke by me" (2 Samuel 23:2).
- "The LORD spoke through His servants the prophets . . ." (2 Kings 21:10).
- "The mouth of the LORD [through Isaiah's words] has spoken" (Isaiah 1:20).
- "All that I command you, you shall speak" (Jeremiah 1:7).
- "Include every word" (Jeremiah 26:2, NLT).
- "The Lord GOD has spoken! Who can but prophesy?" (Amos 3:8).
- ". . . The words which the LORD of hosts had sent by His Spirit through the former prophets . . ." (Zechariah 7:12).

Many passages show that the primary ministry of the prophet was to prophesy—and that means *to speak the message God has given.* Leon Wood adds this extra dimension: "A prophet was one who should speak for God with strong emotional involvement. . . . They were not merely to give recitations; they were to bring vital messages that would change lives. This called for speaking fervently. Thus . . . 'to prophesy' in its fullest significance meant 'to speak fervently for God.'"[2]

The prophets and apostles were less cerebral and more emotional, I believe, than we give them credit for. Their primary calling was to deliver with expediency the word of the living God. This necessitated using their minds, of course, but they were primarily "Spirit people," energetic messengers—not only recipients and bearers of a message, but Spirit-endowed messengers with God-enablement and God-consciousness. It was this spiritual dimension that made their errands possible and successful.

The Lord touched the mouths of three of His servants: Isaiah (6:7), Jeremiah (1:9) and Daniel (10:16). This dramatic action emphasizes the importance of the spoken word and shows God's great concern that words reflect exactly what He wishes. It also explains the fervency and enthusiasm that filled the prophets. Any good salesman who is sold on his product and anxious to make a sale will speak with energy. Over and above this natural enthusiasm and authority, the prophets spoke as people touched by heavenly fire.

The Burden of the Lord

On occasion a prophet ignited by his divine insights would preface his message with a "messenger formula"[3]—an identifying phrase that would leave no doubt about whose word it was and whose authority he invoked. This was the style employed by ancient potentates who sent forth ambassadors and messengers to speak in their behalf (see Ezra 1:2). For example:

- "A man of God came to Eli and said to him, 'Thus says the LORD ...'" (1 Samuel 2:27).
- "Listen to the words of the LORD. 'Thus says the LORD of hosts ...'" (1 Samuel 15:1–2).
- "Go and say to My servant David, 'Thus says the LORD ...'" (2 Samuel 7:5).
- "O altar, altar, thus says the LORD ..." (1 Kings 13:2).
- "Thus says the Lord GOD of hosts ..." (Isaiah 22:15).
- "Then the LORD said ..." (Isaiah 29:13).
- "Therefore, prophesy, son of man, and say to Gog, 'Thus says the Lord GOD ...'" (Ezekiel 38:14).
- "Hear this word which the LORD has spoken against you ..." (Amos 3:1).
- "The word of the LORD came to Jonah the son of Amittai saying ..." (Jonah 1:1).

Edersheim describes with keen insight the prophet, made bold by divine sanction, who brought a word of judgment against the spurious and false altar in Bethel. This epitomizes true prophetic authority: "It was a stranger who spoke, and, as we know him, a Judaean, 'a man of *Elohim*.' He had come 'in [so literally] the word of Jehovah' (1 Kings xiii.1)—not merely in charge of it, nor only in its constraining power, but as if the Word of Jehovah itself had come, and this 'man of God' had been carried in it to deliver the message which he 'cried to the altar in the word of Jehovah' (ver. 2)."[4]

Authority is shown in another messenger formula used frequently by the prophets, expressed in the King James and the New King James Versions as "the burden" of the Lord. The more modern translations call it simply "the message" (NLT, CEV, TEV), whereas the NIV and the NASB call it "the oracle." Perhaps the Amplified says it best: "The burden or oracle, or that which is to be lifted up."

The Hebrew word *massa* undoubtedly implies more than just another "messenger speech" (the term used by textual critics).[5] The underlying thought of "a burden" is too important to ignore. "Cognates of the Hebrew word . . . have mostly the meaning of something lifted up."[6] The word is used both in the sense of a load and in that of an utterance or oracle. Both are something "taken up" or "lifted" and can refer figuratively to "something *taken up* solemnly upon the lips (cf. Exodus 23:1, Psalm 15:3, 16:4, Ezekiel 36:3. . . .)" Such prophecies "were mainly of a threatening character, the burden thus being the threats of punishment imposed upon the place or people concerned."[7] God did not pass judgment on His people lightly; it weighed on Him like a heavy load. The prophet, acutely conscious of the mind of the Lord through his times of prayer, bonded to the feelings of his sender. The servant not only delivered his master's message but felt the hurt and anguish involved.[8]

I have heard such prophetic burdens. One occurred at an Oregon Bible conference several months before the destruction of the wall separating East and West Germany. David Schoch prophesied the word of the Lord to Estonia, Latvia and Lithuania—countries then under the iron hand of Communism. Freedom was declared for those countries as well as the penetration of the Gospel. The emotion or "burden" of the Lord was obvious and powerful, although at the time of the prophecy not everyone was fully persuaded of its authenticity—but it shortly came to pass.

Types of Expression

The prophets of the Bible were a mixed lot: scholastics, sheep-herders, wonder-workers, statesmen, preachers, farmers, priests. Their declarations and writings display a great variety of personal idiosyncrasies and expressions. The bottom line, however, remains the same: They were all devoted to their God and to the faithful delivery of His word to the people, and their authority lay in the authenticity of the revelation they shared. Various commentators have attempted to categorize these prophecies, but there is no established listing.[9] I will mention some broad varieties, but my listing is only representative, not conclusive.

Consider the objective of all this activity. The main driving force behind every prophet's expression was the revelation of God's nature to His people and the will of God for His people in their temporal situation. Undoubtedly the supreme function of their task was "the exposition of the character of God. His holiness and His love were the high themes of their investigation. Above all they had to insist on the practical application of these qualities to the life of the nation, and, later, to that of the individual."[10] There was a continual effort to destroy idolatry and return to true worship of the true God, for this was the benchmark of the people's spirituality. W. S. Towner identifies four themes woven throughout Old Testament prophecy: justice for the disenfranchised, indictment of corruption among leaders, purification of religious establishment and hope.[11]

Let's look at some of the varieties of expression of the prophetic message.

Prayer. Scattered throughout the Old Testament we find prayers punctuating the various themes presented. *Habakkuk* opens his oracle/burden with a sincere cry for help (1:2), then uses the entire third chapter for a prayer of intercession. *Jeremiah* interjects a one-verse prayer in 11:20 (as just one example), then uses the first four verses of chapter 12 for prayer. The various writers do not seem hesitant to insert pungent, sincere prayers into their narratives. This indicates to me that they would just as easily employ prayer in their public speeches and proclamations. Prayers were incorporated into the historical records (1 Samuel 23:10). *Joel* felt the burden of his message so much that he cried out to the Lord (1:19–20), and *Amos* saw a series of five visions that caused him to break forth in prayer (7:2, 5). Many other illustrations indicate the importance of prayer in the prophets' presentations.

Songs or Odes and Poetry. Music has wonderful liberating power and was used by the prophets most effectively. *Miriam* the prophetess led the jubilant people in singing the prophetic ode of Exodus 15. *Samuel* told Saul he would meet a band of prophets playing musical instruments and prophesying (1 Samuel 10:5). *David,* before the Temple was completed, pitched a tent for the Ark of the Covenant on Mount Zion and instituted 24-hour worship every day. He had learned the tremendous power of praise and worship—the ideal environment for prophecy to function. *Certain priests* were ordained to prophesy with instruments (1 Chronicles 25:1–7). When the atmosphere was so full of unbelief that it was hard to prophesy, *Elisha* called for a minstrel, who undoubtedly sang some Davidic psalms (2 Kings 3:15). Sections of the major and minor prophets were originally meant to be sung, and possibly were sung by the prophet when giving it.

The use of music by the prophets is suggested by Edersheim: "The effect of music is to detach from surrounding circumstances, to call forth strong feelings, and to make us yield ourselves implicitly to their influence."[12] Walter C. Kaiser Jr. feels that music "had the effect of quieting the disturbed thoughts and attitudes of the prophets, and of setting theology in the context of doxology."[13]

Poetry was used by the Hebrew prophets, but unlike us they rhymed thoughts rather than words. The Psalms are filled with this kind of parallelism. The prophets spoke and wrote prophetic poetry and sometimes put it to music, which helped perpetuate the message since the people could remember it more easily. Ellison points out that "before the days of printing, the only possibility of a message becoming widely known was for it to be passed from mouth to mouth."[14]

Writing and Recording. *Gad* wrote of the acts of David, while *Nathan* recorded the acts of David (1 Chronicles 29:29) and of Solomon (2 Chronicles 9:29). *Habakkuk* was told to "write the vision, and make it plain" (2:2, KJV). *Shemaiah* recorded certain information (2 Chronicles 12:15). *Iddo* wrote a story about Abijah (2 Chronicles 13:22), "visions . . . against Jeroboam" (2 Chronicles 9:29, KJV) and historical notices regarding "the acts of Rehoboam" (2 Chronicles 12:15). *Jehu* recorded the acts of Jehoshaphat (2 Chronicles 20:34). God instructed *Jeremiah* to write down some judgment prophecies and have them delivered to the king. The manuscripts were shredded and burned, much to the consternation of Baruch the scribe. Then they were to be written again and once again delivered (Jeremiah 36). Jeremiah was also to write down in a book the words that God gave him (Jeremiah 30:1–2). Certain truths were to be recorded as a part of enacted prophecy, as *Ezekiel* recording the day the siege of Jerusalem began (Ezekiel 24:1–2).

Lamentation and Dirge. In many places in the Psalms we find lamentations. These expressions of grief and sorrow (similar to the "burden" of the Lord) were a vital part of the prophet's repertoire. Jeremiah, for instance, "chanted a lament for Josiah" (2 Chronicles 35:25). In fact his entire book of Lamentations is such an expression.

Prediction. Slightly more than one-fourth of the biblical message is predictive.[15] Future events were presented in a variety of styles: simple speech, a written statement, a thundering oracle, a musical expression, a woeful lamentation. Imagine the rough-hewn Elijah declaring to Ahab, "As the LORD, the God of Israel lives, before whom I stand, surely there shall be neither dew nor rain these years, except by my word" (1 Kings 17:1). I would add an exclamation point because I think the prophet was really waxing bold! A sad commentary on the future predictions of the prophets was that their messages were rejected consistently by Israel and Judah; both kingdoms failed to heed the prophetic warnings and were destroyed.

Futuristic prophecy involved contemporary events, the near future and the far-distant future. Clifford Hill lists five categories under the last type:

- The Day of the Lord
- The ingathering of the exiles

- The messianic age
- The conversion of the Gentiles
- Eschatological and apocalyptic concepts[16]

Keep in mind that biblical prophecies can be fulfilled *conditionally* (meaning there are conditions to be met before fulfillment can take place) or they can be *unconditional* (no obligations to be met before fulfillment). Most of the Old Testament prophecies were conditional, based on the texts of Leviticus 26 and Deuteronomy 28.[17] The unconditional prophecies were concerned mainly with the salvation of God's people and the grander cosmic themes.

One of the most fascinating studies of the Bible is that of the prophecies concerning Jesus and their fulfillment. Thirty-eight of these prophecies are laid out in a helpful chart in *The Thompson Chain Reference Bible.*[18] All the messianic prophecies are clearly identified and quoted in the New Testament. I notice that my *New Open Bible Study Edition* lists 22 messianic passages in the Psalms alone identified by direct quote or allusion in the New Testament.[19] The most quoted messianic text in the New Testament is from Psalm 110:4: "Thou art a priest for ever after the order of Melchizedek" (KJV).

Styles of Rhetoric. A number of effective styles were used by the prophets, but they were always connected with the special burden of the word of the Lord. It is safe to say that nearly all, if not all, kinds of communication and Israelite life were reflected in prophetic speech. The prophet used familiar ways of speaking, such as the language of proverbial wisdom, courtroom process, religious expression, the tavern, the funeral, the commercial world and popular songs.

The prophets brought indictment (statement of offense), judgment (punishment to be carried out), instruction and exhortation (expected response), after-condition statements (affirmation of future hope or deliverance), testimonials (of God's acts, ways and nature), historical narratives (describing historical happenings) and parables (true-to-life stories with a spiritual meaning).

One category usually overlooked is the death pronouncement. Some examples: Elisha on the 42 lads (2 Kings 2:24); Isaiah to Shebna (Isaiah 22:18); Jeremiah on Pashhur (Jeremiah 20:6); Amos on Amaziah (Amos 7:17); and Peter to Sapphira (Acts 5:9).

Tucker lists these basic modes of prophetic speech: hymnic units, cultic songs, priestly Torah, sayings, parables, exhortations and admonitions, legal process, dirge, vision reports, symbolic action and woe oracles.[20] The prophet, inspired by the Spirit, sought to bring graphic realism to the message and make it compelling.

Enacted Prophecy

The plan of the fearful Jewish remnant in Jerusalem seemed logical: Flee to Egypt and escape the invading Chaldeans. The prophet Jeremiah, with anguished heart, admonished and threatened his countrymen not to go. His dire warnings were quickly cast aside, however, and the remnant pursued their so-called escape from destruction, compelling the prophet to go with them. The refugees settled in several Egyptian cities but Jeremiah was retained in Tahpanhes, where Pharaoh's palace stood.

Jeremiah had done everything in his power to make his people understand they must submit to Nebuchadnezzar, or else his hordes would devastate Judah. He preached and talked in vain. God enhanced the spoken prophecies with a series of fourteen "signs" that were to be like "acted words"—that is, constant visual reminders of the word of the Lord (see chart on page 105). Jeremiah paraded before the diplomats of Edom, Moab, Ammon and Sidon, for instance, wearing a wooden yoke (Jeremiah 27), an act whose symbolic imagery was easily understood—and which they disdainfully rejected.

While Jeremiah found himself in Tahpanhes under duress, an amazing word of the Lord came to him. The hardened Jews were so dull of hearing that God now chose to give them a mind-boggling exhibition that would make a major statement to three nations—Egypt, Judah and Babylon. This message to Jeremiah, living as he was among idolatrous Egyptians and treacherous Israelites, must have prompted some hesitation, but he proceeded as directed:

> [God] said, "While the people of Judah are watching, bury large rocks between the pavement stones at the entrance of Pharaoh's palace here in Tahpanhes. Then say to the people of Judah, 'The LORD Almighty, the God of Israel, says: I will surely bring my servant Nebuchadnezzar, king of Babylon, here to Egypt. I will set his throne on these stones that I have hidden. He will spread his royal canopy over them. And when he comes, he will destroy the land of Egypt. He will bring death to those destined for death; he will bring captivity to those destined for captivity; he will bring the sword against those destined for the sword. . . . He will pick clean the land of Egypt as a shepherd picks fleas from his cloak. . . .'"[21]
>
> Jeremiah 43:9–12, NLT

Some enacted prophecies are heartrending episodes. Ezekiel's wife died by divine decree, for instance, on the day the siege of Jerusalem began—as a sign of God (Ezekiel 24:16–27). The prophet was not (as we have seen) to lament or show any remorse at his tragic loss; he was to be mute

Jeremiah's Enacted Prophecies

Reference in Jeremiah	Action	Symbolism
1. 13:1–11	*Sign of the Linen Waistband:* Worn, buried, uncovered	God will destroy the pride of Judah and Jerusalem
2. 16:2	Jeremiah not to marry or have children in this place	Children born in Judah will die there
3. 18:1–12	*Sign of the Potter and His Vessel*	God can deal with Israel as a potter handles clay
4. 19:1–13	*Sign of the Jar:* Buy a jar, then break it	Sign of calamity on Judah
5. 20:6	*Sign of Pashhur:* Captivity and death foretold	He and his friends will go into captivity and die there
6. 22:11–12	*Sign of Shallum's Death*	He will die in his captivity
7. 27:2 (28:2)	*Sign of Bonds and Yoke:* Jeremiah wore yoke publicly	Edom, Moab, Ammon, Tyre and Sidon will be given over to Nebuchadnezzar
8. 28:16	*Sign of Hananiah's Death:* Death because of rebellion	Died within 2 months
9. 30:2	*Sign of the Written Book*	A witness that the captivity will return
10. 32:6–15	*Sign of the Real Estate Deal:* Jeremiah bought a field in Anathoth, put documents in earthen jar	A witness that the captivity will return
11. 35	*Sign of the Rechabites:* They refused wine offered them	Judah is rebuked by their example
12. 36:4, 27	*Sign of the Scrolls of Witness:* Dictated to Baruch, who then read them publicly	A statement about Jerusalem's fall
13. 43:8–10	*Sign of the Hidden Stones:* Jeremiah in Egypt hid stones in brick courtyard	To mark the place where Nebuch. will set up his throne
14. 51:59–64	*Sign of the Sunken Scroll:* Wrote calamity of Babylon, read it publicly, threw in Euphrates	A sign that Babylon will sink down and not rise

until the city fell. Another example was Hosea, who was to love a wayward wife regardless of her unfaithfulness and disloyalty (Hosea 1:2).

These dramatized prophecies were not just an alternate way of putting across a particular message more effectively. They were certainly that. But more, they showed the true heart of God in and through the very emotions and lives of His servants. The prophet, like a stage actor caught up in the part being played, experienced and identified with the intensity and reality of God's love in a way not otherwise possible. H. McKeating has a good insight on this: "Thus almost everything a prophet like Jeremiah does can become a prophecy. He *lives* his prophecies. His witness is not simply what he says but what he does. A prophet can be described, then, not only as a proclaimer of truth but as a demonstrator of truth, and he demonstrates truth both in actions that we can define quite narrowly as enacted prophecies and also in wider ways, in his own attitudes and behaviour towards the events of his time."[22]

McKeating also says, "Enacted prophecy has an objective potency which our word 'symbolism' does not convey." In other words, when Jeremiah buried those stones under the pavement in front of Pharaoh's palace, he was not only predicting that Nebuchadnezzar would actually set up his temporary throne on that exact spot, but believing that in some sense it would bring what he prophesied to pass (as it did!). He acted out what God was decreeing would be done. In a sense the authority of God so infused the action that we might say the "acted word" was "more than a symbol; it was a sign, a soul-filled, power-filled reality"; it was more than the word borne by a prophet, for in that moment the prophet himself was an extension of Jehovah's personality, thereby becoming himself the word.[23]

Another example is Ahijah meeting Jeroboam on a country road (1 Kings 11:29–39). Taking his new robe, the prophet tore it into twelve pieces, which symbolized the tribes of Israel, then commanded the king to pick up ten of the pieces. Ahijah did not just symbolize the dividing of the kingdom; he *was* dividing the kingdom. The prophet not only lived out the prophecy but was enacting history.

Once in Chesterfield, Virginia, in the House of Prayer Church, some ministers and I were praying over a native pastor from Nigeria. The unction of the Spirit came on me to prophesy over him. As I began I felt impressed to ask one of the ministers to bring the flag of Nigeria, one of many flags on display for a missionary emphasis, and hold it by him. It was an enacted prophecy, in simple form, to reinforce and bring to pass God's intention for Nigeria.

The miracles of Moses, Elijah, Elisha and Jesus were usually more than just supernatural manifestations. A spiritual message was an integral part of what was conveyed. More and more the Church is realizing that spiritual warfare can involve praying with a prophetic touch and at times with prophetic enactment.[24] Enacting a thought or concept, if done appropriately, upgrades the prophetic strength manyfold. An unexpressed thought is dead; it cannot be considered a prophecy. A thought must be communicated or expressed in such a way that it is understood. And sometimes that thought gains maximum impact through a dramatic action, which secures and holds the attention of the mind.

Old and New Testament prophets performed actions bizarre by our standards, such as Aaron and Hur holding up the hands of Moses (Exodus 17:12) or Agabus binding Paul with his sash (Acts 21:10–11). In our time evangelist Arthur Blessitt has dragged a large wooden cross on his shoulders around the world as a testimony of Christ's love for fallen humanity. When I first heard of this years ago, I thought it farfetched, but Arthur continued on, thank God, in spite of doubters like me, and has done a remarkable job, winning many to Jesus Christ.[25]

An idea from the book *The Language of Love* by Gary Smalley made a big impression on me several years ago. The author emphasized the importance of creating in your listener's mind an image of what you are saying. In that way the thought will make a greater impact and tend to remain. This concept applies to preaching and interpersonal communication, but in enacted prophecy it will be particularly effective. Sometimes it is difficult to remember words of a prophecy, but a word picture stays framed in the mind.

Testimony of David Bryan

In the next chapter we will deal with the subject of false prophets, particularly evaluating Balaam, the highly overrated soothsayer who finally met an untimely death. But first, so that you may see the possibility and importance of prophecy in today's Church, I offer the following testimonial from David Bryan, pastor of the Church of Glad Tidings in Yuba City, California, given in February 1997. The reference to my personal ministry may also help you understand my own deep interest in prophecy.

> In 1974, when I was in the eleventh grade, my father took me to Portland, Oregon, to visit Bible Temple (now called City Bible Church) for the first time. We were then living in Idaho, and my older sister was attending Portland Bible College. She had written home saying there would be a prophetic gathering she hoped we could attend.

So Dad, a minister, decided to go, taking Mom and me along with him and including a pastor friend from a neighboring town. Dad had reached out to Mike Basher in a variety of ways. Our family had been to his church many times. Dad had often preached in his church, and our family, which had traveled with Dad as part of a ministry team, would sing there, too. We were very familiar with Pastor Basher's ministry and the pastoral struggles he was facing in the southern Idaho area.

The prophetic gathering was being held in an old theater building that Bible Temple had converted into a church. We entered the service late, having driven hundreds of miles. We sat in the back on the right-hand side, probably on the third row from the back. As the meeting progressed, we listened to the prophetic ministry over different people, most of whom were candidates who had been in fasting and prayer and were brought forward one at a time. Toward the end of the service Brother Ernest Gentile, one of the prophets, looked toward the back of the auditorium and stopped the meeting. He said he would like to minister prophetically over someone in the congregation, indicating Mike Basher, the pastor who had come with us from Idaho.

Although Mike was a little apprehensive, my father encouraged him to go forward. As Brother Gentile ministered over him prophetically, I was really impressed. I had never experienced anything quite like this. The accuracy and the prophetic gift of God that was unfolded that night amazed me, particularly since I knew so much of the history and current situation Mike Basher was facing in his church.

Brother Basher was told that he was a pastor from out of state from somewhere far away and that he had come to check these prophetic meetings out, which of course was true. Gentile said he saw Basher with a book opened in his hand. He was standing on a foundation, a place where a building was to be built. It was a church foundation, and he was looking at the blueprints (the book in his hand) and was frustrated. He had fabricated the walls. A prefab wall lay on the foundation but needed to be stood up and connected with the other adjacent walls. In the prophetic picture Brother Gentile observed Mike and heard him saying, "I don't understand why it's not working. I have the blueprints. I've done what it says here, and it's still not working." He would put the book down and then lean a wall up, balancing it carefully. Then he would look back at the book he was using as a reference, go to another wall and begin to try to tip that wall up. As he tipped up the second wall, the first would fall over and knock him down, and he would get up, dirty and frustrated, and look once again at the blueprints.

Brother Gentile shared the meaning of the vision with Pastor Basher, a message of the Lord to clarify the vision. Mike wasn't necessarily doing anything wrong. It wasn't a problem with the blueprints, but it was God's wisdom and will for him to work in another setting where he could have some on-the-job training and watch someone else assemble a building—in reference, of course, to building a local church. It was very encouraging because, as we all knew, Brother Basher had been struggling with his pastoral leadership there. A confirmation of the message witnessed in Brother Basher's heart.

Later he resigned his church and moved to Bible Temple. He became part of the eldership of that church, served there for years and learned much about the local church, church structure, government and all of those kinds of things. After some time he went out from Bible Temple to help plant a church elsewhere.

It was thrilling for us to see the clear gift of God being unpackaged at the prophetic gathering that night and to see the positive impact, and the amen, on the heart of Brother Basher as God looked into his life and encouraged him, helping redirect him to the center of God's will. That was tremendously encouraging.

Toward the end of the prophecy, Brother Gentile paused for a moment and said, "I'm hesitant to say this, but brother, if I told you I saw a black man seated near the rear of the sanctuary there in your church, would you know who I was talking about?" Brother Basher nodded his head. Then Gentile said, "I really feel I need to tell you that when you return home, you must pray over him, lay your hands on him and invoke the spirit of prophecy over him—encourage him to prophesy the word of the Lord!"

Now this was a very significant thing to us! We were familiar enough with Mike Basher's ministry to know that there was only one black man who ever went to that church, and he always sat toward the back. I don't think we were ever there when he wasn't sitting there. So to hear God use a man who had never seen Brother Basher before, had never been to his church and had little way of knowing any of these details—to hear God use him to speak something so very clear, so very precise, so very accurate, was a tremendous encouragement and inspiration.

This whole experience framed my understanding of the power, effect and impact of New Testament prophecy, especially as I saw that the end result was to nurture, encourage and guide God's people into a fuller understanding of His will. I am very, very thankful to have experienced this very credible, very clear demonstration of the gifts of the Spirit coming through human instrumentality, yielding great encouragement and comfort to the Body of Christ.

REFLECTIONS

While scholars may try to classify different forms and styles of speech and writing (poetry, history, prophecy, *etc.*), this does not deny that there is one common factor: it is all God's prophetic word, and therefore absolutely authoritative.[26]

Graham Houston

Jehovah revealed the mystery of His divine will to the children of men, teaching them through symbolic signs and types, and through utterances. The signs and types were a very illuminating, lucid and effective way of impressing on [sic] the mind, while the prophets were inspired, on the other hand, to explain the nature and meaning of such symbols. So that the impression had double force on them which they tutored.[27]

D. P. Williams

The prophet thus discovered and proclaimed eternal verities. Yet the garb in which he clothed them was essentially the fashion of his own age. The language, metaphor, style, and still more the 'thought-shape' were such as were current amongst his compatriots and contemporaries.[28]

T. H. Robinson

The prophet, as regarded in the light of Scripture, was simply the recipient and bearer of a message from God; and such a message of course was a prophecy, whatever might be its more specific character—whether the disclosure of some important truth, the inculcation of an imperative duty, or a prospective delineation of coming events. A message, however, that bespoke no supernatural insight into the will and purposes of Heaven could not, except in peculiar circumstances, require a divinely-commissioned person to deliver it.[29]

Patrick Fairbairn

. . . The prophet speaks *primarily* to the men of his own time, and his message springs out of the circumstances in which he lives. . . . But for all this, the source of the message is super-natural, not natural. It is derived neither from observation nor intellectual thought, but from admission to the council chamber of God (Amos 3:7; Jer. 23:18, 22), from knowing God and speaking with Him (Num. 12:6ff; Exod. 33:11).[30]

H. L. Ellison

7

MADNESS: WHAT
COMPELLED
THE FALSE PROPHET?

. . . A dumb donkey . . . restrained the madness of the prophet.

2 Peter 2:16

WHAT WAS THE DRIVING force behind the prophets? Without question the genuine biblical prophet was inspired, carried along and given impetus by the Spirit of God. This chapter will focus on the prophet who brought false prophecy and the "madness" that compelled it.

A strange, idolatrous climate existed in Bible times that encouraged the proliferation of soothsayers, magicians and false prophets. The role of the genuine prophet is set in stark contrast to these deceivers. What was the basic error of the false prophet? Special attention needs to be given to Balaam, the ultimate example of the false prophet for hire. Also, it is important for us to look at the spiritual events surrounding the exodus and the time just prior to Israel's entering the Promised Land. This background will lend depth to our discussion and define the essence of the false prophet.

Moses and the Gods of Egypt

Around 1500 B.C. the entire area from Egypt to Babylon was covered by a sinister shadow of magic and idol worship. At that dark time and place the only true God made a spectacular entrance into human history. He came to set His people free and to raise His banner against every false deity that had corrupted mankind.

For four hundred years the descendants of Jacob had dwelled in the land of Egypt, at first living royally as invited guests but finally held captive as a subjugated people. Gradually Egypt had forgotten Joseph and God's kindness to the nation through him, and a new Pharaoh came to the throne who knew nothing of the former days. With calculated intensity Israel's captors increased the harsh burden of servitude until the people cried out to their invisible God for help.

The time for deliverance finally came, but more was involved than the wisest elder in Israel could imagine. The exodus was to far transcend a mere deliverance of oppressed slaves who needed help (although that was certainly included). God had waited until the religious crafts of Egypt had fallen to their nadir of perfected degradation; and the evil corruption of the tribal nations inhabiting the land of the Jordan, which had been promised Abraham, had plummeted to the depths of horrible heathen practices.

Each nation, tribe and area had its polytheistic hierarchy of primary and secondary gods. Abominable deities took shape in hideous, idolatrous forms and degrading ceremonies that reduced humankind to the lowest forms of bestial depravity—and the people became like the objects of their worship (Psalm 115:8). Evil spirits, preying on the fallen inclinations of man, concocted these awful forms of religion to divert each human's focus from the true God to lifeless objects with sensual, immoral rituals. Men and women had degraded themselves to the lowest possible point.

As the simmering caldron of Egypt's magical abominations (which some say was the graduate school of the day for such practices) was frothing to the overflow state, God met Moses in the Sinai wilderness and commissioned him to go and bring forth Israel from Egypt. Raised as a prince for forty years in the Egyptian society, Moses knew firsthand the rampant polytheistic system (with its profuse lexicon of terms and titles) that granted deification to nature, animals and even man. Ra, the sun god, was represented by a hawk. The river Nile was considered sacred. The leading deities were represented by bulls, cows, goats, crocodiles, apes, frogs, flies, serpents and vultures, and each had a sacred name, ritual, priesthood and temple. The Pharaohs were deified.

That was the setting in Egypt when, in the wilderness, God said to Moses, "Go and set my people free!"

The response of the frightened prophet-to-be was logical and appropriate for a man living in a world of gods galore. Overwhelmed by the startling appearance of the God of fire, Moses was keenly conscious that some name was necessary to distinguish this awesome "God almighty of

Abraham, Isaac and Jacob" from the array of Egyptian deities. Moses' question was basic: "They may say to me, 'What is His name?' What shall I say to them?" (Exodus 3:13).

The true God answered with a profound, simple Name of just four Hebrew consonants: *Yah—He—Vau—He,* the famous Tetragrammaton (the "four-lettered name") that means I AM THAT I AM.[1] This Name declared the eternal, invisible, majestic nature of God's very essence and put a premium on present-tense experience before the worshiper. In a more practical sense we might say that God was giving a blank check to His people. By saying "I AM *(whatever you need),"* the people could fill in by faith their need of a given moment.[2]

Newly commissioned and with heart set ablaze by the revelation of God, Moses returned to his estranged people armed with the invincible Name—and the rod to work miracles. Stubborn Pharaoh, surrounded by his court magicians, soothsayers and priests, considered himself the supreme god of the world. His mistake was to think of the Lord as just another god who could be beaten or compromised. Pharaoh found he was wrong, and mighty Egypt was humbled—in fact, stripped to the bone. As God had told Moses: "Against all the gods of Egypt I will execute judgments—I *am* the LORD" (Exodus 12:12, emphasis added).

Every command issued by Moses, every miracle wrought by his mighty rod, had as its primary objective the destruction of some Egyptian deity and exaltation of the great I AM. Over and over God stated that through these plagues and miracles of judgment both Israel and Egypt would come to "know that I am the LORD" (Exodus 6:7; 7:5, 17; 10:2; 14:4, 18; see 8:22). The entire religious system of Egypt, as well as its crops, animals, military force and civilian population, was left a shambles. The God of the Hebrews, known as "The Jealous One," had set His people free.

Moses was undoubtedly the greatest of the prophets (Numbers 12:6–8). His leadership position and example, expressed through the demolition of Egypt's gods, arches with majestic authority over all the Old Testament prophets.[3] Every succeeding prophet was to contend for the purity of Israel's worship and challenge any form of idolatry; but each was a guardian of the marvelous monotheistic revelation given Moses. False prophets compromised this concept, making the great I AM just another god. Genuine prophets knew that when people's understanding of God is right, everything else will fall into place.

Henry H. Halley comments: "Modern books on the Prophets lay great emphasis on their social message, their denunciation of the political corruption, oppression and moral rottenness of the nation. However, the thing that bothered the prophets most was the IDOLATRY of the nation. It is surprising how largely this is overlooked by modern writers."[4]

The True Character of Heathenism

The electrifying news of Egypt's devastation by Moses and the Hebrew God swept far and wide with surprising rapidity. Along the caravan routes excited traders told and retold of a land stripped of her wealth, vegetation, livestock, firstborn and renowned cavalry and chariots. Egypt's gods had been demolished! Never before in history had a nation been so formed and delivered as Israel had. The great horde of people (the census at Mount Sinai showed 603,550 males above the age of twenty) moved ponderously like a slow lava flow across the sparsely populated Sinai peninsula.

But then the Hebrews' entrance into the Promised Land was postponed. Unbelief brought them forty years of wandering in the wilderness. Gradually those who remembered Egypt died off, and a new, desert-toughened generation made ready to enter Canaan. The people who had been brought out that they might be brought in were finally poised to make their entrance.

The exodus had shown Israel that their God was not just a tribal god, another in a religious menagerie of gods galore. But another lesson had to be learned before they entered their Promised Land—even as they stood on the threshold of their inheritance, kept separate only by the boundary line of the Jordan River. This lesson has deep meaning for the Church today as well, and is a foundation truth espoused by every true prophet.

The heathen nations were more than antagonistic political and military powers that would oppose the Israelites' progress. The intrinsic nature of heathenism was hostility to the purposes of God. Israel, following the true and only God, was to make no alliances, cultivate no relationships, make no treaties. So evil was heathenism, and so diametrically opposed to God and His ways, that Israel was allowed to make no compromise.

Our Western minds find it difficult to think like those ancient peoples. To them the god of the Hebrews was simply one among many (1 Kings 20:23; 2 Kings 18:33–35). To the heathen the question was a practical one: Are their gods stronger than ours? The heathen worshiped different gods, believing that some were more powerful in the valley and others on the mountain. The claim of the Hebrews about their God, therefore, disturbed the neighboring nations. This God was jealous of Israel and would tolerate no variances or insubordination. A people with such a belief system could not coexist comfortably with the tribal peoples already in the land. Israel was not to intermarry with the resident peoples, and Israel felt this land belonged to them!

The invasion of their lands brought great consternation to the nations of the Jordan. The story of God's victory over Egypt was known by all. Jethro, Moses' father-in-law, had heard (Exodus 18:1). Rahab, in Jericho, had heard and told the spies how fear and dread had fallen upon the inhabitants (Joshua 2:10–11). The Amalekites had been thoroughly trounced. The giant people under King Og, the gatekeepers of Canaan, had been overcome. The forces of the Amorites, under Sihon their king, had been virtually exterminated. An awesome, fiery cloud hovered over the Hebrews and they received bread from heaven. How the stories circulated!

Would the Lord, the deity of the Hebrews, be as strong here as He had been in Egypt? The nations were apprehensive but still willing to put their armies and gods to the test. Military battles commonly waged among these ancient peoples were accompanied by intense divination and witchcraft. They would increase sacrifice to appease their deities. If the Hebrew God was indeed stronger than their gods, could they perhaps appease Him as well?

Balaam, Enemy Agent

The vast size of the Israelite host necessitated the most careful of spiritual strategies. God told Israel not to provoke their distant relative Moab to war, and this was probably known by Moab. But the huge alien force in such close proximity was just too uncomfortable and dangerous!

So Balak, the king of Moab, stepped forward as champion of the Jordan Valley tribes. He knew of the heroic accomplishments of Israel's God but still considered Yahweh just another—although impressive—god in the pantheon. Being of Midianitish origin, he most likely sought the advice and alliance of Midian in this threatening situation. Probably through the Midianites, nomadic wanderers of the vast desert area that stretched from Mesopotamia to the Jordan, Balak learned of the celebrated magician Balaam who resided in Pethor, Mesopotamia, on the banks of the Euphrates (Numbers 22:5; 23:7; Deuteronomy 23:4).

It seemed like the right move: Bring in this magician, for such a one had power to influence and persuade gods. Balak did not want a prophet to tell him the future; he wanted someone who could influence the future. Considering the alternative, the price would be negligible. Magicians were noted for their abilities to convince strong gods to transfer their powers and allegiances from one nation to another. Moab would not need to give up her lands, gods and heathen practices if only the Hebrew God would transfer His benediction to Moab. So Balak hoped to cut a deal with the Hebrew God.

Balaam was not ignorant of Abraham's seed and God. A professional soothsayer like him knew such things (note Joshua 13:22); it was part of his trade. He recognized the national God of Israel, and in all probability relished the opportunity of this new adventure, not to mention the wealth and fame that would be his! The fascinating story unfolds in Numbers 21–25.

115

Balaam came as the greatest of the Gentile heathen soothsayers and magicians, representing the full opposition of heathenism to the ways of Israel's God and the claiming by Israel of her inheritance. He came not in the role of genuine prophet but of magician-antagonist. God says, "Balaam was an enemy agent" (Revelation 2:14, Message). He came as the great compromiser, the saboteur of Israel's holy pilgrimage. Yahweh would be added to his stable of gods already compromised and hence under his influence. He functioned as a spiritual infiltrator. He was paid to beguile, humble, disgrace or degrade gods in the eyes of people and local deities. Balak's invitation was just another job offer.

Balaam could and should have advised Balak to bless Israel (Numbers 24:9), giving a truthful explanation of God's intentions and what He would do for Moab. How Balak would have profited from such positive advice! But it did not happen.

Balaam seemed to address God as a devout Hebrew (Numbers 22:8–20), but this appearance is misleading. Communication with god spirits (actually evil spirits) was common to him, and Yahweh simply met him on his own turf in his accustomed style. God told Balaam not to go with Balak's messengers: "You shall not curse the people; for they are blessed" (verse 12). Finally, after giving him grudging permission to go, the Lord became angry at the diviner's eager attitude (verse 22). An angel with drawn sword appeared as an adversary because, in the translation of *The Torah* by W. Gunther Plaut, "the errand is obnoxious to me" (verse 32).

The seer's perceptive donkey saved his life, then spoke directly to him. *The Torah* gives this clever insight: ". . . A great and proud man was incapable of seeing what a dumb beast could behold. . . . His vision was limited and his sureness frail. The main burden of the story, which is full of irony and subtle humor, is not in fact the *speaking* but the *seeing* ass, contrasted with the prophet who looks and yet is blind. Over against both of them stands their Creator, and in their common creatureliness they are bound to the ultimate purposes of God."[5]

Balak hurriedly took Balaam to various mountaintop vantage points to view the vast camp of Israel, where the soothsayer dutifully ordered sacrifices of appeasement to Yahweh. Time and time again God overpowered Balaam so that he was compelled to speak exactly what God wanted. Four marvelous poetic oracles were put into Balaam's mouth as direct divine inspiration.[6] Balaam's confession in Numbers 22:38 indicates that, like his donkey, he could speak only the words put into his mouth. Twice the text states that God "was not willing to listen to Balaam" (Deuteronomy 23:5; Joshua 24:10).[7]

Balak was infuriated at Balaam's blessing of Israel, sending him home in disgrace. Apparently the crafty soothsayer gave some serious thought to the payment he had missed ("Is there still the possibility for some gain?"), for he soon returned with devious but accurate advice for Balak. No divination would work against Israel (note Numbers 23:23), but there was a way! Balaam counseled his client to mingle, not fight. Israel could not be cursed from without, but she herself would bring on God's curse by her own sin and idolatry. Corrupt the nation from within, he advised Balak, thereby inviting divine retribution against her (Deuteronomy 23:3–4).

Tents of Midian and Moab suddenly sprouted like poisonous mushrooms on the periphery of Israel's camp, filled with every imaginable enticement for the lusts of men. Israelites flocked to these tents to commit their whoredom (sexual pleasures carefully intertwined with acts of idolatry), after which the judgment of God broke out on them (Numbers 25). Twenty-four thousand sinners died in the plague, and then an angry Moses sent warriors to take vengeance on the Midianites. Balaam, who had given the cursed advice for "the wages of unrighteousness" (2 Peter 2:15), died by the sword (Numbers 31:8; Joshua 13:22).

The soothsayer's treachery, greed and indecision have made him an infamous example of the corruption of heathenism. He was an impostor and betrayer: God did not send him, nor had He given him a message to deliver. He spoke God's word only because he was overpowered and compelled to do so. He died as a fool and an abomination to God.

The False Prophets

The ministry of Moses, as exemplified in the exodus from Egypt and the entrance to the Promised Land, brought an all-out declaration of spiritual war against every force that would compete with the prophetic revelation of God. From that point on all forms of sorcery, divination, soothsaying, witchcraft, necromancy, interpretation of omens and contacting mediums were expressly forbidden (Leviticus 19:26; Deuteronomy 18:10–14). And false prophets were given dire warning. Surely never again would a case of idolatry, witchcraft or false prophecy ever occur in Israel! But it did, time and again, and the history of the true prophets is the ongoing story of their battle with idolatry.

The term *false prophet* does not occur in the Old Testament, although Jeremiah said that some prophets "prophesy falsely" (Jeremiah 5:31). It appears eleven times in the New Testament. Jesus and Peter both called the misleading prophets of ancient times "false prophets" (Luke 6:26; 2 Peter 2:1), and Jesus foretold more false prophets during the Church age (Matthew 7:15; 24:11, 24; Mark 13:22).

False prophets "delivered messages which were in conflict with the messages of the true prophets of Israel . . . [and] their messages contradicted God's revelation."[8] A good deal is said about false prophets in the Old Testament, but only a few illustrations are given of what they actually said that was wrong.[9] What *is* strongly stated concerns the personal characteristics or character of such prophets and a clear identification of why their messages were wrong. The chart below lists the false prophets in both Testaments.

The False Prophets in Both Testaments		
Name	Description	Scripture
Ahab son of Kolaiah*	Foretold safety	Jeremiah 29:21
Asherah	400 prophets on Mt. Carmel	1 Kings 18:19
Baal	450 prophets on Mt. Carmel	1 Kings 18:9–40
Balaam	The Gentile soothsayer	Numbers 22–24
Daughters	Gave false prophecy	Ezekiel 13:17
Elymas the magician	Withstood Paul	Acts 13:6–11
False prophet	A last-days deceiver	Revelation 16:13; 19:20; 20:10
Hananiah*	Challenged Jeremiah's yoke	Jeremiah 28:1–17
Jaazaniah	Leader of the people	Ezekiel 11:1
Jannes and Jambre†	Withstood Moses	Exodus 7:11; 2 Timothy 3:8
Jerusalem prophets	Adultery and falsehood	Jeremiah 23:14; Ezekiel 13:9
Jezebel	Prophetess in Thyatira	Revelation 2:20
Manasseh	Israelite king who was involved with sorcery	2 Chronicles 33:6
Noadiah	Tried to frighten Nehemiah	Nehemiah 6:14
Pashhur*	Opposed Jeremiah	Jeremiah 20:1–6
Pelatiah*	Leader of the people	Ezekiel 11:1, 13
Samaritan prophets	Prophesied by Baal	Jeremiah 23:13
Shemaiah of Delaiah	Hired against Nehemiah	Nehemiah 6:10, 12
Shemaiah the Nehelamite*	Opposed Jeremiah	Jeremiah 29:24–32
Simon the sorcerer	The insincere convert	Acts 8:9–13, 18–24
Slave girl	A spirit of divination	Acts 16:16
Zedekiah son of Chenaanah	Opposed Micaiah	1 Kings 22:11, 24; 2 Chronicles 18:10, 23
Zedekiah son of Maaseiah*	Opposed Micaiah	Jeremiah 29:21–23

* Note: The six marked with (*) died because of death pronouncements on them.

† The *Expositors Bible Commentary* (p. 408) says: "Jannes and Jambre are not mentioned in the OT. But there was a Jewish tradition that they were two of the Egyptian magicians who withstood Moses and Aaron. They are thus mentioned in the Targum (Aramaic paraphrase) of Jonathan in Exodus 7:11. Pliny in his *Natural History* (A.D. 77) names Jannes along with Moses."

118

Personal characteristics. Before examining the source and nature of the false prophet's falsehood, let's consider a scriptural listing of character flaws in these people. No one person had all these problems (just a few are bad enough!). Obviously people with such deficiencies would not be reliable individuals or messengers, yet, amazingly, people readily followed their lead. Two key texts that furnish information are Jeremiah 23 and 29. False prophets, it seemed, were the greatest hindrance to the acceptance of Jeremiah's preaching. In the name of God these prophets would declare openly and forcefully that Jeremiah was lying. No wonder he had much to say on the subject!

Variously the false prophets were:

- *Adulterous* (Jeremiah 23:14; 29:23)
- *Corrupted or polluted* (Jeremiah 23:11)
- *Deceitful* (from their own hearts, Jeremiah 14:13–16)
- *Drunken* ("befuddled with wine," Isaiah 28:7, Phillips; 56:10–12)
- *False* (Jeremiah 6:13–14; 8:10–11; 23:13, 14, 32; 29:23; Ezekiel 13:2, 17)
- *Foolish* (wasting time on nonsense, Jeremiah 2:8; 29:23; Hosea 9:7)
- *Greedy* (Jeremiah 6:13; 8:10; Micah 3:11; 2 Peter 2:3, 15)
- *Lying* (Jeremiah 6:13–14; 27:9, 10, 14, 18; Isaiah 9:14–16; Ezekiel 22:28)
- *Murderous* (shedding blood, Lamentations 4:13–14)
- *Presumptuous* (Jeremiah 23:21; 29:31)
- *Profane* (impure or defiled, Jeremiah 23:14; Zephaniah 3:4)
- *Reckless and irresponsible* (Jeremiah 23:32)
- *Thieving* (stealing words from each other, Jeremiah 23:30)
- *Treacherous* (Zephaniah 3:4; "snare of a bird catcher," Hosea 9:8)

Reasons for the "madness" of the false prophet. The above character flaws should be sufficient in themselves to invalidate a ministry and message, but these false prophets were seduced, led astray or helped along by their weaknesses. The ultimate madness of the false prophet was to bring a perverted word of human or demonic origin and claim it to be from almighty God, thus making the people discount a true word and trust in a lie.

The heathen prophets were easily identifiable because they spoke in the name of the heathen gods. Apparently some Israelite prophets did this, too, like certain prophets of Baal. Some misguided Israelite prophets spoke in the name of the Lord but had personal agendas. They may or may not have been God's servants, but their messages were so misguided by satanic influence, personal ambition, greed, false prognostications, wrong impressions or wild imaginations that their messages were, for all intents and purposes, no better than that of the heathen false prophets. Such people sometimes spoke by what they perceived to be the Spirit of God, but their impressions were not from God at all; rather, they were self-induced or demonically inspired. Such pseudo-prophets were not always easy to discern.

The false prophet was guilty of:

- *Going without being sent;* speaking without hearing a divine word (Jeremiah 14:15; 23:21; 29:31). These prophets were not commissioned, nor had they come out of the Lord's presence.
- *Listening to seducing spirits* (1 Kings 22:23; 2 Chronicles 18:22; Zechariah 13:2; 1 Timothy 4:1), which involved divination (Jeremiah 14:14; Ezekiel 12:24, "flattering divination"). Some were "being inspired by Baal the no-god, and by such prophesying led the people into error"[10] (Jeremiah 2:8; 23:13). Incredible as it sounds, the deceptive spirit of Baal worship actually made the Israelites forget the Lord (Judges 3:7; 8:33–34; Jeremiah 23:27).
- *Responding to the people's wishes* (who wanted nice, satisfying words, Isaiah 30:10; Jeremiah 5:30–31; Amos 2:12). Micah 2:11 (Phillips) says: "The sort of prophet this people wants is a windbag and a liar, prophesying a future of 'wines and spirits.'"
- *Seeking evil wages* ("her prophets divine for money," Micah 3:11). Like Balaam they "loved the wages of unrighteousness" (2 Peter 2:15); "for pay they have rushed headlong into the error of Balaam" (Jude 11).
- *Proclaiming lies* (Jeremiah 14:13–16; 23:14; 29:23) and false visions (Jeremiah 14:14; 23:16; Lamentations 2:14; Ezekiel 12:24; 22:28; Zechariah 10:2), and doing so in the name of the Lord (Jeremiah 29:21).
- *Yielding to sensual appetites* (Isaiah 28:7; see the fourteen characteristics in the previous list).
- *Following false dreams* (Jeremiah 23:32; 29:8).
- *Declaring their own imaginations* (Jeremiah 23:16); having deceived hearts (Jeremiah 14:14; 23:26; Ezekiel 13:2). "They give out the thoughts of their own hearts to be divine revelation, and promise peace and prosperity to all stiff-necked sinners."[11]

These pseudo-prophets were the tragic result of seduction. They were (and are) the results of misguided minds choosing a course of action that, like a great whirlpool, sucked them to their destruction. The closer to the vortex, the harder to escape, with God Himself finally choosing their delusion (Isaiah 66:3–4), from which there was no escape.

Four steps define the downward course of delusion and falsehood:

- *Degeneration of personal life.* The false prophet tolerates destructive habits that influence thoughts, health and emotions. Because personal spiritual discipline declines and is finally replaced, the personality is opened to the possibility of vain imaginations or demonic thoughts.

- *Misguided thought life.* Vanity and falsehood become the acceptable norm. Willful deceit is easily embraced (Jeremiah 23:31). The laws of God are set aside for a more "appealing" and "exciting" approach to life. The holiness of God is replaced by the pursuit of personal ambition and fulfillment. Flattering dreams and imaginations become the norm.

- *Seduction by evil spirits.* As the false prophet's personal agenda drifts away from that of God, he or she becomes an easy target for seducing spirits that prey on ambitious souls. Gradually the spirit of Satan takes over, a demonic agenda substitutes for the divine agenda and the prophet is found fighting God and all He stands for.

- *Delusion by divine choice.* When a person's rebellion against God and choice of evil ways reach a certain point, no return is possible. Such people love unrighteousness more than truth. As Paul has said, "They did not receive the love of the truth so as to be saved. And for this reason God will send upon them a deluding influence ["strong delusion," NKJV; "A misleading influence," Amplified] so that they might believe what is false" (2 Thessalonians 2:10–11).[12]

The false prophet is driven by the same obsession as Lucifer: "I will make myself like the Most High" (Isaiah 14:14). To communicate with spirits and manipulate them, or to communicate with people and manipulate them, in order to become a final authority in spiritual things—and to be paid handsomely for doing so—is most fulfilling to certain misled personalities. They are experiencing the height of rebellion against the true and living God and are often demonized individuals. These soothsayers, wizards or magicians sell themselves on the great lie of their own importance, casting aside the claims of God and Scripture. They have a certain slant, twist or perversion in their personalities that makes them a law unto themselves.

The Chinese Beggar Children

Some dismiss the visions and spiritual manifestations of others with a shrug. When such visions are received by children, however, it makes you stop and think. This true story of modern times is about not just one child but many. The simplicity and purity of attitude of the young orphans described—involved in one of the most marvelous prophetic happenings in Church history—stands in such stark contrast to the devious nature of Balaam and other false prophets that it seems a fitting close to this chapter.

H. A. and Josephine Baker went to China in the early 1920s as faith missionaries with no denominational sponsorship. They settled in a little town of five thousand called Kotchiu, located in the southwest corner of Yunnan, the most southwest province of China. Said to be the worst town in all China, Kotchiu was controlled by robbers and was unspeakably vile and sinful.

> Almost immediately, [the Bakers] were conscious of the many teenage beggar boys who were starving and dying in the streets. That was when they decided to open the Adullam Home. In addition to dysentery and other internal diseases, the boys had terrible sores all over their bodies. Josephine found real joy and satisfaction in removing their filthy rags and giving them baths. Disheveled hair was cut and clean clothes were given them. Their sores healed rapidly as they responded to the love of Jesus.
>
> There were forty boys in the Home when the great miracle took place. There was an outpouring of the Holy Spirit, the like of which is recorded in few pieces of Christian literature. They fell prostrate on the floor under the power of God. While in the Spirit, they saw into the next world. They saw angels and talked with them; they played in the wonderful parks of Paradise; they saw the saints of old.
>
> This outpouring went on for days and days. Little children preached under the anointing of the Holy Spirit. The lowest, most outcast beggar boys saw revelations of invisible worlds and the glories of the redeemed.[13]

For the most part the children of the story had been beggars on the streets of the city. In the Bakers' words:

> In some cases they were poor children with one or both parents dead and had been brought to the Home. There were also some prodigals who had run away from the homes in more distant parts of this or adjoining provinces.
>
> But from whatever source they came, these children, mostly boys ranging in ages from six to eighteen, had come to us without previous training in morals and without education. Begging is a sort of "gang" system in which stealing is a profitable part. The morals are what would be expected of a "gang" in a godless land.
>
> p. 11

The Bible was taught daily in the Adullam Home and the Gospel preached. Many of the children had a knowledge of the main themes of the Bible before the outpouring of the Spirit began and some had been converted. They attended their classes, taught by a Chinese teacher, and also had schedules for chores or working in the garden. H. A. Baker explains that such uneducated, mentally untrained, unimaginative boys could not have conceived of the things that were spiritually revealed. He insists that "many of these children were too young, too ignorant, or too recently rescued from paganism to know the Bible teaching on these subjects" (p. 13). Amazingly children in different rooms sometimes had simultaneous visions of the same things! The prophetic experiences of the children did not come from any revival atmosphere, mental excitement, religious frenzy or other self-produced condition. "This outpouring of the Holy Spirit," he writes, "came to ordinary children as they went about the not-too-exciting business of going to school" (p. 14).

Baker's description of the outpouring of the Holy Spirit is impressive and gives important background to some of the prophetic incidents of interest to us:

> The morning prayer meeting was lasting longer than usual. The older children left the room one by one to begin their studies in the school room, while a few of the smaller boys remained on their knees, praying earnestly. The Lord was near. We all felt the presence of the Holy Spirit in our midst. Some who had gone out returned to the room.
>
> Such a mighty conviction of sin—a thing for which we had prayed so long—came to all, that with tears streaming from their eyes and arms uplifted they cried out to the Lord for forgiveness for their sins, which now seemed so black. One after another went down under the mighty power of the Holy Spirit until more than twenty were prostrate on the floor. When I saw that the Lord was doing a most unusual thing in our midst, I went over to the school room and told the boys that if they felt led to come and pray they might be excused from their school work. In a short time the Chinese teacher was left sitting alone by the table [he started to leave, then came in to pray, lifting his hands and pleading for the Lord's forgiveness].
>
> pp. 21–22

The meeting continued for hours, with the children seeing visions of the awfulness of hell, the anguish of lost souls and the evil force of the devil. The revelation of the grace of the Lord Jesus was so real that dramatic liberation from the clutches of the evil one occurred. "Their joy, laughter, and peace of soul in the knowledge of what they had been saved from gave them an experience which I am sure they will never be able to forget" (p. 23).

In the first days no one paid much attention to eating and sleeping. Whenever the young folks began to pray, the power of God would fall, prostrating many to the floor. It was impossible to have meals at regular hours without interfering with the work of the Holy Spirit. After the power of God lifted from different ones they would go out for a time to rest or to get a snack and then return to the prayer rooms soon to be under the power of the Holy Spirit again.

These manifestations of the Spirit were so continuous that nearly all day until late in the night some were under His power. . . .

From the very beginning the manifestations of the Spirit, the visions, and the revelations carried everything into the supernatural realm so far beyond our own limited knowledge or experience of supernatural matters that Mrs. Baker and I confessed to each other that these things had already advanced to the stage where the only recourse we had was to believe that God was bigger than the devil. We took refuge behind the promise that those who sought the Father for bread would not get a stone . . . that those with pure motives, like these children, who sought the Holy Spirit would not get evil things or demons, but would get exactly what they sought: the Holy Spirit (Luke 11:13).

pp. 25–27

A confirmation of the reality of these works of the Spirit was that most of the marvelous manifestations were given to those who knew little Bible teaching on the subject. The children had never heard the missionaries refer to the outpouring of the Holy Spirit as "the latter rain," for instance, but they experienced it almost literally. To the children it seemed as though they felt water dropping onto their heads (their eyes were kept closed in prayer), with the downpour increasing until they felt "submerged in this wonderful, life-giving flood from heaven."

One small boy spoke in pure prophecy when in the Spirit he seemed to be in heaven at the feet of Jesus. The Lord spoke through him in the first person clearing up many things the children did not understand and telling them how to tarry and how to seek the Spirit. . . . These Adullam people have also seen the Holy Spirit brighter than the noon-day sun. This manifestation of the Holy Spirit as a great light has been very common. Some children, having opened their eyes to see if it was something about the electric light, could scarcely discern the lights in the room because of the exceeding glory of the light of heaven which seemed to fill the place.

pp. 34–35

The very air of Adullam changed. A joyful atmosphere prevailed with the boys praising the Lord in the garden, and even the neighbors said, "Praise the Lord!" when meeting one of the boys. The children were truly born again, and a number of them spoke in other tongues, as on the day of Pentecost. A number later spoke in prophecy, and the Bakers "marveled more and more at the miracles that were taking place as the Lord spoke the wonderful things of God, revealing His plans and purposes by selecting the outcast 'nothings' of the earth who were recent beggar boys, to make them the mouthpieces of the living God, speaking through them by direct inspiration, edifying and building up this little group of simple blood-washed believers so recently saved out of hopeless physical and spiritual despair" (pp. 39–40).

Within several weeks nearly all the children wanted to preach, so street services were held. Speaking in tongues with interpretation, the boys presented Gospel messages with great power to the throngs gathered on the street. The content of the messages amazed all who heard, for they were prophetically inspired.

Time does not permit me to recount all the prophetic and visionary experiences that occurred in Kotchiu, China, in the early 1920s. The full story presented by H. A. Baker needs to be read on its own. Suffice it to say, some of the boys spoke at times like prophets of old, with the same results, and amazing visions of heaven and the future were unfolded to them. I hope this example of God using the most humble of people as His voice will affect the Church of our own day.

With this chapter we close Part 2, "A Profile of the Ancient Hebrew Prophet." The next two chapters, which constitute Part 3, will help us transition to the heart of the book, New Testament prophecy.

REFLECTIONS

. . . *The* basic problem in prophecy: how to distinguish between the authentic and inauthentic address. . . . Even a pretender could chance on a proper anticipation of the future, and in that case how would one know whether the prophets derived their inspiration from God, their own imagination, or from a demonic source? . . . The Torah suggests that the dividing line between the two was loyalty to God. Negatively, if the pretending prophet counseled disobedience for the divine command or even idolatry, then he was *ipso facto* a pretender, regardless of the accuracy of his predictions.[14]

W. Plaut

There is a simple factor that distinguishes false prophets from the genuine ones. False prophets use their gifts and use other people for their own ends, in order to build up their own influence or ministry.[15]

Rick Joyner

But although words of piety came through [Balaam's] lips, beneath them all his heart was set on evil, and a very small test exposed what was hidden therein. God through his own lips told him not to go with the men; still, deep within was the greed for money. God at last gave him permission to go; his eyes were opened when the mouth of the ass was opened. Although used of the Spirit of God to prophesy in order to defend Israel, he was more degraded than a dumb ass. The self-will and corruption of man's heart is declared here. The sovereignty of God over-ruled him; he prophesied, although he was not a prophet.[16]

D. P. Williams

The figure of Balaam stands out alone in the history of the Old Testament. The only counterpart to it is that of Judas, the traitor. Balaam represented the opposition of heathenism; Judas that of Judaism. Both went some length in following the truth: Balaam honestly acknowledged the God of Israel, and followed His directions; Judas owned the Messianic appearance in Jesus, and joined His disciples. But in the crisis of their inner history, when that came which, in one form or another, must be to every one the decisive question—each failed. Both had stood at the meeting and parting of the two ways, and both chose that course which rapidly ended in their destruction.[17]

Alfred Edersheim

PART 3

THE TRANSITION FROM OLD TO NEW

THE REAPPEARANCE
OF PROPHECY

"... I will pour out My Spirit. ..."

Joel 2:28

GOD WAS ANGRY. Moses was upset. People wept in their tents. The scene was desperate. The miracle food called "manna" no longer satisfied the people's greedy appetites and they cried out, "Our soul is dried away!" (Numbers 11:6, my translation). Weeping swept through the whole encampment as the people longingly remembered the juicy, savory food so abundant in Egypt. Like prisoners banging plates and chanting grievances, Israel raised the strident cry, "Give us meat that we may eat!" (verse 13).

Moses panicked and asked to die. God, ignoring the request, chose instead to make this situation a learning experience. He explained that Moses would share his spiritual mantle—the same power and burden—with the elders of Israel. And, incidentally, meat would be provided—miraculously, of course.

"Then the LORD came down in the cloud and spoke to him; and He took of the Spirit who was upon him and placed Him upon the seventy elders. And it came about that when the Spirit rested upon them, they prophesied" (verse 25).

It was an inspiring moment in Israel. The 68 elders standing before Moses experienced the Holy Spirit and began to speak forth the words of God. Suddenly a breathless messenger hurried forward with startling news. Two of the elders, Eldad and Medad, away in a different part of the camp, had the Spirit also come on them. They were prophesying!

Joshua, overly conscious of discipline and proper protocol, reacted as if he had been struck with a hot coal: "Moses, my lord, restrain them" (verse 28).

Moses, excited and much more perceptive, replied with a wishful statement of classic proportions: "Are you jealous for my sake? Would that all the LORD's people were prophets, that the LORD would put His Spirit upon them!" (verse 29).[1]

The hopeful longing of Moses became actual prediction with later prophets. Joel foretold that the spirit of prophecy will indeed be given to everyone, from the least to the greatest, not just to a select group of prophets. Young and old, male and female, slave and free, Jew and Gentile—all will come under the prophetic canopy: "It will come about after this that I will pour out My Spirit on all mankind; and your sons and daughters will prophesy, your old men will dream dreams, your young men will see visions. And even on the male and female servants I will pour out My Spirit in those days" (Joel 2:28–29).

These astounding words found fulfillment on the Day of Pentecost (Acts 2) when the Holy Spirit era was inaugurated. The apostle Peter explained the grand happenings of that day—the phenomena of miracle language, strange behavior and supernatural signs—as the beginning of Joel's outpouring of the Spirit. He declared that "this is what was spoken of through the prophet Joel" (verse 16),[2] thereby confirming that prophetic activity would characterize the Church age.

Other prophets also foretold this era of the Holy Spirit: Isaiah (2:2–4), Jeremiah (31:31–34) and Ezekiel (36:26–28). Wonderful predictions about the Messiah and the Spirit were given by Isaiah (11:2; 42:1–4; 48:16; 61:1–3). The combined expectation of the coming Spirit and the Spirit-endowed Messiah—the dual emphasis of the messianic age—brought great comfort and hope to the exiled Jewish people.

The Four Hundred Silent Years

The years between Malachi, last of the writing prophets, and the beginning of the Christian era was supposedly a time of prophetic silence. During this intertestamental period no canonical prophets existed in the Hebrew nation. Some say it was as though the prophets were dead or asleep. The prophetic voice, which had been very active in Israel, seemed to fall silent about 400 B.C., its last representatives being Haggai, Zechariah and Malachi. The rabbinic tradition believed the Holy Spirit had withdrawn from Israel after the deaths of these last three prophets.[3] A. A. MacRae says: "There was no declaration that prophecy was ending, nor did anyone realize that this had occurred. Only after a time did realization dawn upon the people."[4] Still, there was apparently no question that prophecy was possible, even if there were no recognized prophets. Greenspahn comments: "It is significant that despite numerous references to the holy spirit's departure, rabbinic tradition does not usually claim that prophecy itself had ceased."[5]

The belief in an absence of prophecy is based mainly on three uncertain references in 1 Maccabees (4:46; 9:27; 14:41).[6] A leading scholar, David E. Aune, says: "The opinion is widespread that prophecy ceased in Judaism during the fifth century B.C., only to break forth once again with the rise of Christianity. The evidence [which Aune presents in his chapter 5] . . . flatly contradicts that view. Israelite prophecy did not disappear. Rather, like all religious and social institutions, it underwent a number of far-reaching and even radical changes during the period of the Second Temple (516 B.C.—A.D. 70)."[7]

Some believe that prophetic phenomena were still operative in a kind of low-level revelation from God that did not, of course, match the high-level prophecy of the Old Testament canon. David Pytches comments: "The fact that God continued to communicate in this way is significant. The rabbis called these revelations 'bat kol'—literally the 'daughter of a voice.' The Jewish Talmuds regarded the 'bat kol' as 'a chance snatch of speech overheard' and interestingly enough some of those who exercise a prophetic ministry today have said that is exactly how their 'words' seem to come to them."[8]

Although canonical prophecy was absent during this period, apocalyptic and religious literature flourished, none of which was classified as canonical and toward which the Palestinian Jews were quite negative. Ernest Best suggests that this apocalypticism probably made its appearance to fill the vacuum left by the end of prophecy.[9] The Jews were concerned about their future, naturally, while at the same time they believed God was working out His own purpose for the redemption of Israel.

One bright spot, as Freeman points out, was the glorious hope: "It was firmly believed among the Hebrews during the period between the Testaments that prophecy would be revived in the Messianic age on the basis of such forecasts as contained in Joel 2:28–29. . . ."[10]

The Ending of the Long Drought

Joel had by the Spirit seen a new age, the messianic age, in which the Holy Spirit would be poured out on the people of God like rain from a cloudburst. A leading characteristic of this spiritual precipitation:

prophecy. The New Testament begins with the inception of heaven's rainy season. It was as though a long drought was over and refreshing raindrops had begun to sprinkle the land, a foretaste of the coming showers. The picture reminds me of the marvelous spectacle in the foothills surrounding my home in the Santa Clara Valley of California. In the fall, when the rains start, dry, brown, thirsty hills are transformed almost overnight into beautiful green carpeting. So it was that the Holy Spirit ended the long, intertestamental spiritual drought. Soon green signs of prophetic activity were beginning to sprout among God's people.

Jesus Christ, of course, is the very heart of the messianic age. We are not to exclude Him in our discussion of the Spirit. But we must not forget that all Jesus did was by the power of the Holy Spirit (*Christ* means "the anointed one"). The teachings and works of Jesus are meaningful only in the light of the Spirit. He taught that the disciples would succeed only by the Spirit's empowerment (Luke 24:49).

The revelation of God to mankind has followed a threefold, sequential manifestation: first, the impressive manifestations of God the Father in the Old Testament; second, the physical appearance of God in and through Jesus Christ, His Son; and now, our experience of God through the presence of the Holy Spirit. We live today in the era of the Holy Spirit, which is to be characterized by His prophetic activity.

Contemporary with the birth and ministry of Jesus, outbursts of prophecy similar to that of the canonical prophets suddenly began to occur. God's voice was being heard again! The opening chapters of the New Testament give no indication that prophecy had been terminated, but rather that what was occurring was expected, natural and in continuity with the noble tradition of biblical prophetism. Everyone apparently believed that prophecy was to be an active part of such a spiritual season.

Six individuals, three men and three women, are significant in the introduction of Jesus' ministry. Luke recorded their marvelous outbursts of prophetic poetry and music associated with the incarnation. In addition to the *evangel* sung by the angel of the Lord over the plains and the *gloria* of the angelic host, we are given the Beatitude of Elizabeth, the Magnificat of Mary, the Benedictus of Zacharias and the *Nunc Dimittis* of Simeon. These four, plus Anna and John the Baptist, make up the six "prophets" who invite us across the threshold into the messianic age.

Elizabeth (Luke 1:39–45) and Mary (1:46–55). Two pregnant women, one an elderly woman and the other a teenager, met in a humble home in the Judean hills. Mary, the younger, had conceived her child by the Holy Spirit and then, having been informed of Elizabeth's six-month pregnancy, traveled hurriedly to her relative's abode. Mary needed all the insight and encouragement she could get at this unbelievable time in her life.

Zacharias and Elizabeth were an elderly priest couple (at least sixty or more years of age, Luke 1:7) who lived humble lives devoted to God. The angel of God had appeared to Zacharias in the Temple and told him his wife would bear a son. Named John, the son would be like Samson and Samuel, a "life Nazirite" dedicated to God from conception. He would turn many to the Lord and be the forerunner of the coming One. The miracle conception happened and six months of pregnancy passed. Then, without announcement, Mary burst in excitedly on the older woman. As Mary greeted her, the unborn John leaped for joy in Elizabeth's womb and she was filled with the Holy Spirit. A loud, prophetic cry escaped her mouth, instantly confirming to Mary that she was truly bearing the Son of God. This was more than an ode to Mary, although it did point up the importance of her office. This first song of the dawning of the new age by this elderly daughter of the Levitical system was the fulfillment of all the past hopes of Israel—an homage to and adoration of the Lord Himself.

Mary responded with a prophetic hymn of majestic proportions. Known as the Magnificat, it is a wonderful statement of God's mercy in lifting up the downtrodden. Interestingly Mary said nothing about the wondrous life in her womb, nor did she reflect the pessimism and disappointment of her generation. The mystic life within her released an artesian well of excitement and blessing, and the marvelous song spontaneously interwove many scattered expressions of the great Hebrew poetical literature. First Mary described her own experience, then declared the glories of Israel's God—His holiness, mercy, might and faithfulness.

Mary lingered for three months with Elizabeth. It must have been a blessed time for the two mothers-to-be, bonded by the miraculous and the call of God.

Zacharias (Luke 1:67–79). Silence had been imposed on the priest because of his hesitancy to believe the angel of God. Finally the nine months passed and Elizabeth gave birth to their son. Excited neighbors and friends hastened to call the child by the father's name, but Elizabeth protested, "He shall be called John" (Luke 1:60). Dissatisfied with her answer, they all turned to the old man, who wrote four simple words: "His name is John" (verse 63). The name means "The Lord Is Gracious."

The written declaration broke loose the inner volcano of his soul, and out gushed one of the most impressive, Spirit-empowered prophecies of the entire Bible. Apparently Zacharias had meditated much during his mute condition, for the booming twelve-verse prophecy is laced with thoughts and quotes from Genesis, the Psalms, Isaiah, Jeremiah, Ezekiel and Malachi. Not only did he declare redemption, salvation and prophetic fulfillment, but the priest dramatically proclaimed—addressing the child even as he spoke—that John was to be "the prophet of the Most High" (verse 76) and would go before Him as herald. Words of the angel that had previously fallen on him like a wet blanket of unbelief were now transformed into blazing, transforming truth—words of fire issuing from the Spirit-baptized lips of God's newest prophet.

Simeon and Anna (Luke 2:25–38). Mary bore her baby in a stable of Bethlehem, after which the parents found a dwelling where they apparently stayed for several years. Wise men from the East later visited, bringing about Herod's anger and the annihilation of the town's small children.

Jesus was circumcised after eight days in accordance with Jewish law; then, when the 41 days for Mary's purification (Leviticus 12:1–8) had been completed, Joseph and Mary brought the baby to the Temple for the mother's purification and the baby's dedication. Little did the parents know that two elderly people, a prophet and a prophetess, would abruptly appear and prophesy over the child.

Simeon lived in watchful expectancy for the coming Messiah. He was a true man of the Spirit: The Spirit was upon him, the Spirit spoke to him and the Spirit now led him to the Temple. Taking baby Jesus in his arms, Simeon praised and thanked God for the Salvation and Light cradled in his bosom. Joseph and Mary "were speechless with surprise" (Luke 2:33, Message). Simeon blessed them as well, specifically foretelling the dark time of the death of Jesus when deep sorrow would pierce Mary's own soul.

A second witness suddenly appeared—an ancient woman known by many as a godly woman of prayer and fasting, and a *prophetess!* Anna broke forth in praise over the child, and when she departed, "continued to speak of Him to all those who were looking for the redemption of Jerusalem" (verse 38).

John the Baptist. John grew up living in the deserts "until he began his public ministry" (Luke 1:80, NLT). Such wilderness areas are made for those who pray and reflect. We know nothing of how his parents influenced him, but surely they explained the spiritual significance of his name and the highlights of his father's powerful prophecy. We can assume that Zacharias made clear the meaning of "the prophet of the Most High" and that John would herald the advent of the Messiah. Zacharias would also have explained John's call to the life of an ascetic Nazirite. As the son of a Levite, John would have been expected to follow in his father's priestly profession. At some point, however, he apparently slipped this course and embraced the solitude of the wilderness life.

I have always thrilled at the dramatic account of John's call. After mentioning seven of the great people of that day, whom God passed up, Luke says "the word of God came to John" (Luke 3:2). Thirty years of patient waiting found fulfillment. Now guided by the inner urgings of the Spirit,

John headed for one of the popular crossings of the Jordan River, where a ready audience awaited him.

He was to prepare the way for the Lord's appearance and to help God's people find forgiveness of their sins and the salvation of God. As "the prophet of the Most High" he was to represent and speak on behalf of the Lord and to point the way to the Christ coming after him (Matthew 3:11; Luke 3:16). He declared himself to be the "voice" mentioned by Isaiah (40:3) and that he must fulfill Isaiah 40 by raising valleys and lowering mountains (encouraging the discouraged and rebuking the proud).

At some point the Lord spoke to him that one of those who would come for baptism would be the Christ (John 1:33). He knew somehow that all interest and importance must focus on this Anointed One, and that it would be his joy simply to be the friend of the Bridegroom and not the Bridegroom Himself (John 3:29). The time would come, John knew, for Christ "to move into the center, while I slip off to the sidelines" (John 3:30, Message). The prophet would introduce the main act.

The impressions of the Spirit let him know that the best way to accomplish this was to preach repentance in open-air settings and baptize those who truly repented. So he began to declare the arrival of the Kingdom of God and the need to repent and live an ethical lifestyle. Throngs of people flocked out to listen to him at the Jordan River. As Dunn describes John: "The divine compulsion was such that he had to go forth and proclaim. So compelling was his conviction that the way of the Lord must be prepared, so urgent his vision of imminent judgment that he could do no other than warn the people and give them opportunity to repent."[11]

John came in the spirit and power of Elijah (Matthew 11:14; 17:11–13; Luke 1:17), although he performed no signs and wonders (John 10:41). John himself was a sign, in the best tradition of the Hebrew prophets (see chapter 6). The multitudes held him to be a prophet (Matthew 14:5; 21:26, 46; Mark 11:32). Jesus called him "one who is more than a prophet" (Matthew 11:9) and the messenger predicted by Malachi (Luke 7:27).

John preached to Israel at the crossroads of the valley and baptized people in droves. He challenged all to repent, showing no favoritism, and clearly stated that he was neither the Christ nor one of the former prophets (John 1:25). His only claim to fame: that he fulfilled Isaiah's prediction of "a voice of one crying in the wilderness" for the people to repent and turn to God (John 1:23).

The great purpose of John's existence found dramatic fulfillment when Jesus of Nazareth came to be baptized by him. John saw the Spirit come upon the Nazarene and knew at that instant that this was indeed the Christ. John baptized Jesus, telling his disciples that this was He of whom he had spoken (John 1:30). Finally, because he challenged King Herod's adultery, John was imprisoned and beheaded (Matthew 14:1–12). John the Baptist was a prophet indeed!

Now we will consider Jesus, *the* Prophet.

Time for a Change

Throughout history God has chosen to work in time segments or dispensations, operating according to the covenant relationship then in force with His people. This perspective gives sharper focus to the ministry of the prophets and sheds insight on any differences between the Old Testament, the New Testament and present-day prophets.[12]

Jesus Christ came to fulfill and climax all that had gone on before and to open a new time period in which God's final salvation could be brought to mankind. He arrived on the human scene "when the proper time had fully come" (Galatians 4:4, Amplified). Jesus made an amazing statement about the new arrangement God had initiated: Although John the Baptist was under the old order the greatest of prophets, the least under the new would be greater than John. Jesus' exact words: "Truly, I say to you, among those born of women there has not arisen anyone greater than John the Baptist; yet he who is least in the kingdom of heaven is greater than he" (Matthew 11:11).[13] John was called a prophet, even "one who is more than a prophet," because he was God's last special messenger sent to prepare the way of the Messiah, foretold in Malachi 3:1. John represented the best the old order could produce; he was its last representative.

But how could anyone be greater than John the Baptist? As T. W. Manson says, "John set up a record of devotion and self-sacrifice not easy to be equaled, much less surpassed." Then he adds, "Where the least in the kingdom has the advantage is in what God does for him here and now."[14] The disciples of Jesus had no superior merit of their own that qualified them for this blessing and greatness, but they lived at the time when Jesus was bringing in the new age of salvation. F. F. Bruce makes this special emphasis: "It is not in moral stature or devotion or service, but in privilege, that those who are least in the kingdom of God are greater than John—greater not for what they do for God (in this John was unsurpassed) but for what God does for them."[15]

The launching of God's new era set in motion new factors that directly influenced, enlarged and enhanced prophetic activity.

Jesus, *the* Prophet

To the Hebrews of Bible times there was a difference between "a" prophet and "the" prophet. A prophet could refer to any one of a number of prophets sent by God, but *the* prophet could refer to only one, very special Prophet. That Prophet was He who would fulfill the prediction of Moses: "The LORD your God will raise up for you a prophet like me from among you, from your countrymen, you shall listen to him. . . . I will raise up a prophet from among their countrymen like you, and I will put My words in his mouth, and he shall speak to them all that I command him. And it shall come about that whoever will not listen to My words which he shall speak in My name, I Myself will require it of him" (Deuteronomy 18:15, 18–19).

Peter made it perfectly clear that Jesus of Nazareth was both the Christ and the promised Prophet. Preaching to an amazed multitude that witnessed the healing of the lame beggar, Peter specifically declared Deuteronomy 18:15, 19 to be fulfilled in Jesus (Acts 3:22–23).

During His earthly ministry, the people and authorities wondered at Jesus' identity. The disciples reported to Him that people thought Him to be John the Baptist, Elijah or one of the prophets (Mark 8:28), and Herod nervously received the same report from his spies (Mark 6:14–15; Luke 9:7–8).

On one occasion, when Jesus stopped a funeral procession in Nain and raised a man from the dead, the multitude of people "began glorifying God, saying, 'A great prophet has arisen among us!' . . . And this report concerning Him went out all over Judea, and in all the surrounding district" (Luke 7:16–17). The Samaritan woman said to Jesus, "Sir, I perceive that You are a prophet" (John 4:19). The blind man healed by Jesus said to the authorities, "He is a prophet" (John 9:17). When Jesus made His triumphal entry into Jerusalem, "the whole city was thrown into an uproar" and the cry went up, "Who is he?" (Matthew 21:10, TEV). The answer came back: "It's Jesus, the prophet from Nazareth in Galilee" (verse 11, NLT). The Temple authorities wanted to seize Him but "became afraid of the multitudes, because they held Him to be a prophet" (Matthew 21:46). The two disciples on the road to Emmaus told the stranger walking with them "about Jesus the Nazarene, who was a prophet mighty in deed and word in the sight of God and all the people" (Luke 24:19).

Clearly Jesus was received as a prophet, and He Himself seemed to have no problem being identified as such (Mark 6:4; Luke 4:23–27; 13:33). As *a* prophet, Jesus was to all outward appearances typical of what the people expected a Hebrew prophet to be, in terms of:

- *Calling.* He was aware of divine direction and empowerment (Luke 3:21–22; 4:1, 18; John 5:19).

- *Intercession.* He was man of prayer (Matthew 14:23; Mark 1:35; Luke 5:16; 6:12; 9:28).
- *Miracles and healing.* Seventeen bodily cures, nine miracles over the forces of nature, six demonic deliverances and three raised from the dead (as recorded).[16]
- *Visions.* Jesus saw the fall of Satan (Luke 10:18).
- *Outward features.* He made authoritative statements ("I say to you") and performed symbolic actions—for example, conducting the Last Supper, cursing the fig tree and entering Jerusalem. (Note the chart below.)
- *Teaching.* His teaching was prophetic in form and content (He spoke in parables, short sayings, poetic form) and brought a prophetic message to His nation.
- *Insight and emphases.* He displayed discernment of human character, prophetic insight into contemporary political, social and international conditions and made predictions.[17]
- *Fate.* Jesus fulfilled the prophet's role of rejection, persecution and martyrdom.

Jesus' Seven Sign Miracles in the Gospel of John		
Reference	Sign Miracle	Meaning
2:1–11	Changed water to wine	His ministry would be miraculous (power over nature), and His new ministry would be better than the old, established traditions
4:46–54	Healed nobleman's son	Faith invalidates the need for Jesus' physical presence
5:2–9	Healed lame man at Bethesda	Jesus challenged Sabbath tradition and the Jews' unwillingness to come to Him
6:5–14	Fed 5,000 with bread and fish	Jesus is the bread of heaven
9:1–16	Healed blind man on Sabbath	Jesus' purpose in coming: "Those who do not see may see; and . . . those who see may become blind" (9:39)
11:43–47; 12:18	Resurrected Lazarus	Whoever "lives and believes in Me shall never die" (11:26)
20:14, 19, 26	Appeared after resurrection	We should believe in His accomplishment (note 2:18)

Note: *Miracle* (KJV), *wonder-work* (Williams), *sign* (NASB), *attesting miracles* (NASB margin), *signs of some underlying reality* (F. F. Bruce). All are explicitly called *signs* except the story of the lame man at Bethesda. Other uses of *sign*: John 2:23; 3:2; 6:2, 26, 30; 7:31; 9:16; 10:41; 12:37.[18]

James D. G. Dunn feels that Jesus' strongest prophetic characteristics were "his insistence that the good news was for 'the poor' and his strong reaction against the formalism of contemporary Judaism."[19]

Jesus identified Himself with the prophetic group, yet without specifying that He was *the* Prophet. The gospel of John, however, picks up this thought. When the people saw the miracle sign of multiplying five barley loaves and two fish to feed five thousand men plus women and children, they said, "This is of a truth the Prophet who is to come into the world" (John 6:14). Also, on the last day of the Jewish feast, Jesus cried out for the people to come to Him to drink so they would experience the flow of living water. "Some of the multitude therefore, when they heard these words, were saying, 'This certainly is the Prophet'" (John 7:40).

As Jesus hastened toward the consummation of His earthly ministry, most of the people acknowledged Him as a prophet, and a discerning few . . . as *the* Prophet.

Moses and Jesus

Jesus as *the* prophet became to the New Covenant what Moses as the greatest of prophets was to the Old Covenant. Moses was the foundation prophet of the Old Testament, distinguished from all other prophets by his privilege of free, open and direct communication with God. The Lord made it clear that He would speak directly with Moses and Moses with Him, not through angels or mysterious visions, and that Moses would be physically able to have such communication without perishing (Numbers 12:6–8).

A general resemblance existed between Moses and all other prophets, but every other was markedly inferior. Moses, by contrast, spoke with God "face to face" (Exodus 33:11) and "mouth to mouth" (Numbers 12:8) and was used by God to structure the Law and theology of Israel. Under God he was the founder and foundation-builder of a great house— the dispensation reaching from the exodus to the first advent of Christ, and in some respects even beyond. Like the other prophets, Moses spoke the words of God in the name of God and was a mediator between God and the people; but his assignment and responsibility carried him to a much loftier position unattained by the ordinary prophet.[20]

It was in this sense that Moses referred to the Prophet to come as "a prophet like me" (Deuteronomy 18:15). This coming Prophet would stand out far superior to the ordinary prophets and leaders of His day. He would be like Moses in the sense of unrestricted communication between Himself and God, and in this resemblance His *likeness* in particular would be exemplified.

When Jesus ministered among His people, they faced the question of whether He was *the* prophet predicted by Moses who also was the Messiah. His disciples said He was, but it was not until Jesus conquered death and hell, ascended back to God the Father and sent the Holy Spirit that His followers began to understand the full implications of this concept. Jesus was indeed *the* Prophet and the Messiah; in fact, He was God manifested among men. So in the end Jesus was not only like Moses, but far superior; and His house, the Church, was made large enough to include believers from both Israel and the Gentiles; and His law was written in human hearts by His Spirit, not merely on stone tablets.

Comparisons between Moses and Jesus	
Moses	Jesus
Met the great I AM	Is the great I AM
Delivered Israel	Liberates all mankind
Interceded between God & Israel	Mediates between God & man
Administered death	Disburses life
Brought Ten Commandments	Accents two Commandments
Interpreted legalistic law	Administers spiritual law
Founded a natural nation	Creates a spiritual people
Awakened carnal awareness	Imparts spiritual knowledge
Wrote laws on stone	Inscribes laws on hearts
Made natural sacrifices	Initiates spiritual sacrifices
Brought atonement through the blood of animals	Provides atonement with His own blood

The Prophetic Consciousness of Jesus

Concerning Others

- Perceived "in His spirit" what was in people and what they were reasoning in their hearts (Mark 2:8)
- Knew Lazarus would be raised (John 11:11)
- Declared the centurion's servant healed (Matthew 8:13)
- Declared the Canaanite woman's daughter healed (Matthew 15:28; Mark 7:29–30)
- Recognized the lie of the Samaritan woman (John 4:17–18)
- Knew a coin would be found in a fish's mouth sufficient to pay the Temple tax for two (Matthew 17:27)

- On two occasions located large shoals of fish whose presence was hidden from experienced local fishermen (Luke 5:4–7; John 21:6)
- Pronounced woes on a certain three cities (Matthew 11:20–24); on Pharisees and lawyers (Luke 11:42–52); on scribes and Pharisees (Matthew 23:13–33); and on the comfortable (Luke 6:24–26)
- Warned daughters of Jerusalem to weep for themselves (Luke 23:28)

Concerning Himself

- Knew He must fulfill Scripture (Luke 22:37)
- Knew He would be betrayed (Mark 14:18; Luke 22:22)
- Identified His betrayer (Matthew 26:25; John 13:26)
- Knew His coming death was imminent (Matthew 16:21; 17:12, 22–23; 26:2; Mark 8:31)
- Knew He must die in Jerusalem (Mark 10:33–34; Luke 13:33)
- Knew He would be buried three days (Matthew 12:40; 17:23; Mark 8:31; 9:31; 10:34)
- Knew He would be raised from the dead (Matthew 16:21)
- Promised to return (Matthew 10:23; 24:42)

Concerning His Disciples

- Saw Nathaniel under the fig tree (John 1:48)
- Had insight into Peter's personality (John 1:42)
- Later rebuked Peter for ungodly remark (Matthew 16:23)
- Knew Peter would deny Him (Luke 22:61) and foretold that a cock would crow at a particular time (Mark 14:30)
- Said a colt would be found (Matthew 21:2; Mark 11:2)
- Said disciples would meet a man carrying a water pitcher (Mark 14:13)
- Foretold deaths of James and John (Matthew 20:23; Mark 10:39)
- Knew Satan wished to sift Peter and disciples (Luke 22:31)
- Knew His followers would be persecuted (Matthew 5:11–12; Mark 13:9–13)
- Knew who would betray Him (John 13:26)
- Predicted Peter's death (John 21:18)

Concerning the Kingdom of God

- Knew the present dimension (Matthew 10:7–8; Mark 1:15; 9:1)
- Understood the future dimension (Matthew 13:28–33)

Concerning the Destruction of Jerusalem

- Foretold all the stones would be torn down (Matthew 24:2; Luke 19:44; 21:6)
- Foretold the city would be surrounded by armies (Luke 19:43; 21:20)
- Foretold the Temple sanctuary would be desecrated (Matthew 24:15; Mark 13:2, 14)
- Foretold it would be a difficult time for those with child, and many would die (Luke 19:44; 21:23)

REFLECTIONS

Intertestamental literature was conscious of the loss of the Spirit. In the apocryphal and pseudepigraphical writings there is an awareness that the period of prophetic inspiration is over. Prophecy is defunct. Prophetic inspiration departed from Israel with the last of the prophets. In rabbinic literature it is expressly stated that the Holy Spirit departed from Israel after the last prophets. . . . There was no longer any inspired revelation.[21]

George Eldon Ladd

Without the living voice of prophecy continuing to direct Judaism, the strongest influence in Jewish politics and faith became in the end the zealotism that destroyed the nation and the rabbinism that petrified the religion.[22]

James D. G. Dunn

The Christian community is therefore primarily a prophetic community, and the Spirit is the spirit of prophecy, taken in its widest sense. If Jesus is the Spirit-anointed servant of Isaiah 61 who opens the age of salvation, the church is the community of the Spirit foretold by Joel.[23]

George T. Montague

The privilege of holding free and open communication with heaven in respect to the secret things of God, however it may have distinguished Moses from other prophets, only attained its perfection in Christ, as in Him also the ground on which it rests becomes immeasurably higher and broader.[24]

Patrick Fairbairn

COMPARING PROPHECY IN BOTH TESTAMENTS

"I am a fellow servant of yours and of your brethren the prophets...."
Revelation 22:9

THE TERM *PROPHET* is used by both ancient Hebrews and the early Church, and the Christians did not seem to struggle with a difference in meaning. They saw continuity between the Hebrew prophets and the New Testament prophets.

The Septuagint, the popular Greek edition of the Old Testament used by many Jews of the time, translated the Hebrew *nabi* into the Greek *prophetes* consistently throughout the Old Testament. The New Testament writers continued the use of the same word, without any abrupt redefinition or explanation, in their discussions of local Christian churches.[1]

Some important variations did exist in the use of prophecy between the two Testaments, as we will see in this chapter, but the essence of prophecy has not changed. God spoke in biblical history to reveal His will and He still speaks today.

The prophets of both Testaments were spokesmen and messengers of God to His people. Because the historical settings were different, we find that although the basic definitions of prophet and prophecy remain constant, new factors influence the contemporary message of God to His people. Clifford Hill identifies the difference for us: "The concept of prophecy in the New Testament is identical with that of the major prophets of Israel under the old covenant. . . . When we come to the function of prophecy, however, there is a major difference. . . ."[2]

There has always been discussion concerning the possible differences between the Old Testament prophets themselves,[3] or the contrast between Old and New Testament prophets,[4] and now the considerations of prophetic activity in modern times.[5] A simple schematic of this continuity, which also illustrates the theme of this book, would be:

Figure 1

Hebrew Prophecy ⟶ NT Prophecy ⟶ Today's Prophecy

Reasons for a Difference

Six concepts are discussed in the following section that contrast Old and New Testament prophecy. A chart at the end of the chapter gives a good summary of the differences.

- The new era brings prophetic changes.
- The Holy Spirit is now an abiding presence in every Christian believer.
- The Hebrew religion has been exchanged for a multiethnic Church led by the Spirit of God.
- The ancient ministries of the prophets, priests and kings have now passed into the lives of ordinary people.
- A new leadership structure allows prophetic ministry to be more practical and functional.
- Limitations were placed on both Old and New Testament prophets.

Let's look at each of these concepts in turn.

The New Era Brings Prophetic Changes

Jesus Christ brought to an end "both the message and the prophetic ministry as it was practiced in the Old Testament."[6] New Testament prophecy is functionally different because we have a New Covenant that places Jesus Himself as Prophet, Priest and King over the people of God. The message has shifted from the knowledge of sin through Moses to the knowledge of grace and mercy through Jesus Christ. Fairbairn, in his classic work on prophecy, says, "The fundamental difference lies in this— that in the Church there is the revelation of God's grace; and grace from its very nature is instinct with the spirit of prophecy."[7]

Like discardable scaffolding used in the erection of a house, the old Mosaic system helped prepare the people of God for the new house called the Church. Now the scaffolding (which included a certain approach in prophecy) is no longer needed. The scaffolding actually fell the day Christ died, when the veil of the Temple was rent. Jesus had said to the Jews that "your house is being left to you desolate [abandoned and empty, TEV]" (Matthew 23:38). The old support structures were important in their time, but now we have the beautiful new house, the Church. Let's not drag back the old (Luke 5:36–38).

The coming of Christ was the great watershed of prophetism. Previously every Old Testament prophet was subordinated to the revelation of Moses. Thank God for that superintending ministry that overshadowed and guided the prophets of old! But then Christ came as *the* prophet (Deuteronomy 18:15; Acts 3:22), fulfilling all that the prophets and Moses himself had foretold and hoped for. He was the very embodiment of the highest aspirations of those who would communicate with God; in fact, He was God manifest among humankind. Jesus came as the perfection of revelation, and His advent drew a crucial dividing line that has settled forever the difference. Jesus was not only the subject and object of all prophecy; He was and is the origin and inherent energy of it (Revelation 19:10).

The Holy Spirit Is Now an Abiding Presence in Every Christian Believer

The Hebrews of the Old Testament era lived in a time when the Holy Spirit was not *in* or *upon* each person all the time. They did not enjoy the continuing inner presence of the Holy Spirit that we Christians do. As Edersheim says, "Under the Old Testament, only the manifold influences of the Spirit were experienced, not His indwelling as the Paraclete."[8] Jesus Himself explained how it would be in the new era (in which we now live): "He who believes in Me, as the Scripture said, 'From his innermost being shall flow rivers of living water.' But this He spoke of the Spirit, whom those who believed in Him were to receive; for the Spirit was not yet given, because Jesus was not yet glorified" (John 7:38–39).

A new relationship between God and His people now exists. In Christ there is a new order. The Holy Spirit is available to all God's people and all may experience the prophetic anointing (1 John 2:20, 27). Kim Clement comments: "No longer would God selectively communicate to chosen individuals. He would reveal His kingdom in the heart of anyone who would believe."[9]

When the era of the Holy Spirit was launched on the Day of Pentecost, the apostle Peter cited the famous prophetic promise of Joel 2:28–32 concerning a Last Days outpouring of the Holy Spirit. Peter, inspired by the Spirit, quoted these verses with such great enthusiasm that the casual reader misses four words (not found in Joel) inserted into the middle of the quotation—words that capture the very essence of this newly birthed Church and how her men, women, sons and daughters will function: *"And they shall prophesy"* (Acts 2:18, emphasis added).

The common Israelite of Old Testament times did not experience the empowerment of the Spirit. This privilege was reserved for special people like prophets, national leaders, kings, wise men or appointed artisans[10]—and even such encounters were limited. Now, thank God, all His people can become familiar with the blessed Holy Spirit! Bruce Yocum summarizes this thought beautifully:

"The difference in the role of the prophets under the old and the new dispensations is the result of a change . . . in the relationship between God and his people as a whole. The Old Testament prophet was a man unique among God's people because of the Holy Spirit's action in him. He was in direct communication with the Lord, while the people as a whole were not. But under the new covenant all of God's people receive the Holy Spirit, all of God's people are in direct communication with God himself. In Old Testament Israel the prophet was thoroughly unique; in the 'new Israel' the prophet is one means among many by which God can speak directly to his people."[11]

Although "we are provided with one clear line of continuity between the classical prophets of the Old Testament and Christian prophets in the New,"[12] we must not ignore the obvious: The very nature of a prophecy given to a fervent New Testament church of Spirit-filled people will necessarily be different from prophecy spoken by a uniquely empowered Old Testament prophet to a lackluster crowd of unspiritual people. In the next chapter, when defining prophecy in the early Church, I will say more along this line.

New Testament prophecy was geared for the benefit of the Spirit-filled followers of Jesus—believers who heard God's Word and acted on it. These people received helpful "edification and exhortation and consolation" (1 Corinthians 14:3). The prophetic words were generally more confirming than directive in nature because the Christian was already in communication with God. Under the Old Covenant the Spiritless nation of Israel is addressed, whereas in New Testament times prophecy is addressed to the *Church,* the Spirit-filled body of believers in Christ Jesus.

Emil Brunner comments: ". . . Through the present fulfilment of what had been previously merely promised . . . an utterly new dimension of salvation has been vouchsafed, namely, life in the Holy Spirit, concerning which the Gospel of St. John roundly declares 'for the Holy Spirit was not yet given'. When Paul affirms: 'If any man is in Christ he is a new creature' he is alluding to a new mode of existence not yet known to the believers of the old covenant."[13]

The Hebrew Religion Has Been Exchanged for a Multiethnic Church Led by the Spirit of God

The Church with Christ as Head now welcomes every race and social class, and gives men and women equal status in spiritual activities (Romans 3:22; 1 Corinthians 12:13; Galatians 3:28; Colossians 3:11). The New Testament writers distinguish between membership in a nation or race and membership in the community of Christian believers.

God's intention was to have "a kingdom of priests and a holy nation" (Exodus 19:6), a theocracy with God as Ruler. The full function of this concept was not accomplished under the old order. The people sinned, rebelled and soon clamored for a king, which the other nations had, so elderly Samuel anointed young Saul as Israel's first earthly monarch (1 Samuel 9–10). Thus the king replaced the prophet-seer-judge as the leader, under God, of Israel.

Most of the kings in Judah and Israel corrupted Hebrew religion by initiating or tolerating various forms of idolatry, and God sent His faithful servants to challenge those destructive practices and religious compromises. The prophets had a difficult job but were strengthened by an intensity of divine energy enabling them to deliver God's word without fear or favor, and despite obstacles and resistance of every kind. As I. Howells says: "Even though the prophets sometimes called the kings to the throne, at the same time they could predict the fall and destruction of the same royal families because of unfaithfulness. Through the mouths of the prophets God exercised His dominion in the national life and the people realised that the government . . . was, in fact, in the hands of God."[14]

The Hebrew found himself part of a society and culture and religion that were all-pervasive. Laws regulated food eaten, clothes worn, even cutting one's beard. The teaching of God and His laws permeated family life, social relationships, even business. This did not automatically produce spiritual people, but a godly worldview enabled Israel to keep a more balanced outlook than her heathen neighbors. Even when the nations of

147

Judah and Israel split from each other, the covenants of Abraham, Moses and David exerted significant influence on people's lives. Unfortunately the kings were not always devoted to maintaining God's laws, so corrupt practices were always at work.

The prophets of the Old Covenant boldly denounced the sinful nations of Judah, Israel and their Gentile neighbors—not always an easy task. Graham Cooke writes that "prophets were sometimes a single voice speaking a righteous word to a corrupt and rebellious nation. They were often hounded individuals, living lives of immense hardship as they shared the joys and often the bitterness of life with the people."[15]

The Hebrew prophets heard the call of God for a very specific task, and they responded. Two-thirds of their message involved declaring the word of God to a people who had failed to obey His moral law. This ethical preaching was interlaced with futuristic predictions about a coming Messiah and the age and Kingdom to come, as well as the future of Israel.

Heathen nations were also addressed. Walter C. Kaiser Jr. points out that "the prophets exercised a surprisingly large ministry to the Gentile nations. Significant portions of their writings are given over to God's challenge to the heathen dominions to likewise return to the one true God, to his standards of righteousness and morality. Large sections of the major prophets' works deal with the Gentiles: Isaiah 13–23; Jeremiah 46–51; Ezekiel 25–32."[16]

Apparently the prophets managed to get their messages to the nations by means of foreign ambassadors who came to Jerusalem (Jeremiah 27:3), staff officers who carried and read the prophets' words (Jeremiah 51:59–64) and, like Jonah, by going personally.

In contrast to these national and international directives, which served as a protective against the abominations of the heathen and of Israel itself, New Testament prophecy is directed to the Church—to the body of believers in Christ Jesus who gathered in local assemblies. Whereas the Hebrew prophet was raised up in Israel during times of national crisis and political upheaval, the early Church had regularly functioning prophets and people who prophesied to maintain the spiritual dynamism within local churches. In Old Testament times the whole world had comparatively few prophets at any given time, each functioning as an estranged mouthpiece for God. In contrast New Testament prophecy functioned regularly, weekly, in the thousands of Christian churches in many countries through a multitude of prophetic ministries whose objectives were to serve as vehicles of individual and congregational inspiration, edification, consolation and exhortation.

Old Testament prophets were involved with specific national and international events. They were part of a national state religion; their religion, culture and national heritage were all one intertwined experience and lifestyle. New Testament prophecy occurred within the churches of various nations and ethnic groups—not as a political force but as an edifying spiritual influence to encourage the domestic lives of the people and to help them withstand persecution.

A Jew was a Jew nationally, racially, culturally and religiously. The Christian, by contrast, was a Christian in religion but was also the citizen of a non-Christian nation who lived in a cultural and social environment foreign to Mosaic standards. The Jew was automatically one with his nationality; the Church was composed of those "called out" ones who lived in the world but were not spiritually part of it.

The New Testament prophet (or person who prophesied) was a member of the Body of Christ, a person involved in the local church family. These people did not live in some exalted, rarefied condition; they were called as servants of Jesus. They did not enjoy the unlimited authority possessed by Old Testament prophets but were "obliged to function in fellowship and co-operation with other related members."[17] The Christian prophet "does not stand above the community; like all the rest he is a member of it."[18] The Christian must merge and coordinate his or her ministry with that of brothers and sisters, submitting all prophetic utterances to the evaluation of fellow Christians. Spiritual judgment among their own members was a new situation for the people of God and a far cry from the Hebrew prophet, who was revered when right—and stoned when wrong! As Rick Joyner says: "The Old Covenant prophets were prophesying *of* Jesus who was to come; the New Covenant prophets are prophesying *in* Jesus, as members of His very body."[19]

Prophets in every nation now have as their primary concern the Church and carrying out of the mission of Jesus Christ, rather than national, military and political interests. Prophetic emphasis shifted dramatically from chasing wayward kings and warning hostile nations to the weekly edification, comfort and spiritual direction of all God's people, even the lowliest of souls. Alex Buchanan remarks: "There were national prophets in Israel in Bible times, but Israel was a theocracy. . . . We are not guided as a nation by prophets, although prophets may speak out within the nation. Prophets today speak mainly to or through the church."[20]

The Ancient Ministries of the Prophets, Priests and Kings Have Now Passed into the Lives of Ordinary People

God's desire for a nation of royal priests (Exodus 19:6) is fulfilled in the members of the Church—all of whom are designated kings and priests, and who all have the potential to prophesy.[21] Jesus "has made us kings

149

and priests to His God and Father, to Him be glory and dominion forever and ever. Amen" (Revelation 1:6, NKJV).

Continuity exists between the Old Testament prophets, priests and kings and their New Testament counterparts in the sense of general definition, but a grand spiritual enhancement occurs in the spiritual fulfillment. Harold Horton says: "In the Old Testament only some were priests, because such intermediaries were necessary; in the New Testament all are priests, because our Antitypical Priest has come and is Himself seated in heaven as our only Intermediary. In the same way in the Old Testament, only some were prophets, because such intermediaries were necessary; but in the New Testament 'all may prophesy' since our Antitypical Prophet has taken up the Office and sent forth a Representative who will lead us all equally into all truth."[22]

Although all may prophesy in the Church (1 Corinthians 14), there is definitely the ministry or calling of the prophet as well. The New Testament prophet comes from the succession of the legitimate prophets of the Old Testament, which helps explain the necessity of maintaining the Hebrew practice of "testing."

A New Leadership Structure Allows Prophetic Ministry to Be More Practical and Functional

The shepherding of God's people now shifts from the paradigm of prophet-priest-king to the New Testament pattern of apostle-prophet-evangelist-pastor-teacher (Ephesians 4:11). The people of God ceased being just one, small ethnic group to become the worldwide family of God composed of innumerable people from all nations. This radical national and geographical change, reinforced by new spiritual empowerment, necessitated a change in leadership approach.

Jesus began the change by recruiting those amenable to His message of humility. The greatest among His people, He taught, would be the most humble, and He began by calling disciples, those willing to obey His teachings and follow His lifestyle. From this pool of followers He selected twelve to be His foundational leaders.

At this point there occurs a radical departure from the Old Testament: Jesus chose not prophets but apostles to found His Church. Jesus' choice of twelve apostles seems to indicate a deliberate, direct break with the institutionalized twelve tribes of Israel. He was launching a new order with new, functional leadership titles that would convey fresh significance to the hearers. The apostles became "the New Testament counterpart of the divinely authoritative Old Testament prophets."[23] Although *apostle* is not the same as *prophet,* there is a sense in which these new leaders were connected with the Old Testament prophets. The Hebrew prophet was a messenger, one sent to speak on God's behalf, and the Greek word *apostolos* conveys the same thought.

The task of writing the inspired Scriptures shifted from the Old Testament prophets to the New Testament apostles. This is borne out by 2 Peter 3:2: "Be mindful of the words which were spoken before by the holy prophets [Old Testament spokesmen], and of the commandment of us the apostles [New Testament spokesmen] of the Lord and Savior" (NKJV).

In the New Testament the apostles were never specifically called prophets. Jesus did say, however, that He would *send* [the verb form of *apostle!*] prophets: "Therefore, behold, I am sending [*apostello*] you prophets and wise men and scribes; some of them you will kill and crucify, and some of them you will scourge in your synagogues, and persecute from city to city" (Matthew 23:34).

The position of prophet was not depreciated but rather enhanced as it was blended with four other leadership ministries to provide broader coverage of service and more loving and suitable outreach. Ephesians 4:11–13 summarizes the new plan: "[God] gave some to be apostles, some to be prophets, some to be evangelists, and some to be pastors and teachers, to prepare God's people for works of service, so that the body of Christ may be built up until we all reach unity in the faith and in the knowledge of the Son of God and become mature, attaining to the whole measure of the fullness of Christ" (NIV).

The New Testament prophet is no longer the primary spokesman for God; still, this ministry is not to be silenced. The prophets of the early churches lived and served as one of the people, members of one Church, fellow believers with one Head—certainly not accorded superstar status! The great burden of being God's only voice (the feeling of the Hebrew prophet) is relieved by the presence of others who can both prophesy and, when needed, give loving evaluation. The ministry of the prophet now comes into its highest use as some perform traveling ministry and others function as local church members. Pastor Mike Bickle gives this practical insight: "Prophetic ministers are validated by their involvement in and with the local church, not by their separateness. The church becomes evangelistic through its evangelists, caring through its pastors, serving through its deacons and prophetic through its prophets. Prophetic ministers serve within the church to help it fulfill its function."[24]

Each of the classical prophets of the Old Testament was far more than a prophet. Each was "a spiritual leader of the times."[25] In a sense these important prophetic leaders of ancient times were the counterparts of the fivefold New Testament leadership ministry: apostles, prophets, evangelists, pastors and teachers. The new order required the creation of new ministry and function. The apostles became the leaders and spokesmen of doctrine and government, and the New Testament prophets continued the great tradition of hearing God's voice, but subject to the authority of the message proclaimed by the apostles. Evangelists, pastors and teachers also came into existence. Thus, from the one ministry of the classical superstar prophet, five new ministries arose to lead the Christian Church—the greatest leaders being those who serve most!

The traveling ministry among the churches was enhanced by the apostle *and* prophet working together.[26] Some feel that the apostles John and Paul were also prophets (a thought considered in chapter 11). Also, it has been argued that the apostle Barnabas (Acts 14:14) was a prophet.[27]

The loving way in which evaluation of prophecy was to be administered in the early Church was an incentive, safeguard and great relief to those who prophesied. The presence of the Holy Spirit in each of the believers, their openness to hear from God and the cooperative concern of apostles, other ministries and elders made for an effective, ongoing prophetic presence in the churches.

Limitations Were Placed on Both Old and New Testament Prophets

Individuals in both Testaments were inspired at divinely initiated times to speak God's very words with absolute divine authority. These prophets were used to inscripturate the revelation of God. Their messages, as originally given, were without mistake and have been collected to form the Bible. Carl F. H. Henry explains: "A special divine activity of inspiration has been operative in their production. . . . The Spirit, in His redemptive outgoing to fallen man, has outbreathed the Scriptures by a special relationship to chosen prophets and apostles."[28]

The inscripturating prophecy that produced the Bible is timeless, vital, special revelation meant for all mankind; it is universal truth. This occurred in both Testaments. The prophets and apostles did not initiate this inspiration; it came from God. This no longer happens in the Church, for the canon of Scripture is complete.

Also, in both Testaments there occurred prophetic activity not recorded for posterity but particularly for individuals and groups of people at the time given. This secondary prophecy occurred for personal enlightenment and enrichment, appropriate for the time and setting but not infallible or inerrant. Such prophecy sometimes proceeded from persons with no proper office of such a kind to fulfill (that is, they were not of a distinct order with a recognized function), yet they were endowed supernaturally for the occasion. In the Old Testament we see this in the prophesying of the elders in Numbers 11:16–29; the prophesying of King Saul in 1 Samuel 10:10–13; and the ministry of people like Samuel whose judgments and prophecies on Israelite domestic activities are not recorded. Such prophecy, which does not lay claim to being absolutely authoritative to all God's people, happened in New Testament times and can occur today.

Remember also that once the Law was given, God still had things to say to His people. The Law was complete in basic principles but did not cover every contingency. Hence God raised up prophets to be His voice as a present, continuing presence.[29] The prophecies preserved in Scripture were those that best expressed the character and purposes of God for all mankind in the future, and this probably explains why we have almost nothing of the messages of men like Samuel, Elijah and Elisha. Although intimately connected with the circumstances of their own times, much of their ministries had slight importance for later generations but serviced the immediate needs of the people at the time.[30]

In the New Testament we find congregational prophecy meant for edification, comfort and exhortation (1 Corinthians 14:3) that was to be evaluated or judged (1 Thessalonians 5:21). Regular prophecy in New Testament times and also today "does not add to Scripture although it should add to our understanding of the unchanging word of God. Its major purpose . . . is to enable the church to receive continuous guidance from the Father in the carrying out of the mission of Christ and the fulfilling of the purposes of God to bring the knowledge of salvation to all the nations."[31]

The God-breathed canon of Scripture (as explained in chapter 5) was given by special dispensation of God. The Bible stands as fundamental truth in written record for all peoples of all times, to be interpreted by spiritual believers; Jesus is the full revelation of God and His truth in human form. The ancient canonical prophets brought revelations that unraveled the plans and purposes of God. Of necessity such inspired utterances were of a higher order, whereas the prophecies in the early churches and today bear on immediate needs and circumstances. As David Blomgren points out: "There is a direct limitation put upon all New Testament prophecy. Paul in 1 Corinthians restricted such prophecy in this age to that which is based upon prior revelation. . . . New Testament prophecy can only operate 'in part', according to the portion of knowledge granted us now in the prior revelation of God's written word. . . . The prophetic function of the New Testament prophet continues . . . parallel to and illuminating that which we 'know in part.'"[32]

I have prepared a chart that contrasts Old and New Testament prophecy in eleven categories, similar to the points I mentioned in chapter 3.

Contrast of Old and New Testament Prophecy

Element	Under the Old Testament	Under the New Testament
Sender	God the Father, the Lord of glory.	Jesus Christ, God's Son, Head of the Church.
Audience	Nations of Judah, Israel, foreign nations; also selected individuals. Non-Spirit-filled people. Most of the time the audiences are in covenant relationship with God through the teachings of Abraham, Moses and David.	The local church made up of Spirit-filled people in right standing with God, through the New Covenant of Jesus Christ, drawn from every nation. The Church at large. Sometimes individuals (as Paul to kings).
Situation	Military threats, religious compromises, social upheaval, crises. All events seen through the grid of the turbulent OT and its covenants.	Local church situations; domestic life of New Covenant believers. Contemporary events including persecution of the early Church.
Messenger	Stands above the community, an Israelite who is in OT covenant relationship, who serves as a spokesman (*nabi*) for the Almighty and a seer (*roeh* or *hozeh*) of divine realities. A solitary figure, usually working independently. A single voice with unlimited authority.	Sons and daughters, New Covenant believers in Christ, all part of the Christian community. A team player working with 5-fold Church leadership and local elders. Not a superstar, part of a plurality. All Christians have the potential to prophesy.
Message	Both foretelling and forthtelling, often involving judgment. A specific, more focused task. Given in crisis, under strong anointing. Objective: national renewal. Usually crisis-oriented foretelling. Directive prophecy. Foundational function: truth about God's nature and ways.	More forthtelling: centered on edification, comfort and exhortation. Given weekly in church setting and dependent on faith level of the person. Primary role: church renewal. Usually help-oriented forthtelling. Usually non-directive, more confirming. Formative function: continuous guidance to carry out Christ's mission.

Mode of Delivery	Great variety: spoken, written and demonstrated. Usually given in crisis. Delivered in private encounters, on city streets or in public declarations.	Spoken, sung or demonstrated in the congregational meetings of the Christian churches, given in love. Sometimes done privately.
Time	Sporadic crisis times. Prior to Christ and His salvation.	Routinely or regularly in congregational meetings, as normal part of church services. After Christ.
Place	Anywhere.	Usually at local church meeting place. Sometimes to individuals.
Evaluation	Prophecy judged mainly on fulfillment and words of Moses. Basically unchallenged, but failures terminated!	Evaluated or tested by leaders and the people. Failures identified and judged; then the person is allowed to prophesy again if penitent and cooperative. Judged mainly on character and content.
The Spirit	External anointing on prophets. A sudden, dramatic, powerful influence or a revelation given to be delivered. Manifold influences for control and direction.	An inner filling of all the people. Prophecy operated by faith. The constantly abiding, indwelling *Paraclete*, mainly for confirmation.
Canon	Produced by prophets/scribes.	Produced by apostles/prophets/scribes.

In Conclusion

God has spoken to His people in many and various ways throughout history; the way in which He speaks is determined by the covenantal dealings of the given time frame. One of the most frequent ways has been prophecy, and this form of divine communication—whether in *logos* declarations of universal significance or in local church prophecies for current encouragement—has continued throughout the Bible. Obviously prophecy functioned differently after Christ ascended. Now we who are part of the Church Jesus founded seek to have that prophecy, and other spiritual gifts that were a vital part of the early Church, restored to today's church operation.

The next chapter opens Part 4, the heart of our discussion on what prophecy in the Church, past and present, is meant to be. All six chapters of this section advocate that the voice of Jesus continues in the Church in the form of prophecy—not as a substitute for preaching and teaching, which are essential, but as a complement to the ministry of the written Word.

REFLECTIONS

Only gradually and after violent struggles was a final release from Judaism attained and did it become recognized in consequence that the Christian society was utterly distinct from and indeed irreconcilable with the Jewish church.[33]

Emil Brunner

... Though prophecy was directive in the Old Testament times because God's people did not have the Holy Spirit within them, in New Testament times, prophecy is not to be directive; it is used to confirm what God has already shown someone.[34]

Roxanne Brant

Since Paul saw prophecy as evidence for the fulfillment of God's eschatological promises, he undoubtedly also saw the New Testament prophets as in the succession of the legitimate prophets of the Old Testament. This explains in part why all such prophecy must be discerned, just as with those in the Old Testament. But the *nature* of the new prophecy was also understood to be of a different kind, precisely because of the church's present eschatological existence. A prophet who speaks encouragement to the church in its between-the-times existence speaks a different word from the predominate word of judgment on ancient Israel.[35]

Gordon D. Fee

The New Covenant prophet is not to go to Mount Sinai to hear God and bring back a fading glory to the Church. The New Covenant prophet is to serve the body in coming to Mount Zion, where they too can hear God and receive an increasing glory.[36]

Ted J. Hanson

PART 4

CHRIST'S CONTINUING VOICE IN THE CHURCH

DEFINITION
OF CHRISTIAN
PROPHECY

Therefore, my brethren, desire earnestly to prophesy, and do not forbid to speak in tongues.

1 Corinthians 14:39

THE EARLY CHURCH embraced an astounding belief—one that could revolutionize today's Church if we would accept and buy it as our own. They were convinced that the Jesus who had walked among humankind in a literal body now resided among them in the invisible Person of the Holy Spirit. The Christ who had spoken to them through His own lips now spoke to His people through the inspired speech of His servants! They called this continuing voice of Jesus in the Church *prophecy.*

This chapter introduces the essential nature of this wonderful New Testament phenomenon, opening our discussion of "Christ's Continuing Voice in the Church." We will treat prophecy as an authentic experience, both then and now. Exciting and dynamic, prophecy provides an essential benefit in our church programs for experiencing God and expanding Christ's Church. Prophecy is a vital part of the renewal of the Church, and Christians must become more enlightened and inspired about its function and use.

The broad scope of prophetic activity in first-century churches is apparent from even a casual reading of the New Testament. The biblical documents that furnish direct information are Paul's letters, Acts and the book of Revelation.[1]

Prophecy seems to have been a normal occurrence in the churches of Judea, Syria, Asia, Italy and Greece, for Scripture indicates that the churches of the following fourteen cities were experiencing prophetic action: Jerusalem, Antioch, Ephesus, Tyre, Caesarea, Corinth, Thessalonica, Smyrna, Pergamum, Thyatira, Sardis, Philadelphia, Laodicea and even Rome, the distant capital of the Empire. Since prophecy was so widely expressed and experienced, we may well conclude that it was commonplace in all the churches of that time.

Prophets like Agabus, Judas and Silas traveled among the churches fanning the prophetic flame of early Christianity (Acts 15:22, 32; 21:10–11). A comment by Paul verifies the far-reaching extent of prophetic participation. While traveling on a serious mission to Jerusalem, Paul stopped in Troas and shared with the Ephesian elders that "the Holy Spirit solemnly testifies to me [probably referring to prophecy] in every city, saying that bonds and afflictions await me" (Acts 20:23). Prophetic warnings at every stop!

Two early extrabiblical sources shed light on the prophecy of that time: *The Didache* (10–13), ostensibly a basic church manual addressed to rural Christian communities in Syria-Palestine by an unknown author around A.D. 100, and *The Shepherd of Hermas,* written in various stages from A.D. 90 to 150 and addressed to Christian congregations in and around Rome.[2]

A Basic Definition

New Testament prophecy occurs when a Spirit-filled Christian receives a "revelation" *(apokalupsis)* from God and then declares that revelation to the gathered church under the impetus of the Holy Spirit. Such revelation "enables the church to know something from the perspective of the Kingdom of God."[3] The essential makeup of a prophecy, based on my definition, is fivefold:

- *God gives a revelation* (communication, divine truth, message, insight)
- *to a Spirit-filled Christian* (one of God's people, a spiritual intermediary)
- *who speaks it forth* (an oral declaration)
- *to the gathered church* (the public assembly of believers)
- *under the impetus of the Holy Spirit* (inspiration, stimulation, prompting, encouragement, empowerment).

A Revelation from God

Insight of the Spirit is essential. Without perception of the divine will, there can be no prophecy. It is not the result of a human mind thinking up a nice religious thought, even if appropriate. It is a word from God, a communication from heaven, a divinely inspired thought for a current situation. Paul's prayer for the Ephesians holds true for today's churches as well: that God "may give to you the spirit of wisdom and revelation in the knowledge of Him, the eyes of your understanding being enlightened . . ." (Ephesians 1:17–18, NKJV).

An event in Matthew 16:16 illustrates the sharp contrast between divine revelation and man's own ideas. Peter's great declaration, "Thou art the Christ, the Son of the living God," was more than a personal conclusion. Jesus pinpointed the divine Source: "Blessed are you, Simon Barjona, because flesh and blood did not reveal this to you, but My Father who is in heaven" (verse 17). Within moments of the commendation, however, Peter was severely rebuked by Jesus for blurting out a hasty statement that challenged the very reason for Jesus' coming (verse 23)!

Prophecy occurs at the influence of God's Spirit. The words spoken while a person is "in the Spirit" come not from reflection, premeditation or study but are initiated by God for the benefit of His people.[4] This revelation "occurs when a Christian either hears, sees or senses a prompting from the Holy Spirit and speaks what he or she has received."[5] James D. G. Dunn comments: "For Paul prophecy is a word of revelation. . . . It is a spontaneous utterance, a revelation given in words to the prophet to be delivered as it is given (1 Cor 14.30). At this point Paul stands wholly within the (Hebraic) tradition of prophecy as inspired utterance."[6]

Some might ask, "Is prophetic revelation some form of ecstasy?" We have already discussed ecstasy in chapter 5. Here I will say simply that Paul teaches that those who prophesy in church are not to be out of control or out of their minds (1 Corinthians 14:32). It is often someone who has not received one of the "utterance gifts"—prophecy, tongues and interpretation of tongues (1 Corinthians 12:10)—who feels that biblical prophecy is an out-of-body ecstatic experience in which the person loses sanity.

Unfortunately various Old Testament scholars have given the impression that the prophets of old were possessed by frenzy or mania in which their normal faculties were suspended. I have already challenged this concept but would like to state again that scriptural support for such an assumption is just not available. There is no authority to compare the Hebrew or Christian prophets with the heathen soothsayer (the *mantis*) who worked himself into a religious frenzy, attempting to gain favor with his observers by undergoing some kind of spirit transport. I agree with

Patrick Fairbairn, a leading commentator on Old Testament prophecy, when he describes the prophetic unction as "the higher impulse stimulating [the prophets'] natural powers, and informing their minds with supernatural revelations, but *never destroying either their personal freedom, or their proper individuality.*"[7]

Spoken Out

A revelation intended for prophecy is not considered prophecy unless it is shared, proclaimed orally, to the assembled church by a Spirit-filled Christian, as these references make clear (emphasis added):

"While they were ministering to the Lord and fasting, the Holy Spirit *said . . .*" (Acts 13:2).

"The Holy Spirit came on them, and they began *speaking* with tongues and prophesying" (Acts 19:6).

"This is what the Holy Spirit *says . . .*" (Acts 21:11).

"One who prophesies *speaks* to men for edification and exhortation and consolation" (1 Corinthians 14:3).

"Let two or three prophets *speak,* and let the others pass judgment. But if a revelation is made to another who is seated, let the first keep silent. For you can all prophesy one by one, so that all may learn and all may be exhorted" (1 Corinthians 14:29–31).

Given to the Church

The setting most conducive to such revelation is the worship environment in the local church. Christians in this atmosphere of Spirit-inspired worship find themselves more open to hearing God's voice and more willing to be channels for that voice to speak through them. Since the human mind attunes more easily to the spiritual dimension through prayer, praise and worship, God's people tend to function best in these surroundings. When our attention has shifted from our bankrupt selves to the glorious Lord, we are in the best possible position to hear from heaven.

Prophecy is a special vehicle God uses to bless His Church. The gathering of the faithful is the ideal place for the Holy Spirit to speak into current needs and situations. The sanctity of the message is enhanced and preserved in the context of the Christian assembly. Here the people are capable of evaluating prophetic manifestations and the spiritual leaders help bring God's immediate purposes to pass. If a prophecy needs correction—and we know from the Bible that this is sometimes necessary (more on this in Part 6)—the loving pastoral care of the church provides the necessary help and enforcement.[8]

An Anointed Word

We have noted that prophecy is more than a good religious thought. Nor is prophecy authentic just because it is spoken by an outstanding citizen or talented member of the congregation, however impressive. *Prophecy is characterized by the inherent involvement of the Holy Spirit in the utterance.* Prophecy is "anointed" because of the attendance of the Holy Spirit's presence with that spoken word. Samuel poured anointing oil over David, giving us a graphic symbol of God's overshadowing power; thus, the word *anointed* is often used by Spirit-filled people to describe the action or empowerment of the Holy Spirit.[9] The person speaking is prompted and moved on by the Spirit. The content and delivery of the message is divinely empowered, causing people to delight in what they hear. The message, if from God, has that unique, "bell-tone" quality that brings peace and assurance.

Different from Public Address

Bible commentators and translators who work their way through 1 Corinthians always find the discussion of tongues and prophecy in chapters 12–14 a formidable challenge. I have known ministers who simply skip over these chapters while preaching through the book.

What were those Corinthians actually doing when they prophesied? The differences between the Greek verbs show that *to prophesy* is not the same as *to preach* or *to teach.* Unfortunately the lack of personal experience or contemporary models causes the uninitiated student to fall back on his or her own (in)experience. Thus, prophecy is sometimes considered synonymous with the public proclamation of the Bible. Examples from six modern translations illustrate how the clear-cut Greek word for "prophecy" *(propheteia)* has been diluted: "the gift of preaching the word of God" (Phillips); "inspired preaching" (Goodspeed); "preaching the messages of God" (LB); "to speak God's Word" (Beck); "the gift of preaching" (TCNT). A marginal note in Williams suggests the meaning is "speaking new spiritual truths."

William Barclay in his commentary on 1 Corinthians said: "This chapter is very difficult to understand because it deals with a phenomenon which, for most of us, is outside our experience." His solution: to treat the gift of prophecy as "the gift of forthtelling the truth in such a way that all can understand it."[10] Eugene Peterson in *The Message* makes prophecy "the proclamation of his truth." Some of the Reformers, like Calvin, considered the office of teacher similar to that of prophet. These thoughts are good but inadequate to explain the phenomenon.

The accuracy-conscious translators of the 1611 King James Version of the English Bible consistently translated the Greek verb *prophetein* as "to prophesy," not "to teach" or "preach." Many of the well-known translations have followed suit. As I mentioned in chapter 3, the Septuagint (the Greek version of the Jewish Scriptures redacted in the third and second centuries B.C. by Jewish scholars and adopted by Greek-speaking Christians) consistently uses the various forms of *prophetein* when translating Hebrew words for "prophecy." The New Testament writers picked up the same Greek word (from *pro,* meaning "forth," and *phemi,* meaning "to speak") and continued its use. This consistency of the same word in both Hebrew and Christian Scriptures illustrates its historic continuity. Paul and his contemporaries apparently had few of our modern hang-ups with words or experiences—or, I might add, with the prophecy and oracles in the Graeco-Roman world.[11] Rather they saw themselves in the same continuing flow of prophetic activity as practiced by the Hebrew prophets.

Prophecy is, as Barclay pointed out, forthtelling or speaking forth, but it is beyond the simple declaration of a lecture or sermon. Prophecy is not prepared oratory, a studied approach to a subject followed by a speech or presentation. It is not the delivery of a previously prepared sermon.[12] It is empowered delivery of a divine insight that comes in a flash (or as a "now-word")[13] to bring spiritual insight for that moment. The early Church realized there was a clear difference. Prophecy to them was "the communication of a word received direct from God, under the operation of the Holy Spirit."[14] J. Rodman Williams points out that "there is no 'scheduling' of prophecy: it just happens."[15] It is an immediate message of God to His people through a divinely anointed utterance.

For example, when Reinhard Bonnke, the well-known German evangelist who has led multiplied thousands to the Lord, was a boy, a woman prophesied that there was a lad in church that morning whom God would someday use mightily on the continent of Africa. Then, turning to young Reinhard, she said, "And you are that boy!" The rest is history.

Paul is careful, when listing the offices and gifts of the Church, to distinguish between prophecy and teaching.[16] Only one conclusion seems plausible: Prophecy is not the same as preaching or teaching. Teachers and preachers work with material already known and make it relevant. Prophecy comes here and now, bypassing rational thinking in the sense that human ingenuity is needed.[17] Prophecy imparts in an *ad hoc* manner the express *purpose* of God for a current situation, whereas teaching and preaching communicate a researched understanding of God's *principles* for life, growth and service.[18]

Prophecy is insight that comes in a flash of inspiration provided by the Holy Spirit. God's thought is then proclaimed, usually in a more energetic way than common speech because of the overwhelming sense of God's presence and power. (Special enablement often accompanies prophetic manifestation.) Agabus the prophet's prediction of a famine (Acts 11:27–30) could have come only through divine insight, not by research or study.

Once, as I laid my hands on a young ministerial candidate couple, not knowing their situation, I said they did not need to wait any longer; they could go. It turned out they were already planning to leave for Japan the following week; they had even purchased their tickets. This kind of personal confirmation, simple as it is, greatly blesses the people involved, but clearly in the realm of the prophetic, not that of teaching or preaching.

Prophesying must not take precedence over teaching. Both of these indispensable gifts require the inspiration of the Spirit, and both cause the local Christian community to increase numerically and to grow healthy in sound doctrine. Prophecy works in tandem with preaching and teaching; teachers and prophets, for instance, worked together at Antioch (Acts 13:1). "Prophecy should be," says David Schoch, "a complement to preaching."[19]

The role of prophecy is to build up the local church; to personalize the great, stated truths of Scripture and make them real in a current, familiar setting. These inspired prophetic utterances should not occupy as much congregational time as preaching and teaching, and they are to be subject to close scrutiny and evaluation. True prophecy does not contradict or replace Scripture, nor is it meant to take over the Church. Neither should prophecy be cast aside or considered insignificant.

Summary of Prophecy

Our discussion has shown that prophecy has nine essential aspects:

- *Divinely originated:* The spokesperson is a mouthpiece for God, declaring in human language a divine communiqué or message.
- *Immediate:* Usually the prophecy is a "now word" that comes suddenly, abruptly, instantly, on the spot.
- *Spontaneous:* The message is humanly unprompted, unbidden, unpremeditated, unplanned, unstudied, unrehearsed.
- *Spirit-inspired:* The words originate with God and are empowered in their inception and delivery by the Holy Spirit.

167

- *Intelligible:* Prophecy is (or should be) a clearly spoken, concisely related message in the contemporary language of the people.
- *Orally delivered:* The voice of God is expressed through human voices, a divinely anointed utterance spoken loudly enough to be heard by those assembled.[20]
- *Addressed to a gathered church:* The message is for God's people, usually delivered to a gathered assembly of Christians, although possibly to an individual.[21]
- *Relevant:* Prophecy is intended for the edification or encouragement of the people in their present situation.
- *Hearer-friendly:* The words of prophecy should ideally be brought in an attractive, sensitive, spiritual, nondistracting style.

The Most Significant Gift

Much teaching on spiritual gifts is being given these days. Christians feel compelled to examine the importance of these gifts so vital to the early Church, and churches that hardly mentioned the subject previously now find it of great interest to their own people as well as to Christendom worldwide.

I would like to suggest eight reasons prophecy can be considered the most significant spiritual gift.[22] It is the:

- Most *mentioned* in the biblical listings of gifts.
- Most *explained* gift in Scripture.
- Most *edifying* to the whole Church.
- Most *revealing* of God's will.
- Most *available* to all.
- Most *used* (with tongues) by the Spirit.
- Most *promoted* of the gifts.
- Most *connected* with Jesus.

Most mentioned in the listings. The chart on page 173 gives an overview of the eight New Testament lists of spiritual gifts. Prophecy is underlined in each list and each occurrence connected with the other listings by dotted lines. The importance can be seen immediately. "Prophecy" or "prophet" is the one gifting in all the lists that remains constant.

Most explained in Scripture. Prophecy is the only gift (along with tongues) having a whole chapter dedicated to its operation in the Church.[23]

Obviously Paul devoted so much space because he considered prophecy important and did not expect it to be discontinued.

Most edifying to the whole Church. The verse most favored by commentators to explain the purpose and function of prophecy is 1 Corinthians 14:3: "One who prophesies speaks to men for edification and exhortation and consolation." Glenn Foster sets it up like this:

Prophecy edifies.
It builds up the believer.
Prophecy exhorts.
It stirs up the believer.
Prophecy comforts.
It cheers up the believer.[24]

Each of these functions can also be fulfilled through other Christian activities. Paul says we are to "pursue the things which make for peace and the building up of one another" (Romans 14:19). One such activity we can pursue is "speaking the truth in love" (Ephesians 4:15–16). Prophecy does not replace other activities that build up, but rather edifies through its own unique application of the Holy Spirit. J. R. Williams comments: "As far as the upbuilding of the fellowship is concerned, prophecy stands out as the most significant of all the Spirit's operations. . . . This edification—or upbuilding—through prophecy consists of consolation, encouragement, stimulation, exhortation, strengthening. . . . It is God's Word to His people for the living of their lives before Him."[25]

In any given assembly, many needs and emotional states are represented. God knows how to touch and motivate His gathered people, individually and collectively, all at the same time. Bill Hamon explains that "prophecy is important in the life of the church, because prophecy is the most edifying gift for a congregation. The other eight are focused 'rifle' gifts, which normally bless one specific person or perhaps a few; prophecy is a 'shotgun' gift that can bless hundreds of people at once."[26]

Most revealing of God's will. Prophecy is significant because it is a revelation of God for the moment when the congregation is assembled. Michael Harper says, "It is a special anointing given at a selected moment by the sovereign Spirit for a distinct purpose."[27] God has something to say *now!* Prophecy comes with relevancy and immediacy, pertinent to the existing needs and spiritual state of the local church. Grudem comments: "Prophecy, then, is superior to the other gifts because the revelation on which it depends allows it to be suited to the specific needs of the moment, needs which may only be known to God (cf. 1 Cor 14:25; Rom 8:26–27)."[28]

169

I have heard simple prophetic statements move a congregation or someone in the congregation profoundly. When a discouraged person forces himself to a worship service, for instance, he may be gripped by a beautiful but simple expression of God's love and concern for His people. As the worshiper opens his heart to the prophecy, he experiences a marvelous release from his burden and is lifted up. To see the statement in print later or to hear what was prophesied when you were not present often seems strange, even meaningless. A prophetic message does not compare with Scripture teaching or preaching because it is directed more to the immediate heart needs of the people than to their intellects.

I write these lines on a Sunday afternoon. This morning my wife and I attended the church in San Jose that we founded more than three decades ago. Because we are usually traveling in ministry, it was good to be home without any ministerial responsibilities. I was uplifted greatly by the worship, although I heard some choruses that were new to me. The atmosphere was one of worship and praise.

Then, utilizing the microphone (see chapter 22), three people gave prophetic expressions that were a great blessing to me. First there was a prophetic song of encouragement by the pastor: "I, the Lord, make streams in the desert, rivers in the valleys. . . . I will bring life to your soul. . . . Be thirsty in your heart. . . . I make a way where there is no way. . . . I am the way; I am your way." Then there was an exhortation by a woman in the church urging people not to be discouraged with this period of transition. We were to move ahead in spite of pain, for when God was finished and brought the answer of life, we would not even remember the pain! Third, my daughter Janice saw a vision of a toddler learning to walk, describing the feeling of distress that the child would experience trying to walk or turn and then falling. The vision illustrated the condition of some of us in the church, but we were assured that God had decreed hope for us and exhorted to remember that our security was not in natural things, "just in Me!"

I cannot begin to do justice to the song, the exhortation and the vision, nor can I repeat the exact words. I can testify, however, of the wonderful uplift that these spontaneous, Spirit-inspired manifestations gave to me, especially as they were enhanced by the preaching of the Bible.

Sometimes such expressions are more complicated or varied, but this simple description is meant to represent just a peek for any reader who has not experienced prophetic utterance and spiritual revelation.

Most available to all. Someone may wonder at calling prophecy the most significant gift, especially if that person feels that his or her own gifting is quite important (or most important) to the body of believers. You should appreciate your own gift or ministry. But remember that in addition to your own gifting, *you can also prophesy* (Acts 2:17–18; 1 Corinthians 14:1, 5)—and this is not true of any other gift except tongues. Some exercise specialized gifts of prophecy, but everyone has the potential (as we see in the next chapter) to participate in prophecy.

Recently in our home church, during the time after worship when the microphone is open to the congregation, Big Jim came sauntering up to the front. The elder monitoring the mike raised it to accommodate Jim's six-four, 250-pound frame. Big Jim does not look like your typical church attender. Tattoos decorate his big, stovepipe arms and he was wearing sunglasses. God has done some remarkable things for Jim and he has become a real prayer warrior and witness for Christ. Usually I close my eyes for prophecy, but the huge figure fascinated me. This was his first time up at the mike. What would he do?

Obviously he was being moved on by the Holy Spirit. He began a singsong chant in his deep, gravelly voice that brought a smile to every face:

> I thank the Lord,
> He set me free.
> I thank the Lord,
> I now can see.

My fascination turned into astonishment and thanksgiving. Jim kept going, tears flowing down his face. He was on a spiritual roll. On and on he went, rhyming away the praise of God:

> I thank the Lord,
> He saved my soul.
> I thank the Lord,
> He made me whole.

After he finished about a dozen of these dynamite sentences, he returned to his seat as the congregation began clapping and praising the Lord. Jim had made a simple yet significant prophetic contribution to the church.

Most used by the Spirit. In the typical New Testament worship service, prophecy was the most common manifestation of the Spirit. We, too, are urged to desire the workings of the Spirit, but our particular focus should be on prophecy (1 Corinthians 14:1–5). Other gifts, such as miracles, healing and a word of wisdom, are comparatively infrequent and sporadic in their manifestations, but prophecy is available to all whenever the church convenes.

Most promoted of the gifts. 1 Corinthians 14 is the basis of this statement, for in terms of sheer bulk of verses in the Bible, prophecy stands out as the most promoted!

Most connected with Jesus. "The spirit of prophecy" is equated to "the testimony of Jesus" (Revelation 19:10). This unusual comparison, made by an angelic guide to the apostle John while in heaven, can be taken two ways: the testimony *about* Jesus or the testimony *by* Jesus. The possible meaning: that prophecy is the continuing voice of Jesus to the Church. Either way this marvelous gift is closely associated with Jesus and His word.[29]

The Eight Lists of Spiritual Gifts in the New Testament

The chart on the next page, although arranged differently, is based on a chart by Michael Griffiths. He says: "A comparison of the different lists amounting to some twenty different items suggests neither Paul nor Peter was intending to produce a single exhaustive list; each was rather illustrating what he meant when emphasizing either the variety of gifts or the unity of the purpose for which they were given."

Admittedly the gift of prophecy is not mentioned specifically by Peter in his short list, but certainly when he says, "If anyone speaks, let him speak as the oracles of God" (NKJV), he is including prophecy in his thought of the ministry of speaking.

Prophetic Accuracy and Gradations of Prophecy

Accuracy and inerrancy are part of any present-day discussion of prophecy.[30] Sometimes unintentional mistakes are serious but amusing, showing why we need supervision and evaluation. There was the man who went on and on with his prophecy describing God's faithfulness. He became focused on the ark and how God helped Moses call the animals inside. "And Moses called the elephants . . . and Moses called the giraffes." And so on. Finally, after a prolonged account of Moses gathering the various animals, the speaker sat down. A deathly silence followed the message. Suddenly the man stood up again: "God saith, 'I made a mistake; it was Noah.'" This true story illustrates that good, sincere folks may need some adjustment in their prophetic ministries!

The Eight Lists of Spiritual Gifts in the New Testament

1 Cor. 12:28	1 Cor. 12:29–30	1 Cor. 12:8–10	Rom. 12:6–8	Eph. 4:11	1 Pet. 4:10–11	1 Cor. 13:1–3	1 Cor. 14:26
Apostleship	Apostleship	Word of wisdom	Prophecy	Apostleship	Speaking	Tongues	Psalm
Prophecy	Prophecy	Word of knowledge	Serving	Prophecy	Serving	Prophecy	Teaching
Teaching	Teaching	Faith	Teaching	Evangelism		Knowledge (all mysteries)	Revelation (*apokalupsis*)
Miracles	Miracles	Healings	Exhortation	Pastor/teacher		Faith	Tongues
Healings	Healings	Miracles	Giving			Giving	Interpretation
Helping		Prophecy	Leading			Martyrdom	
Administrating		Discerning of spirits	Showing mercy				
Tongues	Tongues	Tongues					
	Interpretation of tongues	Interpretation of tongues					

Note: The underlining and dotted lines correspond to my statement on page 168 under "most mentioned in the listings."

Here are five reasons some New Testament prophecy, like all contemporary prophecy, had the possibility of partial or total inaccuracy and is therefore not on a par with Scripture prophecy:

- Prophecy is to be judged.
- Prophecy today is "in part."
- Prophecy was encouraged among the people by Paul, something he would not have done if it was only for creating Scripture.
- Prophecy depends on the faith level of the one speaking.
- Prophecy often contains a conditional aspect.

To be judged. We will discuss fully the subject of testing prophetic utterances in chapters 20 and 21. Three Scripture passages (1 Corinthians 14:29, 1 Thessalonians 5:20–21 and 1 John 4:1, each of which we will examine in those chapters) teach that Christian prophecies should be judged or evaluated. This implies, of course, that prophecy can have error. False prophecy is troublesome for a local congregation, but there are also the challenges of impure, weak or "sloppy" prophecy given by sincere but untrained people.[31] Even the content of "good" prophecy must be gauged by whether the utterance is inspired in general content or exact wording.

In part. The great love chapter, 1 Corinthians 13, sandwiched between two powerful chapters on spiritual gifts, says it simply: "We prophesy in part" (verse 9, NKJV, NIV). The clear meaning of the two Greek words *(ek merous)* is translated consistently: "incomplete" (Williams), "fragmentary (incomplete and imperfect)" (Amplified), "imperfect" (RSV), "only partial" (TEV), "fragmentary" (Berkeley), "not complete" (CEV). We must conclude that today's prophecy, like that of the Corinthian believers and unlike Scripture, was subject to imperfection.

Encouraged. Paul encouraged all the Christians to prophesy in their local settings, but he did not envision that Scripture-level prophecy would be produced by everyone. Only a few apostle-prophets would be inspired on a canonical prophecy level to write the New Testament Scriptures, and those writings alone would be accepted on a par with the Hebrew Scriptures (1 Thessalonians 2:13; 2 Peter 3:16)—that is, binding and authoritative.

The inscripturating prophecy that produced the Bible ceased after the last New Testament books were written. A dire warning is given in Revelation 22:18–19 not to add or detract from the message given to John. These verses are rightly applied to the whole Bible. Note, however, that John was told he would "prophesy again" (Revelation 10:11), indicating that the day of prophecy was not over, even though the writing of Scripture had been completed.

Prophecy in the early and modern Church frequently has been one hundred percent accurate. No present prophecy, however, even if absolutely accurate, is considered in the same class as the inerrant, infallible Scripture. In all the years I have associated with Spirit-filled people, I have known no one who equated modern prophecy with the Scripture (see chapter 5). Prophecy in local church gatherings is directed specifically. Robeck explains: "The gift of prophecy seems to be designed by God to speak ad hoc, to specific people at specific times in specific situations."[32] This is clearly the tenor of Paul's teaching for the prophecy that he expected to occur.

Bible readers have long observed that the words of some Old Testament prophets who spoke to the needs of the people were not preserved or given canonical status. A few examples: Moses' elders (Numbers 11); Saul (1 Samuel 10, 19); the old prophet in Bethel (1 Kings 13:11); Ahijah (1 Kings 14:4–16); the anonymous prophet (1 Kings 20:35–42); Iddo the seer (2 Chronicles 9:29); Uriah, son of Shemiah (Jeremiah 26:20); the prophets in the prophetic schools; and the canonical prophets themselves, whose words at times were not recorded as Scripture. This observation has led some to posit two levels of prophecy in the Old Testament—one more valued, the other less. Graham Houston, for instance, cites "considerable evidence in the Old Testament for at least two types of prophecy, one of which claimed to communicate God's word with an absolute verbal authority, and one which was seen as a powerful sign of God's presence without necessarily bringing a specific message."[33]

Bishop David Pytches suggests caution: "While a two-level category of prophecy may be suggested here we should never insist upon such clear-cut distinctions. The Holy Spirit eludes systemisation. Who can say where the wind is coming from or where it is going (John 3:8)?"[34]

Depends on faith of speaker. If and when a person prophesies in the church, he or she must do so "according to the proportion of his faith" (Romans 12:6). "Proportion" is the translation of *analogia*, which appears only once in the Greek New Testament. As Everett Harrison points out, it seems that Paul in this text is "intent on emphasizing the need for exercising the gifts, and for exercising them in the right way. . . ."[35] Various commentators rightly suggest that "faith" here is to be taken in a subjective way, tied in with the "measure" mentioned in verse 3. So, as Barrett points out, while it is possible to translate "of *the* faith" (with faith representing the Christian religion), Paul is most probably referring to *how* a person is to function.[36]

Some have stronger faith than others, but each of us must minister with the strength of conviction God gives, recognizing an element of launching out in faith. Sometimes we miss an opportunity to minister a spiritual gift because of timidity or false pride. Let's trust that the church body will be gracious in their evaluation of our contribution and move out to express the anointed conviction of our hearts!

Conditional. Just as in prayer, an "if" clause also conditions a prophecy. H. L. Ellison, in his study on Old Testament prophets, points out that a prophecy can be annulled, delayed or suspended. His statement is geared for the Hebrew prophets, but the principle applies to New Testament prophecy as well: "Every prophecy is conditional, even when the condition is unexpressed. A prophecy of good may be annulled or delayed, if men do not obey, while repentance may suspend or reverse a prophecy of evil. We must make an exception when it is confirmed by God's oath."[37]

A clear "if" clause was attached by Paul to prophecies made to Timothy (1 Timothy 1:18). Timothy was exhorted, "according to the prophecies previously made concerning you," to "wage the good warfare" (NKJV). Many times the known will of God is thwarted by the devil, people or circumstances simply because a person will not take a strong, aggressive stand. Prophecy given over me as a young man probably saved my ministry. I learned to wage warfare—that is, claim God's promises and persevere in spite of problems. Like some pastors, I was ready to resign the church every Monday morning! But biblical admonitions and prophetic words of challenge caused me to address problems boldly in Jesus' name.

In the next chapter we will discuss six channels of prophetic expression. One channel operative in the early Church no longer exists; four are particularly important for congregational use today; and a special channel is suggested for utilizing prophetic anointing in reaching out to the lost people beyond the church walls.

REFLECTIONS

Prophetic ministry is the declaration of the mind of God in the power of the Spirit, with a special bearing on the current situation.[38]

F. F. Bruce

It is a spontaneous supernatural manifestation of God, spoken by the Spirit through human tongues in the language of the hearers, that the church might be edified.[39]

Cecil M. Robeck Jr.

Prophecy is the gift by which God speaks through a person a message to an individual or the whole Christian community. It is God making use of someone to tell men what He thinks about the present situation or what His intention is for the future, what He thinks that they should know or be mindful of right now. Prophecy is not necessarily for prediction of the future (although this frequently happens).[40]

Stephen Clark

. . . It was a direct word from God for the situation on hand, through the mouth of one of His people. . . . It was clear speech, which did not need interpretation.[41]

Michael Green

. . . In prophecy God speaks. It is as simple, and profound, and startling as that! . . . It is the operation of the Spirit upon and within the human mind so that the message spoken, while in the language of man, is the direct utterance of God.[42]

J. Rodman Williams

The early Christian prophet was an immediately inspired spokesperson for the risen Jesus, who received intelligible messages that he or she felt impelled to deliver to the Christian community, or, as a representative of the community, to the general public.[43]

M. Eugene Boring

A Christian prophet is a Christian who functions within the Church, occasionally or regularly, as a divinely called and divinely inspired speaker who receives intelligible and authoritative revelations or messages which he is impelled to deliver publicly, in oral or written form, to Christian individuals and/or the Christian community.[44]

David Hill

CHANNELS
OF PROPHETIC
EXPRESSION
IN THE CHURCH

There are distinctive varieties of operation—of working to accomplish things—but it is the same God Who inspires and energizes them all in all.

1 Corinthians 12:6 (Amplified)

A WONDERFUL PART of initiation into the early Church was the experience of the Holy Spirit. The new convert found an awesome awareness of the Spirit of God in gatherings of fellow believers. These encounters with God stood in stark contrast to the dead, useless, tedious ritual of pagan temples. Heathenism gave way to deep despair and dissatisfaction, the desecration of human dignity and sexuality, and futility for women and slaves. But those ordeals were gratefully exchanged for the new, blessed life of joy and hope in serving Christ, even when outward circumstances could not change.

New converts discovered joyfully that Christians were prophetic people in the sense that they shared the same infilling and awareness of the Spirit of Jesus. The manifestation of prophecy and other spiritual gifts was a normal part of Christian living. Not only did God think about His people, but He spoke to and through them by His Spirit.

The constant New Testament references to the Spirit indicate the deep conviction that gripped the first Christians: They believed they lived in the messianic age when God's prophetic Spirit would be poured out on His people (Acts 2:4; 4:8, 31; 9:17–18; 13:9). Their worship times were characterized by prophetic or visionary experiences that gave them purpose and direction in living. They believed Jesus was truly among them in the Person of the Holy Spirit.[1] Gatherings for worship were characterized by several activities, all of which were flexible, inspirational and open to spiritual manifestation:

- Reading, instructing and preaching from the Hebrew Scriptures and the teachings of Jesus
- Praying for each other and the needs of the people
- Performing the sacraments in a way that manifested the presence of Christ
- Praising and worshiping God in enthusiasm, sincerity and reverence that yielded a satisfying emotional release in the adoration and proclamation of God
- Being adjustable in their methods to allow different gifts, ministries and operations of the Spirit to take place[2]

Today's churches need to know the same Holy Spirit presence. God can be more than just invisible, intangible and unfelt. Since He delights in expressing Himself to His people, we can expect the Holy Spirit to take us beyond our human limitations. Such terms as *revelation* or *inspiration* refer to the prophetic transport of the Spirit that lifts us into an awareness of divine reality.

Six channels of prophetic expression seem apparent in the early Church. (My chart illustrates these basic categories of expression.)[3] Five of these can be experienced in the Church today. The sixth channel, the inspiration to produce Scripture, no longer functions. The very phrase *channels of expression* emphasizes the experience of a given moment rather than a person's ministry in the Body of Christ. Also, *channel* suggests merely one of several ways in which prophecy can be manifested. Everyone can realize some degree and aspect of prophetic expression in a church worship service.

The fifth channel deserves special mention. The prophetic unction should not be limited to the church's building and services but can occur in a secular setting as well. In fact, we would probably see more manifestations in church if Christians were more involved in crisis situations

Channels of Prophetic Expression

1. Prophetic Presence	2. Prophetic Opportunity	3. Prophetic Ministry	4. Prophetic Calling	5. Prophetic Outreach	6. Prophetic Scripture
State of Prophecy	*Spirit of Prophecy*	*Gift of Prophecy*	*Office of Prophet*	*Fruitfulness of Prophecy*	*Prophecy of Scripture*
Everyone can receive personalized, direct edification from the Holy Spirit in the worship environment of the local church.	Every believer has the potential on occasion to bring a simple prophetic thought or word to the local church for edification, exhortation or comfort.	Certain gifted people function consistently in the church with the *charism* or grace gift of prophecy.	The NT prophet, given by Christ to the Church, will bring significant prophetic direction and edification in conjunction with other church leadership.	Everyone can have prophetic insights that will enhance personal evangelism.	Apostle-prophets and scribes were divinely inspired to write Scripture, which became part of the canon of the Bible. This no longer occurs.
"We have received . . . the Spirit . . . that we might know. . . ." (1 Cor. 2:12)	". . . Desire earnestly to prophesy" (1 Cor. 14:39)	". . . To another prophecy" (1 Cor. 12:10)	"He gave some as . . . prophets" (Eph. 4:11)	"He arose and went" (Acts 8:27)	". . . the rest of the Scriptures [i.e., the NT]" (2 Pet. 3:16)

in our communities. Such prophetic outreach is not prophecy *per se*, as in our more restricted definitions in chapter 10, yet is essential for New Testament evangelism.

In the rest of this chapter let's look at the five channels of prophetic expression.

Prophetic Presence

State of prophecy. Everyone can receive personalized, direct edification from the Holy Spirit in the worship environment of the local church. An environment of worship and praise seems to be the favorite and most usable situation in which the Holy Spirit causes spiritual gifts to function in His people. The spiritual atmosphere (a kind of "prophetic magnetic field") is produced among the gathered worshipers that best allows the Spirit to bring revelation and spiritual manifestations. Every church member can expect to receive and participate in this spiritual climate.

During worship each Christian should be occupied in giving adoration, thanksgiving and praise to God, and be sensitive to the reception of divine thoughts. In an atmosphere of spiritual worship everyone is capable of tuning into this first channel of prophetic expression. Someone who is not a prophet or does not have a gift of prophecy may still receive prophetic insights from the Spirit—into the Bible, personal life or God's direction—during this time of congregational worship "in spirit and truth" (John 4:23).

The Holy Spirit is spontaneous and works in His own unpredictable way. We should not carry checklists of unsolved problems to worship, expecting immediate divine answers. But many personal needs can be met and many problems solved in a vibrant worship service. Amazing insights for personal life have flashed into my mind while I was concentrating on God in a worship service—thoughts so clear, reasonable and workable that I perceived instantly they were from Him.

A few years ago I heard an anecdote about R. G. LeTourneau that illustrates this truth. LeTourneau's company specialized in producing heavy, dirt-moving machinery. An airplane manufacturer needed special large equipment to handle the fuselage assembly of jet aircraft and came to LeTourneau's engineers with the problem. The answer eluded them until they faced a particular Wednesday deadline with no solution. That evening LeTourneau, to the consternation of his associates, announced that he was going to his church's midweek prayer meeting. As he sought the Lord the solution came suddenly to his mind. The perfect answer supplied at the last minute by a God who cares . . . to a saint who worships!

181

In the setting of spiritual worship, we can all sing or declare our praises to God. The Holy Spirit is present to inspire us with odes that are prophetic in nature and delightfully edifying. The "spiritual songs" mentioned in Ephesians 5:19 and Colossians 3:16 are spontaneous songs of the Spirit—inspired, prophetic expressions that bring an immediate awareness of God's presence and a deep sense of personal edification. The inspiration of the Spirit is for the whole congregation as well as each individual. Truths of God formerly not understood or appreciated become significant as a person sings forth the dynamic insights, blending his or her contribution with songs of praise from other worshipers. Let's make space available in our church worship for such spontaneous praise to be enjoyed by all. It is an entry-level door to prophetic activity.[4]

Paul explains the inability of the natural man to understand spiritual things. He says that "the depths of God" (1 Corinthians 2:10) are inaccessible to man but that the Holy Spirit can explore this vast treasure vault. The Spirit has been given to us so "that we might know the things freely given to us by God" (verse 12). Verse 13 holds the key to understanding this "prophetic state" expression in local church worship. Of these spiritual things, Paul wrote, "we also speak, not in words taught by human wisdom, but in those taught by the Spirit, combining spiritual thoughts with spiritual words."

Michael Green, commenting on this text, observes that "it takes God to reveal God. And Paul claims that God has done so, through the Spirit interpreting spiritual truths to men who possess the Spirit."[5]

Consider that spiritual truths are sometimes communicated through the personal impressions given by the Spirit during congregational worship. Psalmic style worship helps a person relax from natural thoughts and reach upward unhindered in worship. The church thereby enters into what I like to call a "prophetic state."[6] Technically this is not prophecy *per se;* it is spiritual worship, the first step in preparation for congregational prophecy. It is like turning on a computer so it can operate.

Certain scholars of early Church function confirm that prophecy was given in the worship setting of the congregational meeting. David Aune, for instance, says: "On the basis of the evidence in I Cor. 12–14 it appears that prophets, or those who prophesied, were active only within the framework of Christian worship. Further, it appears that prophets were particularly active during particular segments of the service. . . ."[7]

As we involve spirit, mind and body *(pneuma-psycho-somatic)* in a total biblical expression of praise and worship, the Spirit drops truths, encouragement and direction into our hearts. If we participated weekly in such worship, far less pastoral counseling would be needed! Tensions and problems would fade before the wonder of His presence. Experiencing God in worship is one way Christians are taught individually by God. As Jeremiah said:

"This is the covenant which I will make with the house of Israel after those days," declares the LORD, "I will put My law within them, and on their heart I will write it; and I will be their God, and they shall be My people. And they shall not teach again, each man his neighbor and each man his brother, saying, 'Know the LORD,' for they shall all know Me, from the least of them to the greatest of them," declares the LORD, "for I will forgive their iniquity, and their sin I will remember no more."[8]

Jeremiah 31:33–34

Other, more obvious expressions of prophecy were certainly part of the New Testament Church, but the classification and explanation of those manifestations vary. "For most scholars," explains Christopher Forbes, "early Christian prophecy, like Gaul under the Romans, is divided into three parts."

- Wandering Christian prophets, traveling from place to place
- Resident Christian prophets within the congregations
- Christians not considered prophets who occasionally prophesied in church services

"For many scholars," Forbes continues, "a correct description of early Christian prophecy has been a matter of finding the correct mix of these three forms, or arranging them in a broad chronological sequence."[9]

These three classifications seem reasonable and acceptable at first, but several problems present themselves. The threefold breakdown does not provide a sufficiently broad or practical format for the actual function of prophecy in the local church, nor does it sufficiently coordinate with Scripture's discussion of the subject. (I will address the question of wandering prophets later in the chapter.)

My solution is to suggest (as we have been discussing) six channels of prophetic expression. These are practical, functional, biblical and field-tested. The first channel, "Prophetic Presence," has just been presented. The sixth, "Prophetic Scripture," no longer occurs. And the fifth, "Prophetic Outreach," describes the practical application of prophetic expression in reaching out to the lost secular community. This is one important facet of power evangelism that accelerates church growth worldwide.[10]

This leaves three broad categories that make up the kinds of prophecy given in the congregational setting:

- The spirit of prophecy: opportunity for all
- The gift of prophecy: ministry for some
- The office of prophet: calling for a few[11]

Prophetic Opportunity

Spirit of prophecy. Every believer has the potential to bring a simple prophetic thought or word to the local church for the purpose of edification, exhortation or comfort (1 Corinthians 14:3). Scripture does not say we all will prophesy, but it opens to all the door of invitation. It is a matter of being in the manifest presence of Him who is *the* great Prophet, being impressed by the Holy Spirit and then exercising faith for manifestation.

The expression *spirit of prophecy* comes from Revelation 19:10 equating "the testimony of Jesus" with "the spirit of prophecy." Many believers have discovered that from time to time the Holy Spirit comes on a congregation as a mantle of prophetic anointing. This unique presence of the Spirit "is so manifest that anybody that will exercise a measure of faith can, under this anointing, bring forth a prophetic utterance."[12] The spirit of prophecy enables those to prophesy who do not have the gift of prophecy or the office of a prophet.[13]

The wonderful presence of the Lord comes whenever He chooses to send it, but a church that worships fervently in the Spirit will generate more frequent times like this, for God delights in the praises of His people. Also, the greater the presence of prophetic ministries, the more likelihood that this anointing will occur. A person without a prophetic ministry may prophesy in this setting, but it will be simple thoughts that God has brought to mind that deal with encouragement, comfort and exhortation.

This category, as I perceive it, is not the residing "gift" *(charism)* of prophecy (1 Corinthians 12:10) but rather a spontaneous spiritual manifestation that causes the person to share simple, inspired thoughts to the congregation.[14] All the following admonitions are from 1 Corinthians 14 (emphasis added):

- "Pursue love, yet desire earnestly spiritual gifts, but especially that *you* may prophesy" (verse 1).
- "I wish that you *all* spoke in tongues, but even more that *you* would prophesy; and greater is one who prophesies than one who speaks in tongues, unless he interprets, so that the church may receive edifying" (verse 5).
- "If *all* prophesy, and an unbeliever or an ungifted man enters, he is convicted by *all,* he is called to account by *all*" (verse 24).
- "You can *all* prophesy one by one, so that *all* may learn and *all* may be exhorted" (verse 31).

- "Therefore, *my brethren,* desire earnestly to prophesy, and do not forbid to speak in tongues" (verse 39).

A demonstration of spontaneous prophecy is described in Acts 19. After baptizing twelve followers of John the Baptist in water, Paul laid his hands on the men and they were filled with the Holy Spirit and began speaking in tongues and prophesying (verse 6). This was an attendant, miraculous demonstration of God's presence. Since the Spirit is prophetic, it should not seem strange for such a manifestation to occur, even if the men were not prophetically gifted. No one can prophesy unless the Spirit of prophecy is on him or her.

In the Old Testament we see the same phenomenon. Saul and his messengers, although not spiritual men, began to prophesy as they approached the camp of Samuel and his disciples. The prophetic aura of the camp moved even the strangers to speak forth the things of God (1 Samuel 19:20–24). The story in Numbers 11:24–30 illustrates the same concept. The Spirit of God and prophecy on Moses was put on the seventy elders of Israel, who also began to prophesy.

Prophetic prayer. A varied form of prophetic expression is more personalized than prophecy in a congregational meeting. This kind of guidance can be received to some degree by whoever will open his or her mind to it. Called "prophetic encouragement" or "prophetic praying," this approach refers to personalized ministry to selected individuals.

From time to time a Christian will be given a prophetic insight about a certain situation or person, either Christian or non-Christian. In this elementary form of prophecy, insights or impressions are shared with that individual or expressed prayerfully over him or her. Without some grandiose statement ("Thus saith the Lord!"), we simply communicate that impression to the other person. We might say, for instance, "I've been feeling that you need prayer in a particular area," or, "I think the Lord may have shown me something of interest to you." The person's response tells us of our accuracy and his or her willingness to receive our prayerful help.[15] The purpose is to encourage someone by sharing insights or helpful suggestions that have been given by the Holy Spirit. Often after a worship service, when people are praying at the altar or together, this form of ministry, if kept sincere, simple and concerned, can be very effective.[16]

Prophetic intercession. Those who intercede for the work of God locally and worldwide sense a quickening from time to time about a nation, church, community or individual. These insights born of the Holy Spirit— attended by boldness, authority and fervency and interjected prophetically into serious intercession—enhance prayer dramatically and give us power to discern and resist satanic powers. While praying, Peter was given knowledge about God's plan and purpose for the Gentiles (Acts 10:9–16). The early Church had sudden and united insight from the Holy Spirit on how to apply Psalm 2:1–2 to their situation (Acts 4:23–31).

What I describe here is not manifested as prophecy in a congregational meeting of the local church, but it does represent a way in which the voice of the Lord can come to us through the Spirit, so in that sense I call it prophetic.

Prophetic Ministry

The gift of prophecy. Certain gifted people function consistently in church with the charism *or grace gift of prophecy.* It is possible, as we saw in the last section, for any person to prophesy *on occasion.*[17] In fact a person might prophesy once and never again. The grace gift of prophecy is, by contrast, a definite, resident enabling of God placed in the individual so that he or she may bring inspired edification, comfort and exhortation to God's people on a regular basis. "Since we have gifts that differ according to the grace given to us," wrote Paul, "let each exercise them accordingly: if prophecy, according to the proportion of his faith" (Romans 12:6).

Usually this gift does not include correction, new direction or prediction. The gift of prophecy is given primarily for a function in the local church. The gift of a prophet (discussed in the next section) is usually a gift to the universal Church.

In contrast to "the spirit of prophecy" manifested occasionally (and resulting from the benevolent influence of the Holy Spirit moving over a worshiping congregation), the gift of prophecy is the expression of a gift resident in a believer,[18] a sovereign gift of the Holy Spirit implanted in him or her.[19] The key text: "To each one is given the manifestation of the Spirit for the common good. . . . And to another prophecy. . . . But one and the same Spirit works all these things, distributing to each one individually just as He wills" (1 Corinthians 12:7, 10–11). Each one of us is given a manifestation of the Holy Spirit, one of which is prophecy.

There are varying degrees of maturity and experience within the prophetic ministers of the Church, just as there are with every other kind of ministry. The gift of prophecy often begins to manifest itself through various kinds of revelation such as spiritual impressions, visions and dreams. As this gift matures in the believer, it will become more recognized and authorized in the church. Training and nurturing the individual enhances prophetic efficiency and causes the person with such a gift to be a profitable part of team ministry. Someone with the gift of prophecy will be able to prophesy regularly among God's people, enabled by the resident gift to function apart from those special occasions when the Spirit's unction charges the atmosphere of a service.

I realize that neither Romans 12:6 nor 1 Corinthians 11–14 says all this specifically, but the approach seems logical in light of Paul's discussions and has proven workable and practical. I agree with Mike Bickle as he endeavors to clarify the various levels of prophetic activity: "These are not biblical distinctions. These are simply categories that help us to communicate with each other more effectively."[20] My classifications are based on Scripture, insights from serious thinkers and the practical experience that comes from pastoring. This approach also allows each classification to be broad enough to allow for a great variety of manifestations yet still conform to Scripture.

An unusual illustration of the gift of prophecy is the four virgin daughters of Philip the evangelist. The NASB says they were "prophetesses" (Acts 21:9) while the KJV describes them as "daughters . . . which did prophesy." The Greek text does not warrant calling them prophetesses, although we may infer that. The present tense of *propheteuousai* suggests more than a particular prophecy on one occasion; it indicates that they probably exercised the gift of prophecy regularly.[21] Although Paul had been living "many days" in this home with four sisters, all of whom had the gift of prophecy, God chose to send a prophet to give direction to the apostle. Here is a clear example of the diversity of function between the gift of prophecy and the ministry of a prophet. (Since I have three married daughters who prophesy, I can readily understand the blessing on Philip's house!)

Some feel it is more logical to divide into two groups those who prophesied in early Christianity: prophets and others who prophesied.[22] Perhaps no designations at all are needed, since all may prophesy. But needed is an honest attempt to harmonize both scriptural research and practical experience gleaned over a number of years. I certainly have no desire to split hairs! My goal: an efficient and effective prophetic ministry in our churches.

Prophetic Calling

The office of prophet. The New Testament prophet, a gift ministry that the Lord Jesus Himself set in the Church, brings significant prophetic direction and edification in conjunction with other Church leadership. The gift of prophecy is given to the Church by the Holy Spirit, who distributes His gifts "to each one individually just as He wills" (1 Corinthians 12:11); hence it is called a gift of the Holy Spirit. Significantly, however, the office or ministry of prophet is given to the Church by the Lord Jesus Christ Himself: "He gave some as . . . prophets" (Ephesians 4:11). The prophet thus becomes a gift of Christ. Paul describes this in 1 Corinthians 12:28: "God has appointed in the church . . . prophets. . . ." The gift of prophecy is a function of the Spirit, whereas the ministry of a prophet is the gift of a person who has been prepared by Christ. The prophet's ministry is thus linked inseparably to specific individuals.[23]

The New Testament prophet, similar to his or her Old Testament counterpart, is a voice of God to the people. The prophet receives simple impressions but also goes beyond the basic prophecy that edifies, comforts and exhorts. David Blomgren says: "The office of a prophet . . . operates in the realm of guidance, rebuke, judgment, correction, and revelation. The one who has the gift of prophecy but is not a prophet does not function in any of these latter realms."[24] Various people may prophesy but that does not automatically make them prophets. This is a ministerial calling, not just a prophetic tendency.

Teaching and preaching colored by unique prophetic insight lie within the realm of the prophetic office, as well as giving words of warning and direction. The prophet's function is sometimes governmental in nature (determining missionary procedure, Acts 13:1–3; working with apostles in establishing basic doctrine and policy, Ephesians 2:20; 3:5). It can also be predictive (Acts 11:28; 21:10–11; 2 Thessalonians 2:3; Revelation 1:1–3; 22:6). From time to time the prophet, working in conjunction with others in leadership, brings significant direction or prediction for the local church, a group of churches or the Church worldwide.

This ministry, like that of the Old Testament prophet, is open to both male and female,[25] although I realize no woman in Acts or in Paul's writings is actually called a prophetess *(prophetis)*. Women did prophesy occasionally (Acts 2:17–18; 1 Corinthians 11:5), although, as Robeck points out, "There is no explicit evidence that any woman ever occupied the office of prophet."[26] I base my conclusion on two references, Galatians 3:28 and 1 Corinthians 12:13, both of which indicate to me that the gifts and ministries of the Spirit are available to all, regardless of nationality, social status, age or sex. Not everyone can function in a given spiritual gift or occupy the office of a prophet, but no explicit statement in Scripture forbids a woman who is so called to function in either charismatic gifts or prophetic ministry.

One difference between Old and New Testament prophets is in the area of accountability. The Old Testament prophet moved forward on the strength of divine authorization and enabling, usually with little support or encouragement; he was *the* ministry of the hour. The New Testament prophet worked closely with apostles and other church leaders (1 Corinthians 12:28; Ephesians 2:20; 3:5; 4:11; Revelation 18:20). Paul demanded without compromise that the Corinthian prophets come under his guidance and direction (1 Corinthians 14:37). Bryn Jones of the United Kingdom gives this contemporary analysis of the roles of apostle and prophet:

> The apostle is primarily an architect, concerned with the overall design of the local church. The prophet, on the other hand, is first and foremost a seer, who sees beyond the present situation and brings the purposes of God into sharp focus. He has a revelation of the mind of God. . . . The prophet is primarily concerned about keeping things moving, whereas the apostle tends to concentrate more on what is being built and how it is being achieved. . . . People sense that the apostle has an anointing that embraces God's purpose on a scale far wider than the immediate issues. They can respond to a prophet's inspiration for the immediate but they find security in an ongoing relationship with an apostle.[27]

The words of both Old and New Testament prophets were not to be accepted automatically as correct and above question. Prophecy, regardless of the level of proficiency and ministry, was given close scrutiny by the leadership (1 Corinthians 13:9; 1 Thessalonians 5:20–21; 1 John 4:1). This approach served to encourage the people to prophesy, assuring them that they would be supervised, and to hold a restraining hand on fanaticism.

A great deal of prophetic activity is mentioned in the New Testament, but only four people are specifically called prophets: Agabus, Judas, Silas and John (Acts 11:28; 15:32; Revelation 10:8–11). Mention is made of "prophets and teachers" at Antioch (Acts 13:1), but the five men named are not specifically categorized. The four virgin daughters of Philip who prophesied are not, as I said, called "prophetesses" in the Greek text of Acts 21:9, although that is the translation given in the NASB and suggested by *The Expositors Bible Commentary*. Strong arguments are presented to make Barnabas a prophet,[28] and some scholars feel that some of the apostles could also be classified as prophets[29]—or at least they functioned with great prophetic abilities, such as Paul (some would use Acts 13:1 to justify this; note 1 Thessalonians 2:13; 1 Timothy 4:1); James (possibly receiving a prophetic word of wisdom at the council at Jerusalem, Acts 15:19, 28); and John (scribe of the apocalypse, Revelation 10:8–11).[30]

The study of Acts has caused some to believe that the prophets wandered without a settled community (Acts 11:27; 15:32; 21:10–11), although personally I do not infer this from these references. We are given no indication that Agabus or other prophets were wild-eyed wanderers who struck prophetically wherever and whenever they wished. The term *wandering* is both unfortunate and unnecessary. Forbes refutes this description most effectively:

In both cases . . . the place of origin is specified: in the first case, Jerusalem, and in the second case, Judaea. . . . That Agabus is later noted as still being based in Judaea years later is also important. For while it is quite clear that he and his fellows at Antioch did have a ministry which extended beyond their church of origin, it is not proven that their normal ministry was "wandering". Twice Agabus is noted as having made a specific journey. That does not in any way demonstrate that he was an *itinerant* prophet, let alone one who wandered "at random" from place to place.[31]

Also, the two prophets chosen by the elders at Jerusalem to accompany Paul and Barnabas were carefully selected and commissioned to accompany the apostles as they brought the report of the Jerusalem council (Acts 15:22–23). There is no evidence of wandering or aimless itinerancy. Admittedly the Christians of Bible days seem to have been a very mobile group, but for a prophet to operate without a ministerial covering or apostolic oversight is inconsistent with Pauline instruction. (These prophets, by the way, did more than prophesy. They exhorted and preached as well, adding their unique flavor and confirmation to the ministry.)

There is also the question of whether there were settled prophets who ministered regularly in a given community (Acts 10:23; 13:1; 21:4, 9). Although the references only state this, rather than imply it, common sense and practice suggest that they did minister regularly. Prophets who travel on assignment do find themselves in their home churches on occasion, thus fitting this description. Other prophets, probably in secular employment, function as local church prophets. Every prophet, like any other ministry, is only part of the whole. "There are different calls and combinations of gifting among the prophets. No two are exactly the same."[32] God gives different measures of His giftings and ministries, and some function best in a resident ministry working with local leadership.

One godly prophet my wife and I knew for more than forty years was Tom Edmonson. After pastoring a few small churches without great success, he finally settled in Anchorage, Alaska, found his niche and began to function well. He was put on staff of the Abbott Loop Chapel, where he was considered a resident prophet. When he was not teaching or functioning prophetically, he did various odd jobs around the church campus, praying a great deal as he puttered around. Brother Tom impressed me as a very spiritual yet practical prophet. We need more like him.

A team of prophets was sometimes used as a prophetic presbytery. During times when the local church was seriously seeking God, the prophets would lay hands on local church members and bring prophetic confirmation, impartation and blessing. To Timothy, for example: "Do not neglect the spiritual gift within you, which was bestowed upon you through prophetic utterance with the laying on of hands by the presbytery" (1 Timothy 4:14).

This particular function of prophets brings great blessing and inspiration to a local church. During forty years of pastoring, my wife and I have seen the wonderful benefits of this kind of ministry in our congregations. Now we travel extensively as prophetic presbyters, perpetuating this ministry among many churches. We are part of a local church yet are also scheduled as itinerant ministers. (We will discuss this particular function of prophet and its practical application in chapter 22.)

Prophets were sometimes used to bring significant, high-level, predictive prophecy that would be of major importance to a local church or group of churches. Such prophecy comes from time to time, usually through a prophet, and it must be handled carefully by the local leadership. A biblical example: Agabus foretelling coming famine in Judea (Acts 11:28).

In our own home church in San Jose, we have had a number of such prophecies over a thirty-year period. Prophecy gave us major direction, for instance, in our missionary outreach to Brazil. Also, when we were asking God for new church property, a prophetic word came that we would be near "the crossroads of the valley." As time passed and we looked for property, the city erected a major interchange for Highways 101 and 280. The highways were not connected to the interchange, however, so this large structural monstrosity stood glaringly alone for several years, an irritating eyesore to the community. Finally city and state funds became available, and public sympathy was strong, so the local newspaper ran an article referring to "the celebrated crossroads of the valley." Shortly thereafter we purchased seventeen acres near that crossroads, which we had previously decided to buy, now believing that the prophecy (given before the interchange was constructed) was indeed additional confirmation by God of our choice of property. We have not been disappointed with our decision.

Prophetic Outreach

The fruitfulness of prophecy. Every believer has the potential of utilizing the prophetic anointing in outreach to the non-Christian community. A strict definition would keep "prophecy" in the local church setting, and that is correct in the context of Paul's instructions to the Corinthians. The early Church, however, did not confine God's activities to church gatherings. Apparently they experienced the thoughts and guidance of God more easily than many today think possible. The early Christians acted on what they believed to be the revelations of God, and this kept them busy in reaching the lost.

The prophetic Church today must be released to the city. We do not need thousands of Christians running around declaring *Thus saith the Lord* to non-Christians, but positioning themselves to be available in the crisis situations that proliferate throughout a given community. God uses spiritual gifts in these highly charged, desperate conditions to reveal Himself. The River of Life, the Holy Spirit, was not meant to flow into a Dead Sea church and become stagnant. Rather, the saving voice of God must be allowed to resonate through God's people.

Reread the Acts of the Apostles. This book counterbalances the academic teaching of the epistles with vibrant, Spirit-filled living. The early Christians did not go around declaring themselves prophets, but they did learn the secret of Jesus' own success. The Son of God learned to hear His Father's voice and then act on any directions the Spirit gave.

Three prophetic aspects of outreach are needed today:

1. Direction to people. Jesus knew "He had to pass through Samaria" (John 4:4), for a Samaritan woman would come to a certain well for water. Philip did not know that a searching Ethiopian eunuch would be traveling by chariot on the desert road to Gaza, but the Spirit directed him right to that man, who was then converted and baptized (Acts 8:26–39). Both Jesus' Samaritan convert and Philip's African official proceeded to spread the message even further.

In 1952 Tommy Hicks, an evangelist in his mid-forties, saw in a vision a map of South America. Multitudes, like fields of grain, were crying out for help. Finally he managed to get himself on a plane to Buenos Aires. The word *Perón* came forcefully to him. The stewardess informed him that Perón was the president of Argentina, so Hicks felt he must see Perón. All efforts failed. But Hicks was persistent, and in the office of the minister of religion he prayed successfully for the healing of the secretary. The minister of religion promptly arranged an interview with Perón.

> When Hicks met Peron, the President was at that time suffering from eczema which so disfigured him that he allowed no photographs to be taken of himself. His ailment was common knowledge. Listening to Hicks tell of what the Lord wanted to do in Argentina, Peron asked him, "Can God heal me?"
>
> Hicks replied, "Give me your hand." Right there he prayed. Peron's skin was healed instantly. Stepping back in utter amazement, he wiped his hand across his face and exclaimed in astonishment, "Dios mio, estoy curado!" (My God, I am healed!)[33]

Perón then supplied Hicks with the use of a large sports stadium and free access to the state radio and press. The ensuing 52 days of meetings reached a combined total of two hundred thousand people, with many healings recorded. The resistance to the evangelical witness was broken, and the rapid growth of the Pentecostal Church in Argentina was launched.

2. *Awareness and insight.* Jesus was constantly aware of situations and people because the Holy Spirit revealed things to Him (see illustrations in chapter 8). Later Peter rebuked Ananias and Sapphira for lying to the Holy Spirit (Acts 5:1–11) and challenged Simon for his wicked intentions (Acts 8:18–24). These were more than human perceptions; they were revealed by the Spirit, yielding great spiritual results that would otherwise have been lost.

3. *Declaration of message.* Jesus told His disciples that they would be brought before "the rulers and the authorities, but do not become anxious about how or what you should speak in your defense, or what you should say; for the Holy Spirit will teach you in that very hour what you ought to say" (Luke 12:11–12). Apparently the first time this happened is recorded in Acts 4:8–12, which states that Peter, filled with the Holy Spirit, spoke to the rulers and elders. Another example of prophetic preaching is given in Acts 7, where Stephen made his defense with such power of the Spirit that the infuriated crowd killed him.

Your experience need not be that dramatic, but rest assured that whether you talk to the multitudes or to a single soul, God's Spirit will give you the golden key to unlock the situation. Channels of prophetic expression are now open to you! Take advantage of your opportunities to tune in to the voice of the Holy Spirit.

Our next chapter reviews prophets and prophecy in the book of Acts. Thank God for this marvelous historical record of how the early Church functioned! Rich insights are gained about prophecy as a dynamic force in the Church of that time.

REFLECTIONS

The church that is alive and relevant for today's generation must always be a prophetic church. We must therefore listen very carefully in order to discern what God is saying to us TODAY. It will always be in accordance with the teaching of Scripture, and there is no such thing as new revelation or new doctrine—but the Spirit of God will always be wanting to pin-point certain aspects of the total truth of God's word that are especially relevant for TODAY—and that will almost certainly be different from what was especially relevant for yesterday.[34]

David Watson

We are convinced that the Holy Spirit speaks today, and wishes so to do, but the Bible makes it clear that the proper gift for this is prophecy. The ability to prophesy extends to all if they have the needed measure of faith.[35]

Donald Gee

. . . Prophecy and other charismatic gifts flourish in an atmosphere of expectant faith. That is, they operate mainly where they are *expected* by those who receive them.[36]

Bruce Yocum

Practically everyone who is filled with God's Spirit is able to prophesy on an inspirational level . . . especially in a worship service where the Holy Spirit's presence is more easily recognized. . . . The purpose of this type of prophecy is to inspire and refresh our hearts without giving any correction or new direction. This kind of prophecy is usually a reminder from the heart of God about his care and purpose for us, and it often emphasizes some truth we already know from the Bible.[37]

Mike Bickle

Although the prophetic tradition of the OT probably lay behind Pauline understanding, at no point does he understand the prophet to be speaking anything other than an ad hoc word. . . . For Paul it must be "weighed" or "tested." Thus, there is never any sense that a prophetic word was to be raised to the level of "inspired text."[38]

Gordon D. Fee

What authority does prophecy carry? The same authority as that of any other Christian activity in the church, like leadership, counseling, teaching. . . . If it is true, it will prove to be true. Spiritual people will respond warmly to it. Wise and proven leaders will approve and confirm it. The enlightened conscience will embrace it.[39]

Donald Bridge

12

PROPHETS
AND PROPHECY
IN THE BOOK OF ACTS

"Your sons and your daughters shall prophesy. . . ."

Acts 2:17

SOME OF OUR MOST significant documentation about prophecy, a vital part of the early Church, comes from The Acts of the Apostles. The evidence presented is convincing proof that the early Church was operational in prophecy and that the early leaders expected this ministry to continue throughout the Church age.

Our expert witness is Luke, the inspired scribe of the gospel of Luke and the Acts of the Apostles. The written testimony of the "beloved physician" (Colossians 4:14) is most reliable. Luke accompanied Paul on many of his journeys (Acts 16:10–17; 20:5–15; 21:1–18; 27:1–28:16) and was with him during his imprisonment in Rome (2 Timothy 4:11). Luke obviously made the study of Jesus' ministry and early Church history a major research project.[1]

In this chapter I will present Acts passages (in chronological order) related to prophecy, with brief commentary and some personal testimonies added for contemporary flavor.

A Chronological Record

Acts is the only *bona fide* historical record of the first-century Church. As William Barclay said: "In one sense Acts is the most important book in the NT. . . . If we did not possess Acts, we would have, apart from what we could deduce from the letters of Paul, no information whatsoever about the early church."[2]

The book of Acts is also theological, for the history of the Church is in itself a revelation of God. Luke's record of the early Church purposes less to account for the doings of the Church than to account for the doings of God in and through the Church. It shows us what actually happened and how the Church realized life through the Holy Spirit. The primitive Church was the prototype for spiritual concepts designed to work in every generation and society. The religious accouterments of the Church may change as history progresses, but the manifold activities of the Holy Spirit remain consistent with the original principles.

Prophetic Happenings in Acts		
People involved	Happening	Reference in Acts
120 disciples	Spoke in prophetic tongues	1:15; 2:4
120 disciples	A prophetic era dawned	2:17–18
Philip and eunuch	Philip sent to eunuch	8:29–39
Ananias and Saul	Ananias sent to Saul	9:10–17; 22:12–14
Peter	Peter sent to Cornelius	10:9–48
Household of Cornelius	Gentiles received the Holy Spirit	10:44–48; 11:1–18
Agabus and Antioch church	Agabus predicted famine	11:27–28
5 men at Antioch	Prophecy confirmed mission	13:1–4
Paul, magician and magistrate	Paul blinded a magician	13:8–12
Judas and Silas	Prophets selected for mission	15:25–26, 32
Paul and associates	Forbidden to go	16:6–7
Paul and the Ephesians	Spoke in tongues and prophesied	19:6
Paul in the churches	Warnings given Paul	20:22–23
Disciples at Tyre	More warnings given Paul	21:4
Philip's four daughters	Women prophesied	21:9
Agabus and Paul	Agabus enacted a prophecy	21:10–11

The Opening Manifestation (2:4)

"They were all filled with the Holy Spirit and began to speak with other tongues, as the Spirit was giving them utterance."

The astounding miracle of Jesus' disciples speaking in human languages they had not learned was the first prophetic occurrence in the book of Acts. Non-Christian Jews at the Feast of Pentecost in Jerusalem, from far and near regions circling Judea, heard the unlearned disciples speak perfectly in at least fourteen of the numerous languages of the far-flung Roman Empire. These disciples of Christ, mainly Galilean Jews, spoke in assorted native languages, yet it was apparent from dress and manner that they were not native to the languages they spoke.[3] Peter quickly identified this phenomenon as foretold by the prophet Joel (2:28–32), thereby associating these miracle utterances directly to prophecy.

A close link exists between glossolalia and prophecy (Acts 19:6; 1 Corinthians 14)—two gifts of the Spirit that are related yet have distinctive purposes. Both involve oral communication and a special empowerment of the Spirit that bypasses human initiation. Although the flaming fire and wind of Pentecost was not subsequently repeated, speaking in tongues and prophesying did become commonplace among the Christians (Acts 10:46; 19:6).[4]

This first occurrence is a miraculous demonstration that was both tongues and prophecy at the same time: tongues to each of the speakers, who spoke languages they did not know, and prophecy to the hearers, who heard Spirit-inspired communication in their native languages. Peter called the phenomenon of speaking in tongues *prophecy*.[5] It was obvious that the disciples' abilities were not involved in the amazing performance. This first display thereby sets the high standard for all subsequent prophecy in the Church age.

Genesis 11 recounts that God cursed the sinful society of the day by using different languages to confuse and scatter the people. Now, in Acts 2, this alienation of the nations is reversed through Christ. God shows His concern for the nations and sets the course for the era of the Spirit by having the first prophecies of the new age come forth in Gentile tongues, not Hebrew.

Do such literal languages ever occur in our day? A most interesting story from this century involves an early Pentecostal evangelist and missionary named Thomas Hezmalhalch (1848–1934). "Although he was not considered a great preacher by some contemporaries," writes W. E. Warner, "Hezmalhalch's name is legendary in both the U.S. and South Africa as a man who walked in the Spirit and who had great influence in the early Pentecostal movement."[6] He is best known for his ministry in South Africa beginning in 1908 (after he had reached sixty years of age!).

Brother Tom felt God wanted him to preach to the Zulu people. To reach their country he had to cross a river, so he acquired a boat and rowed across. Then he beached the craft, looked up and found himself facing a group of Zulu warriors. Because he did not speak their language, he addressed them as best he could in what he thought was English. But something other than English was coming out of his mouth, and they seemed to understand what he was saying.

Taken captive to their village, Hezmalhalch continued to communicate with the people in Zulu, much to the consternation of the witch doctors, who were apparently planning to kill and cook him. For three days and nights Tom was kept in a hut near the place of assembly. Each night at midnight the drums throbbed as the witch doctors practiced their incantations in preparation for the feast, and Tom prepared to die. But for three days and nights he was left in the hut in safety.

Finally the tribal leadership confronted him.

"Who are those tall men with you?" they demanded.

"No one is with me," Tom answered in amazement.

"Oh, yes, there are. Each night when we've come to kill you, you're surrounded by tall, white-robed figures with flaming swords!"

Brother Tom's amazing ministry continued to the Zulu people. Until his death he was able to communicate with them in their own language with no accent, formulating English words in his mind and finding Zulu words coming spontaneously from his mouth. Thomas Hezmalhalch's was the primary effort that opened that tribe to the Gospel of Jesus Christ.[7]

My first experience of speaking in tongues was wonderful although, like that of many others, it did not involve interpretation. As a fourteen-year old boy I had heard an uneducated preacher speak eloquently on the need for power in the Christian's life. When he gave an altar call in that small skid row mission on Stevens Street in downtown Spokane, Washington, I ran forward for prayer. I knew I needed the power of the Holy Spirit!

The older folks present prayed for me in shifts, urging and exhorting me to "give up," "hang on," "pray through," etc. It was both serious and amusing. Finally, after an hour of intense prayer, I fell backward to the floor (whether from exhaustion or the Holy Spirit I do not know!). A deep peace settled on me and I realized the presence of the Spirit more than I had ever known. I lay on the floor quietly experiencing the wonder of God. Never having seen anyone speak in tongues before, I prayed a simple prayer: "Father, I know that in the Bible, people spoke in tongues when they were filled with the Spirit. And these people here think I'll speak in tongues. I believe You are filling me, so I'm going to open my mouth and speak in tongues."

Suddenly a volcano exploded inside of me! I began to speak fluently and excitedly in a language I had never learned. In fact, I could not speak in English for the rest of the night. I startled the little group of people in the church who had been praying for me and wondering at my prolonged silence on the floor. Now they came alive and bounced with joy. Later I caught the last bus home and burst through the door speaking in tongues. The next day at school I had to speak slowly and carefully in English, or I would break out once again in tongues! And for the past 55 years I have continued to use this inspiring ministry of prayer language in my prayer times, sometimes speaking a number of different languages.[8]

In chapter 13 I will address the question of tongues as a literal language and whether it is for public display or personal devotion.

A New Era Dawns (2:17–18)

"'And it shall be in the last days,' God says, 'that I will pour forth of My Spirit upon all mankind; and your sons and your daughters shall prophesy, and your young men shall see visions, and your old men shall dream dreams; even upon My bondslaves, both men and women, I will in those days pour forth of My Spirit and they shall prophesy.'"

The prophecy of Joel, quoted by Peter, is "the key to the right understanding of the history of primitive Christianity."[9] This astounding prediction found fulfillment in the dramatic events that occurred on the Day of Pentecost. Peter explained the phenomena of miracle language, strange behavior and supernatural signs as the beginning of Joel's prophetic outpouring.[10] He was clearly identifying the Church of the last days as Spirit-filled and prophetic in nature, closely linked with God's action of "pouring forth" His Spirit. The previous restrictions that limited spiritual participation because of nationality, age, sex or social status were superseded by a new law of the Spirit that unifies and reconciles people so they all can share the same spiritual privileges (see Galatians 3:28).

The era of the prophetic people had been launched! The Church of Jesus Christ, composed of believing Jews and Gentiles, became the new Israel of God longed for by Moses (Numbers 11:29) and foretold by Joel.[11] Jesus, who had come as *the* prophet of God,[12] now returned to grace all His followers with the same prophetic mantle in the Person of the Holy Spirit. This "universalizing" of the Spirit among all God's people now replaced the "individualized" Spirit whom Jesus alone had experienced. Clearly the Church is declared a prophetic community.

As Peter quoted from Joel 2:28–32, he inserted four significant, definitive words not found in Joel: *"And they shall prophesy."* This inspired statement hangs like a banner over the book of Acts. It is God's declaration that not just a few have been singled out to manifest the prophetic gift; *all* have been anointed by the prophetic Spirit. The end time has indeed come!

Philip Sent to the Eunuch (8:29–39)

"The Spirit said to Philip, 'Go up and join this chariot.' . . . When they came up out of the water, the Spirit of the Lord snatched Philip away; and the eunuch saw him no more. . . ."

Doesn't the idea of the Spirit speaking to Philip sound like something from an Old Testament Elijah story? The text does not mention prophecy, but the guidance of the Spirit is so similar to prophetic activity that I feel it should be included. This and other references establish that the Spirit did, during this period, speak clearly and distinctly to ordinary people.[13] The fact that Philip had four daughters who prophesied (21:9) indicates that he was very familiar with the prophetic.

Ananias Sent to Saul (9:10–17; 22:12–14)

"There was a certain disciple at Damascus, named Ananias; and the Lord said to him in a vision, 'Ananias.' And he said, 'Behold, here am I, Lord.'"

Ananias is later described (22:12) as a devout Jew in good standing with the Jewish community. Although not designated as an apostle or prophet, this average, devoted Jew received and delivered his message to Saul in much the same manner as an Old Testament prophet would have. Made bold by the Holy Spirit, Ananias declared this prophetic word to Paul (22:14): "The God of our fathers has appointed you to know His will, and to see the righteous One, and to hear an utterance from His mouth. For you will be a witness for Him to all men of what you have seen and heard."

Although usually given in the context of a church gathering, prophecy this time was on a one-to-one basis—directive, predictive and challenging.

Gentiles Receive the Holy Spirit (10:44–48)

"While Peter was still speaking . . . the Holy Spirit fell upon all those who were listening. . . . And all the circumcised believers . . . were amazed, because the gift of the Holy Spirit had been poured out upon the Gentiles also. For they were hearing them speaking with tongues and exalting God."

Peter Reports the Event to the Elders at Jerusalem (11:1–18)

"'The Spirit told me to go with them. . . . And as I began to speak, the Holy Spirit fell upon them, just as He did upon us at the beginning. And

I remembered the word of the Lord, how He used to say, "John baptized with water, but you shall be baptized with the Holy Spirit." If God therefore gave to them the same gift as He gave to us also after believing in the Lord Jesus Christ, who was I that I could stand in God's way?'"

This occasion in the house of Cornelius the Roman centurion was the first time the Holy Spirit was poured out on Gentiles, and it happened even as the apostle to the Jews was speaking. These Romans spoke with tongues and glorified God, just as the Jews had done previously (2:4, 11), and probably also the Samaritans (8:14–18).

Later Peter gave his eyewitness account to some of the nervous, concerned Jewish leaders in Jerusalem, making several important points:

- The prophetic experience of the Holy Spirit was no longer restricted to Jewish Christians; the door was now open to Gentile believers as well.
- Peter and his friends knew that the Romans were undergoing the same experience because they heard them speak with tongues and exalt God, just as the Jews had done on the Day of Pentecost.
- Peter remembered how Jesus "used to say" (that is, it was a repeated topic) that they would be baptized with the Holy Spirit; and Peter apparently believed that the Jews at Jerusalem and the Romans at Caesarea had just experienced what Jesus had foretold.

Agabus and His Team (11:27–28)

"Some prophets came down from Jerusalem to Antioch. And . . . Agabus stood up and began to indicate by the Spirit that there would certainly be a great famine all over the world."

Luke's casual introduction of prophets seems to confirm the commonality of this ministry in the early Church. These prophets were not aimless wanderers but ministers who traveled to certain places to exercise their prophetic gifts in particular ways.[14] This was possibly a prophetic team of elders with Agabus in charge, sent from the church in Jerusalem. When Agabus began to "signify"—that is, to show by sign or to give a sign[15] or to indicate "by the Spirit"—that there would be a great famine, he was actually performing prophetic ministry, bringing a message originated by the Holy Spirit. The Church and the other prophets judged the prophecy dependable, probably relying more on the character of Agabus than on the unknown circumstances, for they then received contributions to send to their brothers in Judea.

The Resident Group in Antioch (13:1–4)

"There were . . . in the church . . . prophets and teachers. . . . And while they were ministering to the Lord and fasting, the Holy Spirit said, 'Set apart for Me Barnabas and Saul for the work to which I have called them.'"

The prophets mentioned in the previous section were "temporary visitors, while these in this verse belonged to the Antiochene church."[16] This is apparently a case of resident prophets who worked closely with resident teachers—an ideal combination for producing a strong local church. Five men are listed, but no attempt was made to specify who had what ministry. Apparently such identification of ministry in Bible days was very acceptable.

This was an ideal setting for prophecy: a group of people gathered for worship, fasting and prayer. Then the Holy Spirit spoke.

But how would He have spoken? Out of the air? From some inanimate object? This surely must have been prophecy—the Spirit communicating through a human spokesperson, one of the prophets. The message was direct, concise and emphatic. The "setting apart" indicates that the time had come for Paul's missionary ministry to begin. The content of the prophecy was nothing new or startling; rather it confirmed Paul's original call and represented an urgent summons for its immediate fulfillment.

One of the great benefits of prophecy in the Church is this time and placement factor. It reminds me of a humorous anecdote told by C. Peter Wagner at one of his church growth seminars.

Wagner had taught on demographic analysis but was also stressing the importance of Spirit guidance. He had talked with his friend Pastor Jack Hayford while they were driving together one day in southern California. Peter mentioned casually that his home church in Pasadena would be starting a congregation in an area they were just passing. Several thousand dollars had been spent in extensive evaluation of selecting this area. Jack smiled, saying their church had also decided to plant a church in that area. Then he added, "The Lord just spoke to me one day while driving through the area." Peter chuckled as he concluded, "Perhaps we could save ourselves a lot of money if we could just learn to listen to the Spirit."

Paul Blinds a Magician (13:8–12)

". . . Paul, filled with the Holy Spirit, fixed his gaze upon him, and said, '. . . Behold, the hand of the Lord is upon you, and you will be blind and not see the sun for a time.'"

This bold action by Paul was certainly in the best prophetic tradition! An astounding word of God thundered through the apostle. As we say,

Paul read his mail that day! He discerned the false prophet for what he was, then denounced him with emphatic, uncompromising words. As he pronounced judgment, a blinding mist of darkness descended on the sorcerer—and the magistrate was converted!

Paul's action resembles that of Peter condemning Ananias and Sapphira for lying to the Holy Spirit (Acts 5:3, 9). Severe judgment was sometimes part of the ministry of the prophet. Consider Ahijah telling Jeroboam's wife that her child would die when she walked into the city (1 Kings 14:12), or Jeremiah declaring that the false prophet Hananiah would die that year (Jeremiah 28:16–17).

A Pair of Prophets Selected (15:25–26, 32)

"Judas and Silas, also being prophets themselves, encouraged and strengthened the brethren. . . ."

After the Council at Jerusalem had solved the problems raised by the presence of Gentiles in the predominantly Jewish Church, the apostles and elders wrote a letter to be circulated among the churches. They deputized two prophets, Judas and Silas, to accompany the apostles Paul and Barnabas (14:14) in delivering the letter. These prophets were seasoned ministers, having risked their lives for Christ. As prophets they did more than just prophesy; they had a unique ability to "encourage and strengthen" the churches. Since assimilating the Gentiles was the most critical problem the young Church had faced, apostles and prophets were teamed to present the Council's conclusions (note Ephesians 2:20).

Churches miss great blessing and spiritual impartation when they do not have prophets visit them from time to time. As a former pastor I can testify of the good and lasting impact that prophetic ministries have had on our church. Not only have people been blessed and inspired uniquely, but the church program is often given special insight and direction. Once our church was facing a special necessity of thirty thousand dollars needed within a few months. Every time the elders met we asked ourselves the question, "Where will we get the money?" It became a faithless obsession! Then David Schoch came to preach for us, not knowing of the financial need. Suddenly, without warning, he declared a word from God for our situation: "You are not to worry about the thirty thousand dollars!" Our worries evaporated and the need was met on time.

Receiving Divine Directives (16:6–7)

". . . Forbidden by the Holy Spirit to speak the word in Asia; . . . and the Spirit of Jesus did not permit them."

The text is not clear how the Holy Spirit made His directives known to Paul and his associates. It could refer to personal, inner revelation of the Spirit or it could indicate prophecy. Either way it was revelation.

New Christians at Ephesus (19:6)

"When Paul had laid his hands upon them, the Holy Spirit came on them, and they began speaking with tongues and prophesying."

Prophesying here is seen as a spontaneous activity that coincides with being filled with the Spirit for the first time. This situation is similar to Acts 8:15–17 in which the Spirit was bestowed after baptism and the imposition of the apostles' hands. Once again (as in 2:4; 10:44–46) the coming of the Spirit was accompanied by unlearned languages and prophecy in the known language. (Compare with the magnifying of God in 2:11; 10:46.)

This should not be an unusual occurrence for a church. Our church, like many others, has made it standard procedure to pray over baptismal candidates. Numerous people come out of the water speaking in tongues or do so standing in the water after being baptized—a jubilee time! Prophecy has also occurred.

A Pervasive Activity in the Churches (20:22–23)

"'. . . Bound in spirit, I am on my way to Jerusalem, not knowing what will happen . . . except that the Holy Spirit solemnly testifies to me in every city, saying that bonds and afflictions await me.'"

As Paul traveled toward Jerusalem, visiting various churches and groups of Christians, a consistent prophetic warning was sounded (for example, the disciples at Tyre in 21:4 and Agabus in 21:11). The prophecies foretold the difficulties and dangers that awaited him. Paul's fellow Christians immediately concluded that he should not enter Jerusalem. But he accepted these warnings as legitimate and informative, unwavering in his decision that his going was definitely in the will of God.

Paul's situation gives us a glimpse of the prophetic activity that was normal and pervasive among the churches of the time.

Disciples at Tyre (21:4)

". . . They kept telling Paul through the Spirit not to set foot in Jerusalem."

This does not mean the Spirit was saying through the prophecies not to go to Jerusalem while at the same time urging Paul to go. The meaning of Acts 21:4, I feel, is simply, "Do not set foot in Jerusalem, or you will be bound." Paul apparently saw no conflict in meaning. Gleason L. Archer says that "it seems best to understand Acts 21:4 as conveying, not an absolute prohibition of Paul's journey to Jerusalem, but only a clear, unmistakable warning that he is not to set foot in Jerusalem—if he wants to avoid danger and stay out of serious trouble."[17]

Four Prophesying Daughters (21:9)

"Now this man had four virgin daughters who were prophetesses."

The mention of Philip's four daughters is significant for several reasons. F. F. Bruce comments: "There is good evidence that from them Luke received much of the information which he gives in the earlier part of Ac., as well as much of the material peculiar to the Third Gospel. He certainly had ample opportunity to learn all he could from them, not only during the 'many days' spent in Caesarea on this occasion, but also during the two years of Paul's imprisonment there (xxiv.27). Eusebius (HE, iii.39) relates on the testimony of Papias, how Philip's daughters were known in later days as informants on the early history of the Church. Eusebius also quotes references to them by Polycrates and Proclus (HE, iii. 31; v. 24)."[18]

Although none of their prophecies is recorded, it is evident that the four daughters were highly esteemed by the Christian community. They are the only women in the Church specifically identified as participating in prophecy. As we noted in the previous chapter, the Greek text does not warrant calling them prophetesses (as the NASB does), although these women prophesied on a regular basis.

This is not a forced, accommodating inclusion in the text, but rather the simple account of a normal activity of the women of that time. When Peter quoted the prophecy of Joel, the door was opened wide for women to participate freely in the spiritual activities of the Church. He declared that "your daughters shall prophesy" (Acts 2:17) and that God would pour out His Spirit on His bondslaves, "both men and women" (verse 18). Mary and other women were part of the original Pentecostal outpouring (Acts 1:14; 2:4). We know also that the women of the church in Corinth prayed and prophesied in the congregation (1 Corinthians 11:5).

Agabus, the Traveling Prophet (21:10–11)

". . . A certain prophet named Agabus . . . took Paul's belt and bound his own feet and hands, and said, 'This is what the Holy Spirit says: "In this way the Jews at Jerusalem will bind the man who owns this belt and deliver him into the hands of the Gentiles."'"

Again we meet Agabus more than ten years after his introduction in Acts 11. He probably made his home somewhere in Judea but from time to time visited the churches. I cannot imagine that Paul would have been receptive to his ministry if Agabus were not considered reliable and submitted to authority.

In the tradition of Ezekiel and Jeremiah (see chapter 6), Agabus acted out his prophecy by using Paul's belt to bind his own hands. This is sometimes referred to as "prophetic symbolism" but is more accurately described as "enacted prophecy." Three surprising examples from the Old Testament:

- Ahijah's tearing of the new cloak (1 Kings 11:29–39)
- Isaiah's going naked and barefoot for three years (Isaiah 20:2–6)
- Ezekiel's shave and haircut (Ezekiel 5:1–17)

In an excellent article on the subject, H. McKeating explains: "The purpose of enacting a prophecy is frequently to create, perhaps in a more powerful way than the spoken word ever could, that prophecy's fulfilment."[19] The enactment is as much a part of the prophecy as the words, and usually the graphic demonstration forms a picture in people's minds that is remembered more easily than mere words would be. Let me use a personal illustration.

Some years ago a group of ministers gathered for a retreat of teaching, prayer and fellowship in the San Bernardino Mountains. Some pastors who were seeking God's direction, realizing there were prophetic ministries present, requested that we have a time in which prophecy might be given over those who so desired. After prayer some of us laid hands on these seekers and prophesied. A Canadian was the most forlorn-looking pastor I had ever seen. Slumped in his chair, he was the picture of dejection. How, I wondered, could the poor man be helped? Then I felt the Lord say, *Take him by the hands, pull him to his feet and make him dance!* I had never seen such a thing done and, frankly, the thought was repulsive to me.

As the impression grew stronger, however, I began speaking to him about the joy of the Lord. Taking him by the hands, I pulled the bewildered fellow to his feet. Then, looking him in the eyes, I told him that the joy of the Lord was his strength and that he was to rejoice with me. God's joy swept over me and I began to laugh and jump up and down. He responded slowly. Then the meaning of it swept over him and faith took hold. He began leaping and shouting and laughing, losing all restraint. The two of us whirled around the room praising God—and my brother was set free! Words alone did not break him of his despondency, but the enactment of the words did (and I mean *really* did!).

Agabus used a formula to introduce his prophecy that had not been used previously in Scripture: "This is what the Holy Spirit says" (NASB, TEV) or "Thus saith the Holy Ghost" (KJV). One must have great assurance to employ such an introduction! The message that followed was clearly foretelling—bringing predictive information to the apostle Paul. In fact, Agabus' word is probably the climactic prophecy of a series of messages given at various places and warning Paul as he journeyed toward Jerusalem.

Agabus' prophecy, although apparently received without fault by the early Christians, has come under some modern criticism. David Hill, for instance, comments: "The fact that his word did not strictly come true would have made his prophecy 'false' by Old Testament standards."[20] Wayne Grudem points out two mistakes in the prophecy: first, Agabus' prediction that "the Jews at Jerusalem" would "bind" Paul, whereas it was not actually the Jews but the Romans who bound him; and second, that the Jews did not "deliver" Paul into the hands of the Gentiles, but rather he had to be forcibly rescued from the Jews by the tribune and his soldiers (Acts 21:32–33).[21]

The best resolution to this question, I think, is given by Cecil M. Robeck Jr.: ". . . Even if Paul was not literally bound hand and foot, the Jews were the ones who cornered him in Jerusalem and laid hands on him, at least metaphorically binding him. While they did not voluntarily bring Paul to the Gentiles and deliver him, nevertheless, the Gentiles (Romans) took Paul from the Jews. Thus, according to Luke, the prophecy seems to have been fulfilled. The prophecy which Agabus delivered to Paul, was given with no addition or elaboration. . . . It was predictively informative. . . . It did not request or demand action with respect to it, nor did Agabus offer a commentary on it."[22]

My own conclusion is that Paul:

- Obeyed the Spirit, since the prophecies did not forbid him to go; they merely warned him of the consequences.
- Believed the inspiration of the Tyrian believers and Agabus, since Paul believed what they said, if he went, would take place.
- Accepted the message without negative criticism and set a good example for the Church, since this was an example of how prophecy is to be judged.
- Appreciated the believers' concern, since this experience made an opportunity for rich *koinonia*.

207

- Fulfilled his prophetic destiny, since Ananias had announced that Paul would bear God's name before the Gentiles and kings.

Agabus' enacted prophecy was accepted, despite some question as to God's will and meaning.[23] This raises the most significant question about prophecy in our day: *How can prophecy be evaluated or judged?* This challenging question will be addressed in chapters 20 and 21. Until then important preliminary information is presented—such as the next chapter in which the controversial fourteenth chapter of 1 Corinthians is examined (where Paul outlines the proper place and use of tongues, interpretation and prophecy in the local church).

Summary of Acts

We may draw nine conclusions about prophetic activity in Acts:

1. Some Christians practiced prophesying regularly, and possibly twelve individuals were labeled "prophets": Agabus (11:27–28; 21:10–11); Judas and Silas (15:32); the four virgin daughters of Philip the evangelist (21:8–9); and at least two of the five men at Antioch (13:1)— Barnabas, Simeon called Niger, Lucius of Cyrene, Manaen the Herodian and Saul. Also, some prophets (unnamed) who accompanied Agabus to Antioch (11:27).
2. Prophecy is a primary manifestation of the outpouring of the Spirit during this era (2:16–21).
3. Acts depicts prophetic activity as normal and pervasive among the churches of that day (20:23; 21:4, 9, 11).
4. Prophesying is an unexpected activity that accompanies being filled with the Spirit for the first time (19:1–6).
5. Prophesying is one among many manifestations of the Spirit taking place in the early Church.
6. It has several functions:
   a. Foretelling or predicting the future (11:27–28; 20:23; 21:10–11; and some would include Paul's revelation in 27:10, 23, 31)
   b. Selecting individuals for tasks (13:1–3; 22:13–16)
   c. Solving religious disputes (15:28, 32)
   d. Receiving guidance in making decisions (16:6–10)
   e. Demonstrating the supernatural (19:6)
7. Some prophets were mobile but they were not aimless and irresponsible (11:27; 15:32; 21:10).
8. Paul received prophecies (gratefully, we assume) from others:

    a. Ananias (9:17)
    b. The prophets at Antioch (13:1–2)
    c. The prophets in various churches (20:23; 21:4)
    d. Agabus (21:10–11)
  9. It is possible that 4:3–12 (Peter on trial) offers the first recorded case of the disciples coming before magistrates and fulfilling Luke 12:11–12.

REFLECTIONS

. . . The primitive Christian communities displayed a fresh outburst of enthusiasm and of prophetism. Prophecy was indeed one of the most distinctive features of early Christianity.[24]

K. S. Latourette

The picture of the prophet which emerges from the pages of Scripture and the early church writings is impressive. Rather than a mere mouthpiece who passively responds when God picks him up, the prophet is a conscious agent of God, gifted by God to be an envoy, a watchman, and a bearer of royal authority.[25]

Bruce Yocum

Although New Testament prophecy never has authority equal to Scripture in our lives, it can carry with it revelation for the hour (or present time) about which the Holy Spirit wants the Church to know. We see this pattern all through the book of Acts.[26]

Cindy Jacobs

I have found that those who move with a remarkable degree of accuracy in the prophetic do so by receiving revelation from God by means that go beyond the "reporting in human words what God brings to mind." On occasion God speaks to his servants in an audible voice. . . . Additionally, open visions of the spiritual realm or of future events are familiar modes of communication to those who move in the prophetic realm with a remarkable degree of accuracy.[27]

Mike Bickle

13

THE PROPHETIC
CONFUSION
AT CORINTH

*. . . So that you are not lacking in any gift [the first occurrence in
1 Corinthians of charisma], awaiting eagerly the revelation of our Lord
Jesus Christ.*

1 Corinthians 1:7

THE CORINTHIAN CHURCH has been much maligned by critics, and the happenings of the worship services there, specifically tongues and prophecy, written off to lack of spirituality or fanaticism. Actually, considering the heathen society of the time, it is amazing that the church did as well as it did! It may someday be seen that the Corinthian church, which demonstrated so much spiritual activity in such a depraved environment, was actually one of the heartiest in the Mediterranean world, and more spiritual than given credit for.

The city of Corinth, which Paul first visited during his second missionary journey, was strategically situated on a narrow isthmus sandwiched between the Aegean and Adriatic Seas. This land bridge connected the Peloponnesus (the strange, handlike southern tip of Greece) with northern Greece. The city had two seaports, one on each sea, which made it a major commercial center, the metropolis of the Peloponnesus and the leading city of Greece. In Paul's day the population of Corinth was approximately seven hundred thousand, about two-thirds of whom were slaves.

A helpful description of the city is provided by Sholem Asch, a Jewish author devoted to historical accuracy, in his well-known novel *The Apostle:*

> Corinth was a young city, which was unfolding into greatness. The old and famous Corinth which had flourished under the rule of the Greek tyrants, the Corinth of ancient temples and ancient treasuries of art, had been completely destroyed by Pompey [146 B.C.]. Julius Caesar had begun the rebuilding of the city [46 B.C.], intending to make of it a Roman commercial center. He settled it with freedmen and encouraged colonists from all parts of the Empire to settle in Corinth and to develop the commercial and industrial possibilities of Achaia, so that Corinth might take the place of Athens. But there was nothing whatsoever in the character of the city which entitled it to the proud title of the capital of Achaia. It was a city without tradition, without a dominant unifying language, without a uniform culture. It was a mixture of races and a Babel of tongues. Freedmen and slaves—the former predominating—worked in the foundries, the potteries, the weaving and dye factories, the oil presses, and the gardens. Phoenician, Egyptian, and Asiatic cults of all kinds took root in the city. Some fame had already been acquired by the temple of a Venus Pandemos who was in reality a Phoenician Ashtoreth. More than a thousand girls served there under the overseership of the priests, conducting a huge trade in prostitution under the cover of a sacred service. The temple was naturally much frequented by transient sailors, who spent there the money saved up on long journeys. The city was always full of drunken sailors, who rioted in the streets, crowded the hostelries and restaurants, and lost their hard-earned demeters and Roman dinarii at dice to the local sharps. From the narrow streets of Corinth there went up continuously the angry shouting of drunken and swindled sailors and the shrill laughter of whores. The visitors who passed through Corinth carried the repute of its wealth and dissoluteness to the ends of the ancient world, and a constant stream of peddlers, merchants, and artisans swelled the population of the city. It also happened, some time before Paul's arrival in Corinth, that riots broke out in the city of Rome because of popular resentment against a certain "Xrestos"; and the Emperor Claudius drove many Jews, both Messianists and non-Messianists, out of the capital. Among those that fled to Corinth were Aquila and Priscilla.[1]

Arriving at Corinth, Paul was sickened to the core: Almost everything violated his Jewish upbringing and Christian character. His misery compounded an already troubled heart. He was arriving somewhat discouraged in spirit, having just come from Athens, where he had attempted to match wits with the philosophers but had meager results to show for his efforts.

The pace picked up quickly in Corinth. Paul made immediate contact with the Jewish community, where he met the zealous husband-wife team of Aquila and Priscilla, fellow tentmakers who were also Messianists (Acts 18:2–3). During the week Paul toiled as an artisan in the marketplace with his new compatriots. From black goat hair they wove material for tents and mantles, which was sold on the spot to passersby. But as he labored at his loom, the apostle boldly shared the Good News to whoever would listen. On the Sabbath he argued the claims of Jesus the Messiah in the synagogue (verse 5). A few Jews responded; many questioned and held back. But some hungry Gentiles snatched up his message eagerly, joining themselves to the Jewish Messianists under Paul's leadership.

Jewish resistance to the apostle's claims flared with such intensity that he pulled out of the synagogue, shaking the dust from his garments. Opening a church next door in the home of Titius Justus, Paul invited believing Jews and anyone interested to come. The friction between the two synagogues grew fierce as the distraught Jews found they could not silence Paul physically, outdebate him theologically or refute his scriptural proof that Jesus was indeed the Messiah. Their only recourse: to drag him before the secular magistrate Gallio, who surprised everyone by throwing them all (and their religious beliefs) out of his court and even allowing the leader of the synagogue to be beaten (Acts 18:17). With his ministry launched so dramatically, Paul continued his efforts for a year and half in the city, and a strong church resulted.

His first epistle to the Corinthians was possibly written in the mid-50s A.D. Evidently the church had written him a letter of inquiry (7:1) and was now sending a delegation of three requesting Paul's judgment on related issues (1 Corinthians 16:17). This epistle was his corrective response to the problems and questions raised by the Corinthian congregation. Paul realized quickly that their Christian testimony was in jeopardy because of immorality, disunity and immoderation. Corrupt Corinth seemed to be invading the church![2]

One area of concern: the disorderly operation of spiritual gifts, particularly tongues and prophecy. This is the focus of 1 Corinthians 14.

This chapter has become very important to contemporary Christians because speaking in tongues and prophesying have once again assumed a position of importance in the Church. As in Bible days, these dynamic spiritual gifts can both benefit and disrupt the local church. Paul was concerned that the worship gatherings of the Corinthians appeal to both believers and nonbelievers, so he boldly addressed their misguided use of tongues and prophecy during congregational worship.

The first 25 verses of 1 Corinthians 14 discuss "the relative value and use of prophecy and speaking in tongues."[3] The great need Paul addresses here is "intelligibility" in the church services. People need to know what is being said or they will not know how to respond. The last fifteen verses discuss orderly conduct in public worship. People should behave properly in church!

Let's look at each of these two sections in more detail.

Appropriate Use of Inspired Utterances

This first section contains four subheads, each containing valuable information to enhance our devotional lives and congregational worship through the proper use of spiritual language. The theme is captured in the word *edification,* used in various forms seven times.

Personal Tongues versus Public Prophecy (verses 1–5)

Verse 1. Pursue . . . desire earnestly . This paragraph opens with a clear directive that we "put love first" (NEB)—that is, "follow the way of love" (NIV, Phillips) or "want love more than anything else" (JB). The Greek word *diokete* appears in the present imperative, implying continuous action: "Keep on pursuing love." Dynamic and challenging, the word means "to run swiftly in order to catch; to seek after eagerly, earnestly endeavor to acquire."[4] With such love in our hearts, we should not have a difficult time fulfilling Paul's objective in this chapter: the edification or building up of the Church.

In addition, we are to "eagerly desire spiritual gifts" (NIV). The word *gifts* is somewhat misleading. In 1 Corinthians 12:31 Paul wrote, "Earnestly desire the greater gifts" *(charismata).* But here we are told to desire *ta pneumatika*—better translated "the things of the Spirit"[5] or the activities of the Holy Spirit. Both exhortations—to pursue love and to seek spiritual gifts—are worded strongly, which means we dare not be casual about either one. We must chase after them both with determination! On the interplay between the two expressions, F. W. Grosheide observes that "'to follow after' indicates a never terminating action, while 'to desire earnestly' stresses the intensity rather than the continuity of the action."[6]

Paul desires "especially that [we] may prophesy" (verse 1). Both tongues and prophecy have individual value, and it would be wrong to minimize the importance of either or to suggest that Paul does so. He does not disparage tongues! As we work through 1 Corinthians 14, keep in mind the theme of verses 1–40: "We are looking at *the church gathered for and practicing worship in the public assembly.*"[7] In the congregational setting, prophecy is the preferred and most appropriate use of inspired speech, since it is the more meaningful and helpful to the most people.

Verse 2. Speaks in a tongue. Some versions and translations can be evasive and even deceptive about what tongues are. For instance: "unknown tongue" (KJV), "strange tongues" (TEV), "a strange language" (Beck), "language of ecstasy" (NEB), "languages that others don't know" (CEV). The Greek word *glosse* simply refers to a language, and in this context to a language "you haven't learned" (LB) or, as the NIV says in a footnote, "another language." Happily the New King James Version has dropped the word *unknown* used in the old Authorized Version. That word was italicized, indicating that the translators knew it was not in the original but felt it added clarification. Unfortunately many have overlooked this important point. Because *tongues* has an archaic ring and an unfortunate reputation, Jack Hayford suggests calling it "spiritual language"[8]—a term I like very much.

This section of 1 Corinthians 14, and most of the chapter, is about two kinds of inspired utterances or spiritual communication, so let me offer a brief definition of each. (See also the definitions in chapter 10.) Both kinds of communication are essential, Paul felt, in maintaining the body life of the Church, but they must be kept in balance and exercised properly.

- *Tongues or spiritual language:* The ability to speak, through the inspiration of the Holy Spirit, in a language not learned through natural means. This language is sometimes recognized as an actual foreign language. It is particularly a spiritual language for a devotional relationship with God through prayer, and one the speaker cannot use without the enablement of the Holy Spirit.[9]
- *Prophecy:* The ability to speak, through the inspiration and enablement of the Holy Spirit, an immediate message from God to a specific group of people in the known language of the speaker and listeners.

Are the languages spoken as "tongues" literal languages? This reasonable question is often raised.[10]

As a teenager, having newly experienced this phenomenon (as I described in the last chapter), I marveled at the beauty of the experience but wondered at its authenticity as strange, unlearned words tumbled out of my mouth. Later I was startled and amazed to hear veteran missionary W. W. Patterson tell of the Holy Spirit's activities in Indonesia. A great visitation of God occurred in that Southeast Asian archipelago in the early 1900s when many of the nationals were filled with the Holy Spirit and spoke in tongues. Some of those speaking in tongues, the missionaries reported, were actually speaking pure, proper English, in which they had no training!

A similar story is told of Carlton Spencer, president of Elim Bible School in New York State, visiting East Africa in the early 1950s. "What a glorious time it was," writes biographer Marion Meloon, "a veritable tidal wave of the Spirit. Carlton was privileged to behold the unusual sight of an African woman lost in worship and speaking in a language unknown to her—English! She sat with her babe at her breast, oblivious to all about her, even the babe's sucking and then slumber, as she worshiped on and on in English. Similar Baptisms swept through the crowds gathered, beyond numbering."[11]

Dennis J. Bennett gives several illustrations. Here is one of them:

> I have encountered many examples of someone speaking in known languages, but unknown to himself. At our Thursday communion service not long ago, an elderly lady presented herself at the altar rail for healing prayer. I had never seen her before and I have not seen her since. I didn't know her needs. Laying my hands on her head, I said the liturgical prayers for healing, and then added some of my own. Then realizing that although I did not know her needs the Holy Spirit did, I prayed quietly in words the Holy Spirit gave me to utter. I did not recognize the language that came to me, and I'm sure the woman did not either. Soon, feeling that my prayer had been completed, I moved along to pray for others. The next day a friend called: "Did you realize that Gloria S. was kneeling next to that woman yesterday, and she says you prayed in Japanese?"
>
> Gloria S. is an old acquaintance, the daughter of a well-known family in the diocese who were occasional attendants at St. Luke's. She and her husband had just returned from four years in Japan, where he had been with the State Department. I called Gloria. "Oh, yes," she said. "You prayed in Japanese." She proceeded to tell me some of the phrases of the prayer in Japanese and then in English. She had not heard the whole prayer but had picked up phrases. "Your conclusion was, 'Because you have asked this thing,'" she said, giving it to me in Japanese and English. "By the way, your accent is perfect!"[12]

After I had demonstrated speaking in tongues in an Oregon church (to show the people the ease of speaking in a devotional prayer language), I was surprised to learn from a couple who had served in China as missionaries that I had spoken in Mandarin Chinese. David Sell, one of our elders who now pastors in Pleasanton, California, prayed once in Spanish at a prayer meeting in our San Jose church, and once later in Portuguese. David did not speak either language, but some in the congregation did and they confirmed hearing these languages.[13]

Verses 2 and 4. Paul includes four excellent reasons for speaking in tongues as he contrasts the beneficial use of tongues for the person with the profitable use of prophecy in a church meeting.

1. To speak to God. The ability to speak privately and directly to God is a wonderful experience, "for you are sharing intimacies just between you and him" (Message). Believers should still use their native language in prayer a good deal of the time, but this additional channel for occasional use is a delightful devotional variation that gives inspiration and confidence. The Bible clearly speaks of both kinds of prayer. "When I pray in tongues," says Jack Hayford, "I'm talking to God. Period! Whatever else anyone may say about the employment of spiritual language, this is the Bible's bottom line. Tongues are connected to heaven's throne; that's all there is to it."[14] Bursting forth in tongues in church because of personal excitement, however, would not build up the Christians present and it could confuse visitors.

2. To speak mysteries. Spiritual language enables a person to understand things that otherwise have been hidden. I have discovered that when I pray in tongues my mind is not disconnected; in fact, it seems sharper and clearer than at any other time. Perception of how to pray for certain missionaries, insights on a certain Scripture, impressions about God's direction for the day—all these can be part of this unveiled understanding.

3. To edify oneself. This may seem self-serving, but actually it is very spiritual! Consider that God has made intentional provision for your encouragement. I have found, to my amazement, that when I am discouraged and hardly know how to express myself to God, praying in the language of the Spirit has lifted me out of my mental quagmire and given me spiritual inspiration. I cannot explain how this "building up" (*edification* is a builder's term)[15] actually happens, but I know it does. When a person gets bogged down, this wonderful channel of the Spirit is a powerful means to break free.

Sometimes it is helpful to allow the Spirit to bring additional new tongues, rather than just the one spiritual tongue you may be accustomed to using. This is easily done: Simply open your mind to the possibility, ask for the Spirit's help, yield to Him, then speak. To flow linguistically in several languages you do not know is truly exhilarating spiritually. Obviously, though, the church service is not the place for you to have your private devotions. This is best accomplished in your own prayer closet.

4. To edify the Church. This takes place when a public interpretation is given with the tongue (verses 27–28). Combining tongues with interpretation is a viable ministry. Usually the Spirit of God utilizes such communication when it is appropriate to have a specific message reach and impress someone speaking a given foreign language (which would be translation) or when the combination tongue-interpretation presents a meaningful devotional message (an interpretation) from God's heart to the congregation.

Unless tongues are used divinely to communicate a message to a foreign visitor[16] or with interpretation as a message to a church, a spiritual tongue is a language best utilized as a form of prayer to God. Prophecy, on the other hand, is God speaking to men and women, communicating what the Spirit is saying to the churches, so it is a word *from* God. Both forms of spiritual language are inspirational, tongues as devotion to and prophecy as communication from God.

Here are nineteen points of comparison and emphasis between tongues and prophecy:

Comparison Chart of 1 Corinthians 14	
Tongues	Prophecy
God-directed, personal, spiritual language, mainly for devotional prayer	People-directed, corporate language to edify all with divine communication
1. Speak to God (v. 2)	Speak to men (v. 2)
2. Speak "mysteries" in Spirit (v. 2)	Speak understandable message of edification, exhortation, consolation (v. 3)
3. Edify self (v. 4)	Edify church (v. 4)
4. Desired for all (v. 5)	Preferred; "greater" (v. 5)
5. Important, esp. with interpretation (v. 5)	More valuable (v. 5)
6. Not profitable to church (v. 6)	Profitable to church (v. 6)
7. Indistinct sounds bring confusion (vv. 7–9)	Distinct sounds have significance (vv. 7–9)
8. "How will it be known?" (v. 9)	Words easily understood (v. 9)
9. Interpretation needed (v. 13)	Edifying to church (v. 12)
10. Spirit prays, mind unfruitful (v. 14)	Spirit and mind pray (v. 15)
11. Spirit sings (v. 15)	Mind sings, too (v. 15)
12. Others not blessed (vv. 16–17)	Others blessed (v. 16)
13. 10,000 meaningless words (v. 19)	Five understandable words (v. 19)
14. In understanding, children (v. 20)	In understanding, men (v. 20)
15. Sign to unbeliever (v. 22)	Sign to believer (v. 22)
16. "You are mad" (v. 23)	"God is among you" (v. 25)
17. 2 or 3 with interpreter (v. 27)	"One by one, so that all may learn" (v. 31)
18. Be silent when no interpreter (v. 28)	Speak to all when inspired (v. 31)
19. *"Forbid not tongues"* (v. 39, KJV)	*"Covet to prophesy"* (v. 39, KJV)

Verse 3. Speaks to men. This key verse carefully sets out the parameters of prophecy in a church body, just like chalking out the boundaries of a volleyball court.[17] This verse defines and identifies the "purpose or

217

result"[18] or "effects"[19] of prophecy. It fixes the "objectives" of prophetic discourse[20] and delineates "the functions of the prophetic word."[21] Three words in this verse give us a thumbnail sketch of New Testament prophecy and show the divine intent or nature of prophecy:

Edification (KJV, NKJV, NASB), Greek *oikodomen:* "strengthening" (NIV), "upbuilding" (RSV, Williams), "power to build" (NEB), "improvement" (JB), "help" (TEV), "helping others grow" (NLT), "helped" (CEV). Prophecy builds up individuals, but more importantly the whole assembled company.[22]

Exhortation (KJV, NKJV, NASB), Greek *paraklesin:* "encouragement" (NIV, RSV, JB, Williams), "encouraging" (NLT), "encouraged" (CEV). Sometimes presented in a fiery, challenging way and other times in soft, beckoning tones, prophecy stirs the people of God to action. Faith is lifted to new levels and believers are filled with great confidence in their God, heartened and inspired to face the burdens of daily life. This word comes from the same root as *Paraclete,* Jesus' term for the Holy Spirit, whom He promised to send to assist and support His disciples (John 14:16, 26; 15:26; 16:7).

Comfort (KJV, NKJV, NIV, TEV, Williams), Greek *paramuthian:* "consolation" (NASB, JB, RSV), "comforting" (NLT), "made to feel better" (CEV). Many people drag themselves to church weighed down with the cares of life. Because I live in the Silicon Valley of California, the electronics center of the world, I know how people can be driven into the ground by the goals of money-hungry management. Such wiped-out workers need the awesome comfort of the Holy Spirit. Like eagles catching a thermal current, the people of God experience gracious spiritual updraft when they come to worship! The emphasis of this word *comfort* is on gentleness.[23] It basically means to speak "in a friendly way."[24] People undergoing depression, sorrow and heartache are comforted and sustained by a nurturing prophetic word.

These three words depicting the divine intent for prophecy mean "to build up, stir up, lift up." Each of them in turn contributes to the substance, motivation and comfort of people's faith.

Verse 5. But even more. Paul wants everyone to experience the edification that comes through personal communion with God in spiritual language, as well as through public prophetic communication from God in the corporate body of the church. Prophecy is preferred in the public setting because it edifies not just one, but all the church. As Fee says, "Thus it is not inherently greater, since all gifts come from the Spirit and are beneficial. It is greater precisely because it is intelligible and therefore can edify [the whole church]."[25]

As Paul writes, he is actually battling on two fronts: "On the one hand he must warn against an overestimation of glossolalia but on the other he must assign to it the place which it deserves as a *charisma* of the Spirit."[26] Paul handles this delicate subject like a tightrope walker who maintains his bearing on the high wire only so long as the pole he is carrying stays perfectly balanced.

Illustrations of Meaningless Sound (verses 6–12)

Paul is not yet satisfied that his point is made. He proceeds to reemphasize that intelligibility of spiritual language is essential for building up the Church. People must understand spiritual communication before they can be helped by it. Four graphic illustrations help visualize his point:

Musical instruments (verse 7) must have clear, distinct, in-tune tones for music to be pleasurable. Improperly used tongues in a service affects a gathering just as discord offends a musical audience. Writes Simon Kistemaker: "Music must be agreeable to the ear to be acceptable to the audience. The musician must skillfully produce pleasing sounds that disclose the distinct characteristics of the instrument that is played, whether the flute or the harp. Thus a relationship is formed between the player and the listener. But if the player produces a cacophony of sounds, everyone will depart from his presence."[27]

The army bugle (verse 8) was valuable in ancient warfare. A faulty bugle call could spell disaster for a military unit, especially when under attack. In such a situation the bugle was the only form of communication. An army's success depended on quick response to the trumpet call, so the sound had to be clear and identifiable. Imagine the impact of a bugler posted on the city wall who lost his lip and made squawking sounds as an enemy force prepared to take the city!

Unclear conversation (verse 9) leaves a person dissatisfied and frustrated. Meaningful conversation depends on the cooperation of two people speaking clearly and understandably.

Every language in the world (verse 10) has its distinctives, and each language carries special meaning for its native people. Unknown foreign words (verse 11) create a significant communication barrier. Words must register meaning in the minds of the hearers.

Paul ties these crystal-clear illustrations to speaking in tongues without interpretation in the church service. It is best, he stresses again, to speak meaningful spiritual language in a public service so that all may benefit. One purpose of congregational worship, after all, is building up the whole church, and we should seek zealously to fulfill this objective in our pursuit of spiritual activities.

Appropriate Use of Personal Tongues (verses 13–19)

The focus in this segment is not prophecy but the public use of tongues.

Verse 13. Pray that he may interpret. If a person wishes to speak in tongues publicly, he or she should pray to be able to give a public interpretation. Paul refers to a public setting, just as he does in verse 28, where he teaches that the person who speaks in tongues should not do so in a public meeting unless an interpreter is present. I understand verse 13 to mean this paraphrased thought: "Therefore the one who speaks out loudly in tongues to be heard by all in the church service should cease crying out in tongues. Rather he should wait and pray that he may interpret any message coming to him, so that when he does speak forth to the whole church, he will use language that everyone present understands." In a public setting it is important for the mind to be "fruitful" (verse 14), not unresponsive or unknowing, like ground that "lies fallow" (Message).

Verse 14. My spirit prays. Praying in tongues indicates that "my spirit" is praying. This is excellent for private, personal, closet prayer. The fact that my mind is "unfruitful," however, is a warning sign that the manifestation of tongues alone is not meant for public congregational edification, since the rest of the people (such as yourself!) will not understand what is being said. I think of *my spirit* as referring to my inner, invisible, spiritual self as it is inspired, enabled and empowered by the Holy Spirit. I cannot help but feel that every use of *spirit* in these verses is a deliberate reference by Paul to the Holy Spirit.[28] We have here a remarkable bonding of human spirit, spiritual gift and Holy Spirit. Thank God I experience and enjoy what Paul is describing, although I have trouble explaining it. It is like enjoying food even when I cannot explain the process of digestion.

Verses 15–17. What is the outcome then? Paul has reached a conclusion about performance in the congregational meeting. He contrasts three activities that benefit the individual with three that benefit the whole church. I like the way the NLT says, "I will do both" (implied but not stated in the Greek).

Edify Self		Edify the Church
• Praying with the spirit	vs.	Praying with the mind (or, "in words I understand")
• Singing with the spirit	vs.	Singing with the mind (or, "in words I understand")
• Blessing with the spirit	vs.	Giving thanks intelligently (in understandable words)

Many people who pray in tongues have discovered the delightful experience of singing with the spirit—that is, in tongues. This is a wonderful adjunct to your prayer ministry. In the church service, however, when singing to bless and inform others, we should sing at appropriate times in the known language or have the song interpreted.

Verse 16. If you bless in the spirit is an attempt to extend toward others the inspiration of God's presence and revelation now upon you. You want to share the blessing. It is a "giving of thanks" in the sense that it expresses prayer and appreciation to God. The person so blessed wishes to draw everyone else into the wonderful magnetic field of the Holy Spirit's presence. This is commendable. But such an expression of prayer and appreciation to God is meaningless to those meant to receive it if they cannot understand it. Paul says, "You are giving thanks well"—that is, "You are having a great private devotion"—but the experience is ineffective for public edification.

The place of the ungifted. Who are these "unlearned" (KJV) people who say amen to an inspired person's giving of thanks? I feel that the term must refer to believers in the church who simply "do not understand" (NIV).[29] Unbelievers are not inclined to say "Amen!" in confirmation of some verbal expression, or even know why they would. Saying amen involves a "wholehearted response to and endorsement of the words of another."[30] My experience is that nonbelievers generally sit, observe and wonder rather than participate vociferously.[31]

The Greek word for *ungifted* is *idiotes*,[32] a word used five times in the New Testament. Each occurrence allows us to believe that such a person is a Christian, even if uninformed. Paul uses the word again in verses 23–24 in contrast with *unbeliever*, to show that both Christians and non-Christians need to understand what is said. The Jewish Temple leadership considered Peter and John *idiotai*—laymen, nonprofessional and uneducated. Paul uses the same word in 2 Corinthians 11:6, describing himself as "unskilled in speech." Bauer's *Lexicon* lists a number of contrasts drawn from ancient secular Greek illustrating that *idiotes* refers to a "*layman* in contrast to an expert or specialist of any kind"—contrasts such as subject and king, soldier and officer, patient and physician.[33]

When Paul alludes to such a person as "occupying the place of" or "filling the place of" the *idiotes*, he need not be referring to an actual, literal location in the meeting place. He may, rather, be referring figuratively to the person's state of mind.

Verses 18–19. I speak in tongues more than you all. Paul is most grateful ("I thank God") for his devotional ability to speak in spiritual language to God. And why not? He has discovered great benefit from this exercise and shares a surprising insight that would greatly benefit the

Church today. Paul is, after all, speaking to God, articulating mysteries of God, edifying himself. All these wonderful activities are highly beneficial and inspiring—*but to the individual alone!* Ten thousand glorious words to uplift oneself yield not one puff of uplift for the rest of the Church.

Is it possible that all this personal, inward edification was the secret of Paul's outward spiritual success? Perhaps his public ministry was effective because his inner spiritual resources were sustained by frequent private devotional prayer in tongues. I believe this to be true while hastening to acknowledge Paul's insistence that many spiritual words are useless to others in a church gathering if those words are meaningless.

Signs of a Mature Approach (verses 20–25)

Verse 20. Be mature. We are to be childlike in our innocence and acceptance of the events of life ("a childlike unfamiliarity with evil," Message), but this must not replace our maturity in handling those same events, especially when it comes to worship services. Experience-oriented Christians can too easily swap mature, well-exercised intelligence for gullibility. We must conclude, then (combining this thought with those from two other verses), that being mature in our worship services means avoiding behavior that is:

- Childish (verse 20)
- Mad (verse 23)
- Confusing (verse 33)

The opening admonition is timely, for many commentators consider this section of the chapter the most difficult in the entire dissertation. Paul wishes to establish an important point: A message from God in a public service in the known language of the people profits Christians and non-Christians alike, but unknown tongues, when uninterpreted, bring confusion to everyone.

Verse 21. It is written. Paul likes to strengthen or authenticate his arguments with Scripture. This approach reminds me of my days as a young man, loading and unloading railroad boxcars for Sunshine Biscuit Company. We stacked packages of cookies side by side and layer upon layer; then, every so often, we built a bulkhead with iron bars nailed into the wooden walls. Those barricades served to keep the merchandise from spilling and breaking during the severe jolting that occurred with the abrupt stopping, starting and slamming of cars together.

"Proof Scriptures" are to a theological argument what my bulkheads were to securing a load. Here Paul builds his bulkhead, securing his discussion with an unfamiliar (to us) translation of an unusual, seldom-used Old Testament reference,[34] Isaiah 28:11–12. Paul's quotation in 1 Corinthians 14:21 is given below in modern English:

New Living Translation:	New King James:
"I will speak to my own people through unknown languages and through the lips of foreigners. But even then, they will not listen to me," says the Lord.	"With men of other tongues and other lips I will speak to this people; and yet, for all that, they will not hear Me."

Other tongues. Paul found Isaiah's unusual text appealing because of its reference to tongues: "With men of other tongues and other lips . . ." (NKJV).

The KJV and NKJV accurately translate the Corinthian text as "other tongues" *(heteroglossois).* "Strange tongues" is used by the NIV and NASB—mainly, it appears, to parallel Isaiah. In this case "other tongues" is not a direct translation of either the Hebrew or the Greek Old Testament, but possibly an unknown translation or personal interpretation. Paraphrasing Old Testament Scripture (more an interpretation than a translation) was a common tendency of New Testament writers.

Barrett says of this difficult text: "This [NT] quotation is not given in agreement with the LXX [the Septuagint]; there is some evidence (Origen, *Philocalia* ix.2) that Paul may have used here a version known also to the later Old Testament translator Aquila. It was probably the word 'men of other tongues' that caught his eye and suggested the application of the passage to his discussion of 'tongues.' . . . His point is simply that (according to the Lord himself) when he speaks to men by means of strange tongues they will not listen—that is, they will not hear in obedience and faith."[35]

Paul extricates one basic truth to illustrate his point, apparently not meaning for every aspect of the Isaiah reference to find an exact application.[36] He makes no literal connection between the Assyrian language and New Testament tongues. Instead his loosely shaped quotation reinforces and secures his basic argument: Unbelievers and outsiders are repulsed by uninterpreted languages, so tongues to them become a *negative* sign of judgment.

The simple point of this verse is often lost because the context is not considered. In the Old Testament setting, Isaiah lamented Israel's spurning of the message of the Hebrew prophets, which was given in clear, unambiguous speech in their mother tongue. Since the people refused to heed God's clear directions to them in their own language, He sent Assyrian invaders in judgment who spoke a strange, foreign tongue. His purpose: that Israel grasp the reason for her mistreatment and humiliation and still respond to the original message. (The Assyrian tongue was even a sign to the unbelieving invaders that Israel was under judgment because the Assyrians could "boss them around" in their own tongue.) Alas, Israel neither listened to the clear words of the Hebrew prophets nor recognized God's hand of judgment in the confusing tongues of the Assyrian invaders. He was actually speaking through both the Hebrew and the Assyrian languages, but His people were deaf to the meaning of each.

Verse 22. A sign. Now, Paul says, the church has a problem: Unintelligible tongues are replacing clearly understood prophecies in the church. These strange, uninterpreted languages become a sign of confusion to all who do not understand what is going on in the church, especially the unbelievers. Grudem comments, "When God speaks to people in a language they cannot understand, it is a form of punishment for unbelief," and, correspondingly, "Prophecy is an indication of God's approval and blessing on the congregation because it shows that God is actively present. . . ."[37] Paul's focus is the confusion that results, either in Israel or the church, when strange, uninterpreted language is used. To the Israelites the Assyrian tongue represented judgment; to the church uninterpreted glossolalia is a sign of confusion.

This verse poses the greatest single problem in interpreting 1 Corinthians 14. Speculation occurs because of what appears to be a glaring contradiction between two sets of Pauline statements. Paul is using a two-thread analogy that can easily be misunderstood, so we must take the section as a whole and seek the total sense, rather than attempt to manufacture a single interpretation based on one word.

Paul says that uninterpreted tongues are a sign for unbelievers, while in the next verse he says that if we speak in tongues in our meetings, those same unbelievers will react negatively! Similarly he says that prophecy is a sign for believers; then he encourages prophecy when unbelievers are present.

Here is where I believe the resolution lies. The word *sign (semeion)* can be used in a dual sense: "an indication of God's approval and blessing" or "an indication of God's disapproval and a warning of judgment."[38] Thus, "the term 'sign' . . . [is] used explicitly in one sense in v. 21, and then . . . in another sense in v. 22b."[39] The purpose of Isaiah 28 was to show God's disapproval and to bring warning, so the "other tongues" of the Assyrians were a *negative* sign to Israel. Paul uses that thought to show that speaking out messages in tongues in church without interpretation is a sign to the unbelievers present—again, a *negative* sign—that something strange is going on. A meaningless tongue, unless interpreted, confuses both visitors and uninformed church members.

This approach maintains the unity of the passage, raises the interpretation out of the nonsensical and says more accurately what Paul meant.

Verse 24. But if all prophesy. The possibility exists that any church member may prophesy. The word *all* appears three times in one sentence: "*All* prophesy . . . an unbeliever or an ungifted man . . . is convicted by *all* . . . called to account by *all*" (emphasis added). Also, note the three "alls" in verse 31. J. Rodman Williams comments: "Whenever the Spirit is outpoured, the result is that people without distinction of sex or class are able to prophesy. . . . Thus at Corinth and in all Spirit-anointed assemblies, everyone may prophesy."[40]

Verse 25. God is certainly among you. It is marvelous to see a person turn to God in repentance because a prophetic word has touched his or her heart! Sometimes in a worship service unsaved people come forward and fall on their knees, calling out to God. These things happen when God is "really" (NIV) among us. Forbes observes that "the effect of prophecy on unbelievers is, in Paul's view, a sign for believers in a quite specialized sense. . . . The unbeliever's confession, provoked by prophetic conviction of his sins, is a sign to believers of the eschatological presence of God among his people."[41] The confession of the unbeliever, "God is certainly among you," lines up with Isaiah 45:14, Zechariah 8:23 and other Old Testament texts emphasizing that God's blessing brings heathen acknowledgment that God is truly among His people.

Recently in a prophetic presbytery in Moses Lake, Washington, three of us were ministering prophetically to church candidates, including a couple who came forward for ministry. Unknown to us, the husband was backslidden and no longer serving God. (He probably should not have come forward at all, but his wife was desperate to see him restored.) Suddenly Bob Isabel, one of the prophets, began to speak forth several secrets of the man's heart. Before we had finished, their two teenage children had run up to the platform and were hugging their parents and crying, while the man was overwhelmed with repentance and the grace of God.

Orderly Conduct in Public Worship

Paul uses his authority to suggest the proper decorum for public services. He is concerned that there be no distractions in the spiritual utterances or the women's behavior.

The Best Procedure for Tongues and Prophecy (verses 26–33)

Verse 26. *When you assemble.* Paul apparently considered it important for the Corinthian saints to assemble (11:17–18, 20; 14:23, 25).[42] When they did, they were to cooperate in a unified effort to share the rich diversity provided in a gathering of Christians. The sharing of a psalm (music, inspired and learned), a teaching (doctrinal lesson), a revelation (prophetic insight), a tongue (an unlearned language given supernaturally) and an interpretation (the intelligent explanation of the tongue) are not meant to be an inclusive list, but rather a suggestion of unified diversity. Paul again pounds home his theme: "Let all things be done for edification."

Verses 27–28. *By two or at the most three.* Paul wants no one to monopolize the service with an overdose of personal ministry. He suggests, therefore, limiting the presentation of a tongue with interpretation to not more than three. This does not mean (as I see it) that only two or three people can participate, but that the same person (literally, "If in a tongue anyone speaks") should not have more than three ministry times. (Each presentation would have a reasonable number of interpreted sections.)

Paul's teaching indicates that the Corinthian believers should from time to time expect tongues with interpretation. Such a manifestation is beneficial in reaching certain foreign-language peoples present, as well as in bringing a beautiful, devotional expression of God's heart to His people.

I feel that tongues with interpretation should be expressed in an alternating, rapid-fire manner, such as when a person is speaking through an interpreter. That is, the message is given in short sections or bursts (so that the interpreter can remember), followed by instantaneous interpretation, alternating in this fashion until the message is finished.

Last Sunday we had a tongues/interpretation/prophecy manifestation in our home church in San Jose. During the time in the service when spiritual gifts are encouraged to function, a woman from Mexico, who has been attending the church for several years, came to the microphone. Recently she had had a wonderful experience in the Holy Spirit and now came to deliver a prophetic utterance. Since she does not speak fluent English, she brought the church's Spanish pastor with her. To facilitate her utterance, she spoke the prophecy in her native Mexican Spanish; then the pastor interpreted to the congregation. It was both a prophecy and a tongue and an interpretation! She gave quick expressions, followed by the pastor's interpretations, until she was done.

The swiftness, spontaneity and uniqueness of such a presentation brings an amazingly fresh touch to a church service.[43]

Verse 28. *If there is no interpreter.* How does a person know if an interpreter is present? Members of a church family soon become aware of the various giftings in that body of believers. Also, if one is not sure, a brief sentence spoken forth, then a pause to see if an interpreter is present to give the interpretation, will answer the question. If the person insists that there is a message requiring interpretation, the leader of the meeting can simply ask publicly if anyone present can interpret.

Verse 29. Let two or three. As with tongues and interpretation, so also with prophecy. Once again Paul advocates the sharing of time, with no one person monopolizing the meeting. Prophecy is subject to judgment, discernment and the weighing of content, and it is most helpful for prophecies to be spaced so that any appropriate pastoral comments can be inserted. Fee suggests: "This does not mean that in any given gathering there must be a limit of only two or three prophecies. . . . Rather it means that there should not be more than three at a time before 'the others discern [what is said, is implied].'"[44]

The evaluation of prophecy is essential, for as George Montague observed: "No prophet can claim absolute authority for what he says, and there can be degrees of validity to prophetic speech."[45]

The term *prophets,* incidentally, is best understood in terms of "functional language"—that is, "similar to the use of 'interpreter' in v. 28, and [meaning], as in v. 3, 'the one who is prophesying.'"[46] This interpretation is borne out by a number of thoughtful commentators. In the light of the context of 1 Corinthians 14, it makes sense that the "prophets" referred to here (but not necessarily elsewhere) are simply those who prophesy.[47]

Verse 30. If a revelation is made. A revelation is initiated by God. It comes spontaneously as an immediate word of communication brought by the Holy Spirit.

Keep silent. When the Holy Spirit is moving, it is not unusual for a number of people to experience prophetic impressions. This does not mean, however, that such an experience justifies jumping up and taking over the meeting. Prophetic people tend to be fluent, so Paul urges them to recognize that others may also have something to say. Everyone should keep in mind that a person prophesies something revealed by God. Church members should not be sitting around trying to think up a message! We must learn to be quiet and listen to whatever the Lord brings through our brother or sister, being sensitive to the spirit of cooperation and sharing.

Sometimes a novice feels that a spiritual thought must be immediately communicated to the church, regardless of who is speaking or what is happening. The Holy Spirit is not quenched or frustrated if a person waits politely for the appropriate opportunity for expression. Prophets can feel impressed by the message they have to deliver, but they must also accept the importance and timeliness of someone else's contribution.

Verse 31. All . . . all . . . all. . . . Paul makes the point strongly that everyone has the opportunity to participate, learn and be exhorted.

Verse 32. Are subject. Paul establishes that prophecy in Christian churches should not be an out-of-control expression. The experience may be ecstatic in an inspirational sense, but the prophesying person can control the impulses (even of the Holy Spirit) and cooperate with the rest of the church toward orderly presentations. This does not mean we are void of emotion, but that our emotion is under control so that everyone can benefit from the contribution of the Holy Spirit.

In Spirit-filled churches there are both spiritual manifestations (such as the nine mentioned in 1 Corinthians 12) and human reactions to the moving of the Spirit (such as falling, laughing, crying, weakness). Human reactions can be either a blessing or a disturbance, depending on how the leadership handles them and whether the people cooperate. It is a shame to stamp out all human reactions, especially among people just coming to God; and it is good to see brothers and sisters moved on by the Holy Spirit, even if they act somewhat strangely. (Some of these reactions may typify their behavior at other events.) At the same time, if a person unwisely incorporates unusual reactions into his or her prophetic ministry, these personally edifying experiences may not be well received by the rest of the congregation.

Paul clearly wishes prophecy to be given in a straightforward, understandable way that does not draw undue attention to the person.[48]

No Women's Chattering in Church (verses 34–35)

Verse 34. Women keep silent. This reference to women's behavior in public services is included in Paul's discussion because controlling unseemly talk bears directly on his main theme of intelligibility and orderliness in church. Women were not to distract the services with their talking—that is, chattering. In those days (in Jewish synagogues as well as in Greek gatherings) women were usually confined to a side room or screened-off balcony where they could barely hear what was being said. To call out to their husbands or to each other in order to find out what was being said was disruptive, so Paul advised the women who did not understand everything to talk with their husbands at home. He was suggesting a solution that would accommodate the social custom of the day and still upgrade the women's education.

This verse does not mean women cannot speak, for in 1 Corinthians 11:5 Paul says that a woman can both pray and prophesy.

Summary with Authority (verses 36–40)

Verses 37–38. Paul closes the chapter with a demand that what he says be recognized as the Lord's commandment. The apostolic foundational teaching must not be tampered with. A test of a person's spirituality is how he or she responds to Paul's Spirit-derived directions.

Verses 39–40. Paul's conclusion should be understood by every church: All of us are to "desire earnestly" to prophesy. At the same time, no church is to forbid speaking in tongues. We must simply be sure everything is done in a proper and orderly manner. Paul has given us the most basic, workable approach for an orderly expression of spiritual language in the church service. He has also heartily endorsed personal spiritual language as a beneficial devotional expression to God.

In the next chapter I contend that prophecy was meant to continue throughout the Church age, and I attempt to address (and refute!) four key arguments of cessationism.

REFLECTIONS

I wish to submit that the languages spoken by people today who employ spiritual language under the enabling power of the Holy Spirit are all actual languages. I'm aware that a few instances of linguistic analysis conducted by experts who have scrutinized tapes of speakers in tongues have made such judgments as "gibberish," or, "This does not contain the usual structures of recognizable speech." But my own experience and that of many other pentecostals and charismatics I have met strongly argue against this laboratorial judgment.[49]

Jack Hayford

It does seem strange that in the face of well-documented evidence to the contrary, some investigators are still insisting that no one ever speaks in a tongue in a real language. Surely such a statement is unscientific! . . . Our friends will not accept documentation from those who have heard these real languages spoken, or who have spoken them themselves. They insist on tape recordings in order to satisfy "objectivity." So they attend meetings with recorders ready, or ask people to come and speak in tongues for the recording machine, searching vainly for a speaking that is recognizable by an objective group of listeners. Perhaps they are overlooking one very important question: If speaking in tongues is indeed the result of the direct guidance of the Holy Spirit, who is very much aware and present in the whole process, is he interested in providing them with the proof they are seeking?[50]

Dennis J. Bennett

The words [of prophecy] *should* be in the vernacular if the congregation was to be edified; but the inspiration *must* be immediately from the

Spirit, the words must be *given* from the Lord. Without rational speech there could be no edification; but without the (often non-rational) inspiration of the Spirit there could be no community, no body of Christ to edify.[51]

James D. G. Dunn

Those who tend to discount [speaking in tongues] as meaningful because of Paul's strong words against it in the assembly need to pay closer attention to his own determination to pray and praise in this way—and his thanksgiving for it. On the other side, those who have rediscovered this gift as a meaningful expression in their personal lives of devotion need to be especially conscious of the greater concern of this paragraph [1 Cor 14:13–19] that the gathered assembly be a time for the building up of others individually and the body as a whole.[52]

Gordon D. Fee

14

DID PROPHECY
CEASE—OR DOES
IT CONTINUE?

Concerning spiritual gifts, brethren, I do not want you to be ignorant.
1 Corinthians 12:1, NKJV

■ OVER THE YEARS scholars have attempted to establish sound principles and rules of interpretation to guide Bible students—a science and art we call hermeneutics. Generally these guidelines are helpful, but a biased rule or application produces a faulty theology and alters the perception of Bible truth.

A student approaching the Bible with an anti-supernatural hermeneutic, for instance, will automatically eliminate the supernatural elements of the Bible, including prophecy. Bultmann and other German theologians carried this approach to the extreme as they "demythologized" the New Testament. Its recorded miracles were not miracles at all, they argued, but merely symbolic stories. This liberal attitude has claimed many unfortunate disciples today.

A more subtle approach is used by some evangelical, ostensibly Bible-believing Christians. They freely accept the miracles and spiritual happenings of Bible days but say such events are not meant for today. This approach is still an anti-supernatural hermeneutic, merely in a different guise. The adherents of this view reject any possibility that miraculous Bible stories or teachings might find literal application or expression in our day. Thus they deftly eliminate the possibility of prophecy in today's Church.

We have already mentioned *cessationism,* the belief that prophecy and other spiritual gifts no longer exist and are no longer needed. This view purports that prophecy and other miraculous gifts ceased functioning once the New Testament was written.[1] The demise of prophecy was simply part of the disappearance of all spiritual gifts from the Church in the post-apostolic age. This position is stated by Charles C. Ryrie, a leading cessationist:

> The gift of prophecy included receiving a message directly from God through special revelation, being guided in declaring it to the people, and having it authenticated in some way by God Himself. The content of that message may have included telling the future (which is what we normally think of as prophesying), but it also included revelation from God concerning the present.
>
> This too was a gift limited in its need and use, for *it was needed during the writing of the New Testament and its usefulness ceased when the books were completed.* God's message then was contained in written form, and no new revelation was given in addition to the written record.[2]
>
> (emphasis added)

The cessationist faces a most difficult task: to prove from the Bible that prophecy and spiritual gifts ceased. The following four arguments are the ones most commonly used to substantiate cessationism:

1. The Bible teaches that the miraculous gifts of the Holy Spirit ceased when the original apostles died.
2. Such so-called prophecy becomes a substitute for or addition to apostolic teaching and Scripture.
3. Church history does not confirm the continuance of miraculous gifts.
4. Prophecy and spiritual manifestations are dangerous and to be avoided because they are easily exploited and misused.

Before answering these four arguments, let me pose an illustration.

If a person was marooned on a desert island and the only book he had was a Bible, the contents of which were unknown to him, what conclusions would he draw about Christ and the Church as he began to read? He would understand the great purpose of the coming of Jesus Christ and His death, burial and resurrection. From the gospels, Acts and the epistles he would gain a picture of the miracle-working power of God. He would also see that the miraculous ministry of Jesus in one small nation was then carried forth by the Church to reach all nations.

Would this new Bible reader find anything to indicate that the miracles and gifts of the Spirit ceased after the early Church?

Quite the contrary. Our reader would find lists of spiritual gifts and ministries scattered throughout the New Testament.[3] He would acknowledge the assumption of the apostles that the spiritual gifts were standard ministries in the Church. He would affirm statements like the one by Peter in Acts 2:39 about Gentiles: "The promise [of the Holy Spirit] is for you and your children, and for all who are far off, as many as the Lord our God shall call to Himself." Our friend would find no teaching about the cessation of prophecy anywhere in Scripture. This marvelous book filled with miraculous stories and statements would register only one thought in his mind: that the early Church believed in the miraculous and that miracles are normative in the lives of God's people today.

Once rescued and brought back to civilization, our friend would seek to find the church he had read about in the Bible. Instead he would find, to his amazement, that many Christians do not believe in the miraculous at all, while others conclude that signs and wonders were only for Bible days and not for modern believers. Although he had discovered on the island that Scripture teaches the existence of miracles and the gifts of the Spirit, he would find a strange situation: Many purport to revere the Bible but do not believe what it says. These people have a conviction based not on Scripture but on their own bereft experience.

Answer 1: The Bible Does Not Teach Cessationism

Five Scripture passages are used by prominent cessationists in their contention that the gift of prophecy no longer operates: Romans 15:18–19; 1 Corinthians 13:8–13; 2 Corinthians 12:12; Ephesians 2:20; Revelation 22:18–19.[4] We will look at each passage, then consider some brief, cogent thoughts about the meaning of the text that will set the tone for the rest of the book.

1. Romans 15:18–19 (NIV)

I will not venture to speak of anything except what Christ has accomplished through me in leading the Gentiles to obey God by what I have said and done—by the power of signs and miracles, through the power of the Spirit. So from Jerusalem all the way around to Illyricum, I have fully proclaimed the gospel of Christ.

Modern-day cessationists argue that the main purpose of miracles is to *authenticate the apostles as trustworthy authors* of holy Scripture. Once these authors wrote their material and died, goes the theory, miracles were no longer needed because there is no more Scripture to be written or authors to authenticate. The possibility of prophecy in today's Church is thereby eliminated.

A more immediate purpose for signs and wonders, however, is shown in the above text. The miracles authenticated the *message* of salvation through Jesus Christ, which Paul preached to the Gentiles. At that moment those heathen did not even know Paul would be a writer of New Testament books. It was the message that gripped their hearts—but only after the miraculous had gained their attention! We preach the very same message to the people of our day. Miracles are needed as much today as they were then.

The purpose of signs and wonders is scarcely mentioned in the New Testament. But a thoughtful examination of all possible references shows only two reasons for miracles: to authenticate the character of the Lord Jesus and His relationship with His heavenly Father; and to authenticate the message proclaimed about Him.[5]

2. 1 Corinthians 13:8–13

> Love never fails; but if there are gifts of prophecy, they will be done away; if there are tongues, they will cease; if there is knowledge, it will be done away. For we know in part, and we prophesy in part; but when the perfect[6] comes, the partial will be done away. When I was a child, I used to speak as a child, think as a child, reason as a child; when I became a man, I did away with childish things. For now we see in a mirror dimly, but then face to face; now I know in part, but then I shall know fully just as I also have been fully known. But now abide faith, hope, love, these three; but the greatest of these is love.

Everyone agrees that verse 10 of this chapter identifies prophecy and other gifts as temporary. The main issue is *when* these gifts will cease. The answer lies in the meaning of the phrase *when the perfect comes*. Various interpretations have been drawn from Paul's statement.

The meaning that came to my mind as I read this remarkable text for the first time remains unchanged more than fifty years later. I believe the coming of "the perfect" refers to the Second Coming of Christ, when we shall see the Lord "face to face."[7] Some cessationists agree with this interpretation but must then compensate by making the time of the cessation of prophecy an open question, to be decided on the basis of other passages.[8]

Other cessationists believe "the perfect" (or "perfection") refers to the New Testament writings that completed the canon of Scripture. Since the Church now possesses the full message of God—that is, the completed Bible—we no longer need prophecy.[9] But this position disregards the function of continuing prophecy as described in New Testament churches: for comfort, edification, exhortation and future prediction (1 Corinthians 14:3; Acts 11:28). The written scriptural record is complete but the activity of the Spirit in applying the principles of Scripture to our current needs continues just as it did in the early Church.

F. David Farnell feels that the most viable interpretation is to translate *to teleion* as "mature" or "complete" rather than "the perfect state."[10] He stresses the growing up of the collective Church of Christ during the Church age. This view is comprehensive enough to embrace the relative maturity implied by the illustration in verse 11, Farnell believes, as well as the absolute maturity depicted in verse 12.[11] Eventually, according to this position, we will arrive at complete maturity, but we are sufficiently mature enough now not to need prophecy and spiritual gifts.

This argument neglects Paul's strong teaching on the place of prophecy in the church program. Since he boldly includes prophecy with other doctrinal teachings (which are not ignored, incidentally, by the cessationists), we are not at liberty to cut and paste doctrines according to personal prejudices or to turn a cold shoulder to significant information.

Paul wanted no church of his day to be deficient in spiritual gifts. His comment to the Corinthians is significant. He did not want them to be "lacking in any gift, awaiting eagerly the revelation [the Second Coming] of our Lord Jesus Christ" (1 Corinthians 1:7). This indicates to me that all *charismata* can and will be in effect until the Second Coming of Christ.

3. 2 Corinthians 12:12 (NIV)

The things that mark an apostle—signs, wonders and miracles—were done among you with great perseverance.

Written in this way, the text does seem to say that signs and wonders authenticate the apostles. Jack Deere, however, casts reasonable doubt:

This translation . . . is inaccurate. A literal translation is, *"The signs of an apostle were performed among you in all endurance with signs and wonders and miracles."* In this passage Paul uses "sign" (Greek *semeion*) in two different ways. The first use of "sign" in the phrase "signs of an apostle" cannot refer to miracles, for then Paul would be saying that "the miracles of an apostle were done among you with signs and wonders and miracles." What would be the point of such a statement? Paul does not say that "the

235

signs of an apostle" are miracles, but rather that "the signs of an apostle" are accompanied by signs, wonders and miracles. If Paul had meant that the signs of his apostleship were signs and wonders and miracles, then he would have used a different construction in the Greek language.[12]

The vindications of Paul's apostleship were not his miracles but his suffering, his blameless life, his endless care of the churches and the many conversions among those to whom he preached (2 Corinthians 6:3–10; 11:22–33). The miracles authenticated not himself but the message he preached.

4. Ephesians 2:20

[The church] having been built upon the foundation of the apostles and prophets, Christ Jesus Himself being the corner stone.

Farnell says, "Once that foundation had been laid by those in the first century who possessed the gifts of apostleship and prophecy, no further need to relay the foundation by subsequent generations is implied."[13] The early apostles and prophets certainly set a solid theological foundation that does not need to be laid again. (We do not, for example, need to have the Scripture reinvented.) The LB says, "What a foundation you stand on now: the apostles and prophets."

The original theological and doctrinal foundation of the Christian Church was given by revelation and written through inspiration by the first-century apostles and prophets. Most commentators would agree. This was special and enduring revelation for the Church of all time.

The activity of the apostles and prophets, however, was broader in the early Church than writing the canon of Scripture. There were other apostles in the early Church in addition to the original Twelve, and there were prophets who wrote no Scripture. All these functioned according to the objective mentioned in Ephesians 4:11–13, the perfecting or maturing of the Church: "Till we all come in the unity of the faith, and of the knowledge of the Son of God, unto a perfect man, unto the measure of the stature of the fulness of Christ" (verse 13, KJV). The principle of apostles and prophets working together to establish the Church is illustrated in the appointment of a team of apostles, Paul and Barnabas (Acts 14:14), and prophets, Judas and Silas (Acts 15:22, 32), to bring the doctrinal verdict of the Jerusalem Council to the Gentile churches.

The theological foundation is truly set in place, but the growing, maturing body of Christ must have the ongoing fivefold ministries mentioned in this text to maintain the spirit and correctness of what was instituted in the first century. Ephesians was written at that time in history, but its spiritual agenda was expected to continue uninterrupted until the coming of Christ, which necessitated the continuation of those five ministries to hold, guide and govern the Church.

I cannot believe, after reading the clear operating procedure given for the Church in Ephesians 4:11–13, that Farnell is right when he says: "The gift of prophecy played a vital role in the foundational aspects of the church. With the church firmly established through the ministry of the first-century apostles and New Testament prophets, prophecy passed from the scene."[14] Are we to pay no heed to the essential, supernatural teachings of the early Church? Are we to write off the ministries and gifts that made the early Church great? God forbid!

5. Revelation 22:18–19

> I testify to everyone who hears the words of the prophecy of this book: if anyone adds to them, God shall add to him the plagues which are written in this book; and if anyone takes away from the words of the book of this prophecy, God shall take away his part from the tree of life and from the holy city, which are written in this book.

Robert L. Thomas, a strong cessationist, explains his viewpoint of these verses: "With the completion of the last book of the New Testament, the gift of prophecy became obsolete. . . . Since the Book of Revelation covers events occurring from the time John wrote it until the eternal state, any alleged prophecy subsequent to the book of Revelation is counterfeit."[15]

Prophecies given in first-century churches were never intended to be an addition to the Scripture. A prophetic utterance bringing comfort to a band of persecuted Christians was in no danger of replacing, superseding or being added to the Bible. Prophecy received by Timothy with the laying on of the hands of the presbytery was not equated with Scripture. Rather, these two examples illustrate the "now word" of encouragement inspired by the Spirit to help God's people at a specific time and place.

Let me use a personal illustration. My second daughter, Debbie, was soon to move with her family from San Jose, where we all lived, to another city in northern California. She wanted to be a teacher but had no credentials or even a college degree to meet the standards. Then David Schoch, a prophet of God, visited our church for prophetic presbytery meetings and told her with no explanation that she need not worry about having a teaching certificate. After moving, Debbie enrolled her children in the large Christian school there. The fascinating story is too long to tell here, but suffice it to say she did, in fact, become a very popular sixth-grade teacher, and then a third-grade teacher in that school. This unusual story is not meant to excuse a lack of education or to advocate hiring teachers without credentials, but to show that even in highly structured and standardized settings, it is possible for God to make exceptions for those qualified by Him. This remarkably gifted teacher had been given a prophetic word that not only gave her a glimpse of a future possibility, but it released in her the faith that enabled God to bring it to pass.

I do not put this prophetic word on a par with the eternal *logos* of God, of course, but affirm that the simple little prophecy was one hundred percent accurate and a remarkable assurance to Debbie.

Prophecy in the Church does not add to the Scripture but complements it and encourages the people. Three simple proofs confirm this:

- Prophecy is included in the listings of spiritual gifts in 1 Corinthians 12–14, indicating it would be part of the standard operation in a local church.
- Prophecy occurred in at least fourteen of the local churches mentioned in the New Testament (see chapter 10). "The charismata were present in every geographical area in which the church was found."[16] This obvious noncanonical use of prophecy in the ancient churches set a standard for the entire Church age and includes the churches of today.
- Three references in the New Testament about "judging" prophecy (see chapters 20 and 21) clearly indicate that prophecy in the churches did not compete with the canon of Scripture, either then or now.

Answer 2: Prophecy Complements Scripture

Cessationism assumes that the only purpose of biblical prophecy was to supply us with a "canonized" Scripture. Now, with the full canon given, we must assume prophecy is no longer needed. Some also feel that to affirm prophecy for today compromises the unique authority of the Bible, causing a shift from an objective confidence in Scripture to unreliable (or even deceptive) subjective experience.

Proponents of this view misunderstand the nature of prophecy that functioned in the early churches. Much prophesying took place to aid in daily living on a personal and practical level. (We discussed this thoroughly in chapter 10, so my comments here will be limited.) I agree with Michael Harper: "In the New Testament sense prophecy is concerned mainly with the domestic life of the Church."[17]

The text of both Testaments was inspired prophetically by God's Spirit. In addition, a unique, common prophetic ministry was taught and experienced in the New Testament that, because of possible fallibility, required testing and approval. Such prophecy, properly handled, is not just subjective but wonderfully edifying to the church body. Although it can be one hundred percent accurate, it is not considered canonical.

Later I will emphasize that prophecy, along with every other spiritual manifestation, is subject to and evaluated by the supreme standard: the canonized Scripture given by divine revelation to the prophets and apostles. The Bible text is exalted over local prophecy, which can never substitute for or add to apostolic doctrine and Scripture.

Personally, I do not want my theology to depend on experience rather than Scripture. The thought that a spiritual experience can alone validate itself is repugnant to me. Certainly personal experience is important, but prophecy is safeguarded by the sanctified biblical thinking of the rest of the local church—and above all by the written Word of God.

Answer 3: Historical Evidence Exists for Miraculous Gifts

This view has already been argued successfully elsewhere,[18] so I will content myself with continuing to scatter convincing illustrations of prophecy throughout this book as we proceed, and let Jack Deere strike forcefully at the heart of the cessationist argument:

> There is one basic reason why Bible-believing Christians do not believe in the miraculous gifts of the Spirit today. It is simply this: they have not seen them. Their tradition, of course, supports their lack of belief, but their tradition would have no chance of success if it were not coupled with their lack of *experience* of the miraculous. . . . No cessationist writer that I am aware of tries to make his case on Scripture alone. All of these writers appeal both to Scripture and to either present or past history to support their case. It often goes unnoticed that this appeal to history, either past or present, is actually an argument from *experience,* or better, an argument from the *lack of experience.*[19]

Answer 4: Proper Use Invalidates Misuse

Prophecy is sometimes misused, and the approach of a new millennium causes more doomsday prophets to arise.[20] But I like this positive attitude by Joseph Hogan: "As soon as we speak of prophets, people are immediately worried about false prophets. On the contrary, it seems to me that we should pray for prophecy! The problem now is an absence of prophets. It seems that the Holy Spirit is raising up prophets in our midst. We should be attentive. The community can judge the worth of prophecy after it happens, but let it happen first."[21]

Every thoughtful, responsible leader I know who believes in the gifts of the Spirit for today also believes that prophecy should be evaluated, tested and examined.[22] This is the strength and safeguard of the Church as false prophets proliferate in these last days. Let's reclaim the vibrant, positive belief in spiritual gifts and their operation that the early Christians had! They were confident that the same God who gave gifts to His children would give them adequate insight to exercise them. Gordon Fee wisely counsels that "the antidote for abuse is proper use."[23]

A Proper Perspective

It is encouraging to see material now appearing that treats spiritual gifts in a personal, positive way. A noticeable handicap that has confronted commentators in the past has been a lack of practical, personal experience. William Barclay, the brilliant Scottish Presbyterian scholar, confessed while commenting on prophecy in 1 Corinthians 14: "This chapter is very difficult to understand because it deals with a phenomenon which, for most of us, is outside our experience."[24] Dedicated scholarship will miss or overlook certain insights when denied the experience of the activity being discussed. Mark Cartledge brings out this very point in a thought-provoking article for *Themelios*:

> Usually the interpreter's understanding of what the NT has to say influences how the contemporary phenomenon is perceived. With the NT as a starting point, it is possible to beg the question with respect to *contemporary* experience. This is the danger that all interpreters face, and could succumb to. The lack of academic material inevitably contributes to this problem. The material which scholars present as relating to modern experience is often the better quality of popular literature, but nevertheless the selection is often small and possibly unrepresentative. If there is a central weakness in the scholarship considering this question, it lies on the contemporary side, in contrast to their NT discussion.[25]

My participation in prophetic activity during the past fifty years has been both joyful and educational. We do need the scholar's insight of the biblical text, but we must also have meaningful contemporary experience and pastoral application. Let's be wary of the dangers yet appreciative of the blessings, always watching that we do not push the experience beyond reasonable scriptural application. But please, do not shut the church doors on prophecy!

Prophecy did continue after the first apostles passed from the scene, but by approximately A.D. 260 the ominous force of institutionalization had snuffed out the prophetic flame in the mainline Church. How and why did this happen? Is it really necessary to sacrifice the prophetic dimension to ecclesiastical structure as a church becomes more formalized? This is our subject in the next chapter.

REFLECTIONS

C. S. Lewis, in his *Screwtape Letters,* once said that "there are two equal and opposite errors into which our race can fall about . . . devils. One is to disbelieve in their existence. The other is to believe, and to feel an excessive and unhealthy interest in them." We might say something similar to Christians today on the subject of claims to revelations from God: one is to disbelieve any such thing, while the other is to believe all such claims without exercising proper discernment.[26]

David Pytches

I have been enormously heartened by the fact that there are thousands of people who are sick of narrowness and churchiness, and who long for the fresh air of the New Testament. I am greatly encouraged too by the obvious fact that thousands of people deplore the spiritual loss that the church has plainly sustained since the days of Pentecost. There is I find a hunger—sometimes almost a desperate hunger to regain the shining certainties and revel in the freedom and power of the new-born church. . . . I am firmly of the opinion that so great is the longing for New Testament Christianity that it will be along this line that true spiritual revival will come.[27]

J. B. Phillips

. . . Our theologizing must stop paying mere lip service to the Spirit and recognize his crucial role in Pauline theology; and it means that the church must risk freeing the Spirit from being boxed into the creed and getting him back into the experienced life of the believer and the believing community.[28]

Gordon Fee

The prophetic gifts are not just an optional novelty for the super-spiritual; they are essential tools for effective functioning in pastoral, teaching, evangelistic or apostolic ministry.[29]

Rick Joyner

The gift of Prophecy is not to be discouraged, but is to be "earnestly desired." Paul makes it clear that the Corinthian problem . . . was not charismatic excuses, but misdirection and misuse of God's grace. Paul did not take either of the two extremes used in coping with this problem common today: (1) to suggest that the manifestation of certain gifts was evidence of high spiritual status or (2) to squelch all manifestations of the Spirit—to the contrary, he actually encouraged them.[30]

Jon Ruthven

15

WHEN BISHOPS
REPLACE PROPHETS

Are you so foolish? Having begun by the Spirit, are you now being perfected by the flesh?

Galatians 3:3

THIS CHAPTER ADDRESSES a process much considered and often repeated during Church history: institutionalization. Two Protestant ministers, one a Presbyterian and the other a Lutheran, open our discussion with some serious questions.

First, from Ernest Best: "There is a residual question for the Presbyterian [and every other Christian] who believes that his system of Church order reproduces that of the New Testament. . . . If there was an order of prophets in the first two centuries, why has it disappeared? If our pattern of ministry is the same as that of the first two centuries, should we not still possess it?"[1]

Second, from Larry Christenson: "Can free-flowing charismatic power live under the discipline of the church without losing its spiritual dynamic? Can a church rejoice in the free exercise of spiritual gifts and yet retain structure and order?"[2]

The institutionalizing of the early Church accompanied (perhaps even caused) the squeezing out and ultimate demise of prophecy and prophets. It is also probable that undisciplined and unrestrained prophecy forced the imposition of this ecclesiastical restriction and oversight. Why did institutional form conflict with charismatic freedom? Or, phrased differently, why have ecclesiastical authority and spiritual power clashed over and over throughout Church history?

Let's look at the pattern of change that occurs when a religious group institutionalizes. I define *institutionalization* as the process whereby the Church of Jesus Christ becomes an established, recognized organization, a structured and highly formalized institution, often at the expense of certain spiritual factors originally thought to be important.

Let me add Derek Tidball's definition: "It is the process by which the activities, values, experiences and relationships of the [religious] group become formalised and stabilised so that relatively predictable behaviour and more rigid organisational structures emerge. It is the name for the way in which free spontaneous and living [Church] movements become structured and inflexible."[3]

Although we will focus mainly on the Church of the first three centuries, this process tends to happen in all religious bodies—and it sends warning signals to us today. The basic answer we seek: Must the Church be a non-prophet organization?

The 25-Year Principle

The year was 1984 and I was talking with Marvin Rickard, a fellow pastor in San Jose. We were discussing a principle we had known in concept but now found to be active in our churches. Each of us was then in his twenty-fifth year of ministry in the area. Marvin had started with an existing church of about 120 people; I had started with just my family. After 25 years he had six thousand people, the largest church in town, and I had six hundred. We both pastored nondenominational congregations. Our traditions and beliefs in regard to denominationalism were similar: The local church, like those in New Testament times, was to be sovereign and self-governing, free from control by a religious organization. Both of our churches were thus proudly independent. Yet we shared the same dilemma.

Each of our two churches was succumbing to the insidious force of institutionalism. The sheer weight of structure maintenance and development seemed to be stifling the vitality that once had been the driving force of each congregation. Although we were dedicated, long-term pastors, we found it harder and harder to maintain our churches' love and devotion—although we had thought only the denominational churches experienced such things!

After some time our discussion ended. Marvin and I separated and went our ways, each to fight the growing menace as best he could.

There is a law of religion that seems as settled and proven as the natural law of gravity: A religious order that begins with an experience of the Holy Spirit, enthusiasm, sincere love, a burning message, effervescent vitality and crusading leaders will evolve, with the passing of time, into a settled organization with established rules and tenets of faith, maintaining its onward momentum more by its structure and set message than by the inspirational experience of its founders.

Usually this sociologically predisposed evolution occurs within about 25 years in a local church and involves several generations. With the passage of time the children and grandchildren of the founding families attempt to perform the impossible: perpetuate the message and belief system of their grandparents *without* the spiritual experience and dynamic that characterized the original movement.

As things and people change, as society advances, social evolution cannot but help affect the Christian community. Clifford Hill, a trained sociologist and minister, summarizes the process like this: "The first generation in any new movement is always the creative period, the second generation is the time of consolidation, whereas the third generation moves into a period of accommodation, *ie* conformity with prevailing norms and the establishment of harmonious relationships with other institutions that increase credibility."[4] Societal influences and the inevitable inner dynamics of a developing Christian community usually change the church from a Spirit-controlled and -inspired organism to a man-controlled, predictable organization.

No divine decree, however, says that restriction of form has to replace freedom of the Spirit. Christopher Forbes, who gives a good review of this subject, concludes, "There is nothing that can demonstrate *a priori* that prophecy is incompatible with growing institutionalism."[5]

Robeck suggests an ideal balance: "Ecclesiastical position or office without the accompanying charisma would seem to bring lifeless organization to the fore. On the other extreme, gifts exercised without proper ecclesiastical structure or order often lead to bedlam. The two, properly balanced, bring stability and growth to the Church as a whole."[6]

The Process of Aging

David Moberg identifies five stages in a church's development, which I have incorporated into the following outline:[7]

Moberg's Five Stages

1. *Incipient Organization*
   - Earliest days are a period of emergence.
   - Structures are relatively formless.
   - Life centers on strong new leadership.
   - This stage generates much collective excitement.
2. *Formal Organization*
   - Leadership attempts to impose greater sense of cohesion.
   - Leadership encourages commitment to the movement.
   - System of membership evolves.
   - Distinctives (ethical codes, religious practices) become more important.
3. *Maximum Efficiency*
   - There is decreased emotionalism, better response in recruitment, stability.
   - Leaders act more like statesmen.
   - Programs and committees are put into place.
4. *Institutional Phase*
   - Bureaucracy develops merely to advance its own interests.
   - Leadership is self-perpetuating.
   - Little spontaneity is found in worship.
   - Belief is in a creed merely as a relic of past ages.
   - Toleration reigns; organization no longer sees itself as distinctive.
5. *Disintegration or Decline*
   - The original vision is dead.
   - A reason for continuing no longer exists.

The process of institutionalization should not automatically be considered bad. No movement can function without structure, and it is naïve and incorrect to think it can. It is beneficial, moreover, to formalize and establish the belief system, activities, spiritual experiences and social relationships so that a reasonable predictability exists. Humans need framework.

Derek Tidball puts his finger on the problem: "Institutionalisation refers to structures . . . when they have ceased to function in the best interests of the movement they are supposedly serving."[8] In the case of the Church, the problem becomes apparent when the religious system develops and formalizes its structure *at the expense of the spiritual factors that Jesus and the founding apostles taught were essential*. Prophecy, meant to be a continuing part of the Church, is often the casualty of a formalizing religious organization.

The issue seems clearly focused: Is the Church really the Church *as Jesus meant it to be* or is it an evolved institution that merely displays a dazzling outer religious appearance while hiding a Spiritless, lifeless experience within? Inevitably, it seems, the organized Church gravitates toward spiritual deterioration like a moth drawn to a flame.

The Cycle of Deterioration

The study of the sociological cycle of church development is not a new endeavor, as Elmer L. Towns pointed out: "Ernst Troeltsch, a German theologian and philosopher, described the social forces of the sect-denominational paradigm over 150 years ago.[9] He indicated that sectarian churches grew into denominational churches, then deteriorated. He has been called the Grandfather of Sociology because of his observation and classification of the factors and dynamics that make up the outward institution of the Church."[10]

Towns, along with C. Peter Wagner, focused on the "postdenominational" church as the successful model in Christendom today. Since then Wagner has renamed this religious phenomenon "The New Apostolic Churches" and edited a book by that name featuring articles by eighteen leaders of such churches.[11] This model promotes apostolic-style leadership, weekly revival, spiritual gifts, indigenous independence (yet fellowship with other churches) and, rather than theological distinctives, an application of biblical principles to culture.[12] Wagner says, "I am sure we are seeing before our very eyes the most radical change in the way of doing church since the Protestant Reformation. . . . In virtually every region of the world, these new apostolic churches constitute the fastest-growing segment of Christianity."[13]

It seems once again that the cycle of deterioration has run its course and we are seeing the broadest, most far-reaching reaction against the institutionalized Church since the Reformation. Many if not most of these "new apostolic churches" believe in present-day prophecy, which further testifies to my thesis that contemporary prophecy is a vital force in church renewal.

Based on the style used by Towns in diagramming his concepts, I have concocted my own four-stage illustration of "The Cycle of Deterioration" that takes place in a religious movement or church. (Shown on the following page.)

Let's look at each of the four stages in this cycle.

1. An aggressive sect. The original leader or founder displays a rigid single-mindedness. He and the people are on a mission for God, reflected in their sacrificial service to the church. This is a period of revelation and inspiration. The first generation always displays exuberance and vitality. Prophetic leaders give birth to new churches as the contemporary Church lies in spiritual stagnation. Leaders of the new movement want to right the wrongs, purify the believers and release the true Church to fulfill her

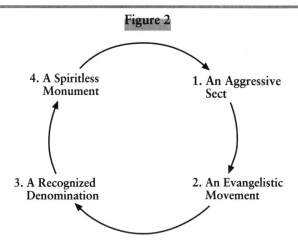

Figure 2

destiny in the world. Persecution rolls off the fledgling church members like water off a duck's back—in fact, it adds fuel to their fiery zeal. "The white heat of passion in the members' hearts drives these churches. As a result these churches [grow] in attendance, offering and membership."[14] The creative juices are flowing as everyone pitches in to launch the new congregation. It is a joyful experience and people aggressively invite their friends. Small wonder church growth experts say that church planting is one of the best ways to win souls!

2. An evangelistic movement. As time passes and the church grows, it continues in missionary zeal, maintains much vitality and retains doctrinal distinctives. It is a time of consolidation. But as the congregation becomes more structured, organized and acceptable in the community, the religious experience tends to become more rational, with less emphasis on spiritual gifts and the spontaneity of prophetic direction. "The original purpose of the church is retained," Towns says, "but an efficient administration keeps the church in motion."[15] Prophetic activity is a possibility but not a probability. During the first and second generations, the freshness and flexibility of new spiritual experience begin to settle and harden into the set form of religious tradition.

3. A recognized denomination. Usually at the beginning of this stage, numbers continue to grow because of organizational efficiency. The lack of spiritual dynamic, however, soon slows natural and spiritual growth. The church loses its drive and enthusiasm and there is an increased secular pull on its membership. The adherents settle into the comfortable, predictable structures of formalized religion and neglect the vitality of present religious experience.

Originally the group reached out to the responsive poor and gained followers, but now "redemption lift" settles in and the members (under the blessing of God) begin to prosper and forget their roots. It is a time of accommodation, a period of establishing harmonious relationships. If the church has spiritual manifestations, these are relegated to special, out-of-the-way times and places. The ministry depends more on academic training than on spiritual gifts and prayer. The prophetic voice is silenced by neglect.

4. A *Spiritless monument*. Finally the church stands as a mute monument to that which once was but no longer is. People do not know God as they did in the beginning. Missionary zeal is gone. If the Holy Spirit removed Himself from the property, the organization would carry on its program and none would recognize any difference. If the founders of the first church could pay a visit, they would see the same system that originally drove them out of their home church and forced them to start a new one.

David Watson says: "Often through the history of the church, the pattern has been the same: God breathes into his church fresh life by the renewing power of the Holy Spirit: man likes what he sees, organizes it, regiments it; and the patterns thereof continue for decades, if not for centuries, after the Spirit has quietly made his departure."[16]

New beginnings. At this point, by the providence of God and the hunger of sincere believers, the cycle begins again. Sincere, spiritual people—discouraged with the lackadaisical attitude of their church leaders—begin to pray and seek God. They start once again to experience the things of the Spirit. Conversions take place and the joy of the Lord sweeps into people's hearts. But, alas, the old wineskins are too dried and cracked to withstand the pressure of the fomenting new wine of the Spirit (Luke 5:37). Hungry people want to hear and believe the Bible. Sincere hearts want to experience the things of the Spirit. A wooden, outdated liturgy will not meet the needs of a restless new generation. Unless a church contends for the Spirit and the Word, there will eventually be an exodus of disenamored people who want to go on with God.

This does not mean every new religious movement or doctrine must be accepted without being tested. Every new surge of religious fervor, with its accompanying "revival phenomena," need not be embraced as authentic or appropriate. Like the Bereans of old, we must search things out in the Scripture to make sure they are genuine, and we must ever be open to the possibilities that the Spirit brings to us. Remember, none of us has yet seen all God can do!

The *Ecclesia*

The essence of the Church (Greek, *ecclesia*),[17] the special nature of the select group who followed Jesus, lay not in a formalized or heavily structured organization. Jesus founded an organism—a living fellowship of spiritual people in love with God and each other. They were a brother-hood, a *koinonia* of people sharing the love and lifestyle of Jesus of Nazareth. They were unified in purpose and called themselves the Body of Christ.[18]

The Spirit of Jesus filled this early Church, joining their hearts by mir-acle bonds of love. The same Spirit who had enshrouded Jesus with power baptized them as well. They carried on the mission begun by the One anointed to reach a single small nation. His followers, similarly endowed, now carry the message forth until all nations receive the witness. Jesus the Prophet has put His Spirit on each of them, and they now go to be God's voice to a lost world. They pick up His torch and run for their generation.

The *ecclesia*, the Body of Christ, was not an institution in early New Tes-tament times such as it became in later times. Transformed by a slow, steady and hence almost unnoticed process, it was eventually found bereft of Holy Spirit ministries and gifting. The *ecclesia* changed from a living organism filled with the Holy Spirit to a staid organization living on the memory of a bygone era, relying for its authority on ecclesiastical succession.

In the light of the above description, one might wonder at the neces-sity of even church buildings, let alone ecclesiastical structures! Jesus did not seem to need all those accessories. He traveled wherever He wanted and seemed bound to nothing—not even His own family.

When the Jesus People movement of the 1960s was taking place, many of those young people rebelled at the religious establishment and adopted what they perceived to be the right mode of the Christian Church: Be mobile, unconnected, unhampered by restraints and answerable only to Jesus. Some even baptized themselves to be free from any influence of the established Church.

Time has proven this approach wrong. Adherents of the early Church, our true model, quickly learned the benefits of gathering regularly under spiritual leadership.[19] They understood that the Church was not some house or building where they gathered; they themselves were the Church. *Ecclesia* has often (and rightly) been translated "called-out ones," but the meaning is as much "assembled together" as it is "called out." The term in nonbiblical Greek referred to the recognized citizenry of a town assem-bled for political purposes. In the Greek Old Testament (the Septuagint, a copy of the ancient Hebrew Scriptures in Greek for the Greek-speaking Jews), *ecclesia* translates the Hebrew word *qahal*, a word referring to the assembled people of God.[20]

The challenge lies before us as it did for the early Church: How can we gather responsibly under spiritual leadership, maintain reasonable guide-lines, structures, programs and properties and yet promote the spontaneity and liveliness of Holy Spirit activity and manifestations among us?

The First Three Centuries

The first three hundred years of the Christian era both fascinate and frustrate the student of Church history. Fascinate because of the imperial persecutions, colorful personalities, societal changes, religious heresies and the astounding transformation of the simple, richly gifted Church of Jesus into a religious institution. Frustrate because we lack information in many areas and must often second-guess the meanings and implications of the extant writings of the time.

The developing Church of this period faced certain problems unknown to us. Sluggish communication, transportation and lack of electronic gadgetry slowed things down immeasurably by our standards. Few people possessed a Bible manuscript, many were uneducated, many were slaves. The Holy Spirit was "not yet a topic of great theological discussion; consequently, the treatment of the Spirit in this period suffered from imperfect formulae and a lack of precise terminology."[21] In addition:

- The Church lived under constant threat from the Roman state.
- Other religions competed actively for the allegiance of the people.
- Secular philosophers challenged the validity of Christianity.
- Heresies broke out periodically within the Church itself.
- The doctrine of the divinity of Christ was not fully developed.
- The Church leadership was kept busy with local congregational problems.

It is reasonable to conclude that the gifts of the Spirit, including prophecy, remained important to the Church throughout the first and second centuries and even into the third. Ronald A. N. Kydd, in his careful analysis, records the references of the time to prophecy and spiritual gifts, offering this poignant conclusion: "These three centuries saw dramatic changes in the Christian Church. In the midst of all this, the gifts of the Spirit vanished. There came a point around A.D. 260 at which they no longer fitted in the highly organized, well-educated, wealthy, socially powerful Christian communities. The Church did not lose its soul, but it did lose these special moments when God broke into the lives of men and women."[22]

Since many of the extant writings of the first three centuries mention prophecy and spiritual gifts, I have included an abbreviated chart that shows where some of these references (particularly concerning prophecy) can be found. Prophecy, although declining, was clearly active in various forms. The Notes on p. 252 particularly reference the works of Bruce, Burgess, Kydd and Robeck—four capable, sympathetic scholars who have researched this material extensively and made thought-provoking comments.

Writings from the First Three Centuries

Author /Source	Date	Document and Reference
The Didache	90–100	*Didache* 10:7; 11:3–12; 12:1–5; 13:1–7; 15:1–2*
Ignatius	107–110	*Epistle to the Philadelphians 7; Letter to Polycarp 2; Letter to Ephesians 17; Letter to Smyrnaeans,* superscription†
Shepherd of Hermas	120–130	Book II, *Mandate* 11‡
Justin Martyr	155	*Dialogue with Trypho* 39; 82; 87; 89§
Montanism	172	Eusebius *Ecclesiastical History* 5.16.8–9; 5.18.5; 5.19.2; Epiphanius *Panarion* 48; Cyril of Jerusalem *Catechetical Lecture* 16:8**
Irenaeus of Lyons	185	*Against Heresies* 2.32.4; 3.24.1; 3.11.12; 4.7.3; 4.53.2; 5.6.1.††
Hippolytus	219	*The Refutation of All Heresies* 8.12; 9.22; 10.21; *Treatise on Christ and Antichrist* 2; 31; *The Apostolic Tradition* 1.1; 15; 35.2–3‡‡
Tertullian	200	*Against Marcion* 5, 8; *Concerning His Soul* 9.3; *Concerning Monogamy* 1.2; *Passion of Petua and Felicitas* 1; *Concerning Baptism* 20.5§§
Cyprian of Carthage	250	*Epistle* 1.5; 7.3,5,6; 7.3, 5, 6, 20; 8.4; 9.4; 14.1; 33:1, 4; 35; 44.4; 55:1; 62:1; 68.5, 10; 69.3; 72.23–24; 78.1,2; *Treatise* 7.19***
Origen	240	*Against Celsus* 1.2, 46; 7.9; *On First Principles* preface 3; 7.8†††

* See F. F. Bruce, *The Spreading Flame* (Grand Rapids: Eerdmans, 1973 reprint), pp. 214–216; Kydd, *Charismatic Gifts*, pp. 6–11; Burgess, *Spirit and the Church*, p. 21; Cecil M. Robeck Jr., "The Prophet in the *Didache*," *Paraclete* 18:1 (winter 1984), pp. 16–19.

† Bruce, *Spreading Flame*, p. 217; Robeck, "Authority," pp. 19–20; Burgess, *Spirit and the Church*, pp. 19–20; Kydd, *Charismatic Gifts*, pp. 14–18.

‡ Cecil M. Robeck Jr., "Prophecy in *The Shepherd of Hermas*," *Paraclete* 18:2 (spring 1984), pp. 12–17; Burgess, *Spirit and the Church*, pp. 22–24; Kydd, *Charismatic Gifts*, pp. 18–21; Bruce, *Spreading Flame*, p. 218.

§ Kydd, *Charismatic Gifts*, pp. 25–29; Burgess, *Spirit and the Church*, pp. 28–30.

** Cecil M. Robeck Jr., "Montanism: A Problematic Spirit Movement," *Paraclete* 15:3 (summer 1981), pp. 24–29; Kydd, *Charismatic Gifts*, pp. 31–36; Burgess, *Spirit and the Church*, pp. 49–53; Hans von Campenhausen, *Ecclesiastical Authority and Spiritual Power in the Church of the First Three Centuries* (Peabody: Hendrickson, 1997 reprint), pp. 181–182; Bruce, *Spreading Flame*, pp. 218–220.

†† Burgess, *Spirit and the Church*, pp. 58–62; Kydd, *Charismatic Gifts*, pp. 42–46.

‡‡ Cecil M. Robeck Jr. "Hippolytus on the Gift of Prophecy," *Paraclete* 17:3 (summer 1983), pp. 22–27; Burgess, *Spirit and the Church*, pp. 80–84; Kydd, *Charismatic Gifts*, pp. 57–60.

§§ Kydd, *Charismatic Gifts*, pp. 66–70; Burgess, *Spirit and the Church*, pp. 62–68.

*** Cecil M. Robeck Jr., "Visions and Prophecy in the Writings of Cyprian," *Paraclete* 16:3 (summer 1982), pp. 21–25; Burgess, *Spirit and the Church*, pp. 84–86; Kydd, *Charismatic Gifts*, pp. 70–74.

††† Cecil M. Robeck Jr., "Origen, Celsus, and Prophetic Utterance," *Paraclete* 11:1 (winter 1977), pp. 19–23; Burgess, *Spirit and the Church*, pp. 72–78; Kydd, *Charismatic Gifts*, pp. 75–81.

The Montanist Movement

The Montanist movement deserves special notice in that it represented the most significant manifestation of prophetism in the post-apostolic age. This influential movement eventually spread to all corners of the Greco-Roman world, bringing significant pressure on the mainline Church of the day. A significant achievement of Montanism was that in the first years of the third century it made a convert of one of the great thinkers of that day, Tertullian. His capable presentations broadcast the tenets of the movement throughout the Christian world.

In some ways Montanism resembled the charismatic movement of our day. History has an interesting way of repeating itself, and I think the lessons from the Montanists can be of great value in the renewal of today's Church. David E. Aune feels that "in general, Montanism should be viewed as a renewal movement within the second-century church. . . ."[23]

The Montanist movement had its beginnings in the latter part of the second century, about A.D. 172, in an obscure, mountainous area of Phrygia in Asia Minor. It took its name from its founder, Montanus. Von Campenhausen calls it "a volcanic revival movement,"[24] a spirited movement within Christianity that drew many people because of its sincere enthusiasm and claims to the supernatural. By the end of the second century it had reached the province of Africa.

Although it was later branded heretical, the Montanists were orthodox in their theology, agreeing in all essential points with the early Catholic Church.[25] The new movement was above all a prophetic movement that raised its voice against a worldly Church and an unspiritual leadership. It was the first major movement that demanded reform. Philip Schaff points out that Montanism was not originally a departure from the faith but a stressful emphasis on morality and discipline: "It was an excessive supernaturalism and puritanism against Gnostic rationalism and catholic laxity."[26] Montanists encouraged women in prophetic ministry, banned second marriages, exercised a stern and exacting standard of morality and discipline, courted martyrdom, believed that a literal millennium would begin shortly and that Jesus' Second Coming was near at hand.

The biggest controversy came in the area of spiritual gifts. Montanists claimed that the Holy Spirit (*Paraclete,* as in John's gospel) was now operative in their meetings. They affirmed the continuance of prophecy and that they were, in fact, experiencing true prophecy.[27] But the Montanists preferred to believe their prophets more than their bishops, which irritated the church leadership. Also, their tenet that spiritual gifts were available to all believers constituted a veiled threat, in that any layperson could use prophecy to challenge the lifestyle or teaching of the clergy. So critics

253

(some among the bishops) branded the prophecies as false because of a perceived lack of conscious control by the prophets.

Geoffrey W. Bromiley comments: "The element of new revelation seems in the last analysis to have been the main cause of offense in the church at large. No objection is raised against prophesying as such, only against an extravagant (and possibly pagan) style and then against the claim to be advancing new truth."[28]

It was a major test for the Church of the hour. That which apparently had begun as a genuine work of the Holy Spirit began to go astray and even become unscriptural. The bishops felt threatened by the new prophetic voice that did not seek their confirmation. The Montanists, for their side, refused to have their teaching tested and their prophets and prophetesses exorcised by unspiritual bishops, declaring their submission to God alone. All the leading bishops of Asia Minor finally declared against Montanism, despite some sympathy in the Western Church.[29]

Each side could have benefited much from the insights of the other. The manner of prophesying that occurred in the Montanist churches, for instance, could and should have been tempered and adjusted. The false concept of the New Jerusalem being set up in Pepuza, a town of Phrygia, should have been judged. The bishops in turn needed to accept the challenge to their worldliness and seek fresh spiritual renewal. Both sides should have remained one Church, seeking solutions with prayer and humility.

But the prophet and his oracles gave way to the bishop and his authority. The prophetic movement of the day, because of its unwillingness to submit, was ostracized from the rest of the Body of Christ. According to Clifford Hill: "If the bishops had been prepared to deal with the Montanists according to the teaching of the New Testament the split need never have occurred and prophetic revelation could have been not simply contained, but used to continue to pour spiritual life and energy into the church to counter the deadening effects of institutionalisation."[30]

Paul Tillich observes that the victory of the Christian Church over Montanism really resulted in loss:

> This loss is visible in four ways: (1) the canon was victorious against the possibility of new revelations. The solution of the Fourth Gospel that there will be new insights, always standing under the criticism of the Christ, was at least reduced in power and meaning. (2) The traditional hierarchy was confirmed against the prophetic spirit. This meant that the prophetic spirit was more or less excluded from the organized church and had to flee into sectarian movements. (3) Eschatology became less significant than it had

been in the apostolic age. The ecclesiastical establishment became much more important. The expectation of the end was reduced to an appeal to each individual to be prepared for his end which can come at any moment. The idea of an end of history was not important in the church after that. (4) The strict discipline of the Montanists was lost, giving way to a growing laxity in the church. Here again something happened which has frequently happened in the history of the church. Small groups arise with a strict discipline; they are regarded with suspicion by the church; they form themselves into larger churches; then they lose their original disciplinary power in themselves.[31]

The first three centuries, then, saw the gradual elimination of the prophetic and the accompanying ecclesiastical strengthening of the Church hierarchy. The following chart shows the process that increased ecclesiastical authority and diminished Holy Spirit power.

Becoming an Institution	
The Church Felt the Need to . . .	**With the Following Results:**
1. Withstand heresies • *to preserve the purity of faith.*	A canon was established, a dogma was assented to and Church office was strengthened.
2. Develop teachers and theologians • *to bring accurate and uniform inter-* *pretation of Scripture and creeds.*	A shift took place from the prophetic to the rational.
3. Install ecclesiarchal authority • *to safeguard the Church against fan-* *aticism, exclusivism and schism.*	Spiritual gifts became identified with office.

4. Ordain minister-priests
• *to allow recognition of and spiritual*
  endowment on certain pre-qualified,
  prescribed priests.
	A distinction was made between clergy and laity.

5. Perpetuate apostolic authority • *to keep the connection with the* *Church founders.*	Priest-bishops inherited the apostolic authority.

6. Unify and formalize worship
• *to lift the responsibility from the con-*
  gregation and shift the focus of wor-
  ship to the minister and sacramental
  objects and actions.
	The Church subtly became more "sophisticated."

7. Establish tradition and practice
• *to assure continuity and longevity*
  and to forestall any excesses or ex-
  tremes that might alienate the Church.
	A tragic loss of expectant faith took place.

Let's briefly explore each of these seven developments and their ramifications.

1. Withstanding Heresies

The young Church faced a formidable challenge, especially with the departure of her founding apostles. Paul had warned: "Be on guard for yourselves and for all the flock, among which the Holy Spirit has made you overseers, to shepherd the church of God which He purchased with His own blood. I know that after my departure savage wolves will come in among you, not sparing the flock; and from among your own selves men will arise, speaking perverse things, to draw away the disciples after them. Therefore be on the alert . . ." (Acts 20:28–31).

Two troublesome heretical movements during this period, Gnosticism and Marcionism, accelerated the formation of the New Testament canon. It was a time to define orthodox Christian faith. The Church saw the great need for a recognized collection of Christian documents to which it could appeal in refuting false doctrines and heresies. The purity of faith was at stake. Latourette says that "by at least the end of the second century a body of writings embracing a majority of the present twenty-seven was being regarded in the Catholic Church as the New Testament and was being placed alongside the Jewish scriptures."[32]

Gradually a basic dogma of belief was developed and Church office—referring to ministerial status, ecclesiastic authority, religious power—was strengthened. Some have said that the formation of the canon occurred because the time of revelation was past, but this idea has been thoroughly challenged by those who have studied the period, showing that prophecy and spiritual gifts were still functioning in the Church.[33] It would have been ideal if the Church had carefully maintained her enthusiasm and spiritual manifestations as she worked on the canon, dogma and Church office. Unfortunately, as in our day, some felt that to avoid wildfire it was necessary to eliminate all fire.

2. Developing Teachers and Theologians

Because accurate, uniform interpretation of Scripture and creeds was needed, an increasing emphasis was placed on developing teachers and theologians. This was an important requirement, of course, and continues to be. But our need for a rational approach to Christianity must be balanced with our need for spiritual revelation and inspiration. Academic and prophetic brothers and sisters should walk hand in hand, as in Antioch, where teachers and prophets worked together (Acts 13:1).

Thank God for the careful, meticulous approach of the researcher-teacher-theologian! Form, logic and consistency are his or her trademark. How the Church needs this, and how wonderful to have this fund of information on tap to be called forth as needed! Nothing can replace the clear exposition of the Scriptures for the instruction and edification of God's people.

Prophecy, in contrast, is uncomfortable with excessive constraints and cannot be put at the beck and call of ecclesiastical leaders. Prophetic oracles cannot be conscripted to time, place or form; they are not served up like hamburgers at a fast-food drive-in. Spontaneity and "givenness" is the very nature of prophecy—and it is as valuable to the Church as the predictability of teaching. Prophecy is the language of higher inspiration rather than of logical exposition and demonstration. It is the disclosure of the hidden counsel of God.

Both elements are essential for balance. But the fledgling Church leaders apparently felt a cap must be put on the prophetic fountain while they addressed present dangers. They must have felt that to allow prophetic activity would only add more problems.[34]

3. Installing Ecclesiarchal Authority

The sly introduction of ecclesiarchal authority (the investment of religious power in the ruling church leadership) allowed the key leaders to capture that authority for their own purposes, thereby eliminating the need for God's voice in prophetic form. An unspiritual, ungifted bureaucratic leadership arose that put out the gifted leadership. At this point prophetic gifts became identified with the offices of Church leadership, especially the bishops. Although the Holy Spirit was mentioned in prayers, the actual, dynamic, confirming Presence was gone. Unpredictable prophets were exchanged for the very predictable and reliable bishops.

If only the two had worked together! But spontaneity was exchanged for routine and religious practices became standardized. With the loss of messianic consciousness came the emergence of ecclesiastical rule.[35] Undoubtedly the increased ecclesiastical authority was thought to be a safeguard. Bishops were created to perpetuate a tradition. But the sacred Presence was sacrificed.

4. Ordaining Minister-Priests

Church order and ministry became sanctified through prescribed method and orders. The impartation or exercise of spiritual gifts became sacramentalized and routinized, thereby minimizing any prophetic activity. Prophecy must be exercised or it will be marginalized, and this is what

257

happened.[36] Ordered forms of ministry replaced unpredictable and enthusiastic ones. The rite of ordination now controlled the Spirit.[37] Leadership became more priestly than prophetic. This emphasis shifted ministry from every member of the Body of Christ to only certain "ordained" ones, giving birth to the clergy-laity division. As in ancient Israel, the priests overpowered the prophets. Standardization of practice, service and worship occurred. Creativity was stifled.

5. Perpetuating Apostolic Authority

To keep connection with her founders without "endangering" the Church by depending on unpredictable prophetic manifestation, the leadership decided to let the office inherit the apostolic authority, even if the man occupying the office lacked the power of the Spirit. Thus was the authority passed from one generation to another. Called "apostolic succession," it merely represented the passing on of a religious family business rather than the fresh impartation and call of the Holy Spirit. This sealed the demise of the ecstatic prophet.[38] It was the time of the sophistication of the Church and the domestication of the Spirit.

6. Unifying and Formalizing Worship

The responsibility for worship shifted increasingly from the people to the clergy. The focus of worship changed to the minister and to sacramental objects and actions. The greatest aid to maintaining spiritual gift activity in the Church—worship in Spirit and truth—was lifted from the congregation. In its place a more rigid, liturgical approach to worship allowed form and pattern to snuff out the spontaneity and givenness of prophecy. Personal participation was no longer extemporaneous and demonstrative. Sacramental unity replaced spiritual unity.

7. Establishing Tradition and Practice

These developments assured continuity and longevity and forestalled any excesses or extremes that might alienate the mainline Church from the secular community. At the same time believers experienced a tragic loss of expectant faith. Holy Spirit activity was quenched by abandoning the atmosphere of anticipation in which spiritual gifts flourish. The Church had become institutionalized in the sense that she no longer served God and the people in the manner originally planned. Even a shift in what constituted salvation (that is, the substitution of religious works for salvation by faith in Christ) had taken place.

Staying Spiritually Alive

The stifling of the prophetic move of the Spirit in the first three centuries is too tragic to be ignored. We can and must learn from the early Church's mistakes. Christians at the end of the twentieth century can maintain spiritual life in our churches and forestall the negative influences of institutionalization if we pursue the following nine suggestions. Remember, in natural bodies and the Church alike, life and health require vigilance and diligence. The Church, like any organization, requires attention to form and structure, but she also requires, like any organism, care for the maintenance of her life system and purpose for existence.[39]

1. Insist on Spirit-Filled Leadership

Everyone in the church should be urged—and expected—to be filled with the Holy Spirit (Ephesians 5:18). The following leaders considered it vital: Jesus (Luke 4:1; 24:49); Peter (Acts 4:8); the twelve disciples (Acts 6:2–3); Stephen (Acts 7:55); Paul (Acts 9:17); and Barnabas (Acts 11:24). Our leadership today, including bishops, must consider this a personal requirement. Nor is being filled with the Spirit something we should assume or take by faith; it is a tangible lifestyle marked by the power of the Spirit and the demonstration of spiritual gifts.

The word *filled* is conspicuous by its consistent appearance in Scripture, and it means we are to be crammed full, clear up to the top and even overflowing. All true leaders must demonstrate the fruit of the Spirit, and they must maintain a prophetic consciousness (an awareness of the Spirit's guidance)—even if they are not prophets. Leaders can lead people only when they themselves are led by the Lord. Leaders must be filled with the Holy Spirit!

Bishops (or any other title- or position-holder) must demonstrate spiritual gifts, and this means more than exercising natural administrative skills and bureaucratic activities. Leaders expectant in the Spirit—who walk in the Spirit, are led by the Spirit, bear the fruit of the Spirit, live by the Spirit and sow to the Spirit—will offset the inbred tendency to organize at the expense of the Spirit (Galatians 5:5, 16, 18, 22, 25; 6:8). If prophecy is to be promoted in the Church—and everyone, as we have seen, has the potential to prophesy on occasion—it is not inappropriate for us to expect our Church leaders to be prophetic. Such leaders must be careful to use and control the fire, not snuff it out.

2. Incorporate the Ministries of Apostle and Prophet

Paul indicated in Ephesians 4:11–13 that the fivefold leadership ministries are essential for the growth and development of the Church. But two of these ministries have been sadly neglected and unrecognized when they did exist: those of apostle and prophet. Their input and leadership are needed *now*. One important way we can offset the bad effects of institutionalization is to reinstate Spirit-filled, apostolic leaders consumed with the fulfillment of the Great Commission and the care of the churches. We can stop the creeping secularism in the Church by promoting once again the ministry of the prophet. Such a voice brings divine direction, challenges worldliness and inspires people to serve God. When prophecy is modeled properly, God's people will also minister prophetically, releasing edification, comfort and exhortation to the members of the congregation.

Genuine apostles and prophets are meant to be team players, not lone rangers. They must earn the trust of the people and then they will be followed. They can also be challenged to improve, change and cooperate. A church is bigger than any one person and cannot be fed and led by only one independent ministry.

3. Promote an Active Holy Spirit

Any church should live in the expectant faith that the supernatural will be evident and that spiritual gifts will flourish. This philosophy should be preached and taught, and also reflected in the church schedule and functions. I saw a church bulletin once that showed a very full schedule for the morning service. One small entry was asterisked with a footnoted explanation that at that point—barely a few seconds—everyone was to allow the Holy Spirit to speak to their hearts!

Holy Spirit activity is promoted not only by preaching but when each church member does things that allow the Spirit to work. Such activities as prayer, fasting, Bible reading and reaching out to the lost must be pursued by every member—and particularly the leadership. Everyone should maintain an openness to Holy Spirit manifestation and an *expectation* that it will happen. This attitude churchwide will keep at bay the forces that promote formality and organization and stifle the Spirit.

4. Seek Balance between Structure and Prophecy

Ecclesiastical structure goes hand in hand with charismatic expression. We have not an either-or choice but a both-and situation. Structure and liberty are not opposites but two vital ingredients that must both be present for the overall well-being of the Church. The leadership team of a local church should see the management of this balance as one of their primary jobs. Consistent, regular review is necessary, as well as quick follow-through on suggestions.

The seven deacons appointed in Acts 6 to administer a food program are an ideal example of believers given ecclesiastical position and authority by the laying on of the apostles' hands. Yet they were men "full of the Spirit and of wisdom" (verse 3) and demonstrated spiritual power in their lives. They took over a job performed originally by the apostles, but they were not to carry on a routine program; they were to maintain the apostolic spirit and function.

Every ministry in the church should seek to emulate these servants who did their duties while evidencing the power of the Spirit. Remember that one of the seven, Stephen, performed signs and wonders by the Spirit, preached the great sermon recorded in Acts 7 and died as the Church's first martyr. Although he accomplished his appointed tasks, he refused to be put into an organizational box that would stifle the work of the Holy Spirit. I think those first servants of the Church are meant to be role models for the rest of us.

5. Maintain a Strong Church Prayer Life

People arriving early at my home church find people praying around the altars and see this announcement on the projection screen in the sanctuary: *You have just entered a* HOUSE OF PRAYER *for all nations. Please come in and join us in the front or be seated. Feel free to pray individually until further instructions are given.*

Greeting people is important, of course, but beginning a worship service with prayer is vital. Sometimes we can be so concerned with church image and visitor friendliness that we forget what we are there for! Let everything be done appropriately and correctly, and everyone, including children and visitors, will profit.

Prayer should envelop our church services and activities. Prayer before, prayer during, prayer after. Concerts of prayer, meetings to pray, praying over people and requests, praying for the missionaries. Using every type and form of prayer possible, we should seek to fulfill Isaiah 56:7 (the "house of prayer" Scripture). Such prayer activity, especially when "in the Spirit" (Ephesians 6:18; see Jude 20), will keep the form and structure of our churches alive with the Spirit as we focus on Him.

6. Provide a Flexible Worship Structure

Our worship service should not be for spectator sport but for participation in experiencing God. A happy, reasonable casualness will allow worshipers to enjoy God and one another. Contemporary worship styles are presently having a major impact on churches everywhere. Heart worship is emphasized—a major way to keep churches from formalizing so much that the Spirit is hindered. When spiritual people worship together in unity, wonderful spiritual cleansing takes place.

The emphasis should be on worship, not just music. All types and styles should be utilized, especially the Davidic worship forms that involve the mouth (speaking, singing, shouting), the hands (lifting, playing instruments, clapping) and posture (standing, bowing, dancing).[40]

7. Encourage a Harvest Mentality

The Church is not a banking institution; it is a missionary enterprise. Church people should be seeking constantly to win their friends to the Lord and bring them to the house of God. Just as a business needs to advertise its products, we are the sales force of the Kingdom of God. Everyone is a missionary, regardless of where he or she lives. If the Church maintains a "harvest mentality"—a driving ambition to see souls saved and brought into the Church—we will experience yet another great deterrent to church death and help build the Kingdom of God.

If we tithe for the support of the local church and give above that for the extension of God's work at home and abroad, a great spirit of faith and liberality will be birthed and maintained in the Church. The spirit of joyful giving encourages faith and expectancy. The gifts of the Spirit work liberally among people who are generous in giving time, money and effort for world outreach.

8. Develop an "Every-Person" Ministry Concept

Everyone is important and part of the team. Those with technical skills that may not be classified by some as "spiritual" are nevertheless essential. The Church is like a racing shell—one of those long, narrow racing boats propelled by people pulling oars. Every church member, when functioning in the proper gifts and ministries (1 Corinthians 12), is pulling his or her oar. Today's Church needs a multitude of volunteers (not just paid staff members) who consider service to God and His Church a privilege, not an obligation. When a church is filled with people active in their ministries, worshiping God fervently, witnessing continuously and praying for the continual outpouring of the Holy Spirit, there is little danger of institutionalization. The prophetic ministry is at home in such an environment.

9. Define and Repeat the Mission Statement

Today's churches function best when they are purpose-driven—that is, fueled by a vision of what God is doing worldwide and what He wishes to do with a particular church. His vision is greater than for us to renew a church heritage of bygone days; it is for the principles and reality of the early, Bible-days Church to take place in the contemporary scene.

The story of why the Church exists needs to be told over and over, and it should be declared each time with fresh fervency of spirit so that new converts become imbued with the same driving ambition.

Conclusion

It is doubtful that a congregation that does these things will institutionalize. Such a church may be structured, excellent in its performance, even very sophisticated in its use of electronics and marketing techniques. But it will not lose its soul. Where the Holy Spirit is active, a church is alive. And an active Holy Spirit will soon manifest Himself in spiritual gifts, one of which is prophecy.

REFLECTIONS

The near ubiquity of prophecy . . . is impressive . . . . There is not a single instance [in the NT] in which the widespread phenomenon of the prophetic gifts is condemned or even questioned. It is regarded as part of the normal life.[41]

J. E. C. Welldon

If the gifts were lost in history, the most important question is not *whether* they were lost, but *why* they were lost. . . . it is possible that God never intended that these gifts should cease, but rather it is *the church* that has rejected these gifts. The loss of these gifts could be due to the rise of an ungifted bureaucratic leadership who put out gifted people.[42]

Jack Deere

Without support from the society, or at least from a group within it, prophets can find no permanent place within the social order and are likely to be regarded simply as sick individuals who must be cured or expelled.[43]

R. R. Wilson

It was the process of institutionalization, to which all new movements are subjected, that was the real cause of the disappearance of prophecy from the early church.[44]

Clifford Hill

Increasing institutionalization is the clearest mark of early catholicism—when church becomes increasingly identified with institution, when authority becomes increasingly coterminous with office, when a basic distinction between clergy and laity becomes increasingly self-evident, when grace becomes increasingly narrowed to well defined ritual acts. . . . Such features were absent from first generation Christianity . . . though in the second generation the picture was beginning to change.[45]

James D. G. Dunn

There is, in fact, an inevitable tension between the ordered forms of regular ministry and the more unpredictable and enthusiastic forms. It frequently happens that those who appreciate one form cannot abide the other.[46]

F. F. Bruce

PART 5

INSIGHTS FROM MODERN CHURCH HISTORY (A.D. 1830–1980)

EDWARD IRVING, MORNING STAR OF RENEWAL

". . . You shall receive the gift of the Holy Spirit. For the promise is for you and your children, and for all who are far off, as many as the Lord our God shall call to Himself."

Acts 2:38–39

HISTORY ABOUNDS with various revivalist or renewal movements seeking to return to the apostolic root system of the early Church. Three relatively recent movements stand out as interesting case studies for the subject of prophecy. More contemporary evangelical or charismatic groups could have been used as examples, but with these three sufficient time has passed to allow historical insights to develop:

- Edward Irving and the Catholic Apostolic Church (A.D. 1830)
- The Apostolic Church of Great Britain (A.D. 1916)
- The Latter Rain Movement (A.D. 1948)

Each of these evangelical groups was thoroughly devoted to Christ and the Bible and characterized by the ministry of prophecy in the local church, a belief in glossolalia and a belief in contemporary apostles and prophets.

267

These three renewal movements (in contrast to the larger Pentecostal and charismatic renewal movements) provide convenient windows for easier viewing of the blessings and problems connected with spiritual manifestations, particularly prophecy. Since these movements have each made a significant impact on the Christian world, viewing their strengths and weaknesses is a helpful exercise for today's churches. In this section, therefore, I will devote a chapter to each movement.

During my Christian experience of 57 years, I have been impressed by the followers and teachings of these three renewals, so my approach is both sympathetic and cautious. They are close enough to each other in history to have had some overlap, with each later renewal having opportunity to learn from its predecessor(s). They are like three segments of a connected time sequence.[1]

Thank God for people who have seen the need for the Church to experience renewal and return to Bible patterns! Although I may not agree with all they did and believed (I offer free advice for their problems from my armchair!), I sit as a sympathetic observer of these zealous Christians of yesteryear, identifying with their holy objectives. We can learn from them and, I hope, avoid some of the pitfalls that befell them.

Background of Edward Irving

In his biography *The Life of Edward Irving,* Arnold Dallimore makes this dramatic opening:

> Edward Irving was a Presbyterian minister who served in London from 1822 till his death in 1834.
>
> But he could also be termed a Pentecostal.
>
> That is, during his last five years his doctrinal position was virtually that of the Pentecostal body of today. He believed God was then granting a restoration of the Apostolic gifts, especially those of "tongues," "healing" and "prophecy", and his views were such that, although he preceded our day by a century and a half, he well deserves the recognition he has recently begun to receive: "The fore-runner of the Charismatic Movement".[2]

This controversial Church of Scotland minister, famous preacher and close friend of Carlyle, Coleridge and Lamb was a man of great piety, compassion and pulpit eloquence. He was born at Annan, Dumfries, studied at the University of Edinburgh, spent several years as a schoolmaster, then served three years as assistant to Dr. Thomas Chalmers at St. John's in Glasgow, where he had great influence among the poor in the slums.

In 1822 he was appointed minister of the Caledonian Church in Hatton Garden, London—possibly one of the lowest assignments a minister of that day could receive! "Little more than a chapel to the Caledonian Orphanage, [it] was in desperate plight. . . . Probably only a desperate church would have come to him in the first place."[3] Soon, however, Irving's dramatic sermons and magnetic personality had filled the chapel, and "two years to the month after Irving's first arrival in London, the foundation stone was laid for a church big enough to accommodate his new congregation [in Regent Square]."[4] Writes Larry Christenson: "High society and low flocked to hear the Scotsman preach, rather smitten than deterred by three-hour long services, and thundering denunciations of their irreligion and immorality."[5]

In 1826, through Irving's participation in a prophecy conference at Albury Park, he was stimulated to seek for and expect a restoration of spiritual gifts to the Church.[6] In 1828 "prayer groups were established to seek a new outpouring of the Holy Spirit, and many were led, by Irving's assistant, Alexander Scott, to seek the 'charismata' described in the NT as part of early Christian spirituality."[7]

Irving conducted preaching tours to Scotland in 1828, 1829 and 1830, which helped fan anticipation for spiritual manifestations.[8] "In early 1830 parishioners near Glasgow began to experience charismata, especially glossolalia, and understood these in light of Irving's analysis. A delegation from Albury [where the prophecy conference had taken place] was sent to investigate and concluded that the manifestations were indeed of divine origin."[9]

At this time, unfortunately, the London area general presbytery of the Church of Scotland challenged Irving concerning his views on the human nature of Christ—an indictment that cast a dark shadow over his ministry.[10] Meanwhile the reports of the appearance of the gifts of tongues and healing near Glasgow reached London, and Irving himself investigated. He was intrigued by what he discovered.

> Irving, in London, immediately began special prayer meetings with the sole object of receiving the gifts, especially the gift of tongues. The magnitude of the yearning was attested by the crowds in attendance at the 6:30 a.m. services. By July, 1831, tongues and interpretations had begun to occur. At first, Irving restrained them, but the illogical position of admitting that they were utterances inspired by the Holy Spirit and yet trying to restrain them became increasingly untenable. His decision to permit tongues in any service isolated his more sedate parishioners, who objected to the frequent disruptions during the Sunday morning sermon.[11]

269

Irving allowed women and men not properly ordained to speak out in tongues, interpretation and prophecy during the services. To put it another way, he "allowed public services to be interrupted by persons not members or licentiates of the church of Scotland."[12] For this he was censured by the London presbytery in 1832, then expelled from his own pulpit on April 26 of the same year. The trustees refused to deal with the substantive issue of the manifestations themselves—whether they were genuine or not—but moved against Irving on the purely technical grounds that he had allowed non-ordained persons to "minister" in the church building.[13]

On May 3, the day after the London presbytery rendered its guilty verdict, "the press celebrated the victory of the trustees with unanimous congratulations. Irving was everywhere dismissed with contempt."[14] The next day those who gathered for the early morning prayer meeting found the church doors locked against them. So eight hundred members proceeded to form the first congregation of what would later become the Catholic Apostolic Church, assembling in a large, remodeled picture gallery on Newman Street.

The sad story continues. Irving was defrocked as a clergyman in the Church of Scotland on March 13, 1833, "over a hair-splitting theological issue unrelated to the question of the charismata."[15] The biggest surprise, however, came from the local church. Returning to London after traveling in ministry, Irving found that the "Apostles and Prophets dominated the work, and they even reprimanded him for preaching when his ordination had been revoked. All authority rested with them and Irving had become little more than a servant, subject to their utterances and therefore to their commands."[16] Considering the newly emerging church a work of the Holy Spirit, Irving graciously, quietly accepted a subordinate position (to the astonishment of many) and rendered spiritual obedience to those who were his own children in the faith.

The problems continued. Irving's young son died. People in his church lost their faith. The doctrine of healing was challenged. He died soon after of pneumonia in Glasgow and was buried there in the cathedral crypt. Fittingly, perhaps ironically, the window over his tomb is of John the Baptist.

Some of the grandest compliments ever penned about a servant of God have been directed toward Edward Irving after his death—some by his critics. Surely this was one of the saddest and most challenging chapters in Church history. Yet as Larry Christenson points out in his gracious evaluation:

> A sober reading of the evidence, in the light of the Church's experience with the Pentecostal, and more recently with the charismatic movement, renders possible a new understanding of Irving's place in Church history: He was a man ahead of his time, pointing to things yet future for the great

body of the Church. He was a forerunner not only of the Catholic Apostolic Church in a direct sense, but of the entire Pentecostal phenomenon of the 20th century. The things he said and did, his emphases and concerns, largely rejected in his own day, have become commonplace in the Pentecostal and neo-Pentecostal movements of our time.[17]

Six Insights from the Catholic Apostolic Church

1. Christian churches should maintain a New Testament outlook, expecting a miraculous dimension in the congregational meetings. Irving was convinced that the Holy Spirit manifestations described in the Bible are rightly claimed by the contemporary Church. He saw no reason, so far as God is concerned, to believe in their cessation. A church that refuses to declare a Bible truth and contend for it will not possess it! If a congregation does not believe a spiritual resource is for them, they will not seek it. Every church body must face the issue of whether the charismatic phenomena of the New Testament are for today.

Writes Gordon Strachan: "[Irving] said that he could not see why the baptized Church should not still receive the complete gift of the Holy Spirit 'as it had been received by Jesus Christ when he ascended into glory and which was poured out upon his Church on the day of Pentecost' and why this gift should not still be in operation in the church 'in all the ways recorded in the book of Acts and the apostolic letters'. He could find no text in Scripture to the contrary."[18]

2. Patience and wise leadership are required during times of spiritual transition, requiring the full cooperation of the leadership and people. It is sad when church leaders, both locally and denominationally, cannot or will not sit down and discuss in a trusting manner the scriptural life of God's people. The Head of the Church is still Jesus, but church leaders often take to themselves undue authority, making decisions from their minds instead of from prayer-filled hearts.

The Church of Scotland need not have lost a praying church and one of her most ardent sons. Irving himself obviously needed wise counsel to handle the strange new developments in his church; his leaders failed him when he needed them most. Larry Christenson's advice is good for then and for now: "Church officials must recognize their own measure of responsibility for some of the unwholesome developments of the charismatic movement, *for they have in too many cases abdicated responsible and caring leadership.*"[19]

The media of that day, similar to our own, jumped at the opportunity to discredit the work of a man of God, and in a sense pushed the Church to wrong decisions. If only prayer and careful thinking had prevailed! The awful effect of gossip destroyed a godly man and split a church.

3. The goal of restoration should be uppermost in dealing with leaders who appear to be straying away. Religious people are sometimes more animated about preserving their perception of religion and doctrine than contending for "the faith that was once for all entrusted to the saints" (Jude 3, NIV). Prayer and communication should have prevailed. Irving violated no teachings of the Scottish Church. Sometimes the defrocking of a minister is motivated more by jealousy than by a sincere desire to help. In love elders and leaders should seek above all the care of God's people, the restoration of the fallen and the will of God.

4. A successful pastor should not automatically be disqualified from being a spiritual leader just because he does not possess certain spiritual gifts. At the same time a leader must lead, which means he must be able to interpret the dealings of God with the people. Irving's eloquent teaching and preaching about spiritual gifts created an atmosphere of receptivity, although "he himself never spoke in a 'tongue', or interpreted, or prophesied, or worked a miracle. He looked on and approved and perhaps allowed himself to become the victim of the extravagances of those who had gathered around him."[20] It was a difficult time in that none of the church leaders had the experience to guide the neophyte charismatics in their manifestations.

Writes George H. Williams: "The situation for Irving did, indeed, quickly assume tragic dimensions. He himself never spoke in tongues; but his inability to lead those who did cost him significant support and evoked the ridicule of the fashionable classes who had once thronged to hear him and the alienation of those whom at a spiritual distance he actually trusted."[21]

Irving's leadership was so easily dismissed that it violated the sanctity of his shepherdhood. Forgetting his great contributions and spirituality, those who possessed the gifts claimed the spiritual authority to reorganize the church and direct all aspects of church life. The man who had contended for the Spirit and opened the door for spiritual manifestations was silenced by his former followers in the name of the Spirit.

At the same time he himself needed to seek and experience that which he was allowing in his church. It is difficult for a man of intellectual prowess to humble his mind to the simple reception of the Spirit. Irving prayed and preached for the church to receive spiritual gifts and manifestations, yet his own faith was insufficient to bring to him what others were receiving. As Paul told Timothy, "The hard-working farmer ought to be the first to receive his share of the crops" (2 Timothy 2:6).

5. Strong pastoral leadership is required in dealing with spiritual manifestations. While Irving himself seems to have had great patience, it might have been more resignation to what would happen. He may not have perceived that as pastor he had the authority to correct and challenge. Irving's neglect in handling the spiritual manifestations in the congregation was probably his major error.

This neglect developed honestly, if unjustifiably. Irving had no models to follow in responding to the new spiritual manifestations, so he yielded his pastoral authority and responsibility—wrongly yet in genuine humility—to those who were spiritually gifted.

This mistake has been made many times in Church history, springing out of the immature belief that people are infallible in their exercise of the spiritual gifts. One of the great lessons (which seems to be relearned in every spiritual renewal) is that *gifting does not imply infallibility.* Pastoral ministry and responsibility take precedence over spiritual manifestation. Even if a leader is wrong in his evaluation, a church still benefits by obedience to his sincere directions.

The testing, evaluation and supervision of spiritual gifts is mandatory, and although Irving and some of his associates seem to have made investigation, they showed an almost spooky acceptance of whatever happened.[22] Later Pentecostal groups discovered that it is not necessary for people to interrupt the pastor frequently while he is preaching. Parishioners can be taught to cooperate with God and the rest of the church body. The timing of manifestations represents a proper balance between spontaneity and control.

True patience with maturing saints requires not passivity but the personal involvement of leaders who love the people yet are unafraid to challenge discrepancies, correct errors and work patiently to perfect a mature spiritual manifestation in public services.[23]

6. During times of renewal, people sometimes assume authoritative titles that are unwarranted and divisive. When Irving returned to his congregation, he found that his position as pastor had been superseded by those claiming the lofty titles of "apostle" and "prophet." Possibly the individuals claiming those titles had such potential, but the shortness of time that had passed indicates an undue infatuation with titles and a disregard for function and ethics. The man who had built a small problem church into a mighty force was no longer thought worthy of leading. The decision was apparently based on hurried prophetic utterances that should have been tested and evaluated in the light of all God had done.

Groups attempting to return to the practices and standards of the early Church invariably face the need for apostles and prophets. But the challenge of recognizing and appreciating such ministries has always been a problem. Some words of Jesus seem appropriate here:

> "You are not to be called rabbi (teacher), for One is your Teacher, and
> you are all brothers. And do not call any one [in the church] on earth father,

for you have one Father, Who is in heaven. And you must not be called masters (leaders), for you have one Master (Leader), the Christ. He who is greatest among you shall be your servant. Whoever exalts himself [with haughtiness and empty pride] shall be humbled (brought low); and whoever humbles himself—who has a modest opinion of himself and behaves accordingly—shall be raised to honor."

Matthew 23:8–12, Amplified

There is no question that the Church needs apostles (Ephesians 4:11), and various renewal groups have attempted to meet this need in various ways. The emerging Catholic Apostolic Church (CAC) believed that the unity of their church centered in the "college of the twelve apostles," men who gradually were appointed to that office. Since the CAC saw itself as a model more than a missionary organization, it displayed a virtual disregard for expanding or perpetuating itself as a body.[24] Accordingly the twelve apostles were not to be replaced, and neither were the priests they ordained. Gradually those apostles and priests died off and the church dwindled to insignificance.

Surely in the light of the development of the CAC, it would be well for us to consider the purpose of apostolic and prophetic ministries and how these ministries can be perpetuated and expanded. The evangelistic function of the CAC was apparently lost in the glory of a restored, sedate apostolate. They fulfilled divine destiny, they felt, by pursuing their course, so they had no regrets.

As the CAC matured, there was a noticeable moderation of the spiritual gifts. By 1847 John Cardale, one of the leading apostles, shared his concern about a "crisis of apathy" in the movement. This challenge initiated a renewed seeking of God and a crystallization of theology about the baptism with the Holy Spirit. The term that became formalized in the CAC was *sealing with the Holy Spirit*,[25] and this was to be received by the laying on of the apostles' hands.

The age-old problem of religious "cooling off" that has challenged every religious movement gradually came, it appears, to the Catholic Apostolic Church. As the movement became institutionalized, a gradual soft-pedaling of the charismatic manifestations took place. I pointed out in chapter 15 that the prophetic voice goes silent from neglect. The body was left without its dynamic life force, the Holy Spirit.

In view of historical developments, it seems apparent that God was indeed restoring spiritual gifts to the Church, but immaturity and reticence in both people and leadership, plus the harping and criticism of the media, caused the developing spirituality to be thwarted, even derailed. It was a tragic loss to the restoration process of the Church, yet an amazing "morning star" contribution to Church history. When the morning skies of modern Church history were void of any glimmer of light testifying to spiritual gifts and the prophetic voice, Edward Irving's ministry burst forth like a morning star of hope, a promise of better things to come.

REFLECTIONS

Irving and his church became important features of Pentecostal historiography as historical precedents were sought for revivals with emphasis on the charismata, especially glossolalia. It is evident from early periodical articles that the Irving phenomenon became an interpretative grid by which Pentecostal theologians came to understand and evaluate their own experience.[26]

D. D. Bundy

Read the lives of the Reformers, of the Puritans, of the covenanters, written by sound and zealous Protestants . . . and show me whether these writers hold it blasphemy to say that a man may be, and hath been gifted with both these gifts, especially that of prophecy?[27]

Edward Irving

Irving would have denied that . . . he was a rebel against the church, but he was always a sharp critic of its ways and manners. He did, however, believe that the structure of its life required change. He brought to sharp focus the question which faces us just as urgently to-day—how to reform the Church from within.[28]

H. C. Whitley

Irving taught that the outward gifts of the Spirit had generally ceased not because they were intended to be temporary, as the Reformers had taught, or because believing Christians had not received a second blessing in the gift of the Holy Spirit, as most Pentecostals were to teach, but simply because of a lack of faith, over the centuries. According to him, miraculous gifts and ministries would be received both by the church and individual members, if only there was faith.[29]

—from the final report of the Panel on Doctrine of the Church
of Scotland, 1974

The fact of the matter is that the name of Edward Irving, for all the notability which it enjoyed during his own lifetime, is today little more than a name to most students of church history, somewhat vaguely identified with speaking in tongues, prophecy, and other sundry fanaticisms.[30]

Larry Christenson

17

THE APOSTOLIC
CHURCH
OF GREAT BRITAIN

And He gave some . . . as prophets. . . .

Ephesians 4:11

THE FIRST ORGANIZED Pentecostal movement in Great Britain was the Apostolic Faith Church, out of which was formed the Apostolic Church of Great Britain in A.D. 1916.[1] Both churches are often overlooked by church historians, which is unfortunate because they were both effusive in the spiritual gifts, particularly prophecy, and influential worldwide.[2] The Apostolic Church today is the smallest of the mainline Pentecostal groups in Britain.

The founders were brothers Daniel Powell Williams and William Jones Williams. "Both were converted in the Welsh revival 1904–05. Early association was with the Apostolic Faith Church founded by W. O. Hutchinson (1864–1928) in Bournemouth in 1908. D. P. Williams entered the full-time ministry in 1911 and was called to be an apostle in 1913. Following disagreement with the Bournemouth parent body, the majority of the Welsh assemblies broke away at the end of 1915 to form the nucleus of the Apostolic Church."[3]

James E. Worsfold, Pentecostal historian, feels that "Hutchinson is most definitely the father of the twentieth century apostolic-type of Pentecostal movements in Great Britain. The Apostolic Faith Church, Bournemouth, the Apostolic church, Penygroes, and the United Apostolic Faith Church, London, all owe their introduction to the ministry apostolic to this valiant pioneer preacher who believed that God would restore the New Testament ministries and offices of apostle and prophet."[4]

As the Pentecostal revival gained momentum, prophetic utterance became more and more common, and certain ministers were publicly acknowledged as prophets. Some major decisions in church operation were made, and certain ministers sent as missionaries or placed in pastorates, through prophetic guidance.

The eventual split between the Apostolic Faith Church (AFC) and the Apostolic Church (AC) is a story too long to be told here, but we can say that certain issues became controversial enough to bring division: the reception and use of tithes and offerings; the leadership problem (in this case, the choice of apostolic leadership); Welsh national sentiment (centered on the use of the Welsh language); the particular way in which the Welsh were using prophecy to guide the affairs of the church; and the ominous foreboding of the first World War.[5]

Eight Insights from the Apostolic Church

Our concern in this chapter is the use of prophecy and prophets in the AC. Because these sincere, Spirit-filled Christians utilized prophecy in a remarkable way, they provide an interesting case study.[6] Here is a brief statement of eight helpful renewal principles that can be gleaned from this zealous, dedicated movement:

1. *The function and fulfillment of prophecy is a great blessing to a church.* The people of the AC, as well as of their parent organization, the AFC, considered prophecy a great blessing, and took great care not to miss any direction the Lord might bring. They felt God was speaking to them.

James E. Worsfold writes that "prophecy in the Apostolic Faith Church was recorded and transcribed by very many highly-skilled shorthand-writers, both men and women, members of the congregation. . . . Clearly without their work . . . there would have been no opportunity to see the extraordinary way in which so many prophecies were fulfilled."[7] The practice of scribes recording prophecy carried over into the AC and continued all the way into the 1970s.[8]

D. P. Williams, one of the founders of the AC, published an interesting treatise on the subject of prophecy in 1931 in which he clearly states their high esteem for prophetic ministry in the church: "If we are called

277

as an Apostolic Church to witness for some thing above another, we witness to the unassailable truth that we are a standing Body that is an evidence of the existence and value of the prophetic ministry."[9]

Another interesting quote by Williams is given by I. Howells: "In a witness to the prophetic manifestations which were new at the beginning of the century, Pastor D. P. Williams said: 'When prophecy began, after the 1904–5 revival, I asked myself if I could trust it or would it be seen to be only a rotten bridge. At the beginning I walked dubiously on the bridge, but there came the moment, after having proved the prophecy, that I could have jumped on the bridge! It was not rotten but safe'. His great faith in prophecy was a proved faith. And this was the experience of Paul in the early church."[10]

Worsfold gives this glowing comment: "Some of the prophecies coming through Jones Williams, in particular, had a profundity that can only be described as awesome. It must be said that under the ministry of the restored apostleship (especially that of D. P. Williams) the restored office and ministry of the NT prophet in the church matured and soon became a powerful, penetrating, spiritual force that was later felt around the world in the pioneering and developing years of the Apostolic Church."[11]

2. Prophecies are not infallible. It is essential to maintain the testing of prophecy and prophets. The dynamic nature of prophecy lends itself to an air of infallibility. In the excitement and rush of activity associated with the beginning of a new religious movement, the blessing of God is often interpreted to mean that all that is said and done is right. After all, would God be blessing us so much if what we are doing and believing is not right? In the beginning of the AFC, adherents kept a strong belief in prophetic infallibility. Three quotes from Worsfold bear this out:

"In this matter, the Apostolic Faith Church was in serious error in equating the interpretation of tongues and prophetic utterance with the Word of God and of also giving all utterance a life of its own."[12]

"The subject of the gifts of the Holy Ghost was carefully examined by Hutchinson [founder of the AFC]. His article on this subject must have been amongst the earliest published this century in Great Britain. He took the view that the gifts of the Holy Spirit cannot be contaminated by the human spirit. From this premise stemmed the once universal Pentecostal teaching that the operation of spiritual gifts is a one hundred percent supernatural exercise. This view is no longer general among classical Pentecostals as they have come to see that it actually denies the cooperation of man with God—denies that he is the Lord's instrument in manifesting spiritual phenomena."[13]

"Regrettably, Hutchinson-Dennis equated the prophetic words given in their movement with the Word of God. . . . It is to be regretted that the

Apostolic Faith Church failed to settle on biblical criteria to test the prophetic inspiration coming in their midst."[14]

While the AFC may in the beginning have regarded prophecy as infallible, John Hewitt questions whether this carried over into the AC. He pointed out to me that while great respect was given to prophetic utterance—people responding to the word, to the extent of traveling across the sea—there was always a sense of safety because the prophetic word was being tested by the apostleship. I. Howells makes this emphatic statement: "We do not believe in the infallibility of prophets and prophecy. . . . Allow me . . . [to quote] W. R. Thomas: 'Prophets are not infallible but rarely do true prophets make a mistake'. Nevertheless the possibility exists and for this reason prophecy must be judged."[15]

Prophetic movements tend to be so enraptured with the concepts of the apostolic and prophetic—and, of course, the exciting manifestations of the present move of the Spirit—that the balancing ministry of the teacher is lacking. In our day, happily, we have available the insightful research necessary to safeguard these attitudes. The differences and similarities between Old and New Testament prophets (see chapter 11) are now more clearly understood. Also, the infallibility of the Scripture given by prophecy is seen more clearly today as on a higher level than congregational prophecy, which is meant only to edify, comfort and exhort.[16]

We will address the subject of testing prophecy in chapter 20. But the fact that prophecy given in the early churches had to be evaluated should be argument enough that we must not assume prophetic infallibility. Sometimes a young movement feels it will compromise the divine authenticity of its message by subjecting its doctrine and prophetic activities to careful scrutiny. Actually just the opposite is true! An excellent statement by Cecil M. Robeck Jr. capsulates the attitude of the early Church about those who prophesied: "If they were willing to submit themselves to testing, they established their authority to speak, but if they were unwilling to submit to such testing, they were not to be given any credibility."[17]

3. Although prophecy is spontaneous and inspirational in nature, it nevertheless functions best in a congregational setting that has governmental order. In this area the Apostolics seemed to have learned an important truth, which was seriously neglected in the early days of the manifestations at Edward Irving's church in London (which we looked at in the last chapter).

W. A. C. Rowe's *One Lord One Faith* is an excellent book that gives great insight on the "doctrine as fundamentally and universally held by the Apostolic Church fellowship."[18] The subject of spiritual gifts, and the gift of prophecy in particular, is given strong emphasis and shows the wise approach that was sought in the proliferating congregations. One theme intertwined through the teaching is on the subject of order and control in the use of prophecy. In commenting on 1 Corinthians 14 Rowe says:

> All will be done in an orderly fashion. For instance, apart from an exceptional activity of divine sovereignty, it would not be expected that the Holy Spirit would operate the gift of Tongues, Interpretation, or Prophecy in such a manner as to break in upon another activity in the service which He Himself has inspired—say prayer or preaching. That would be an unwarranted intrusion and would tend to imply that the Holy Spirit was divided in His activities. Such a disorderly exercise generally happens because of limited knowledge or a lack of experience of knowing how to hold the focus of divine power while it is concentrating in the Gift deep down in the spirit of the believer in order to come forth later with greater richness of purpose.[19]

Every prophetic person and movement must face the necessity of governing the prophetic activity in public services. I am impressed with the wisdom with which W. A. C. Rowe instructs his fellow believers in the AC, such as: "Some uninformed opinions resist any suggestion of government or control in the sphere of prophecy. This has led to much fanaticism, which has marred the testimony of Holy Ghost movements throughout the world. There are principles for the government of Prophets and prophecy laid down in the Scriptures."[20]

Rowe stresses that there must be personal control by the individual; the governing of prophecy in local meetings by the elders; the subjection of one prophet to other prophets; and the overseeing of the whole church through apostolic responsibility.

4. Inquiring of the Lord through a prophet can produce many unwarranted problems in a church. There is a personal relationship between the believer and His Lord that should not be violated. Especially in seeking God's guidance we must be careful to wait on God first and let Him deal personally with us. The tendency in a prophetic movement, however, is for people to seek prophetic shortcuts in finding God's will. Unfortunately, fervent people sometimes spend large sums of money and travel far distances to "get a prophecy" if they feel they can ascertain God's will without having to wait.

One of the dangers of promoting the prophetic in a local church is that people will start gravitating toward those who will give them a prophetic word. This sort of pursuit should not be promoted, for the sake of all involved. It is best controlled by practical pastoral teaching. "The widespread use of the practice of inquiring of the Lord through a prophet," writes Worsfold, "began to be questioned after the Second World War. It was ultimately restricted to the apostleship and then only in reference to a very important spiritual matter."[21]

He also writes: "The practice of allowing the office of prophet to be used for nominations to local offices, e.g., as elders, deacons and deaconesses, became widespread in the AFC. This raised the ire of many who, while having a Pentecostal experience and attending house meetings to maintain fellowship, vehemently opposed having a prophecy used in this way."[22]

Since the 1940s the use of prophecy by the AFC for nominating local offices was gradually abandoned and these appointments were made by the apostleship. "Prophetical ministry through prophets often played an important role in arriving at a decision regarding a minister's location."[23] In August 1913 in the Bournemouth conference, Hutchinson was selected and put into office "through gifts of the Holy Ghost."[24] He "was the first Pentecostal leader in Great Britain to allow the ministry of prophecy to guide the affairs of the church. It was this use of prophecy that became the incalculable factor that set the stage for him to play chess, perhaps unconsciously, with the national leadership closest to him."[25]

A new movement in the first flush of enthusiasm and miraculous manifestation assumes that God will sovereignly overshadow and superintend everything. They may feel that "all we have to do is pray!" Alas, this has not proven to be so, and the AC gradually discovered that along with sensitivity to spiritual manifestation must come a sanctified, critical, analytical use of wise minds. Certainly there is biblical evidence that ministries in the early Church were identified and sent forth by prophecy.[26] This charismatic dimension, however, is balanced with evaluation, such as in selecting deacons,[27] or in determining the character qualifications that must exist in an elder candidate.[28] Also, many leaders now realize that much of prophetic direction does more confirming than providing brand-new, startling information.[29]

To the credit of the AC, their leadership gradually realized that prophecy was not necessary for every occasion. Yet the challenge remained: How to maintain Pentecostal fervor and manifestation without the excitement of the prophetic at every decision?

5. The appointment of specialized prophets to local, national or international spheres sets up an unnecessary tension between prophetic ministries. When the ministry of prophecy is legally categorized and assigned, there are two unfortunate ramifications. First, spontaneity of the Holy Spirit is greatly affected, even shutting the door on certain things the Spirit might wish to say at a given time through a given prophet—even if the time and place does not meet with human approval. Second, the prophets themselves, being human, are put into a position of comparison, favoritism or popularity, thereby allowing the church to consider some prophets of greater importance than others.

With the inauguration of the Constitution in 1937 a practice was formalized: "With the appropriate jurisdiction, a prophet was allowed the freedom to prophesy on any matter, including the life and work of ministers."[30]

When prophecy becomes too common and too inclusive within a church movement, the people will find cause to speak out. So it was in the early 1940s that "the Council decided to put some restraints on the function of prophets. It was thought, for instance, that prophets were nominating people for too wide a variety of ministries in the church, so it was agreed that apostles also should make appointments—for instance to the ministry of Sunday School teaching—rather than use the prophet calling."[31]

The general system worked well for about thirty years but by the 1950s became cause for severe criticism. Although the prophets themselves were becoming increasingly dissatisfied with being restricted to certain spheres, a change finally came when a Scottish prophet, Charles Forrest, declared in the General Council in 1951 that the hedges that the movement had built up around the prophets had to be torn down.

It was a controversial decision, but now the prophets were free to speak on any matter worldwide, although usually they restricted their prophesying to the meetings of which they were members.

6. A prophetic movement tends to gravitate from a renewal of spontaneity to a routine under ecclesiastical authority. It is both a blessing and a curse that the inherent nature of any religious movement or institution is to formalize or institutionalize. Efficiency and organization certainly help maintain standards and ensure a consistent image to both members and outsiders. But when well-defined doctrines and ecclesial procedures are set in place, the members gradually accept the resulting modicum of spiritual manifestations that take place. There is now an assurance, created by the rigid, formalized structure, that the ways and traditions of the founding fathers will not be violated.

Generally the effort to preserve the historic message and history of a movement tends to settle that movement into a hardening commitment that defies change. We looked at the cycle of deterioration in chapter 15 and saw that this formalism is the enemy of spontaneous prophetic activity. Unless church leadership continually crusades for a program that also includes the prophetic, that gift will gradually pass away.

It is probably true that the AC originally had too much confidence in the prophetic, hardly making a move without prophetic confirmation. The prophets were sometimes accorded an infallible status by some of the people because of the freshness of the experience and the fear of quenching the Spirit or missing God. Now, however, "Present day prophets are not infallible."[32]

282

The pendulum has tended to swing to the opposite extreme, away from an open prophetism. The devotion and allegiance given the original eleven tenets of faith (see endnote #6 of this chapter) has transferred over to include the methodologies gradually introduced through the years. As in most movements, the methods gradually assume the claim to infallibility once reserved only for the prophetic.

Part of the problem connected with institutionalizing is the difficulty the original leaders have in sharing leadership. Others must be called and assume responsibility, and this usually involves more transfer of information and natural management skills than prophetic gifting. So one day the organization wakes up and wonders, "What happened to the Ark of His Presence"?[33] The community of the Spirit has successfully become the Organization of Human Endeavor.

7. A prophet tends to settle for the manifestation of the gift of prophecy rather than maintain the higher level associated with the ministry of prophet. Connecting with the process of institutionalization would be the change in the prophet himself. Not wishing to break rules, offend leadership or be spiritually presumptuous, the cooperative prophet finds that the original high level of prophetism is easily exchanged for a watered-down version of simple prophecy that any believer should be capable of delivering. I found this comment by Worsfold very interesting: "It is the observation of this writer that since the 1950s the function of the prophet in the Apostolic Church around the world has, in many instances, settled for a manifestation of the gift of prophecy. It would have needed in this movement a minister (who was also recognized as a prophet) to receive a charism of exceptional spiritual boldness to rise to the level of prophetic ministry that was given in the first twenty years of the movement's life."[34]

8. Religious movements should learn lessons from the movements that precede them historically and be willing to relate to the new order with fresh insights and vitality. The Apostolic Church came 86 years after Edward Irving entered Church history, and the AC began some 32 years before the Latter Rain Movement. All three movements emphasized prophecy and believed in prophets. In a sense these three groups looped the rope of Scripture around the Church to pull her out of her quagmire of unbelief. With great effort and prayer—and in spite of many mistakes and problems—they have successfully restored to the Church universal, with the help of others, the awareness of the need for spiritual gifts in today's churches.

I find this comment on Edward Irving and his associates offered by D. P. Williams, founder of the Apostolic Church, both interesting and insightful. Living so close to Irving's time lends weight to his comments and indicates Williams' efforts to learn from the past.

> It is said that Edward Irving, who became the prominent figure of the movement, was of a most noble character, holy and faithful in his unwearied labour, and has never been surpassed in zeal. The gifts of the Holy Ghost were publicly manifested in his Church. The writer of this booklet has been confirmed by, and has found many lessons in, the history of his labour that are of great benefit. That there were impulsive actions and a lawless spirit in those that had the prophetic utterances is, unfortunately, clear from his accounts. The channels were not submissive, and acted disorderly in the meetings, created excitement under the Power, not holding themselves in steadiness and quietness. This led to much confusion. The operation of the Gifts in the Church are supposed to work in a Divine solemnity, decently and in order, and because of the unmannerly and self-important activities of many that are blessed, it has brought reproach on the work of God, and the cause has suffered.[35]

Fortunately Williams could learn from Edwards, but this did not adequately prepare the AC for the new move that came on the scene in 1948, the Latter Rain Movement, with its fresh emphasis on the prophetic. That movement swept through the United States and Canada and made an impact in Europe as well. The AC as a religious body unfortunately did not welcome the renewal with its emphasis on prophecy. Worsfold comments:

"The Apostolic Church in Britain simply rode out the storm of 'Latter Rain' rather than taking the opportunity to introduce reforms. This state of affairs lasted at least another ten years. Being 'Apostolic' simply continued to mean believing certain doctrines, doing certain things in a certain ordered way, and supporting the centralized system of administration in matters of government, finance and property."

This next statement by Worsfold seems significant:

"A careful reading of the literature available to this writer about the Apostolic church and the 'Latter Rain' highlights one thing above all: that if church leadership and congregations do not remain open to God and His sovereign will, they run the risk of acting as pious conservatives, and will, in the end, sit down to a banquet of consequences. Self-preservationists often lean towards opting for comfort while reformers seek (through spiritual renewal) to initiate changes which often result in challenges to the status quo."[36]

I hope the historical review and prophetic insights of the past two chapters have been helpful. Next we will review one of the most controversial prophetic movements of all time: the so-called "Latter Rain movement." A living contemporary of (but not part of) that movement will be discussed: the mystical prophet-healer William Marrion Branham. Again, insights will be drawn to help us in our quest for prophetic balance in the Church.

REFLECTIONS

Prophecy is not restricted to a few men and women in primitive Christianity. . . . It is a specific mark of the age of fulfillment that the Spirit does not only lay hold of individuals, but that all members of the eschatological community without distinction are called to prophesy.[37]

Gerhard Friedrich

The New Testament balance that all can prophesy, yet some are called to be prophets, needs to be kept in view today. The mantle of prophecy on one person does not preclude other believers from exercising a gift of prophecy. In fact, it is the free access of all to prophesy which confirms the ability of any particular prophet.[38]

George Mallone

The prophet can err. Therefore he or she must be open to correction by the rest of the Body. True prophets are willing for this. They want their words to be tested, and when they are wrong they will admit it. They want their prophecies to be confirmed by the Word of God and by the body as a whole.[39]

C. Peter Wagner

A view of the gifts of the Spirit contained in a slogan that they are "a hundred per cent miraculous" has obtained considerable acceptance in some quarters. We are told that "there is no element of the natural in them at all." This is the pardonable language of enthusiasm for enforcing the truth that there is a supernatural element in spiritual gifts, and we can respect it as such. But it will not do as a statement to cover all the facts. We need a more balanced view. If we do not achieve it we shall perpetuate the extremes that have marred the Pentecostal testimony from its beginning. Indeed, in that way lies considerable danger.[40]

Donald Gee

18

THE LATTER RAIN
MOVEMENT

Remember ye not the former things, neither consider the things of old. Behold, I will do a new thing; now it shall spring forth; shall ye not know it? I will even make a way in the wilderness, and rivers in the desert.

Isaiah 43:18–19 (KJV)

I SAT WITH A GROUP of fellow ministers in the large meeting hall at the Santa Clara County Fairgrounds in San Jose, California. I was in my late twenties, a young pastor newly arrived in San Jose in 1959 to start a church. We ministers were cooperating in an area-wide meeting with one of the most famous traveling ministers of the day, William Marrion Branham. His fame in Pentecostal circles was phenomenal. He was known as a man with a ministry of healing and the ability to "call out" the circumstances and diseases of people he had never met. Many considered him a prophet. The atmosphere of the meeting was charged with expectancy.

Sitting in the front row of the ministers on the platform, directly behind the speaker, I had direct exposure to one of the most amazing religious meetings of my life.

William Branham was an uneducated country Baptist minister. He did not speak well and his messages were not always as clear as they might be. But in spite of these shortcomings, he seemed to convey the dynamic presence of God, especially when he ministered to people.

At one point Branham pointed to three people in the third row near the middle aisle—a father, mother and grown daughter. The girl looked extremely ill. Branham told us who they were and of their battle with a terrible disease. The young woman was barely sustained, he said, by the large amounts of drugs that her pharmacist father supplied her. Standing before several thousand people, the three wept copiously for the accuracy of the prophetic word and the joy of the announced healing. It was awesome!

When the series of meetings was over, we pastors were given the follow-up names of people who had received ministry. I went out to visit my assigned families, not realizing whom I would be calling on but filled with confidence and anticipating success. To my surprise, at one home the pharmacist opened the door. Inside I was introduced to the two other people who had received Branham's prophetic words so joyfully.

Immediately I knew something was wrong. Like waters gushing from a broken dam, their story poured forth from anguished hearts. They had abruptly stopped the prescribed medications and testified to family and friends of the healing. But the girl was not healed. They felt shocked by the absence of a miracle and shamed before the community.

Nothing I could say helped. A bitter disillusionment possessed these dear people and they declared their abhorrence of all that had happened. I left discouraged, disappointed and disillusioned myself.

Now, some 40 years later, I am still numb telling the story. The accuracy with which Branham described the situation had been uncanny, yet his faith for the healing—or the manner in which the public announcement about the healing had been made—was certainly faulty. This traumatic experience launched me on a personal quest to understand better the reality of spiritual manifestations and their importance for today's Church.

I am an advocate of spiritual gifts and prophecy. Why, then, talk of failure, especially since thousands testified of miraculous signs and miracles during Branham's ministry, and multitudes were converted to Christ? The simple fact is, prophets and prophecies can fail or be wrong. Religious leaders can make mistakes or even be misled. This is a fact of life we must live with, but it does not invalidate the Word of God. In spite of stories like the above, I find myself an even stronger (although wiser) advocate of God speaking in our day.

There are reasons such tragedies occur, and our all-too-brief study in Parts 5 and 6 of this book will, I hope, make some of the reasons clear. We must learn from the strengths and weaknesses of those who have pioneered in the restoration of spiritual gifts.

William Branham, part of the healing movement of the mid-twentieth-century awakening, represents a legendary figure in American Pentecostalism, known worldwide as a preacher and healer and prophet.[1] The above story occurred as his successful ministry was beginning to wane. Unknown to me at the time, many things were not going well for him and confusion was settling into his troubled life. I am convinced God used Branham in a remarkable way during his early years, but I also feel some of his beliefs, teachings and announcements were completely unjustified. The present-day cult that has sprung up around some of his bizarre ideas is lamentable. Branham is considered by many the initiator and pacesetter of the healing revivals of 1947, as well as the precursor of the entirely separate Latter Rain movement of 1948.

In this chapter, as in the last two previous chapters, we will consider helpful insights about prophecy and prophets from the Latter Rain movement and also from the life of William Branham. First, an overview of religious awakenings in this century and a brief sketch of Latter Rain history.

Overview of Twentieth-Century Revivals

"In the Twentieth Century there have been at least three major re-awakenings of Christian faith in North America."[2] This is the opening sentence of Richard M. Riss' book on twentieth-century revival movements. His approach may seem simplistic, but its accurate overview provides a convenient framework for my brief discussion of prophecy. All three of these renewal periods demonstrated Pentecostal and non-Pentecostal components. Some of the more popular figures and events are well known, but there were also many lesser-known figures and events whose impact was tremendous.

My focus is on prophecy and spiritual gifts, so the discussion of this intensely interesting period of Church history is unfortunately limited. Having lived through the last two periods, I can assure you that God was moving in many wonderful ways!

The three periods of evangelical reawakening in North America:

- The first great reawakening, 1905–1906
- The mid-century awakening, 1947-1952
- The revival of the 1960s and '70s

The first great reawakening of the Spirit in North America during this century was the Pentecostal movement, which originated with the 1906 Azusa Street revival in Los Angeles.[3] The well-known 1904 Welsh revival had reached worldwide proportions by 1905, and Pentecostalism was part of the resulting spiritual chain reaction that awakened multitudes in the United States and abroad. "Pentecostalism," observes Richard Riss, "eventually became one of the most potent and numerically significant Christian movements of the twentieth century."[4] This movement brought back to the Church a strong emphasis on the activity of the Holy Spirit and spiritual gifts, and it brought into existence hundreds of religious organizations and denominations worldwide. Many of these groups have become some of the fastest-growing religious bodies in the world.

The second great reawakening is not so clearly defined as the first. This mid-century revival, occurring shortly after the close of the second World War, saw the rise to prominence of such evangelists as Billy Graham and Oral Roberts. It had its beginnings among the Pentecostals with the healing and Latter Rain movements in 1947 and 1948. This whole period could be described as the confluence of several religious rivers—evangelical evangelism, Pentecostal mass healing revivals and the uniquely prophetic Latter Rain movement.[5] These concurrent activities yielded a tremendous number of conversions and reawakenings throughout America and the entire world.

The third reawakening occurred in the 1960s and early '70s as three new expressions of God's grace appeared:

- *The charismatic renewal,* breaking on the religious scene with mighty force and invading the mainline denominations
- *The Jesus movement,* originating in San Francisco and bringing Christ to untold numbers of young adults, who in turn brought a fresh, new approach to staid Christianity
- *Evangelicalism,* making a noticeable impact on American life through campus revivals, Campus Crusade and great evangelistic crusades

Now we turn our focus to the Latter Rain movement, an unusual awakening of the mid–twentieth century that placed a heavy emphasis on prophecy and spiritual gifts.

A Great Visitation of the Spirit

Like the stable at Bethlehem, the small orphanage and agricultural Bible college in North Battleford, Saskatchewan, Canada, called "Sharon Orphanage and Schools," set the stage for the humble beginnings of a spiritual movement that would reach around the world. Many Pentecostal groups in the late 1940s had a great hunger to see God revive His people, and Sharon was one of the places where leaders and people alike were deeply serious about a divine visitation and the restoration of spiritual gifts. The pastors and teachers associated with the work at Sharon included two brothers, George and Ern Hawtin, along with P. G. Hunt, Herrick Holt and George Hawtin's brother-in-law, Milford Kirkpatrick.

The arrival on the American religious scene of a hitherto-unknown healing evangelist by the name of William Branham brought a new surge of hope and life to the stalemated Pentecostal movement. Claiming angelic visitations (the first on May 7, 1946), miraculous healings and the power to discern people's illnesses and thoughts, Branham was soon filling the biggest auditoriums in the United States. Outstanding healings and conversions were reported. Branham's method of laying hands on the sick for healing was innovative and criticized by some. David Harrell makes this comment: "The power of a Branham service . . . remains a legend unparalleled in the history of the charismatic movement."[6]

Finally Branham came to Vancouver, British Columbia. Some of the leaders at Sharon were so impressed by the reports of Branham's meetings that they decided to make the long trip and see for themselves. Richard M. Riss, quoting from several sources, describes the Vancouver meetings:

> During the first of a series of meetings in Vancouver, B. C., in the fall of 1947, W. J. Ern Baxter began ministering with Branham, continuing from four to eight months during every year for a period of six years. According to historian David Edwin Harrell, Jr., Branham's campaign in the Pacific Northwest, beginning in Vancouver that fall, "was a stirring success." According to Gordon Lindsay, "In 14 days of services in 4 cities, with only a modest amount of advertising, some 70,000 people attended." During that time, Ern Baxter said that he never saw Branham's discernment miss once. According to James Watt, "They would turn in to brother Baxter the card that was filled out, of the medical history of the person (brother Branham never saw the thing), and he could tell that person what was wrong with him every time. Brother Baxter said he never saw him miss once in six years. Ern Baxter was the preacher-teacher and brother Branham was the evangelist and healer." A historian of Pentecostalism, Walter J. Hollenweger, has made reference to ". . . Branham's ability to name with astonishing accuracy the sickness, and often also the hidden sins, of people whom he had never seen. The author, who knew Branham personally and interpreted for him in Zurich, is not aware of any case in which he was mistaken in the often detailed statements he made."[7]

The leaders from Sharon were sufficiently impressed with Branham's ministry in Vancouver that they returned to North Battleford and initiated prayer and fasting.[8] Three months passed. "On February 12, 1948, the revival suddenly began in the largest classroom, where the student body had gathered for devotional exercises."[9] Ern Hawtin reported: "Some students were under the power of God on the floor, others were kneeling in devotion and worship before the Lord. The anointing deepened until the awe of God was upon everyone." A revelation was given concerning a certain student's life and ministry, followed by a long prophecy by Ern Hawtin detailing the great thing God was about to do. There was strong exhortation to holiness and dedication.

Part of Hawtin's prophecy is of particular interest to us (emphasis added):

> These are the last days, my people. The coming of the Lord draweth nigh, and I shall move in the midst of mine own. The gifts of the Spirit will be restored to my church. If thou shalt obey me I shall immediately restore them. . . . *Thou hast obeyed me and I shall restore my gifts to you, I shall indicate from time to time those who are to receive the gifts of my Spirit. They shall be received by prophecy and the laying on of the hands of the presbytery.*[10]

George Hawtin describes those days in early 1948:

> During the past six weeks we have enjoyed a great visitation of the Spirit of God. Some of us have been praying for twenty years that the nine gifts of the Spirit would be restored to the church. The Spirit [of] fasting and prayer has rested upon the whole school all winter. Finally the great "Break Through" came and the spiritual gifts began to operate among us . . . . The revival is spreading all over the province. . . . The Gifts of the Spirit are definitely being restored to the Church. A new era is dawning.[11]

News of these happenings spread so rapidly that Sharon's annual camp meeting at North Battleford from July 7–18, 1948, was overflowing with people who had flocked from all over the continent. One of the key attractions was that "the North Battleford brethren were successful in imparting spiritual gifts by the laying on of their hands."[12]

Since this approach was not practiced in Pentecostal churches, the leadership at Sharon had followed the initial prophecy with diligent Bible study to ascertain if they were truly on scriptural grounds. After determining that they were, they felt the freedom under God to proceed cautiously. They did not indulge in a wholesale laying on of hands for any and all who came to the camp.

Those present tell of the godly atmosphere and deep reverence manifested at the meetings. Candidates seeking prophecy and the laying on of hands were instructed to fast and pray, and when it seemed appropriate to the Holy Spirit and the leadership, they would receive ministry. But this cautious procedure did not always sit well with some of the eager visitors.

Reg Layzell, pastor from Vancouver, British Columbia, describes the approach used:

> There was no religious hysteria present, but much sincere worship and praise. Jesus was the center of attraction. His presence was desired, cultivated and felt. The laying on of hands was regarded by all as a solemn holy ministry:—holy to those ministering and to those being ministered to. . . . In those days it was necessary to fast. There was no such thing as a "wholesale" invitation to all who wanted hands laid upon them. . . . You will see by this that there was not a hard and fast rule,—but a sincere attempt was made to follow the indication of the Spirit as was first given with the revelation of laying on of hands. In the beginning God said, "I will indicate from time to time upon whom hands are to be laid." All ministers did not take part in the laying on of hands—only those whom the Spirit indicated had such a ministry. It was generally recognized as the ministry of prophets and apostles. When hands were being laid upon a brother or sister in the beginning it was something that was solemn. All in the meeting entered into the ministry in the Spirit. God was present in such a spirit of unity. It was easy to prophesy and the prophecies were very accurate. The prophets sincerely sought God,—they were almost fearful lest they might say something that was not God. The utterances were not just "nice" things,—many hearts were searched.[13]

Based on 1 Timothy 4:14, alluding to "the laying on of hands by the presbytery," the North Battleford leaders applied the term *presbytery* to those so ministering. Then, as the movement began to spread and this group of ministers traveled to other cities, the term continued to be used of those so functioning in prophecy.[14]

Although warned not to name the visitation taking place, those near and far seemed to focus on the term *latter rain,* probably because of the continued emphasis on Joel 2:23. Like many in the Pentecostal movement who also used the term *latter rain,* people touched by the Holy Spirit in this 1948 visitation believed there had been an "early" outpouring of the Spirit on the day of Pentecost (Acts 2) and that there was to be another great outpouring immediately preceding the coming of the Lord.

Certain points of emphasis emerged in the teaching, some of which were strongly resisted by Pentecostal denominational leaders. (The same points of opposition, incidentally, are presently acceptable in many evangelical circles, even among non-Pentecostals.) Some historical analysts feel that the Latter Rain movement (LRM) exerted a strong influence on the charismatic renewal some thirty years later. Some main points of emphasis:

- Apostles and prophets can exist in the Church today.
- The Church is one Church; there is only one Body of Christ, and denominationalism or sectarianism divides its unity.

292

- The premillennial return of Jesus Christ is imminent and will be preceded by an outpouring of God's Spirit.
- God is restoring the gifts of the Holy Spirit in our day, which can be experienced through the laying on of hands by the presbytery.
- A worldwide missionary vision is essential to the Church.
- Spiritual worship is of utmost importance and the atmosphere most conducive to prophetic manifestations.

As news got out about the happenings at North Battleford, people from all over North America and many parts of the world flocked to the camp meeting conventions at Sharon that had been publicized by *The Sharon Star*.[15] Soon the leaders at North Battleford were receiving invitations to minister in many places in North America.

Pastor Reg Layzell invited the Hawtin brothers to come to Glad Tidings Temple in Vancouver, B.C., for fourteen days in November 1948. Shortly thereafter he wrote:

> It is nearly two months since they left us and the revival continues. Hallelujah! It is a wonderful thing when the revival partly leaves the revival with you when they go. . . .
> I have seen more souls saved in the last two months than I saw in two years of ordinary church life while in Toronto. . . .
> People were healed! There were many outstanding healings and thanks be to God they are lasting healings.
> Saints were baptised in the Holy Ghost as hands were laid on them and they were prayed for. Great liberty in the Spirit was among the people and the singing in the Spirit was and is heavenly. . . .[16]

Mrs. Myrtle D. Beall, pastor of Bethesda Missionary Temple, an Assemblies of God church in Detroit, Michigan, was one of those present in the Vancouver meetings. Deeply impressed by what she saw and experienced, she returned to Detroit to lead her church forward in this visitation of the Spirit. The newly completed, large sanctuary in Detroit was dedicated on February 13, 1949, filled to overflowing with people and the blessings of God.[17] Hungry people from all over the world flocked to the church. Ivan Q. Spencer, founder of Elim Bible Institute in New York State, was one who came and was greatly influenced. Both Bethesda and Elim became centers for the LRM in the United States.[18]

Stanley Frodsham, a leader in the Assemblies of God and editor of *The Pentecostal Evangel,* accepted Pastor Beall's invitation to come and see what was happening. He was deeply moved by what he saw, and his experience helped precipitate a great controversy in the Assemblies of God over the LRM.[19]

The Rain Falls on Me

My wife, Joy, and I were zealous young Pentecostal ministers when the LRM began. We were soon hearing reports of what was happening in northern Canada. In my junior year at San Jose State University, I was also the youth minister at the First Assembly of God in San Jose.

One day the pastor called me into his office and laid a letter before me. It was from the headquarters of the Assemblies of God in Springfield, Missouri—a warning about the fanatical activities and heretical doctrines coming out of the North Battleford group. Since I knew little of what was happening, I just read the letter and told the pastor I did not know about those things. Inwardly, however, I was excited that God was possibly moving again.

Joy and I began to hear more and more positive reports from friends about what was happening in the north. We moved to Joy's hometown of Spokane, Washington, where I finished college. After our first baby arrived and we began our pastoral ministry, we continued to hear about the great meetings in Vancouver and how Glad Tidings had an annual camp meeting at Crescent Beach, British Columbia. This was our chance to see firsthand what was happening. The year was 1950. We were twenty years old.

The camp meeting setting was rustic. In fact, the accommodations were so poor that we almost decided not to stay.

I stared and listened in amazement as I observed the large congregation in the old tabernacle worshiping God in a genuine, biblical fashion. People were caught up in the joy of praising God. Sincere, fervent worship continued for nearly an hour as I watched with awe. It disturbed me that I was unprepared emotionally and spiritually for free participation in such glorious, lengthy, total and intense adoration of God.

As the service progressed, I was astounded at the order, the intensity and the spiritual flow. The people employed psalmic worship forms in a natural, free-flowing style. With hands raised they praised the Lord audibly. They stood and worshiped for a long time, yet their awareness of God seemed to dispel their tiredness. Prophetic messages were spoken and the service well controlled by the leaders. I was seeing the worship I had read about in the book of Psalms, and it was coupled with the special emphases and manifestations of the worship of the early Church!

I was also impressed by the amount of prayer. An hour before the services began, people gathered at the altar to pray. Many knelt, while others stood or sat. All prayed with fervency. Many spoke or sang praises to the Lord. The meetings so challenged me that I left a service one afternoon in despair. Wandering into the woods and falling beside an old log, I cried out to the Lord, confessing my pride, arrogance, lack of spirituality and everything else I could think of. I truly broke before the Lord. It was the beginning of a great work of God in me.

An unusual procedure was part of the services at the camp. Candidates who had fasted at least three days were called to the platform, where they knelt to receive the laying on of hands by a presbytery of local and visiting prophetic ministers (see chapter 22). These presbyters spoke prophetically, bringing confirmation and impartation to people about their callings, giftings and ministries.

In the next five years that Joy and I attended the annual camp at Crescent Beach, this ministry of prophecy was an important and ongoing part of the program. Gradually the prophetic gift began to develop in me (as described in chapter 23). Within a year of the start of this move of God's Spirit in North Battleford, there were a number of strange happenings throughout North America also labeled "Latter Rain." Many visitors to North Battleford, and influential churches across the United States, caught the excitement of what was happening, but missed the basic truths and experience. Thus, as in every movement, characteristics were attributed to the Latter Rain movement that were not part of the original.

Insights from the Latter Rain Movement

1. Established religious groups are usually unwilling to consider the need for their own biblical restoration, especially if the leaders are offended by teaching or manifestations in the new movement that are different. All the great movements of the Spirit are characterized by brokenness before God—true humility that allows Him to deal with the heart. As a church body enters the second and third generation of its membership, it tends to rely more on the established structure of its theology and methodology and less on a personal heart experience and encounter with God. The new generation tends to live by the faith of its founding fathers and less on its own relationship with God. The institutionalizing of the Church—a process we addressed in chapter 15—seems to happen in spite of the best intentions of religious leaders and people. Eventually the original revival movement becomes set in its own lifeless, cemented, organizational pattern, just like the settled institution from which it initially exited as a protest movement.

Several things were different in the LRM. Hands were laid on people, for instance, to receive the Holy Spirit—an approach that seemed to violate the old-fashioned, "tarry-and-seek" method of prolonged praying that would eventually bring the baptism of the Holy Spirit. Now people

295

were receiving the Spirit as a gift by the imposition of hands. In fact, both methods achieve the same goal, but the LRM approach had scriptural backing (Acts 8:18; 19:6) and should have been considered more carefully and then graciously received. Well-meaning religious groups that believe the Bible, however, may still reject a clear biblical teaching or experience simply because it is not part of their religious tradition.

One of the biggest problems was the laying on of the hands of the presbytery to impart and confirm spiritual gifts, ministries and callings. Every denomination has maintained this approach in the ordination to ministry, but eventually the religious presbytery has only empty hands to lay on empty heads. The action is no longer a vehicle for dynamic Holy Spirit activity; the form has replaced the fire.

The startling thing about the LRM approach was that this kind of confirmation was bestowed on *any* member of the Body of Christ seeking a deeper experience of God, not just on licensed or ordained clergy. Also, established clergy can be intimidated to find seemingly unqualified people who are mighty channels for the Holy Spirit, and that He speaks through them. The LRM movement was reactivating Scriptures that had been overlooked (1 Timothy 1:18; 4:14; 2 Timothy 1:6; Hebrews 6:2)—which was glorious to some but strange to others.

2. The requirement of fasting before receiving the laying on of hands can be a formidable challenge. One of the characteristics of revival is that God's people are willing to sacrifice in fasting and prayer. There is a direct relationship between the readiness of a candidate's heart and the sincerity with which he or she seeks God. When a seeking saint has fasted for several days in preparation to hear from God, a wonderful simplicity and sincerity comes. Broken of human ambition and stripped of vanity and foolishness, the candidate is ready to hear God's direction.

Some religious leaders during the LRM, sad to say, came to receive but were rebuffed by the requirement to fast, feeling that position alone should qualify them. The first Beatitude is appropriate here: "God blesses those who realize their need for him, for the Kingdom of Heaven is given to them" (Matthew 5:3, NLT).

3. The lack of testing of prophecy produces confusion and rejection. Since we will explore the testing or evaluation of prophecy in chapters 20 and 21, I will simply reiterate here the importance of guarding the sanctity of prophetic ministry by judging the things said in an appropriate manner.

Pastor Layzell describes the simplicity of the first North Battleford camp:

> We tried to be in the Spirit and impartial in judging them and we found a true witness with the utterances. The prophecies of the first camp meeting were not extravagant or unscriptural. They were powerfully uttered,

yet stayed well within the Scripture which states that prophecy is for edification, exhortation and comfort. Except during the time when hands were being laid upon ones for the Gifts of the Spirit, we saw no evidence of the office of a prophet in operation. The prophecies were simply the Gift of Prophecy in operation.[20]

Unfortunately the simplicity and reality of those first meetings were not always maintained as the message, prophetic activity and excitement were carried around the world. The most difficult aspect of maintaining a pure prophetic flow, as with most prophetic movements, is the willingness and ability to submit to evaluation. A challenging statement on the lack of testing in the LRM is given by Pastor Dick Iverson of Portland, Oregon:

> The Latter Rain movement, in my estimation, was destroyed by an unbridled prophetic utterance. Men and women were going around prophesying all kinds of words over people and they were not being judged. They were not under any authority and there was no respect for the local resident ministry. They had a word from God and no man was going to tell them they were not going to be able to minister it. Church after church was ruined and Latter Rain became a reproach and stench across the nation. When something like this happens, the tendency is to "throw the baby out with the bath water."
>
> . . . I believe at this time that there are those who are so caught up with the prophetic spirit and emphasis that they are ignoring some dangerous lessons we've learned in history. Starting "prophetic churches" is very dangerous. That implies that the church is going to be guided by the prophetic. I don't believe that is God's plan. I believe the church is guided by the word of God and God has given ministries to that church. The prophetic was only to confirm the mind and will of God, not to govern or control churches or pastors.[21]

4. Money and prophetic activity are not compatible. Whenever prophets require money for their services, especially for "the-bigger-the-offering-the-better-the-prophecy" ministry, the Church must say no. Prophecy is the voice of God and cannot be bought. As Peter told Simon, "May your silver perish with you, because you thought you could obtain the gift of God with money!" (Acts 8:20).

A challenging prophecy came at Emmanuel Gospel Temple in Los Angeles in 1948: "There will be many that will come and want to be involved and flow along with what I am doing, but they are not of me and I have not drawn them, and you will know them by their love of money."[22]

5. A sectarian spirit arises when any group feels it is the sole custodian of God's revelation. The LRM began, as many revivals do, with the wonderful realization that God loves all His people and that there should be no divisions among them. At North Battleford, fellowship was declared to be around the Person of Jesus, not on what was believed (for example, concerning secondary doctrines). There were to be no supreme leaders. As the visitation spread, however, it became increasingly difficult to correct errors and maintain proper teaching. Because the position of the original Sharon presbytery became somewhat tenuous, it was understandable that they demanded absolute authority, regardless of geographical location, so the integrity of God's move could be protected and maintained. But that was the beginning of the end for the LRM, just as a sectarian spirit has always been the downfall of new religious movements.

The sectarianism that developed among the Battleford leaders further alienated them from LRM leaders in America, as well as from the denominations. Layzell reacted strongly to this sectarian trend:

> At the first camp meeting you were made a member of the Body of Christ by the Spirit of God. And even if you said you were not in the Body you still were. No man could put you in or take you out. Now the error: they claim you are only put in by them and can be put out by them. The laying on of hands, they say, puts you in the body. What foolishness for simple people to follow!
>
> At the first camp meeting we were each one responsible before God and had to stand before God according to our own decisions. Now the error: you must obey the so-called apostles even if they are wrong. They say God will hold them responsible, not you. This is blasphemy and challenges the very words of Jesus.[23]

Ivan Q. Spencer also reacted strongly. By January 1950 he concluded that the North Battleford brothers were not the guardians of the LRM. He wrote an article strongly affirming the oneness of the Body of Christ and striking at the exclusivism being promoted. The title of his article asked a question that should be repeated with every visitation: "Who are the Custodians of Latter Rain?"[24]

When a sectarian attitude grips the leadership of a religious movement, the original, spontaneous spiritual experience—which was so life-giving to the Church and so pleasing to God—becomes deadlocked. This is especially true when the prophetic is involved. The cloak of humility is easily shed for the robe of authority. Soon the prophetic flow, so dependent on human brokenness, becomes tainted and finally dries up.

6. Revival manifestations, characteristics and Scripture applications take on the various idiosyncrasies of the churches in which they occur. This is true to a degree of all religious organizations. But the Latter Rain movement, because of the rapidity of its spread and its lack of organizational unity (which a denomination would have provided), showed an

298

amazing proliferation of odd approaches, strange applications and personal interpretations.

The simple, humble, careful approach to laying hands on people who have prepared their hearts through prayer and fasting soon proved too cumbersome to some ministers, especially traveling evangelists. The spectacular nature of prophecy has an amazing way of drawing people, and the manifestations in some places were pushed, to the detriment of proper preparation.

When people are enthralled with prophetic ministry, it is easy to assume that a minister's odd traits (and doctrines!) are part of the anointing and revelation that God is restoring to the Church. This, of course, is not so. Also, a simple word from God can be embellished with additional supplemental, grandiose words that only serve to promote the messenger and not the Sender. These factors all dilute the simplicity that is in Christ and His gifts.

One group I knew began specializing in laying hands on certain parts of the head for certain kinds of blessing and ministry. Catch words or phrases that excite an audience should not be repeated just to promote audience response. Whenever a "long-lost" truth is restored to a church, it must be presented wisely and free of strange applications. God says, "I am watching over My word to perform it" (Jeremiah 1:12).

Why does He allow human foolishness? It is the same with preaching as with prophesying or with any other ministry of the Church. God is longsuffering, but foolishness will eventually take its toll and a group will find itself left with the form but not the power.

7. *Unworthy actions by unspiritual persons who participate in the manifestations sometimes create offense.* Unspiritual people always seem to commit offenses. Sometimes they have a sincere desire to do God's will and simply blunder or make mistakes. Unintentional mistakes made by sincere people should be overlooked—but the church leadership should talk to such people, especially if they are administering prophecy incorrectly. In the excitement of a prophetic environment, a person can attribute too much authority to his or her own words and experience. The safeguard: the ability to judge prophecy and monitor those who minister.

8. *People should not be bound to a church through prophecy.* Prophecy is not given to hold people in a given fellowship. Believers belong where they are fed and led spiritually. Sometimes they get the impression they will be cursed if they leave a church home, especially if a prophetic word has been given to them there. But prophecy should not hang over people's heads like a sword; this is cultish. We should be careful to follow the guidance of the Spirit, and if an individual or family feels God is leading them to leave a church, we should be willing to commend them to His grace.

The Healer-Prophet

William Branham continues to be an enigma in religious history. He began his ministry in 1933 as an ordained independent Baptist, "pastoring the church he founded in Jeffersonville, Indiana, the Branham Tabernacle. The pivotal point of his career came in May 1946 when he experienced an angelic visitation in which he was promised the gift of healing and opportunities to preach before thousands."[25] Branham's rise to fame was meteoric and he filled the largest stadiums and meeting halls in the world. Outstanding miracles were reported, one of the most famous being that "effected by Branham on William Upshaw, a U.S. Congressman from California who had been crippled from birth. This healing in 1951 made Branham's healing power a world-wide legend."[26]

The following paragraph gives some idea of his influence:

> The great healing crusades that Branham initiated in 1946 revitalized the American Pentecostal movement and popularized the doctrine of divine healing in America as never before. When the healing revival attracted hundreds of thousands of Americans from all denominational and cultural backgrounds, the charismatic movement was born. As the pacesetter of the healing revival, Branham was the primary source of inspiration in the development of other healing ministries. He inspired hundreds of ministers to enter the healing ministry and a multitude of evangelists paid tribute to him for the impact he had upon their work. As early as 1950, over 1,000 healing evangelists gathered at a *Voice of Healing* convention to acknowledge the profound influence of Branham on the healing movement.[27]

We may draw at least four insights from the ministry of William Branham, who was acclaimed by many to be a prophet of God.

1. Prophetic ministry needs the "covering" of a responsible authority. When Branham was associated with J. Ern Baxter, his ministry was probably at its best. Baxter, a sound theologian and outstanding teacher and preacher, brought a solid doctrinal base to the ministry and to Branham personally. Baxter esteemed his associate highly but finally left him to go back to pastoring. Although Baxter honored Branham for his honesty and handling of money, and felt him to be a sincere and godly man, their doctrinal differences became too great for continued compatibility. Afterward it was as though someone had "switched angels" and Branham's teaching went weird. Three months before Branham died, according to one of Baxter's students, he called Baxter and told him his meetings had not been the same since Baxter had left.

Prophetic and healing ministries, sensitive and susceptible to spiritual influences, need the stability of apostolic oversight.

2. Prophets must work hard at maintaining sound doctrine. A prophet's blessed ministry does not automatically make him a credible Bible scholar. Doctrine is not formulated by prophecy. Blessing in one ministry does not confirm it in another. God blesses a ministry in response to faith and an open heart and not as the result of flawless doctrine. Nor does the gift of prophecy ensure that a person also has the gift of teaching. Mike Bickle comments:

> The problem is that people with strong power and prophetic ministries often aren't satisfied. Being used by God in prophecy and healing miracles becomes common to them, and they don't get a zing out of prophesying anymore. They often want to become teachers. One of the tough parts of effective prophetic ministry is keeping personal opinions out of the way. . . . Prophetic people often chafe against this restraint on them that is not upon teachers. It is so important that prophetic ministers are part of a local church team that includes gifted teachers. . . . When prophetic people and evangelists become separate from the local church [and the influence of the leadership team], they are often tempted to establish doctrine, just as a gifted teacher with a large following sometimes does.[28]

3. A prophet can become disoriented by the enthusiasm of his or her followers. Popular acclaim exercises a heady influence, and the regard of enthusiastic followers can lead to an unhealthy exclusivity that declares, "I alone have the message that will usher in the Second Coming of Christ." Prophets sometimes tend to embellish their messages to maintain public support and enthusiasm, even resorting to spurious claims and misrepresentation. Leaders held in high esteem can be given too much authority— too much for their own good as well as for the people's. We can all learn a lesson from Jesus. When He had miraculously fed more than five thousand people with bread and fish, and was probably at the height of His popular acclaim, He dismissed the crowds and disciples and went off into the hills by Himself to pray (Matthew 14:23).

4. Prophetic leaders sometimes use their gifts to reinforce their position. The word of an angel, for instance, should not be held over others to the exclusion of the clear teaching of the Word of God. A prophetic gift or ministry should be held in balance by other ministries. The greatness of a New Testament prophet is his or her ability to cooperate with other ministries in the edification of the Church. A prophetic ministry is only one part of the Body, not the brain that controls all. Any revealed word or vision from God is meant for the exaltation of God and not of the messenger.

We can learn a lesson in humility from King David. As he fled Jerusalem during the uprising of his son Absalom, an uncouth man named Shimei cursed David and threw stones at him. David restrained his men from hurting the outspoken fellow, instead submitting himself and his future to God (2 Samuel 16:5–13).

God is our vindicator; we do not need to promote ourselves. As Psalm 75:6–7 states: "Not from the east, nor from the west, nor from the desert comes exaltation [*promotion,* KJV]; but God is the Judge; He puts down one, and exalts another." Our security, like that of David, rests in the call of God and the power of His Spirit. Let's entrust our ministries to Him, regardless of what people say or do.

REFLECTIONS

There is nothing that can ever take the place of the Holy Spirit in the church. Let us pray for a greater outpouring than ever, and remember when the floods come it will not keep to our well prepared channels but it will overflow and most probably cause chaos in our regular programs.[29]

David J. du Plessis

Those of our day who oppose speaking in tongues and prophecy use the Irvingite movement as an argument against them, because of misleadings resulting from prophetic ministry among them. . . . But we as Pentecostals heartily endorse these gifts they brought to the forefront, though we do not endorse some of their doctrines. . . . Why should we not appreciate the pioneers of our day in the things of God, and if they make mistakes, profit by their experiences—gathering out the precious and leaving the rest?[30]

Ivan Spencer

The restoration of this ministry of laying on of hands was the revolutionary teaching and practice which caused the greatest controversy among Pentecostal churches. The Pentecostals were not greatly disturbed doctrinally by the *Deliverance Evangelists* since all Pentecostals believed in divine healing. . . . The Latter Rain Movement, with its doctrine of laying on of hands for *other* than deliverance and healing, brought about a revolution within Pentecostal circles.[31]

Bill Hamon

It is clear that what Branham achieved was not of equal value on every occasion and in every place. To be fair, one must take into account his extremely limited education and his inadequate English. . . . And in his writings [he] asks for indulgence because of his poor education. However generously he is judged, it must be admitted that his sermons were not merely simple, but often naive as well, and that by contrast to what he claimed, only a small percentage of those who sought healing were in fact healed.[32]

Walter J. Hollenweger

19

DENOMINATIONAL RESPONSE TO PROPHECY IN THE CHARISMATIC RENEWAL

Indeed, can anyone understand the spreading of clouds, the thunder from His canopy?

Job 36:29, NKJV

THE RELIGIOUS PHENOMENON of our time is the charismatic renewal movement among Christians worldwide. Pentecostal-style Christianity has swept both historic church traditions as well as nondenominational settings. Certain distinctive Pentecostal blessings and phenomena have been taking place for more than three decades reminiscent of the Christianity of Bible days: the baptism in the Holy Spirit with the spiritual gifts of 1 Corinthians 12:8–10, spontaneous praise and worship, love for the Scriptures, evangelism and missions, and a personal relationship with God in Jesus.[1]

Combining all the peoples in the world who have come into this strong common bond of conviction—*the Holy Spirit is active in the Church!*—we discover a surging tide of 540 million charismatic Christians![2] Lyle E. Schaller, a leading contemporary church renewal expert, says, "From this observer's perspective the most significant development on the American religious scene during the past half century was the emergence of the Charismatic Renewal Movement during the 1960s."[3]

Much could be said on this exciting subject,[4] but we are focusing on prophecy, a vital part of New Testament Christianity. The charismatic renewal has reactivated in today's Christians a worldwide conviction that God does indeed speak in our time. P. D. Hocken makes this comment: "What is new within the mainline churches with the advent of CR is not the occurrence of any of these gifts, but the expectation that they are currently available and the conviction that the gifts as a whole form an intrinsic part of God's equipment of each local church for its mission."[5]

In 1980 a remarkable three-volume set of books was published. Called *Presence, Power, Praise* and edited by Catholic scholar Kilian McDonnell, this trilogy draws together an astounding 104 documents on the charismatic renewal. These documents were initially published by the historic churches and classical Pentecostal denominations between 1960 and 1980, and they illustrate the relationship of these denominations to the renewal.

McDonnell says in the opening remarks of his introduction: "The charismatic renewal is a prophetic renewal movement. To a large degree its prophetic protest and its renewal goals are directed to the churches. Directly or indirectly those in the movement are saying 'the churches need renewal.' How do the churches react to this implied criticism? What does the renewal offer which so many in the churches find compelling?"[6]

The many documents quoted are vitally concerned with the activity of the Holy Spirit in today's churches. Several activities attracted the studied attention of the various denominational groups, including speaking in tongues, the gifts of the Spirit, the baptism in the Spirit, worship, and maintaining balance between structure and freedom. Since prophecy is one of the primary gifts and manifestations taking place, it receives some mention in the documents.

I thought it would be of interest to quote, without comment, some of the denominational statements about prophecy. The following excerpts from McDonnell's trilogy should give a feel for the reaction that has taken place in the historic churches as well as in the Pentecostal and charismatic renewal.

Definitions of Prophecy from the Historic Documents

Re-Reformed Church, Holland, 1967

Now, what is prophesying? Prophecy is the gift of understanding and expressing what the will of God is in a given situation (Ac. 11:28; 13:1–2; 15:32; 21:10–11; 1 Tim. 1:18; 4:14). The prophet does not speak out of his mind. His spirit is subordinate to the control of his mind and will.

Vol. I, p. 183

Commission Report, United Presbyterian Church (U.S.A.), 1970

Prophesying in the early church was not so much the predicting of future events (though this sometimes occurred, e.g., Agabus in Acts 11:28), but was chiefly the gift of understanding and expressing through teaching or preaching what the will of God was for a given situation, resulting in "upbuilding and encouragement and consolation" (1 Cor. 14:3).

Vol. I, pp. 226–227

Commission on Theology and Church Relations, Lutheran Church, Missouri Synod (U.S.A.), 1972

"Prophecy" is a rather difficult term to understand, since it is used in various ways in Scripture. It does not refer primarily to the gift of declaring coming events in advance, although this did occur in the apostolic church (Acts 11:28: Agabus). It includes also the God-given ability to interpret Scripture correctly and to apply its message of Law and Gospel to the needs of men. It is the gift of expressing what the will of God was in a given situation.

Vol. I, p. 342

Final Report, Panel on Doctrine, Church of Scotland (Presbyterian), 1974

Prophecy is not to be identified with inspiring preaching. It is a charismatic utterance in intelligible language. On occasion, the prophet can foretell the future (e.g., Agabus, Acts 11:28) but primarily it is the gift of interpreting the will of God for the present, disclosing the very secrets of God's purpose, for the upbuilding of the church.

Vol. I, p. 532

Lutheran Church in America (U.S.A.), 1974

As it is reflected in the New Testament generally, prophecy is authoritative proclamation of the will and purposes of God with appropriate exhortation to action on the part of the Christian community.

Vol. I, p. 558

Malines Document I, Roman Catholic Church (International), 1974

1. *Prophecy as Integral to the Church's Ministry*— . . . The Holy Spirit is the origin and the source of the corporate life of the Church. The prophet was seen as integral to the Church's corporate ministry and mission.

2. *Prophecies Are to be Tested*—Therefore, the charism of prophecy belongs to the ordinary life of a given local church and should not be looked upon as an unusual grace. Authentic prophecy proclaims God's will and God's word, and focuses God's light on the present. Prophecy exhorts, warns, comforts, and corrects, and is directed to the upbuilding of the church (1 Cor. 14:1–5). Extreme care is used with both predictive and directive prophecy. Predictive prophecy is not to be acted upon except as tested and confirmed in other ways.

As with all the gifts, prophetic utterance can vary in quality, power, and purity. It also undergoes a maturing process. Furthermore there is a great variety of prophecies as to types, modes, purpose, and expression. Prophecy can be a simple word of encouragement, an admonition, a prophetic act, or a decision for a new line of action. For this reason all prophecies are not to be understood or received at the same level.

The prophet is a member of the church and is not set above it, even when he confronts the church with God's will and word. Neither the prophet nor his prophecy is self-authenticating. Prophecies are to be submitted to the Christian community: "Let two or three prophets speak, and let the other weigh what is said" (1 Cor. 14:29). They are also submitted to those who have pastoral responsibilities. When necessary, they are submitted to the discernment of the bishop (Lumen Gentium, art. 12).

Vol. III, pp. 58–59

Lutheran Church, Mekane Yesus (Ethiopia), 1976

Prophecy: It is a special gift that calls and enables certain persons to convey revelations of God to His church. The revelation is: (a) From God to man, (b) For the edification of Community, (c) For laying bare the secrets of their hearts (1 Cor. 14:24–25), (d) Revealing God's presence, (e) For predicting future events (Acts 11:27–28; 21:10). The criterion by which we judge the claims of a prophet is the Scripture. "Let us prophesy in proportion to our faith" (Rom. 12:6). 1. Do not go beyond the given. 2. Do not withhold the truth.

Vol. II, p. 165

Special Committee to Study Charismatic Renewal, Presbyterian Church (Canada), 1976

Many Neo-Pentecostals [people still within the denomination], especially those in the Reformed tradition, see prophecy as outward-looking. They are concerned with bringing back the voice of the biblical prophet whose ministry is directed toward the world where God is at work in the lives of men and women.

Vol. II, p. 234

Antilles Episcopal Conference, Roman Catholic Church (Antilles), 1976

Recognizing that the gift of prophecy continues in the Church of today, we must remember the danger of false prophecy. True prophecy must be in keeping with the Scriptures and the teachings of the Church, to whose teaching authority it belongs to pronounce on its authenticity.[7]

Vol. II, p. 262

Joint Document, Anglican Church (Great Britain), 1977

While estimates and interpretations of the New Testament phenomenon of prophecy vary, it is not identified there with the gift and ministry of teaching. Immediacy in receiving and declaring God's present message to men is the hallmark of New Testament prophecy, as of its Old Testament counterpart. Preaching may at times approximate more to prophecy, although its basic character is one of teaching and exhortation.

If the possibility of prophecy in the sense of speaking a word from the Lord under the direct prompting of the Holy Spirit is admissible today, what is said will be tested by its general agreement with scripture, and will not be accepted as adding materially to the Bible's basic revelation of God and his saving purposes in Christ. It will not be required that such utterances be cast in the first person singular, nor will those that are so cast be thought to have greater authority on that account.[8]

Vol. II, p. 304

Summary Statement, Mennonite Church (U.S.A.), 1977

While occasionally in the New Testament church prophecy may have included prediction (e.g., Acts 11:28), its usual content was exhortation or encouragement (1 Cor. 14:3). The prophet spoke under immediate and evident inspiration. "Givenness" rather than novelty is the characteristic feature of prophecy.

Inspiration of itself does not guarantee the authenticity of the prophetic word. Prophecy must be tested (1 Cor. 14:19; 1 Thess. 5:20–21;

cf. also the gift of discerning of spirits, 1 Cor. 12:10). One such test is whether or not it exalts Christ (1 Cor. 12:3).

Vol. II, p. 337

Commission on Doctrine and Current Affairs, Dutch Reformed Church (Republic of South Africa), 1978

We do not know precisely what constituted prophecy in the early church, but it would not be correct to equate it with preaching or the exegesis of scripture by ordinary ministers of the word in the assembly, for there is a too distinct differentiation between prophets and teachers in the New Testament (cp. Acts 13:1; 1 Cor. 12:19; Eph. 4:11). . . . The prophets spoke primarily on the grounds of specific revelations which they received from the Holy Spirit (cp. 1 Cor. 14:30, etc.).

Vol. II, p. 413

Conclusion

There is still some debate on the charismatic renewal, but the movement must be acknowledged as of major significance. It is presently found in all the continents of the world and in virtually every denomination, Roman Catholic as well as Protestant. To many it has been a breath of heavenly air, to others a major frustration.

All the evidence points to charismatic renewal as not just a prayer or evangelistic movement but an authentic gracing of the Church for renewal in all its dimensions. Perhaps its most notable (and controversial) emphasis is the restoration of spiritual gifts (1 Corinthians 12:8–10)—vital elements of Christian life relatively unknown since the early days of Christianity. One of those gifts is prophecy, the concern of this book.

The quotations used above are not meant to imply that all denominations are open to prophetic activity, but that there is serious concern in many circles to consider the possibilities of prophecy for the contemporary Church. We can safely say there is now a high expectation for this gift to function in our local churches.[9]

REFLECTIONS

There was some concern that the charismatic renewal represented an overblown pneumatology, attributing an exaggerated role to the Spirit and a diminished one to the saving work effected by Jesus Christ. . . . Whatever may be the relationship of Christology to pneumatology in individual cases, the charismatic renewal was and is more in danger of slipping into a Jesus cult than into a Spirit cult. The experience and on-going life is wholly centered on Jesus Christ.[10]

Kilian McDonnell

. . . The renewal restored the gifts of the Spirit to the realm of the ordinary, where they belong to the everyday functioning of the normal Christian community. "A church that is fully alive undoubtedly possesses all the gifts of the Spirit." They are signs that the community is truly alive. Fundamentally they are not adjuncts to the life of the church; rather they belong to the basic structure of the church. "If anything in history is to be rightly called 'the charismatic movement,' it is the church itself."[11]

Kilian McDonnell

But it would be churlish to end this brief evaluation of the charismatic movement on a negative note. I believe it has done much more good than harm. I believe that it has emphases which the modern churches will neglect at their peril. It has taught us to believe in God's reality and his ability to break into the even tenor of our lives with the invading power of his Spirit. It has taken the doctrine of the Spirit off the dusty shelf and put the person of the Spirit right in the heart of the living-room. It has taken the formality, the stuffiness, the professional domination, the dreary predictability out of worship, and made it living, corporate, uplifting and joyful. It has recognised the variety of gifts God has given to his people, discovered some which had been forgotten for a long time, and increasingly insists on a structure of church life where these gifts can be exercised. It has brought together in intimate fellowship men and women of the most diverse backgrounds. It has driven the silent Christians into bearing joyous and courageous witness to their Lord. It has taken seriously the dark element of Satan and the demonic, and has revived among Christians the sense of spiritual battle. It has opened the flood gates to prayer and praise in many a heart that had run dry. In every generation, God raises up some counterpoise to the current weakness and abuses in his Church. In our own day he has raised up this remarkable movement which we call charismatic. It would be tragic if the Church did not learn from it what God wants us to learn.[12]

Michael Green

A comparison with other Christian movements also underlines the importance of CR. Its genesis indicates that it had no one human founder, that its arrival was unexpected and unplanned, that it did not come as a set of coherent ideas or with any strategic methodology, and that it was not in its origins the product of any one Christian tradition more than others. People were first baptized in the Spirit, and then they faced the question of its meaning and what to do with it.[13]

P. D. Hocken

PART 6

THE USE
OF PROPHECY
IN CHURCH TODAY

20

GUIDELINES FOR
TESTING PROPHETIC
UTTERANCES

Dear friends, do not believe everyone who claims to speak by the Spirit. You must test them to see if the spirit they have comes from God. For there are many false prophets in the world.

1 John 4:1 (NLT)

JESUS WARNED THAT "many false prophets will arise, and will mislead many" (Matthew 24:11), and, in contrast, that He Himself would be "sending [*apostello*] you prophets and wise men and scribes" (Matthew 23:34). False prophets often garner quite a following, and true prophets are sometimes ostracized for their efforts. Christians need the ability to discern between the right and the wrong.

Jesus also said, "Beware of the false prophets, who come to you in sheep's clothing, but inwardly are ravenous wolves" (Matthew 7:15). Such false ministers, He assured us, can be recognized: "You will know them by their fruits" (verse 20). Jesus also put the Church on guard against "false prophets [that] will arise and will show great signs and wonders, so as to mislead, if possible, even the elect" (Matthew 24:24). He cautioned His disciples not to heed such demonstrations or make unnecessary trips to places where He has supposedly appeared.

Jesus was deliberately alerting the future leaders of the Church to the need of testing prophecy. He even supplied them with several basic principles that would later be amplified to handle the full range of prophetic activities.

The early Church leaders soon discovered that incorrect prophecies can also be given by dedicated Christians who are mistaken and have no intent to mislead the Church. Thus, the need to judge became more important than ever as false prophets proliferated and true disciples sometimes gave questionable prophecies.

Is it worth the risk to allow prophecy in the Church if it can be misguided, wrong or even evil? Clifford Hill counters this worrisome thought with sound advice: "The opposite of false prophecy is not no prophecy, but carefully weighed and tested prophecy."[1] Graham Cooke suggests helpfully that "the answer always to mis-use is not non-use but proper use. Every leader and ministry must take it upon himself to establish lines of credibility and integrity so that the whole body is safeguarded."[2]

Because of the high-powered nature of prophecy, both the person prophesying and the people listening can be caught up in a justifiable excitement. This enthusiasm characterizes both the Church of Bible days and churches today that make room for the Spirit's activity. James D. G. Dunn describes this magnetic, prophetic environment: ". . . We are here dealing not with a few isolated instances of poetic vision or charismatic potency or prophetic rapture, but with a community where such experiences were characteristic, a community which largely depended on such experiences for its spiritual sustenance and sense of direction. Such a community has to be called an enthusiastic community."[3]

The exciting manifestations in such church gatherings accentuate the need to evaluate what is said and done. A good rule to remember: "Neither the prophet nor his prophecy is self-authenticating."[4] This means the prophet and message are not right because they say so, or even because the people think so,[5] but only if prophet and message fulfill the apostolic criteria for the edification or building up of the Church.

Any problems connected with prophecy, Paul reasoned, were far outweighed by the impartation of life that occurs, and many of us in today's Church have discovered the same truth. This rousing, inspirational gift must not be silenced!

J. Rodman Williams argues for the value of prophecy and its evaluation: ". . . The fellowship finds it imperative to weigh judiciously what is said. . . . Since it is verily God's message to His people, there must be quite serious and careful consideration given to each word spoken, and application made within the life of the fellowship. . . . A delicate balance is needed between complete openness to the Word and sensitivity to its distortion. . . . No one who has experienced prophecy can question its tremendous value for the church of today."[6]

The Implications of *Testing*

Three key texts substantiate the need to test or evaluate prophecy: 1 Thessalonians 5:20–21, 1 Corinthians 14:29 and 1 John 4:1. The first two references are significant because in the context of each Paul discusses the functioning of prophecy in the local church. The third passage refers to the ability to discern the spiritual origin of a prophecy: Is it from the Spirit of God or from other spirits?

From the time that local church congregations began to form, the possibility of prophetic problems was apparent, so it was deemed reasonable to subject prophetic utterances to evaluation. "Indeed," comments Cecil M. Robeck Jr., "it seems Paul never saw the gift of prophecy as separate from the necessity of evaluation."[7] Fee adds: "The awe with which many contemporary charismatics hold prophecy and 'prophets,' which in effect causes them almost never to be 'tested,' stands in basic contradiction to this Pauline injunction."[8]

The English word generally used for evaluating prophecy is *testing*. Although two different Greek words are used in the New Testament, both carry the same basic meaning as that of the English word. The chart on the next page illustrates.

I particularly like the way Williams renders the first two texts: "Stop treating the message of prophecy with contempt, but continue to prove all things until you can approve them, and then hold on to what is good." And, "Dearly beloved, stop believing every so-called spiritual utterance, but keep testing them to see whether they come from God. . . ."

Testing prophecy in the local church should not be a factious but rather a health-ensuring activity! Let's say I go to the doctor for a checkup and my blood test indicates that my cholesterol level is too high. If the good doctor tells me I must exercise more and eat fewer fatty foods, I should not get upset at him! Similarly when an orchard owner checks out the fruit of one of his trees, he is exercising a healthy, positive concern. And when an ancient trader took a coin offered him and hastily weighed it on his hand-held scales, he was merely assuring himself that the coin was true and what it purported to be.

Some might feel uncomfortable about "judging" or "testing" the prophecies of others, but it is of utmost importance. Keep in mind this succinct, practical, five-point synopsis by Graham Cooke: "Firstly, that it is scriptural and right to do so. Secondly, that no person's ministry is exempt from the judging process. Thirdly, that it is not disrespectful or disloyal to weigh the words of others. Fourthly, that local leaders as well as international ministries are to submit themselves for judgment. Fifthly, that the judging process is vital because it removes any enemy influence, whilst cementing the purposes of God into our conscious minds."[9]

Testing Prophecies			
Key Reference	Greek Word Used	Meaning of Greek Word	Translations
1. 1 Thess. 5:21	*Dokimadzo*	Test; examine; interpret, discern, discover, approve; prove, demonstrate.* To scrutinize (to see whether a thing is genuine or not) as with metals†	Prove all things (KJV) Test all things (NKJV) Test everything that is said to be sure it is true (LB) Test everything (RSV, NIV) Put all things to the test (TEV) Bring them all to the test (NEB) Examine everything carefully (NASB)
2. 1 John 4:1	Same as above	Same as above	Try the spirits (KJV) Test the spirits (NKJV, RSV, NIV, NEB, NASB) Test them (Phillips, TEV, JB) Carefully weigh and examine (Message)
3. 1 Cor. 14:29	*Diakrino*	Evaluate, judge; recognize, discern‡	Let the other judge (KJV) Let the others judge (NKJV) Let the others weigh what is said (RSV) The others should weigh carefully what is said (NIV) The rest consider carefully what is said (Williams) Let the others pass judgment (NASB)§

* Barclay M. Newman Jr., *A Concise Greek-English Dictionary of the New Testament* (London: United Bible Societies, 1971), p. 48.
† Thayer, *Greek-English Lexicon*, p. 154.
‡ Newman, *Greek-English Dictionary*, p. 42.
§ Who "others" are will be discussed in the next chapter, "Who Judges the Prophecies?"

The two Greek words identified in the chart are also used in 1 Corinthians 11:28–29, 31 in which Christians are told to examine [*dokimadzo*] and judge themselves [*diakrino*] in preparation for Communion. The evaluation and testing of public prophecy, it would seem, is the logical extension of an activity that individual church members were already applying regularly to themselves!

Any "rules of testing" should not be mechanical and heartless. Those who judge themselves honestly develop the appropriate grace to judge the prophetic utterances of others. The caring, pastoral ministers of the Church are particularly gifted to lead in this area. Although *judging* is the correct term, it has a harsh sound and must be interpreted graciously in the light of the loving community of Jesus' servants. We should avoid any hint of shaming sincere worshipers who may have made a mistake.[10] A congregation should not sit with arms folded, gripping pencils and checklists like pharisaic judges.[11]

On the other hand, the Church should not be gullible either. Dunn comments that "these early communities did not simply sit gape-mouthed drinking in every word spoken under inspiration as a word from the Lord. The prophetic spirit was given freedom, but was subject to safeguards and controls (1 Cor. 14:32). If God had a word to speak through prophecy the congregation were ready to hear; but not every word of prophecy was necessarily taken as a word of God."[12]

We should approach the prophetic gift, despite the possibility of false prophecy, as we do currency, despite the possibility of the counterfeit: It is absolutely necessary, even if there are bogus bills floating around! We must simply learn to recognize the good. This illustration by David Pytches has remarkable application to our subject: "The United States Treasury once taught people how to distinguish counterfeit dollar bills without allowing them ever to see one. They argued correctly that to know the false it is only necessary—but very necessary—to know the true well. So the workers spent their time examining genuine money. They were not allowed to look at counterfeits. Clearly, in the same way, the best way to recognize false prophets will be to have close acquaintance with genuine prophets."[13]

Prophecy is a calculated risk that can bring great blessing, but it necessitates faith, spiritual vigilance and pastoral diligence. As Robeck says, "How these utterances affect the faith of believers and the health of the church depends upon the manner in which they are handled and delivered."[14] The beneficial results of a wise approach are well worth the effort. The New Testament teaches that we can determine the source, accuracy and benefit of prophecy. This is accomplished by testing or weighing a given prophecy.

How to Test Prophecy

I have collected nearly two dozen lists from various authors on how to judge prophecy. These authors suggest from three to twelve helpful ways, mainly in the form of questions.[15] I have grouped my own ideas and the questions of others under seven major headings.[16] My purpose here is not to give a quick checklist but to present the deeper, broader implications that will bring caution, reflection and openness to prophetic activity.

The seven broad categories are:

- The source
- The objective
- The message
- The person
- The delivery
- The recipient
- The response

That seventh category is significant enough to warrant taking the entire next chapter, "Who Judges the Prophecies?" The actual procedure for the public evaluation of prophecy will be covered there.

Judging prophecy is much like enjoying a good basketball game. The audience knows the rules and many have played the game themselves. The umpire calls any questionable moves and shots. But the game would lose the interest of players and audience alike if the rules were constantly being repeated and applied. Similarly the questions in this chapter supply the foundational concepts for discerning authentic prophecy. This theological reasoning should be built into the Church, especially the leadership, so that during a worship service we no more need to go through all the prophetic questions than the umpire must recite all the NBA basketball rules. Having grasped the rules, you can simply enjoy the game.

The Source of Prophecy

1. Is this prophecy of God? The mystery of prophetic operation is diminished when we realize that it springs from one of three sources:[17]

- The Holy Spirit—the Spirit of God, the Spirit of truth
- The human self—the flesh, our old nature or carnal mind or soulish nature
- An evil spirit—a lying spirit, the spirit of error

The Holy Spirit will not discredit or misrepresent the Bible, for He is the Spirit of truth. A genuine prophecy follows the tenor of Scripture. A wonderful, clear, bell-tone quality—the ring of authenticity—characterizes a true prophetic message. Such prophecy produces good feelings and continues to add deepening satisfaction upon reflection. Experienced leadership responds appropriately and good spiritual fruit results.

Christians are usually not motivated by demonic inspiration but are more likely to have problems (if at all) with their own imaginations and feelings, as well as with proper timing. The character and reputation of the person speaking, as well as his or her spiritual level, are usually a clear indication of source.

Demonic prophetic expression does not ring true to the spiritual believer. Such a message (which seldom occurs) is misguided and inappropriate—ecstasy gone awry. Discomfort results from the violation of spiritual sensitivity. Those in the congregation with a gift of prophecy, word of knowledge, discerning of spirits or pastoral guidance are instantly uncomfortable when a demonic expression occurs. W. A. C. Rowe, one of the early leaders and prophets of the Apostolic Church of Great Britain, gave this wise and assuring word: "We do not look upon the possibility of these Satanic intrusions as a prevalent danger in sound, healthy and divinely led Holy Ghost communities. . . . The divine provision is a strong and complete bulwark against every threat."[18]

2. Does the gift of discernment help determine the authenticity of a prophecy? In listing various spiritual giftings, Paul notes that some people have "discerning[s] of spirits" (for example, 1 Corinthians 12:10, KJV, NKJV). This is a noun form of one of the verbs mentioned in the last section.[19] The translators seem almost unanimous that the expression denotes *distinguishing* between various or different spirits (NASB, RSV, NEB, NIV). Williams translates it "the power to discriminate between the true Spirit and false spirits," and the NEB incorporates this interpretation right into the translation of the phrase: "[the] ability to distinguish true spirits from false."[20]

A clear illustration of the gift of discernment is given in Acts 16:16–18. A young slave girl, owned by ruthless masters and further enslaved by a spirit of divination, was crying out truthful things about Paul and his associates. The apostle, annoyed and wearied over a period of days by the girl's actions, finally turned on her and cast out the demonic spirit. Here is a case of an inspired message being truthful and accurate but the source being evil and wrong. The enemy was masquerading as an angel of light.

Some feel it is significant that in the listing of 1 Corinthians 12:8–10, *distinguishing of spirits* comes immediately after *prophecy* (verse 10). Then follows the pairing of *various kinds of tongues* and *the interpretation of tongues*. The pairing of discernment and prophecy possibly indicates that the function of discernment is for the judging of inspired utterances.[21] Personally I feel that discerning of spirits can be used for both prophetic utterances and for the deliverance of those who are demonized.

People in a local church who can identify the utterances and activities of evil spirits are of great value. In the case of the young slave girl, Paul weighed the spirit behind the prophecy and was grieved. The content and accuracy of her prophesying was one hundred percent correct, but Paul's inner unrest exposed the evil spirit. If such discernment takes place in a church service, the information should be given to the leadership, which has the authority to take proper action.

3. What is the objective of an utterance caused by an evil spirit? Satan's greatest desire is to foul up our relationship with God, and this is best achieved through idolatry, or the misdirection of our worship and service. Invariably the false prophets of the Old Testament were corrupters of true worship. Even accurate prophecies could mislead, so additional tests were imposed. Deuteronomy 13:2–3 states that if a sign or wonder comes true, it is nevertheless false if it causes you to "go after other gods."[22] The Bible stresses "the theocentric nature of true prophecy: no true prophet can recommend disobedience to the Lord God or the worship of other gods. This is precisely the test used in the New Testament: only the true Spirit of prophecy can say, 'Jesus is . . . Lord' (1 Corinthians 12:3)."[23]

The Objective

1. Does the message exalt and glorify Jesus Christ? True prophecy will without compromise exalt the Bible's high claim to Christ's deity, miraculous ministry and redemptive accomplishment. The apostle Peter warned that "destructive heresies" secretly introduced by false prophets and teachers will "[deny] the Master" (2 Peter 2:1). David Hill makes this good comment: "The test of all genuine Christian prophecy—in the New Testament church and today—is its Jesus-reference. . . . The message of God's action in and through Jesus . . . is the norm by which all Christian prophecy is to be assessed."[24]

This benchmark concept is clearly stated in 1 John 4:2: "By this you know the Spirit of God: every spirit that confesses that Jesus Christ has come in the flesh is from God." Sometimes called "the confessional test," this question is essential!

The great purpose of any prophetic utterance should be "that in all things God may be glorified through Jesus Christ" (1 Peter 4:11). A Holy Spirit–inspired prophecy will "bear witness of" Christ (John 15:26). Jesus said, "He shall glorify Me; for He shall take of Mine, and shall disclose it to you" (John 16:14).

Invariably if a prophecy's content draws too much attention to the person rather than to Christ, it is wrong. The manner of presentation can also detract from Christ: a falsetto voice, grandiose gestures, clandestine behavior, a mysterious air about the person, a strange application of Scripture. All these shift the focus from the glorious Lord to bankrupt flesh.

2. *Does the prophecy edify the church?* The first objective of prophecy is theological: the glorification of Jesus Christ. The second is extremely practical: Does it build up, admonish and encourage the people of God? A prophecy will produce either liberty or bondage; the key lies in its ability to edify the Body of Christ. We have already seen that *edification,* the theme of 1 Corinthians 14, is a carpenter's term meaning "to build up" (verses 3–5, 12, 26), and this is exactly what good prophecy does.

The Message Given

1. *Is the prophecy in accord with the letter and spirit of Scripture?* Does it contradict the Bible? John Blattner comments: "The principle here is simple: the Holy Spirit does not contradict himself. We can trust that any message that is authentically inspired will be in accord with previous revelation."[25] Isaiah 8:20 clearly establishes God's Word as the standard: "To the law and to the testimony! If [a people] do not speak according to this word, it is because they have no dawn." Or, as the Phillips translation puts it: "Consult the message and the teaching, for unless they speak according to these, their light is but a false dawn."

2. *Is the theological or doctrinal content solid?* The purpose of prophecy is not to add new doctrine or come up with something sensational to supersede Scripture. Some good advice from Graham Houston: "We can be protected from false prophecy only if our faith is thoroughly grounded on the balanced teaching of the whole Bible. One of the greatest dangers we as evangelical people face is to exchange our biblical inheritance for a mess of 'prophetic' pottage!"[26]

I like this phrase from John 10:35: "The Scripture cannot be set aside *or* cancelled *or* broken *or* annulled" (Amplified). The Bible is our divine, objective standard of judgment; it is our plumbline against which all exposition is measured. A true prophecy will not change—add to, subtract from or mix up—the straightforward teaching of the Bible. "Thy word is truth" (John 17:17).

3. *Does the message have substance?* Does it say something worthwhile? Is it just glorified advice or counseling? A prophecy "must be in agreement with the Word of God and not just a lot of nonsense."[27] Some

call this "the test of purpose." "True prophecy will always say something worth listening to."[28]

C. K. Barrett makes a good point in his introduction to spiritual gifts. He explains that in 1 Corinthians 12 Paul "is dealing with the phenomena of inspired, ecstatic speech, and indicating how such speech should be judged." Barrett feels—rightly, I believe—that Paul is "claiming that content, not manner, is the criterion." This "fundamental proposition" has to precede the discussion of spiritual gifts and persons.[29]

4. *Does the prophecy have value within specific limits of time and space?* Robeck calls this "context specificity" and points out (using as an illustration Agabus' foretelling of a famine) that sometimes a prophecy has certain limitations, "and the ability to test the prophetic gift adequately also lies within that context."[30] As it happened, the church at Antioch exercised faith in the prophet and rallied to the immediate challenge. To respond later with an offering would have been too late.

Another "limited-time" prophecy was apparently given to the church at Jerusalem just before the city was put under siege by the Roman general Titus. According to Eusebius, the third-century historian, all the believers fled from Jerusalem in response to prophecy, thereby saving their lives. The city was destroyed shortly thereafter in A.D. 70. "The whole body, however, of the church at Jerusalem, having been commanded by a divine revelation, given to men of approved piety there before the war, removed from the city, and dwelt at a certain town beyond the Jordan, called Pella."[31]

5. *Do predictions come to pass and lead people to God?* Obviously if a clear, unconditional prediction does not come to pass, it was not initiated by God (Deuteronomy 18:22). This means, of course, that time must be allowed for the accomplishment of such prophecies. Outlandish prophecies (such as, California will slide into the sea on a certain date) can be evaluated by responsible Christian leaders.

A prophecy might not come to pass for several reasons. If there is a condition involved, such as a call to repentance, the outcome depends on the recipient's obedience. Or sometimes persevering faith is needed to bring a word to pass, such as when Paul challenged Timothy to "war a good warfare" (KJV) or "fight the good fight" (NIV) according to the prophecies that had once been made about him (1 Timothy 1:18).

6. *Does the message give hope to the people?* Is the prophetic theme one of helpful restoration or judgmental condemnation? One of God's great attributes is love (1 John 4:8, 16), and a prophecy that reflects this aspect will be of great benefit to the Church. True prophecy produces life, not death, and presents a promise of God to a hopeful people.

The Person Who Prophesies

1. Is Jesus Lord of this person's life?[32] The local church has a right to expect that anyone who prophesies in a worship service is a devoted follower of Jesus Christ. The leadership should ascertain a person's spiritual credentials before he or she is allowed to minister or minister again. Some call this "the relationship test": Does this person know the Lord? Is the fruit of his or her life and ministry good?

2. Is this person filled with the Holy Spirit? Prophecy is, after all, a manifestation of the Holy Spirit. "No one can say, 'Jesus is Lord,' except by the Holy Spirit" (1 Corinthians 12:3; see Revelation 19:10), so we may logically conclude that no one can speak forth the words of Jesus prophetically without the empowerment of the Holy Spirit. Ronald A. N. Kydd supports this conclusion: "Basic to the understanding of a 'spiritual gift' is the idea that it is an ability which is given to someone by God. He is its source. It is not at the disposal of a man, but rather it comes into play when God chooses."[33]

3. Is there a reasonable measure of true godliness and holiness about the person? We expect those who preach to us to live a lifestyle free from the covetous, immoral and materialistic attitudes of today's world. This should also be the lifestyle of those who minister in the gifts of the Spirit. "Is this a praying person?" is also a logical question.

The *Didache,* dating from the last half of the first century, instructed the early Christians to beware of prophets who demanded money and wanted to make extended visits to the local church, thereby abusing hospitality.[34] The first-century Church, it seems, was more "concerned with discerning prophets [and motives] rather than prophecies. The warnings of the epistles are directed towards false prophets, not specific false prophecies."[35]

4. Does this person display the fruit of the Holy Spirit in his or her life? Galatians 5 contrasts the "deeds of the flesh" (verse 19) and the "fruit of the Spirit" (verse 22). All of us respond more positively to a prophecy if we sense in that person a loving humility that reflects the life of Jesus. Does this person's life add up? Does he or she demonstrate the character of Christ? Some call this "the moral test," and it is an important one. *The Didache* says that "not everybody making ecstatic utterances is a prophet, but only if he behaves like the Lord" (11:8) and that "every prophet who teaches the truth but fails to practice what he preaches is a false prophet" (11:10). True prophecy produces fruit in character and conduct consistent with the fruit of the Holy Spirit.

George Mallone suggests a cautious response when hearing prophecy: "Without a character reference, we are to remain quietly agnostic about what is said. . . . Churches should not let those unknown to the community share their prophetic words until the character of such persons has been proven over a period of time."[36]

The gifts of the Spirit that may be functioning in a person's life do not automatically endorse that person's character. The Lord uses all kinds of people on various spiritual levels. The local church must monitor those who minister in their midst and be a safeguard against each person's falling away. It is possible for someone to become so self-confident and enraptured with spiritual accomplishments that he or she neglects character. God is merciful and longsuffering, however, and does not quickly jerk away spiritual ministry because of mistakes or negligence. Nevertheless He urges His Church to exercise discipline.

5. *Does this person submit to the Word of God and the government of the local church?* Those with a "messianic complex" should not be prophesying. The apostle Paul demanded that prospective prophetic ministries recognize the guidelines given him by the Lord (1 Corinthians 14:37–38). Visiting or resident prophets must come under the authority of the local church government and not use the Word of God for their own ends.

David Watson, renowned English Anglican pastor who pioneered Spirit gift activity in the local church, asks bluntly, "Is there submission to the church leaders? Does the person allow others to judge and weigh what is said or done? . . . When I note this independence or the attitude of an authoritarian, then all the red lights flash. The more mature are quite willing to be tested."[37] Accountability is essential.

6. *How well is this person known?* What is the track record? If a person has caused problems in various places, he or she should not be allowed to minister until everything has been cleared up. Have previous prophecies proven accurate? Is this a responsible, reliable person?

7. *What kind of fruit comes from his or her ministry?* Jesus said we "will know [those who are genuine] by their fruits" (Matthew 7:20). Roxanne Brant gives good advice: "Any ministry which produces rebellion, delusion, division and dissension as well as exclusiveness is not of God. Let intention be what it may, if the fruit is bad the minister and his ministry are false."[38]

The Delivery Used

1. *Can the people understand the prophecy?* A person blessed with the presence of God may understandably be excited. We are not talking about his or her private devotional times, however, but about public edification (1 Corinthians 14:3, 5, 29–33), and it is essential that those who minister publicly not dress up the simple message of the Lord with emotional excitement or personal idiosyncrasies, preventing the people from hear-

ing it. The words must be articulated loudly, understandably and without melodrama.

James Ryle gives us a humorous insight in "Don't Be Theatrical or Pretentious": "Thus saith the Lord, 'One needeth not to speaketh in ye olde King James language, yea verily, to be speaking forth a word from God to whomsoever believeth. Amen.' This style of prophesying comes from an outdated ministry model and is exclusive and irrelevant. While it may sound spiritual, it is nevertheless lacking in any real substance."[39]

Sometimes a prophet brings a demonstrative prophecy, such as that of Agabus in Acts 21:11 (which the church immediately perceived and accepted). The same advice goes for actions as for words. Unless the audience sees, hears and understands a message without any unreasonable distractions from the messenger, the message may as well not have been given.

2. *Does the prophecy fit in with the flow and order of service?* Usually God will not disrupt a service since a flow of interrelated events enables Him to better accomplish His will.

It is helpful to have an elder or minister monitor those who prophesy, ensuring that a potential prophecy not shatter rather than build the service.[40] Sometimes what the Spirit brings to a person's mind is meant for him or her alone and not for the whole congregation. Prophetic insights often occur throughout a congregation, but everything prophetic is not necessarily intended for the entire group at that time. All should realize that an abrupt, harsh, loud prophecy that cuts through the theme and flow of a meeting is disruptive, even if the words alone are meaningful.

3. *What is the speaker's state of mind?* For a prophecy to edify, comfort or exhort, the thoughts and words must originate with almighty God and not in an insecure, troubled human mind.[41]

Prophecy springing from personal strain, imagination, vexed emotions or personal problems sends a confusing, disturbing message. A hypertense person should find personal comfort before attempting to comfort others in a church service. A speaker is not justified in waxing eloquent or speaking out of prior knowledge or presenting a prejudiced viewpoint. Church people diagnose such improprieties quickly.

Sometimes God's most profound communications are simple, direct, loving statements, and we do them an injustice if we seek to go beyond the anointing by embellishing them.

4. *Is this person out of control?* The sane, understandable delivery of a message must be a primary concern of the messenger. Is the prophecy presented in an orderly fashion? If the mode of presentation is threatening, the audience will be too distracted to appreciate and respond to the actual message. Usually prophecy does not violate the sanctified common sense of a reasonably spiritual, lively congregation.

Prophecy certainly can be delivered in an excited, animated fashion, but it should not be hysterical, fanatical or out of hand. To receive the empowerment or anointing of the Holy Spirit is a forceful experience, and a person so inspired senses more than just mild excitement! But 1 Corinthians 14:32 says that "the spirits of prophets are subject to prophets," meaning that the person prophesying is in control of himself or herself while prophesying. Keep in mind that someone can be emotional, excited and demonstrative yet still have reasonable control. A congregation needs to see and feel the force and impetus of a Holy Spirit–inspired prophecy!

Prophecy may be inspiring and overwhelming, yet the actions of the person prophesying should not come across to an outsider as hallucination, frenzy, mania, unconsciousness, clairvoyance or any other negative textbook term. The Living Bible for 1 Corinthians 14:40 exhorts us to "be sure that everything is done properly in a good and orderly way."

5. *Is the prophecy manipulative or controlling?* Manipulation and control are sometimes the underlying objectives of a person bringing a prophecy. (This can be true of preaching as well.) This presents a challenge to church leadership, for such an attitude must not be allowed to continue. A good question to ask ourselves is: Does this message promote the speaker's feelings or the thoughts of God?

Graham Cooke gives twelve informative pages on this subject in his practical handbook *Developing Your Prophetic Gifting.*[42] Seven signs of manipulation are:

1. Usurping the will of others (acting as an infallible oracle)
2. Pulling rank (pushing a superior attitude)
3. Flattering (taking advantage of someone's vulnerability)
4. Giving dire warnings (employing implied threat)
5. Allowing no outside perspective (locking others into one's own view)
6. Using the phrase *the Lord told me so* (eliminating the need for feedback)
7. Promoting super-spirituality (boasting of personal accomplishment)

6. *Is it wrong to be suspicious?* It is always right to be alert. We must maintain open minds but guard against gullibility. Russell Chandler, who has researched false prophets, gives this advice: ". . . Theories about the future can seldom be tested by present facts. But when the theories turn out to be projects for self-promotion or propaganda for a particular political or religious ideology, we do well to be suspicious. The same holds for aggrandizement of an individual or an elite fellowship or an interest group. Or when the smell of money wafts from a 'for profit' prophet's pockets.

Questions about the use of prophecy should always include raising the moral issues."[43] It is always right to be alert.

7. *Does the person bringing the prophecy do so in love?* Our heavenly Father can be very direct and stern with us but He always speaks from a heart of love. Everyone prophesying should reflect His attitude. Restoration, not condemnation, is God's objective.

Just as we expect a certain decorum at our dinner tables, so we can rightfully expect reasonable, loving behavior in our church services. It is essential that prophecy be given in love and humility. The joining of the congregation with the Father's attitude maintains the family atmosphere of the local church. For those who need direction: "The kindness of God leads you to repentance" (Romans 2:4).

The Recipient of the Prophecy

1. *Does my spirit witness that this is the Holy Spirit?* The human spirit has a marvelous affinity with God's Spirit. Jesus likened it to sheep who hear their shepherd: "The sheep follow him, for they know [recognize] his voice. Yet they will by no means follow a stranger, but will flee from him, for they do not know the voice of strangers" (John 10:4–5, KJV). True prophecy—that inspired by the Holy Spirit—is attested to or confirmed within each believer who hears it.

Sometimes good, meaningful words, even a Bible quotation, are used. Simply testing the words alone will tell you only if the message is true, but not if it is a true prophecy. Inspiration by the Holy Spirit is something the spiritual Christian must discern. John talks of the abiding presence of the Spirit as an "anointing" that causes us to know things (1 John 2:20, 27)—a kind of internal guidance system.

An illustration I like to use is "sympathetic vibration." Hold a guitar near a piano and strike middle C on the keyboard of the piano. A vibration will be picked up by the guitar. The strings of the guitar will respond to the sound waves generated by the piano string and the guitar will begin to pulsate on the same frequency. You can feel the vibration! Certain objects have characteristic frequencies at which they vibrate, and when two such objects are placed close together, the vibration of one causes the other to vibrate as well. The principle of resonance is perhaps the best illustration from nature to show what we experience in spiritual "witness."[44]

This approach is admittedly subjective and should not by itself be considered conclusive. Nevertheless, the response of our own hearts and spirits is of great significance and remains an important aspect of judging prophecy.

2. Am I experiencing the peaceful assurance of the Holy Spirit? When an inspired prophecy, prophetic song, exhortation or prophetic vision is given in a congregational worship service, there is a deeply satisfying assurance that God is with us and deeply concerned about each person's particular needs. We get the same feeling when we have just been fed a sermon or teaching that is deeply meaningful. Faith is renewed. Peace floods in as we realize everything is in God's hands and that He will care for us.

3. Do I now feel inspired, highly motivated to follow through with the challenge of the message? People who heard Jesus teach were uplifted and inspired to follow in His ways. Prophecy is the continuing voice of Jesus speaking through His Spirit to His people.

4. Am I seeing an upgrading of character and conduct? If prophecy has no positive effect on us, its value is questionable. Every ministry in the Body of Christ, including prophecy, is for the betterment of the people of God.

Now, what do we do with all these test questions? How should the Church respond to both good and bad prophecies? Can we judge utterances without destroying the flow and inspiration of the services? Who does the judging? These are the subjects of our next chapter.

REFLECTIONS

If we are desiring to prophesy, we must be equally as willing to have the prophecy judged. . . . If we are not willing to be corrected, to be instructed, to be disciplined in the function of the Spirit, we should not minister. We must have a teachable spirit. God will always vindicate what is scriptural and right![45]

David E. Schoch

The final answer to erroneous prophetical movements wherever they arise in the Church is not only to expose the false but to provide a proper place for the true. The inspirational element must be allowed legitimate expression and honour.[46]

Donald Gee

. . . To ask questions of those who prophesy, and to evaluate their lives and words, is not sin. Words given by inspiration of the Spirit can stand up under such scrutiny. It is those which only seem to be from God that will be revealed as false. If a prophetic word needs explanation or application, it is often the act of testing which can make the explanation or application clear, and it is surely the act of testing which will discourage the proliferation of false teaching in the guise of a word from the Lord.[47]

Cecil M. Robeck Jr.

If and when prophecy occurs in the church today, it is equally in need of examination by others in the Christian community, not with prejudice (1 Thess. 5:20) but with a wisdom that is both biblically informed and filled with the Spirit. Thus regulated, true prophecy can be affirmed and misguided expressions corrected in order that this ministry, so important in the early days of our faith, may in the grace of God once again be used to build up Christ's church.[48]

E. Earl Ellis

Allowing prophecy without testing it . . . leads to abuse within the ministry, a discrediting of the gift in general, a poor model for local believers to follow, and frustration of the purpose for which true prophecy is given.[49]

Graham Cooke

21

WHO JUDGES THE
PROPHECIES?

*Do not stifle inspiration, and do not despise prophetic utterances,
but bring them all to the test and then keep what is good in them and
avoid the bad of whatever kind.*

1 Thessalonians 5:19–22 (NEB)

STRIDING DOWN ONE of the aisles of our church sanctuary came
a youngish, bearded man right out of the pages of the Old Testament. Dressed in a flowing white garment and sandals, the visitor
announced in stentorian tones that he was the prophet Elijah. We drew
our collective breath and every head snapped around to view the outlandish newcomer.

It happened during a Sunday morning service some 38 years ago when
my wife and I first began our church in San Jose, California. Sitting on
the platform facing the people, I knew on the spot that an alien spirit had
invaded our sanctuary. The ushers roused themselves, preparing nervously for action. I moved quickly to the pulpit to intercept the intruder.

The determined, no-nonsense look on my face must have been apparent, for "Elijah" jerked to a halt midway down the aisle, whirled around
and stamped out of the church, shaking the dust from his garments and
announcing that God was going to judge this place!

His words never came to pass, of course. No one in our church thought
they would. But the episode added a little excitement to the meeting!

When word gets around that a church allows spiritual manifestations to occur during worship services, the news acts like a magnet to draw both the sincere and curious as well as the spooky and strange. Some people search for a church open to spiritual manifestations—or, more specifically, for a service that might be free enough to allow them to perform their ministries, at least for a while.

David Pytches, in his excellent book *Prophecy in the Local Church*, has a section on "Beware of Theopaths"—a word coined to describe certain good Christians who seem to have abandoned their God-given common sense, seeing significance in everything that happens.[1]

Cindy Jacobs has observed some of the same activity: "Some weird people are attracted to the prophetic movement in the Church. This is a shame because there are many more genuine, balanced prophetic leaders than there are flaky ones. Those who have severe emotional and personal problems have caused real damage to the body of Christ, and have created a severe backlash against others who are used to prophesy. Although this damage may occur, the Bible is clear about the need to be able to receive the prophetic gifts in our midst."[2]

Some churches and religious leaders toss the blessings and problems of spiritual manifestations into one bag and then simply ignore the whole thing. Why take the risk? Others shy away from spiritual manifestations because they do not know how to govern or control any manifestation that might occur. Still others simply cannot accept the reality of spiritual gifts. It reminds me of Bishop Butler's rebuke to John Wesley when he invaded the diocese of Bristol: "To pretend to extraordinary revelations from the Holy Ghost is a horrid thing, a very horrid thing."[3]

Nevertheless, the Bible is too specific about the importance of spiritual gifts in the Church to take the good bishop's advice and lose the great benefit that God's Word promises. Our answer must be, "Yes, it *is* worth the slight risk to get the big blessing!"

An important suggestion when considering pouring "new wine" (the activity of the Holy Spirit) into our "old wineskins" (established, dried-out church structures) is that some changes may be in order. Jesus advises: "New wine must be put into new wineskins, and both are preserved" (Luke 5:38, NKJV). This approach neither destroys the Church nor wastes the energy of the Holy Spirit, but it does require a new or refurbished wineskin.

Gordon Fee's perceptive statement about prophecy in the Church is sadly true and merits serious reflection: "Most contemporary churches would have to be radically reconstructed in terms of their self-understanding for such [i.e., prophecy] to take place."[4]

The Necessity of Structure and Order

If a church wishes spiritual gifts to operate, a structure must be in place to govern and shepherd prophetic manifestations. A pastor and his people should have appropriate procedures in mind for handling spiritual happenings. Teaching the church *before* manifestations occur is ideal but not always possible. Also, having the leadership in agreement with the procedures is a good safeguard. Every church member should understand that responsibility accompanies prophetic manifestations. He or she must not only believe in and anticipate the movement of the Spirit, but be equally concerned to cooperate with pastoral leadership in honoring reasonable guidelines so that the service is meaningful to everyone. Faith is essential for prophetic activity, in both the giving and the receiving.

It is exciting to work with a group of praying people who are full of faith and expectancy about the supernatural—and it is equally deflating to promote spiritual manifestations among lethargic people who have little or no interest. Sometimes people are so scrupulously "rules-conscious" that they tie themselves up with concern and very little happens. If nothing is ventured, nothing will be gained.

I like this squib by Michael Harper: ". . . The rules are of no use *if the gifts are not operating.* What we need today, for the most part, are not rules to save the gifts from being abused and to see that everything is done decently and in order—but the apostolic injunction 'so, my brethren, earnestly desire to prophesy, and do not forbid speaking in tongues'. The Highway Code is valueless if the car stays in the garage. But it becomes a most important document when we are on the road."[5]

Since the Lord called me to the ministry when I was fourteen, I had some time to think about pastoring. One of the biggest problems in my mind, frankly, was how to cooperate with the Holy Spirit in what He was doing, and at the same time supervise the response and activity of the people in such a setting. It seemed to me that churches went to either one extreme of doing nothing for fear of quenching the Spirit, or the opposite extreme of overmanagement, allowing no manifestations at all. This dilemma almost kept me from going into the ministry.

It was a great relief when I realized that a praying, God-fearing pastor with the best interests of the people in his heart can actually guide a church to glorify God and edify themselves. Pastors are supposed to lead! By the very nature of their spiritual ministry, they have the built-in gifting and discernment necessary to govern and supervise people and renewal manifestations. Most of the time a wise, Spirit-filled pastor knows what to do. He may make a mistake from time to time, but the Lord will honor his concern to protect and preserve the integrity of spiritual activity. The principle of pastoral oversight takes precedent over every other rule.

Often I have prayed in our church sanctuary on a Saturday night for wisdom to guide the services the next day, praying fervently at the same time that God would influence the people and manifest His presence among us. Also, I bind the power of the devil in the name of the Lord Jesus Christ, as well as of any troublemakers who might show up. I have found it helpful to open my mind to any impressions God has for me about the services the next day. (Does He have a special word for the congregation?) Then, backed by personal prayer, Bible study, spiritual insight for the occasion and assurance over the devil's power, I find it a joy to open a Sunday service, fully expecting God to be active among the people.

Prophecy in church gatherings is to encourage, edify and exhort the people concerning their daily living and enrich their relationship with the Lord. As C. Douglas Weaver explains: "Modern prophecy does not reveal new doctrine, but edifies the mysteries of the Christian faith with greater clarity and, in doing so, provides reassurance for the recipient. The primary purpose of revelation through the gifts is the bringing of God's message to a specific time and place, as opposed to the abiding and universal role of biblical revelation."[6]

This kind of prophecy can and should be evaluated. Paul's advice: "Do not stifle the Holy Spirit. Do not scoff at prophecies, but test everything that is said. Hold on to what is good" (1 Thessalonians 5:19–21, NLT). Let's explore further how to do that.

A Practical Approach

I hope the list of 29 questions in the last chapter did not seem too tedious or technical! These are not meant to be a literal checklist for every spiritual manifestation, nor does each item need approval before a church can proceed with the service. We are not like a jet pilot who cannot take off without personally checking each takeoff requirement!

Questions about prophecy should already be a settled part of our theological framework as we go into a church service. This fundamental teaching should be so subsumed into our spiritual thinking that it automatically guides and directs our activities. We do not expect a fan in a basketball game to come running out of the stands and take over the ball! (If he did, he would be quickly removed.) In the same way, we expect people who prophesy in church to be qualified and in good standing. Demonic manifestation and bizarre behavior, we assume, will not be tolerated. We know that the leadership will handle mistakes, just as an unbiased referee calls the shots.

Praying people who are Bible-readers, open to the moving of the Holy Spirit and who have been worshiping fervently in Spirit and in truth will be able to flow with the program of prophetic activity.

Consider the opening episode of this chapter. What if the young man in flowing garments had not turned and left? What if he had continued to shout out his thoughts in defiance of our wishes? This kind of situation should be handled in a straightforward manner.

As he came striding down the aisle, I was not going over some mental checklist. The man was an intruder and had to be treated as one. If a burglar attempted to break into *your* house, what would you do? You would defend your loved ones, property and goods to the best of your ability. It is the same in a church service. If the man had not left the sanctuary peacefully, escorted by our ushers, we would probably have asked the people to stand and then led them in a loud, victorious chorus; this action would have refocused everyone's attention on the Lord, frustrated any evil spirit activity and made it difficult for the intruder to retain any attention. If the man had been belligerent, one of our staff would have called the police to handle the troublemaker.

A perfectly good word from the Lord can be canceled, misunderstood or misinterpreted if the hearts and minds of the people are not in a positive, receptive mode. Eight suggestions can assist everyone's cooperation:[7]

1. *Desire to hear and understand.* Unfortunately many are dull of hearing or have no ears to hear (Jeremiah 6:10; Ezekiel 12:2; Matthew 13:9–17).
2. *Be neither skeptical nor gullible.* Neither despise prophecy nor swallow it without "proving" it (1 Thessalonians 5:20–21).
3. *Listen with a willing heart.* Be ready to attend to God's direction (Zechariah 7:11–14).
4. *Pay attention.* Carelessness or lack of interest can cancel God's best for you (Ezekiel 33:30–33; Mark 4:23–25; Hebrews 2:1–4).
5. *Seek further confirmation.* Even when you believe the word is from the Lord, wait on Him for further confirmation (2 Corinthians 13:1–3).
6. *Hear in faith.* Do not let opportunity be lost by an attitude of unbelief (Hebrews 4:1–3).
7. *Face strong words with confidence.* Excuses are easy to find when a challenging word comes (Amos 7:10; John 16:12; 1 Corinthians 3:2; 2 Timothy 4:4; Hebrews 12:19–20).

8. *Hear, then do, the word.* The hearer of the word is obligated to perform it (Matthew 7:26; James 1:23–24).

Who Does the Judging?

Three New Testament references tell us to evaluate prophecy but they do not spell out who is to do the judging and how it is to be done.

- 1 Corinthians 14:29: "Let two or three prophets speak, and let the others pass judgment" (NASB). "Let two or three prophesy, and let the others evaluate what is said" (NLT). "Let two or three prophets speak, and let the others judge" (NKJV). "Two or three prophets should speak, and the others should weigh carefully what is said" (NIV).
- 1 Thessalonians 5:19–21: "Do not put out the Spirit's fire; do not treat prophecies with contempt. Test everything . . ." (NIV). "Stop stifling the Spirit. Stop treating the messages of prophecy with contempt, but continue to prove all things until you can approve them, and then hold on to what is good" (Williams).
- 1 John 4:1: "Do not believe every spirit, but test the spirits, whether they are of God; because many false prophets have gone out into the world" (NKJV). "Do not believe every inspired utterance" (Goodspeed). "Not all prophetic spirits, brethren, deserve your credence" (Knox).

The only direct advice about who is to judge is given in 1 Corinthians 14:29 (NKJV): "Let the *others* judge."[8] Unfortunately the identification of who the "others" are is not clear and has been the subject of scholarly debate. There are four possibilities:

1. *The other prophets present.* In the light of just the immediate context, this would seem the most logical interpretation,[9] although the Greek word itself suggests differently.[10]
2. *Those with the gift of distinguishing of spirits* (or "the ability to know whether it is really the Spirit of God or another spirit that is speaking," NLT), 1 Corinthians 12:10.[11]
3. *The other church members present listening to the prophecies.*[12] Cecil M. Robeck Jr. comments that "if this injunction in 14:29 is read in the light of Paul's words to the Thessalonian Christians, the pool of 'testers' is broadened to include members from throughout

335

the congregation. The 'others' may well be the rest of the congregation, including the other 'prophets.' This interpretation is also possible from the text, provides more consistency with Paul's overall argument, and allows for a wider dimension of the Spirit's activity in the whole congregation."[13]

4. *The resident leadership*—that is, the senior pastor and eldership.[14]

Each possibility has a certain logic. Consider also that Paul was not trying to make a definitive rule for every situation. If so he could have been much clearer.

The fourth choice, carried through appropriately, ultimately proves, in my view, to be the most workable, practical and scriptural approach. It allows for the input of the others, yet does not destroy the inspiration and integrity of the meeting. The long-term results are much greater.

Five basic considerations, concluded from my pastoral experience, cause me to prefer this fourth position.

1. Who Is Responsible for What Has Been Said?

The local church must assume responsibility for any prophecy given in the areas of its jurisdiction. If no clarifying comment is made publicly, the silence implies tacit approval. Unchecked prophecies will eventually tarnish the reputation of a church.

If prophecy to an individual is deemed accurate, the pastoral leadership of the church is responsible to help that person find implementation. Fulfillment of prophecy often depends on the faith of the person or persons involved to follow through in confidence (1 Timothy 1:18), and this confidence is greatly strengthened by the loving concern of the church body. Everyone involved should be able to rely on a prophetic word approved by the church, and work together for its realization.

Prophecy is not the sole responsibility of the recipient. Such an approach would let the visiting prophet off the hook as far as accuracy, follow-up and any obligation about fulfillment. Some people are incapable of the faith or determination to see a prophecy through to culmination, so they need the support of the church leadership and family.

Visiting prophets must work closely with church leadership, not feeling they are a law unto themselves. They, too, must assume responsibility (along with the leadership) for all that transpires. It is not enough that a prophet tells you what God wants for your future and then departs. I have known cases in which church members were told that they or their sick loved ones would not die—and then they did. This is heartless, irresponsible and without biblical warrant, and it places an unnecessary responsibility on the church.

2. Prophecy Should Be Overseen by the Local Church Leadership.

Every prophetic person and movement faces the necessity of governing prophetic activity in public services. W. A. C. Rowe was wise in giving this advice to his fellow believers in the Apostolic Church of Great Britain (see my chapter 17): "Some uninformed opinions resist any suggestion of government or control in the sphere of prophecy. This has led to much fanaticism, which has marred the testimony of Holy Ghost movements through-out the world. There are principles for the government of Prophets and prophecy laid down in the Scriptures."[15]

Bruce Yocum, experienced in the ministry of a charismatic Catholic community, confirms that "the early church benefited from the tremendous resource of the prophetic gift, and yet avoided the dangers of false prophecy, by entrusting the final authority for determining the authenticity of prophecy to the heads of the community. The heads, in turn, based their judgment upon observation of the life of the prophet and the effects of his prophecy."[16]

The New Testament local churches were governed by elders, one of whom functioned as the senior pastor. Two terms were used for these members of the church who were gifted and ordained to shepherd God's flock:

- Elder *(presbuteros):* Indicates maturity, spirituality, experience and dignity. This term refers to his status by virtue of position and accreditation.
- Bishop or overseer *(episcopos):* Defines the ministry or duties of a guardian, supervisor, shepherd. This term refers to responsibility, activity and function—the nature of his work.[17]

These people were given the responsibility of feeding, tending, healing and caring for the spiritual needs of the congregations.

Prophecy and other spiritual manifestations fall under the oversight of the church elders. Prophecy should be under the scrutiny of the prophets present and the whole congregation as well, but prophets (local and visiting) as well as church members are to be subject to the spiritual guidance of the eldership. The elders bear the ultimate responsibility for the care and protection of the church. If there should be any controversial prophecy, the prophets and those with the gift of distinguishing spirits should be consulted by the elders, but the final decision rests with the elders.

Consider, too, this question: Who will enforce the frequency of tongues, interpretation and prophecies? Certainly not the people, but the elders.

If the "others" are visiting or resident prophets or local people who prophesy, it would seem highly inappropriate—and, by New Testament standards, unthinkable—that they could or would make an important spiritual decision without the elders' participation. Certainly the elders would have the final say, but wise leaders listen to the insights of prophetic ministries.

3. Who Acts as Spokesman for the Congregation?

There are seven groupings of people who will hear and judge a prophecy given in a local church, but ultimately the acceptance or rejection must come in an authoritative statement from a suitable spokesperson. Each of these seven groups must have at least a general idea of the acceptability of what is said:

1. *The person who prophesies.* This person must trust in God and be open to evaluation, yet be assured that the body of Christians in a local church will be receptive of him or her personally, while at the same time carefully analytical of the prophetic utterance. He or she needs to know if the message is accepted or rejected or needs adjustment or correction.
2. *The others present who prophesy.* Although in 1 Corinthians 14:29 *prophets* is the usual translation, this is better understood as "functional language, similar to the use of 'interpreter' in v. 28, and means, as in v. 3, 'the one who is prophesying.'"[18] This is a group that understands the complexities of prophecy, the frailty of people so used and the seriousness of misrepresenting God's message. They have all had their own prophecies judged by the same church system.
3. *The pastor of the church.* This person is called to lead, feed and care for the flock. His or her insights and reactions to a prophecy are of paramount importance. The people of the church are basically followers and respond like sheep to a given situation. Sheep can be panicked by the bark of a small, insecure dog, while the shepherd to them epitomizes confidence, assurance, reliability. The people are led and fed regularly by the shepherd's voice. Certainly when judging a prophecy or other manifestation, it is highly appropriate for his or her voice to be heard.

4. *The elders or others on the leadership team.* The "others" could refer to the elders of the local church.[19] They, along with the senior pastor, are the shepherds and guardians of the flock, with the pastor acting as spokesperson. Paul's admonition to the elders of Ephesus captures this responsibility, especially as related to prophecy: "Be on guard for yourselves and for all the flock, among which the Holy Spirit has made you overseers, to shepherd [*the complete care,* Jay Adams] the church of God which He purchased with His own blood. I know that after my departure savage wolves will come in among you, not sparing the flock; and from among your own selves men will arise, speaking perverse things, to draw away the disciples after them. Therefore be on the alert . . ." (Acts 20:28–31).

The early churches were locally sovereign bodies, related by apostolic spirit, doctrine and practice but without the harsh, inflexible oversight of an institutional church system. Those churches were elder-led, elder-fed, elder-cared for. It was not possible for apostles and prophets always to be present with their more seasoned, highly polished ministries, so elders were the final word. Even if a visiting apostle was present, the local elders were in charge and reserved the last word of authority and decision.

5. *The church membership present.* Trained and guided by the elders, members tend to think and react as their shepherds do. Although each member has his or her own subjective reaction to a prophetic utterance, the inclination is to follow the instruction of the spiritual leaders.

6. *The rest of the people present (visitors, unlearned, uninitiated).* Nonmembers were often present in the services, even as in our day. Some were Christians visiting or just getting established in the church. Some were non-Christians, uninitiated in the things of God. Some were newly learning Christ and participated in the "Amen!" response to ideas proposed. These people would be impressed by spiritual manifestations, but as non-members bore no responsibility for such things.

7. *Those not present in the service who heard about it from others.* It would not be unusual for a church member to share some experience that had happened in the service, retelling a prophetic message to friends, relatives, neighbors, friends or fellow workers. At this level the message is reaching far afield, so it is essential that the prophecy be approved and endorsed by the local church.

An important point to consider: Whenever something happens in a church service, especially prophecy, *everyone* has an opinion of what just occurred. Each person may not be bold enough to speak up or share his or her opinion (nor would it be appropriate), but it is the nature of the human mind to observe a situation and draw a conclusion. All seven groups of people described above are involved in the reception and evaluation of a prophecy, but only certain ones, particularly the pastor and elders, are the authorized spokesmen and decision-makers for the church.

To open a public meeting for anyone to voice his or her opinion about a prophecy allows for great confusion and argumentation. Anyone may draw a silent, personal conclusion, but this is not the same as publicly declaring approval, rejection or questions. The people of New Testament times had great respect for their pastoral oversight, and undoubtedly most, if not all, surrendered personal opinion to the final judgment of the local church leadership.

The key, I feel, is this: Who is responsible for what is done in the service? The answer to that question unlocks who the "others" might be. I strongly believe that the whole church body becomes publicly responsible for the procedures followed and the doctrines taught, and its decisions are made known through the eldership. Individual members may affirm some false doctrine or have strange standards of behavior, but the image of the church itself and its message are preserved by the standards maintained by the membership as interpreted by the eldership.

When it comes to prophecy, someone must be responsible for the accuracy of a prophetic word, its effect on the people, the procedure for allowing and evaluating it, and ascertaining the trustworthiness of those participating. The church itself, composed of all its members, is responsible for its doctrines and behavior. That same church confirms its officials as the leadership and spokesmen. In that sense the whole church participates, but the public spiritual leadership, public confirmation and policy implementation are put into the hands of the shepherd-overseers.

4. Let There Be Closure to Prophecy.

The church needs closure on a prophetic manifestation. Is it to be acted on? Ignored? Shared with others? Do the people understand what has been said? It is not enough to simply "leave it up to God" or allow everyone to take it however they like. Some statement from the leadership should confirm, correct or adjust whatever has been said, so that people will leave the service with correct impressions.

A simple comment often brings appropriate closure to the spoken word. The pastor of the flock is the ideal person to summarize and endorse any beneficial prophecies or, working with the elders, make any correction needed.

5. Public Response Should Be Appropriate.

The joyful inspiration of the moment can be lost by a careless congregational response to a stirring prophecy. I have heard of some situations in which the people responded militantly to a prophecy by declaring, "I confirm!" or, "I don't confirm!" This boisterous response leads to confusion, imbalance and lack of love, and can discourage those with prophetic gifts from even trying.

Clapping after a prophecy can also dilute the sacred effectiveness of the moment. Prophecy is not meant to be received as a performance, although a word from God should be given appropriate, enthusiastic reception. I agree with Jack Hayford when he says, "I lament the glib habit of applauding prophetic words as though the whole idea of the gift were to excite us."[20]

The church must constantly guard the sanctity of spiritual gifts by refusing to bestow foolish adulation on the messenger instead of on the message. It is appropriate to express appreciation for a prophetic word and tell of its benefit to the individual, but an inordinate praise for the conduit depreciates the value of the water flowing through it.

How Judging Can Be Done

With all this discussion, an actual procedure has not been given. The Bible does not give the practical outworking of *how* we are to manage this wonderfully spontaneous and explosive gift of the Spirit. The next two chapters of this book will be devoted to practical procedure; there we will talk about preparation for prophecy in the Church and the practical management and development of all who want to participate. Our purpose at the moment is to focus on how a pastoral statement can be given that confirms, applies, disallows or corrects a prophecy given in a church service in order to facilitate proper congregational response.

Here are ten examples of how various churches and groups handle prophecy in their public meetings.

1. Our Own Experience

When my wife, Joy, and I and our three small children started Christian Community Church in San Jose "from scratch," we were not a denominational church so we had opportunity to experiment and be flexible. Our simple approach has proven very workable through the years.

341

We developed a climate of expectancy for spiritual manifestations, and I taught from time to time on how I believed prophecy and tongues should function in the local church. We have felt it wise to reserve prophecy and spiritual gift manifestation for a time after or near the end of spiritual worship and singing. Since prophecy functions best in an atmosphere of praise and worship, it seems reasonable to concentrate as much as possible on great worship.

It is counterproductive to allow people to interrupt the worship with prophecy. Spiritual worship has a way of building to a climax in which everyone is blessed, so we advise anyone desiring to prophesy to wait in a designated area near the front and continue worshiping.[21]

We place a microphone at floor level near the front of the sanctuary with an elder acting as monitor. This elder quietly inquires as to the basic content of each person's contribution, making a quick judgment of the content and its ability to flow with the service. This is part of the testing process—a pre-prophecy screening that helps sift out potential problems. Both monitor and candidate are aware of the importance to coordinate with the worship leader's intent and actions. At an appropriate time, when the message does not interrupt the worship flow, the elder suggests that the one who has come forward for ministry go to the mike and speak. Usually what is said (prophecy) or described (from a vision) or sung (a Spirit-inspired ode) or shared (a revelation) or exhorted (a challenge) is so uplifting and challenging that little needs to be said or added.

Bruce Yocum agrees: ". . . Most prophecies do not require any significant direct response. The majority of prophecies serve purposes of encouragement and exhortation. They do not of themselves demand any decision as to whether or not they are directly inspired."[22]

If the import of the prophecy is true and faith-building, a public discussion about whether it was inspired would be counterproductive and disrupt the service. If a message was not misleading or unscriptural, yet some of the elders feel uneasy about what was said, they can discuss the matter later. Then one of them can go privately to that person and talk it over, bringing proper alignment.

If the pastor or leader senses that what has been said is troubling some of the people, yet a public statement of correction would be awkward, he or she may ask the person publicly to remain after the service for a few moments, "because I would like to talk to you about prophecy and give some suggestions about how we do things here." In this way everyone knows that any improprieties will be handled. The pastoral concern encourages people to invite their friends and reassure them that spiritual manifestations will not get out of hand.

When people are starting out in prophecy, they often get nervous or make mistakes. One young man in our church came to the microphone and said just a few words. Then he repeated the words. Nothing additional came. Rather than let the poor fellow flounder in embarrassment, I walked over beside him, put my arm around his shoulder and used it as a teaching session for him and the rest of the church, explaining what was happening and what the Lord wished to do.

2. Apostolic Church of Great Britain

This statement by W. A. C. Rowe, a key leader in the Apostolic Church of Great Britain, is good advice:

> Should there be any unwise use of the Gifts in Assembly meetings, either through lack of understanding or teachableness, then the Pastor or qualified person representing the presbytery should take such a one apart and graciously but clearly explain the principles involved in order that there should be no repetition. It is not wise or considerate to do this publicly during the service, if it can be possibly avoided. The persons concerned will generally respond to the directions of the Scriptures and the spiritual experience of the appointed leaders, if this is conveyed in the spirit of the love of Christ. If, for some reason, there should be an unintentional repetition, the same course can be followed in order that the person may be won for the Lord and for the ordained workings of the Holy Spirit. But if there is willfulness and insistence on the part of any person who is gifted, or thinks himself to be gifted, then the over-sight may need to be firm and definite in correcting the difficulty in the service itself. Members must be amenable to the government of the Church.[23]

3. Congress at New Orleans

Prophecy can be beneficial in both small and large gatherings and churches. I was impressed by the way it was provided for at the North American Congress on the Holy Spirit and World Evangelization at New Orleans in 1987. More than forty thousand Christians convened in the Superdome from just about every Protestant and Catholic background. Provision was made for prophecy during these massive gatherings by encouraging approved ministers with prophetic gifts to sit in a special section near the speakers' platform. An approved person monitored those who wished to bring a prophecy to the convention. This approach weeded out any wild statements, and accomplished in those meetings what our approach has accomplished in much smaller church services.

4. Small Groups or Cells

Many churches these days are finding great benefit in home groups within the church family that meet on a regular basis. The format is usually simple: fellowship, worship, Bible study, testimonies, prayer and refreshments. In this setting the operation of spiritual gifts is both a blessing and a challenge, especially prophecy. It is not unusual in a gathering of saints who believe in the gifts of the Spirit to have prophetic perception, especially during worship or prayer times.

I suggest the church family be instructed that the principal purpose for such gatherings is not for prophecy (evangelism is a better objective), but that they remain open to any special manifestation of the Spirit. This requires a vigilant leader in each cell. In this setting any contributions need not be given in a grandiose, "thus-saith-the-Lord" style, but in a humble, relational manner that reflects God's love for His people.

The leader must assume closure for whatever is done. More about this at the end of the chapter.

5. The Church on the Way (Van Nuys, California)

Pastor Jack Hayford gives an interesting description of the function of the gifts of the Spirit in their services: "We expect gifts to flow through all members of the body (1 Corinthians 12); and we maintain order (1 Corinthians 14). Taking these as axiomatic, how do we proceed?" His answer shows that even in a large church it is possible to have beneficial spiritual manifestations:

> Two guidelines serve our congregation well in this regard.
>
> First, since "the spirit of the prophet is subject to the prophet" (1 Cor. 14:32), we do not believe a gift must of necessity "burst forth" uncontrollably. The individual who feels that the Holy Spirit has prompted him or her to prophesy, speak in a tongue, interpret or exercise some other gift is expected to indicate this to one of those leading the service.
>
> There are several times and ways to do this. During worship times, greeting times, ministry times or prayer times, the individual may go to one of the pastors or elders and say what he thinks God is giving him at the moment. Alternatively, an individual could lift his hand and, when recognized, say what he is receiving that he believes to be for the assembly.
>
> Then—and this is the second guideline—it is up to those leading the service to decide what to do. They are not compelled to admit the proposed gift then and there, or even at all. If it does not seem the timing is right, they may ask the individual to wait, or even to share it at another service.
>
> At times sincere people have beautiful insights that are so "electric" to their own soul, since God is dealing with *them,* that they are sure they should

share it. Consequently, we often ask people to share what they feel with an elder [i.e., present the gist of the message][24] before they do so with the congregation. The elder may recognize it as a personal insight that is either unnecessary or inappropriate for the congregation at that time.

We risk hurting people's feelings by doing it this way, though I believe we seldom do, but it seems the path of balance between two entirely undesirable courses: (1) giving no place to the Spirit's working; or (2) exercising no control whatever. Both would be offensive to God.[25]

Hayford also shares this straightforward approach to a questionable prophecy:

Prophecies may be corrected. If there is something clearly erroneous, correct it. And if it is unclear, ask the persons bringing the word to clarify it. If they say they don't know what they mean, then a later contact to clarify their own thinking about prophesying may be necessary. On occasion, if a word seemed erratic, judgmental, or bizarre, I have simply asked openly of elders and deacons present, "Who of you confirm this word?" In such obvious cases, there are usually none whatsoever. Thus, much to the congregation's comfort, the situation is immediately addressed and it is made evident again that our openness to the supernatural has not surrendered us to the stupid or the superstitious. (Incidentally, the few times the above has happened, the persons bringing the word have always been visitors. I can almost assure any congregation seeking to open their worship to a place for the prophetic that such visitors will appear. I sometimes think they're beamed down from somewhere in outer space, but even if that's not true, I can tell you for sure they're from somewhere in deep left field!)[26]

6. Clifford Hill

Sometimes we miss a potentially great opportunity for the Holy Spirit to be poured out on the assembled church. If a powerful prophecy comes to a group of people, the leadership should handle it carefully to gain maximum effect. Such a prophecy could be followed, for instance, by prayer; then the leader could ask all those who felt the spoken word was from God to stand. While everyone is standing, various leaders could be asked to pray for guidance from the Holy Spirit as to how the word should be handled and what response the Spirit is directing.[27]

7. Faith Church (New Orleans)

This congregation has always successfully promoted prophecy and spiritual gifts. Pastor Charles Green has used a three-level approach through the years.

The first level occurs when the person in charge of the meeting publicly reviews and comments on the prophecies that have been brought, carefully *not* including a comment about a questionable contribution. A perceptive person and congregation will note the absence of comment. (This is not the procedure for something blatantly unscriptural, which would receive public comment.)

The second level takes place when the person who gave a questionable prophecy comes again and gives another dubious word. One of the elders or ministers of the church goes to that person, explains that he or she has come to the mike two or three times, then asks, "Did you notice that what you said was not included in the summary?" The omission, it is explained, was because the leadership did not feel it contributed to the church. The person is then asked not to come forward for the next three months to minister, regardless of how he or she feels. This gives the person time to observe how others participate, and reflect on his or her own approach. After three months the person is invited to come back to the elder and talk about prophecy and its evaluation.

The third level occurs if that same person walks up to the mike to minister when he or she has been told not to do so. The mike is refused and the person sent back to sit down. If this is refused, he or she is escorted out of the sanctuary.

8. St. Andrew's (Chorleywood, England)

Bishop David Pytches is the retired vicar of this successful charismatic Anglican church. Although the congregation believes strongly in order and structure, it "is not really a matter of strict rules so much as a sound relationship." Here are eight of Pytches' suggestions:

- An announcement is made in the service about the use of spiritual gifts for the benefit of visitors and to forestall any misuse.
- The right of ministry is reserved for regular worshipers in the church *for the sake of decency and order.*
- Prophecies in the worship service are limited to two or three.
- The leader summarizes key thoughts to the congregation through a microphone.
- They prefer not to give the mike to those who prophesy, although admitting it does function well in some places.
- A prophecy discussed beforehand may be selected to be given over the microphone.
- Space is allowed for this ministry, even if it is not used.

- "The opportunity must be made, the explanation of what it is all about must be given and any limitation felt necessary must be imposed."[28]

9. Abbott Loop Chapel (Anchorage, Alaska)

I first visited this efficient, spiritual congregation a number of years ago at the invitation of my friend Pastor Dick Benjamin. I was pleasantly surprised at the large size of this church in a comparatively small city. The worship was lively and spiritual. Those who felt they had spiritual gifts waited until the main worship was concluded, at which point the opportunity was given for those who had something to share to come forward. The people were well trained and their presentation of prophetic gifts orderly and impressive. Coming to the microphone one at a time, at the invitation of the leader, each person prophesied, shared an appropriate insight, gave a word of knowledge (perhaps about the sickness of someone present), prayed for certain people. If any comment or summary was appropriate, the leader also shared.

10. Metro Christian Fellowship (Kansas City, Missouri)

Mike Bickle pastors this well-known prophetic church. As a young pastor not inclined personally toward prophecy, he was taken by surprise at the upsurge of the gift in his own church. His book *Growing in the Prophetic*, written originally to instruct his own people, is an excellent resource book. That congregation's approach to supervising the prophetic word in public worship is given:

> We have a microphone down on the front row near one of our pastors who has the oversight of prophetic ministry for that meeting. We invite and encourage people to come to the front at any time during the service to speak with the pastor.
>
> If the pastor knows the person is credible, he simply hands the microphone to them. If he doesn't know the person, he quietly helps them discern if the prophetic word is for the whole church or just for them personally.
>
> Also, he seeks to understand if this is the right time to share it. People can have a legitimate prophetic word but the wrong timing. Maybe it should be shared after the preaching and just before the ministry prayer time instead of during the worship time.
>
> If several people approach the pastor at once, he will usually determine in which order the words should be given. Many times several people come with the same word. In this case, the pastor sums them all up and shares it with the church instead of having each person give his word individually. At the proper time, he will get the attention of the worship leader who will make a place in the service for the prophetic word.

If it seems more appropriate, he may come up and summarize some of the different prophetic words himself, or he may also have one or two of the people come up to the microphone and speak to the whole church.[29]

Occasionally someone gives a non-edifying prophecy.

> ... We will usually let it go the first time and probably the second. However, after two so-called prophetic words that seem to contain no anointing or edification, we will go to the person and gently *suggest* that they submit their word to the leaders sitting at the front.
>
> If it happens a third time, we then *require* them to submit their prophetic word to the leadership before speaking it out in the church service. If the person does not heed this third private correction from the leadership, then we will stop them on the fourth time and correct them publicly.[30]

There are two kinds of prophetic words that this church publicly corrects immediately: "a rebuke or correction to the church by someone who did not first go through our leadership team"[31] and a message containing unorthodox doctrinal implications.

Closure Is Important

If several manifestations occur in one service—prophecies, spiritual songs, visions, exhortations—it is helpful for the pastor or one of the elders to review quickly the main points of emphasis that have been brought to the church. Having someone assigned to record the highlights may be helpful to the leadership. This capsulated summary of beneficial points that need to be remembered reinforces their importance. This simple yet effective way of confirming or judging prophecy does not take a lot of time or interrupt the flow of the service. The elder-monitor has already anticipated any potential problems by preventing any non-member from participating and screening out any uncertain or misleading messages that might be brought by members.

As at Faith Church in New Orleans, when a prophetic word is ignored in the summary, it sends a subtle message of disapproval that is usually not missed by the membership. If there is such disapproval, the person can be contacted after the service by one of the elders or ministers. If a person consistently delivers a poor communication, he or she should be counseled discreetly but directly. Possibly such a person should be asked to discontinue participation until he or she is better tuned in on how that church functions.

A public correction from the church leadership is justified when an unscriptural statement is made, an immoral suggestion given, a condemnatory prophecy pronounced on an individual or church, an accusation made that demands verification, or any statement that would create confusion in the minds of the people or destroy their unity or the spirit of worship.

We need to guard against wrong prophecy, but also against throwing a wet blanket on the whole procedure of prophecy in the local church. The elders should not be waiting to pounce on some unwary soul! We are there to help the people and to encourage prophecy, not discourage it. Whatever course of action is needed for prophetic correction, we should seek to do what will best serve the interests of the whole congregation.

If someone's message is borderline, or it has problems and might trouble some of the people, it may be wise for the pastor to ask that person publicly to meet with him after the service (as we do in our church). This sends an immediate message to any nervous sheep that the person who has just given this troubling word will have pastoral counseling and will not be repeating the mistake.

Prophecy holds a potential blessing for both the small church and the megachurch, but it must be handled in both cases wisely and discreetly. It is possible in any location, with any size congregation, to have spiritual order that controls fanaticism yet allows freedom for spiritual manifestations.

REFLECTIONS

To permit the exercise of prophecy, without requiring it to be subjected to scriptural judgment, is against the teaching of the New Testament, and commonly leads to abuses which discredit prophecy as a whole, and frustrate the purposes for which true prophecy is given.[32]

Derek Prince

The root reason inspirational movements in the past have so frequently come to grief has either been, on the one hand, attaching too much infallibility and authority to prophetic utterance, or on the other hand, of "despising" this particular manifestation of the Holy Spirit until it has been thereby "quenched."[33]

Donald Gee

The prophetic word should be judged by those who are established leadership. Those who are not leadership should not presume to make this judgment alone, but trust those who are prophets and [have] mature oversight to determine this matter.[34]

David Blomgren

The whole of 1 John provides guidelines for testing prophecy. . . . Nowhere does it suggest that Christian prophecy is obsolete. As the last survivor of the apostles, the aged John could have dealt with the matter simply by rejecting any prophecy which was not from the apostolic circle. That he did not do.[35]

Graham Houston

. . . Prophecy is meant to be understood as a gift that is inspired by God through the Holy Spirit; granted to individuals for purposes of edification, exhortation, and comfort; and intended to communicate the mind of God. But for someone to claim that he or she is speaking on behalf of God makes the issue of discerning between true and false claims a critical one.[36]

Cecil M. Robeck Jr.

SUGGESTIONS
FOR PUBLIC SERVICES

Everything must always be done in a proper and orderly way.
1 Corinthians 14:40 (Williams)

THE FIRST TIME I PROPHESIED was exciting, but confusing and unproductive. It happened in 1949 at the First Assembly of God in San Jose, California. I was a junior at San Jose State University and Joy and I were newly married. We were the young people's leaders at the church, already ordained and anxious to go into full-time ministry.

The First Assembly was then located across the street from SJSU, so I found it convenient to go into the sanctuary during the lunch period each day to pray. I had heard that God was moving in various places with new manifestations of spiritual gifts and prophecy taking place (see chapter 18). It sounded pretty exciting to me, so I began intensifying my prayers for God's guidance and asking for manifestations to occur.

One Sunday morning during the worship service it happened. I think the manifestation startled everyone else as much as it did me. No one in the church, including the pastor, was trained to prophesy or had been exposed to prophecy. The only expected (and infrequent) spiritual happening in the church was tongues and interpretation, with the pastor usually giving the interpretation to some unrecognizable tongue spoken out by one of just a few church members. These expressions lacked power and magnetism and were more tolerated than heeded—the surviving relic of a bygone era. The content was usually about the Second Coming of Christ and our need to be ready. There was little exhortation and encouragement about God's activity in today's Church or world.

As I sat in the congregation that Sunday, a strong presence of the Lord came upon me and I realized He wanted me to prophesy. I stood trembling, gripping the pew ahead of me tightly, shaking from head to foot. Anointed English words were attempting to come forth just as tongues do—with conviction yet without premeditation. A torrent of confusing sounds (English? Tongues? Gibberish? I don't know!) poured out. Finally I sat down, exhausted. There was a moment of embarrassing silence. Then the service went on just as though nothing had happened! The pastor said nothing, either then or later. No one else did either. It seemed best for everyone to just forget that anything had occurred. But in my heart was birthed, in that moment of frustration, a desire to acquire an understanding of this activity of prophesying.

Now, after fifty years of prophesying, and studying and observing prophetic activity, as well as working with the prophetically gifted, I share this book with you on what I believe the Bible teaches on this remarkable gift. In these closing two chapters I will present some practical insights and conclusions on how I perceive prophecy is to function in the local church. Since "we prophesy in part" (1 Corinthians 13:9), no one has all the answers, so let me share out of my present understanding. Many of these thoughts may seem subjective, but they have worked well where they have been tried. The successful churches that enjoy prophecy invariably have workable guidelines—usually very similar to what I am suggesting here.

Because of the spontaneous, unpredictable nature of prophecy, some might think it should be allowed to happen at will. No one wants to be guilty of quenching the Spirit (1 Thessalonians 5:19). Actually, however, prophecy in a congregational setting functions best with reasonably defined parameters. A mighty river looks beautiful as it flows through a city following its prescribed course, but it becomes dangerous and destructive when it overflows its banks and floods the streets. A church is wise to allow the prophetic to flow in productive channels rather than either curb or ignore it.

Our only scriptural insight to a New Testament service active in the gifts is 1 Corinthians 14 (see chapter 13). The spiritual excitement of those first-century believers, with the attendant blessings and problems, was much as it is now. Paul's teaching, therefore, is timely for our present season of spiritual renewal manifestations. He stresses balance between reasonable, flexible structure and Spirit-inspired activity.

God always has the prerogative to do what He wants in a service, but His highest objective is to work with and through His people. He knows the most consistent, lasting results are obtained when a church makes allowance, under wise pastoral supervision, for spiritual manifestations. So it seems ideal for us to allow a portion of service time for spiritual manifestation, particularly for communication gifts like prophecy. After a period of genuine, heartfelt worship, as we have seen, the atmosphere is most conductive to prophecy.

There are three general ways in which prophecy occurs in a public worship service, and each of these expressions functions best when basic guidelines are considered:

- Congregational prophecy
- Prophetic presbytery
- Prophetic ministry to individuals

Congregational Prophecy

Most people are encouraged, not intimidated, by pastoral supervision. The average person is hesitant to come forward on his own in front of the church and speak. People are fearful of missing what God wants and of failing in front of the congregation. They do not always know how to express themselves or how to determine whether what they want to do is proper and edifying.

Since the main way a person learns to function prophetically is by experience and observation, public supervision is necessary for best results. Many of us want spiritual manifestations, but we also want to invite unsaved friends to church. If the church family knows that the service will be managed properly, with any needed explanations given, members will feel freer to invite friends, assured that any spiritual manifestations that occur will enhance the service and impress the visitor. Pastoral supervision and guidance put most people at ease because they know the screening process is for the good of the individual as well as for the people. It saves mistakes and possible humiliation.

Some Lessons Learned

As our church developed, we had seven different locations. While we were occupying a former Mennonite church building, we had an aggressive, younger congregation of 250–300 enthusiastic people. We were learning about spiritual manifestations, and it seemed to me that we needed to use a microphone for prophecies so everyone could hear clearly. Also, I thought, this would enable us to have better sound quality.

I was unprepared for the negative reaction. To my amazement, when we asked people to come forward to the mike and be recognized from the platform, some felt that such supervision was a spiritual insult. If God wants a person to minister, they thought, why should man have to give his approval? (I should have done a better job explaining things!)

Then we bought seventeen acres of land and began construction. We had to sell the former Mennonite property to help raise funds, so we needed temporary housing for the congregation. A Lutheran church was made available to us on Sunday afternoons. We planned to be in this location only about six months, but due to construction complications we ended up being there for three years.

Everything about this sanctuary was different and challenging, but we had nowhere else to go, so we made do. The acoustics were ideal for the pipe organ in the rear loft (the ceiling was eighty feet high) but, as the Lutheran pastor had explained, terrible for speaking. We faced some immediate decisions. Where do we put our choir? The orchestra? The piano? We had two encircling pulpits that restricted my movements, and an immovable marble Communion table. The Lutheran prayer altar was raised up one step from the floor, so that people knelt on the step—an approach that severely tested the patience of those accustomed to thirty minutes of prayer directly on the floor before every service. It even seemed that the elements of nature were against us! The sun streamed in through the huge stained glass window (remember, it was Sunday afternoon), and many people used their bulletins to shield their eyes during the sermon—an uninspiring sight for a preacher!

We adjusted gradually, but the high ceiling and poor acoustics created a challenging problem for both worship and spiritual manifestations. What had happened to our praise? We were accustomed to fervent praise and worship with the sound enveloping the congregation. But in this new sanctuary the sound went up and up and up—and never came back down![1] People would stand to prophesy, and only those close by could hear them.

It was a blessing in disguise, however, because this time the idea of microphones for prophecy and exhortation was found acceptable and we were enabled to give better spiritual oversight, as well as hear clearly.

The manifestation of spiritual gifts in our churches happens best if reasonable guidelines exist and everyone cooperates to see it happen. The lessons our church learned in the Lutheran sanctuary helped us develop principles and guidelines that are appropriate for congregations large and small.

Microphone Use

The microphone enables everyone to hear clearly, have the messages recorded and pre-screen the speakers. The larger the auditorium, the more difficult it is to prophesy or sing a message that can be heard distinctly. A monitored mike also keeps more than one person from speaking at the same time in different parts of the auditorium.

The microphone should be placed at the front of the sanctuary and be under the supervision of an appointed person. (See the next chapter for suggestions on microphone procedure for the person prophesying.)

Screening Those Who Come

A good screening process encourages those in the church, both members and non-members, with something worthwhile to say and discourages those who have something conflicting to say.

Since a number of people in a Spirit-active meeting will be experiencing the presence of the Lord, it is essential that everyone be able to differentiate between what is for personal edification and what is for congregational edification. This is determined by evaluating content, direction and the nature of the revelation. The church leadership hopes everyone is experiencing the Holy Spirit on a personal basis, but the Spirit also uses selected people from time to time to bring congregational prophecy for the benefit of everyone assembled. Creating a time slot in the service for pre-screened prophetic manifestations allows for spiritual spontaneity while, at the same time, bringing reasonable control.

My suggestion is to have an appointed person, probably an elder, stationed by the microphone to act as monitor. This person should be sufficiently prophetic so as to judge with fair accuracy, and thoroughly aware of the church's qualifications and criteria for those coming forward. Several seats should be left open to accommodate prospective speakers. Anyone who feels that he or she has a prophetic word to give should go up to the monitor in charge of the mike and review, quickly and quietly, what he or she has to say. People in the choir or worship team on the platform can use their leader as a monitor.

"What do you have to share?" should be answered in a simple, direct summary statement as quietly as possible. It is also helpful if the person coming identifies what he or she has—such as, "I have an exhortation [or a prophecy or Scripture]"—and then gives the basic content. Personal testimonies should be discouraged during this time and utilized on other occasions. (This preserves the time for the prophetic and actually enhances the testimonies.) But when people have received something that flows with the service, they should be encouraged as much as possible.

If a church member has any insecurity about the relevancy, accuracy or timing, it should be shared with the microphone monitor. This preliminary step is one practical way of judging or evaluating prophecy. By being identified *before* the prophecy is given, a possible problem can be handled quietly and efficiently. A good monitor, for instance, would have intercepted the following prophecy before it got out to the congregation: "I am sending you two prophets and a third man, whose name I can't remember." Another example is this humorous little admonition, told me by a friend, which was actually given in a small Alaska church:

> Hick—a—mo—see,
> I say unto thee,
> Thou shalt only watch
> News on thy TV.

The worship leader will greatly benefit by this system. By relying on the monitor to allow the proper contribution at the proper time, he or she is freed to concentrate more fully on the Lord and on the quality of worship. This system also maintains organized continuity and prophetic flow so that those on the platform are better informed as to what is happening.

The microphone monitor can be instrumental in training and encouraging both first-timers and veterans in stepping out in faith. The mike can be adjusted and personal suggestions given. The monitor has the authority of the leadership to disallow a person to share and also to bring correction discreetly if someone at the mike is going on too long, violating microphone guidelines or saying something unbiblical. If a person needs correction or adjustment, the situation presents the microphone monitor with a real teaching and pastoral opportunity.

Suggestions on how to prophesy and how to cooperate with the church leadership for this congregational prophecy will be discussed in the next chapter.

The Prophetic Presbytery

Most churches schedule special events, from church picnics to worship seminars. It is practical, efficient and beneficial to plan times of concentrated effort for some aspect of church life needing emphasis or reinforcement. These calendar events become the highlights of a given year and help reinforce a church's priorities. A missions conference reinforces the apostolic function of the church. A marriage seminar strengthens the pastoral function of the church. Evangelism and outreach keep before us the need to reach people for Christ.

I am suggesting services geared to emphasize the prophetic dimension. This approach keeps prophecy alive in a church.

What Is It?

A "prophetic presbytery meeting" or prophetic conference is a specially called series of services in a local church that focuses on prophetic revelation for both the individual and collective members of that church. The word *presbytery,* as used in this way, refers to invited ministers—usually three prophets or those with prophetic ministries—who come and bring prophetic guidance to the whole church, as well as minister by the laying on of hands and prophecy over certain prepared candidates.[2] This is an effective way to obey the admonition of Paul to Timothy: "Do not neglect the spiritual gift within you, which was bestowed upon you through prophetic utterance with the laying on of hands by the presbytery" (1 Timothy 4:14).

I have participated in several hundred of these prophetic gatherings in churches in the U.S. and abroad. My observation is that this approach has a revolutionary effect on local church life. People are dramatically and dynamically awakened to God's great concern for each person and the part each one plays in His program. Usually fasting, prayer and intensified worship bring a more acute awareness of God and a renewed consciousness of church purpose. A great spirit of camaraderie and dedication takes place in the church family.[3]

How Does It Work?

Here is a brief description of my understanding of a prophetic presbytery, followed by scriptural illustrations from both Old and New Testaments to substantiate the importance of such prophetic activity.

A prophetic presbytery meeting generally lasts from three days to a week. (With people's tight schedules these days, a church will reap better results by marketing and scheduling any important aspect of its program, including the prophetic.) Sometimes people gather only in the evenings, but frequently the services include morning or afternoon gatherings, too. The schedule depends on the number of people to receive ministry, as well as the work requirements of the congregation.

Ideally the prophetic conference is a pleasant blend of both structure and spontaneity. Properly organized, such a meeting provides a beautiful atmosphere for the gifts of the Spirit to function. This type of conference should have ample lead-in time for the congregation to set their hearts to seek the Lord. In fact, announcing such a meeting several months in advance has a remarkable effect on the people. It is not unusual for this kind of meeting to be more exciting and better attended than any other kind of conference.

The services are deceptively simple and extremely powerful. People are urged to gather early for corporate prayer. A half hour of intense, sincere seeking of God sets the climate. The meetings open with "psalmic" worship that allows everyone to wait on God. Special musical numbers and events are minimized, and even the sermon by one of the visiting ministers is abbreviated. Usually about an hour and a half to two and a half hours are given to the presbyters' ministry. This allows ministry to about a dozen people each meeting.

Previous to the meetings, active church members who wish ministry fill out an application form. The candidates are approved by the church leadership. This ministry is not for troubled people, those about to leave the church, those disgruntled with the leadership or those who need personal counseling. Nor is prophetic ministry intended to tie people to the church. The candidates are people who are already a solid part of the local fellowship and willing to fast and pray for three days prior to the meetings.

During the meetings the candidates are seated in the front middle section of the auditorium. This makes it easier to call them forward if the presbyters so desire. Two chairs are placed on the platform for the candidates (either individuals or a couple), so they can come and be seated (or kneel) in front of the congregation. There are chairs nearby for the presbyters.

The presbyters gather around the person or couple. Taking turns, but in no set order, the presbyters minister to the candidate(s) as God directs. These prophetic expressions come in the form of exhortations, descriptions, admonitions, words of wisdom or knowledge, visions and statements of definition. God's will is confirmed to each person (what the candidate already knows) and spiritual empowerment for ministry in the Body of Christ imparted. After ministry the pastor and leaders gather around to close with a validating prayer. If anything needs immediate clarification, the pastor should initiate it at this point.

Foretelling

Sometimes what is said does not always seem right to a candidate, especially if he or she has other plans in mind. Anything futuristic, of course, has to be put on the shelf for time to prove.

Leonard Fox, a man used prophetically all over the country, informed a woman that she would have a children's ministry. She felt this was wrong since she had no desire to work with children. She was told not to worry about it, but wait and see how things worked out. Several years later she became a children's minister (really liking it!) and went on to become a teacher of children's ministers in different churches.

Glenn Foster shares this interesting thought: "The prophet Samuel told King Saul that the kingdom of Israel was torn from him by the Lord *that day.* Yet twenty-four years passed before David was crowned King of Israel. When God spoke that word by His prophet, it was a settled fact in the spiritual realm. But it took a process of time before it was evidenced in the natural realm."[4]

Joe Livesay of Meridian, Idaho, had an interesting prophetic word in his home church in Portland several years ago. After a few other things, Dave Hubert, a prophet from Abbottsford, British Columbia, said, "I see you working at a desk helping influential people with financial matters." Then Hubert added, "Does this make sense?" Joe nodded his assent, although he was mystified.

Later, when Joe was counseling with his pastor, he said the prophecy had been great to that point, but much of it did not make sense to him. He was counseled to put the prophecy on the shelf for now—that is, wait and see. Joe had been in the banking industry for several years, but at the time of the prophecy had taken a new job that in no way resembled the one described in the prophetic word.

About a year and a half later, returning to the investment industry, Joe went to work with a credit union whose members were City of Portland employees. This gave him opportunity to work with many of the leaders of the city. Looking back three years later, Joe could see that the words spoken over him had indeed come to pass.

Sometimes what seems an imminent word is still in the future. It is like looking at a mountain that appears very close, yet in reality is many miles away.

Frequently in a prophetic presbytery meeting, a prophecy is addressed to the whole church about future development. Such a message can be expected, because when a church has been fasting and praying, the setting is ideal for God to speak.

In 1996 I was in a presbytery meeting in a church in Moses Lake, Washington, that had beautiful banners spaced around the auditorium walls. Suddenly I saw in a vision flags of various nations hanging between the banners, which indicated to me that God wanted to enlarge the church's missionary outreach. I had hardly finished expressing this when Mike

Herron, one of the other prophets, jumped up, saying, "And the first flag is Ecuador!"

Neither of us knew of the church's plans and desires to enlarge their missions efforts—especially that they had just committed to support a couple in Ecuador. The first support pledge had been sent just one month before our meeting, but only the elders and staff at that point knew about the arrangement. This really encouraged the faith of the people! The pastor later said that the prophecies were one hundred percent accurate— and a flag of Ecuador now hangs in the church sanctuary.

Recording the Messages

After presbytery meetings are over, the recorded messages should be typed out by either the candidate or the church secretary and then reviewed with pastoral leadership. If the candidate transcribes and types the message out, the mental concentration will greatly enhance the process of recalling important information.

Scriptural Background, Old Testament

The following five examples from the Old Testament establish a principle and precedent for prophetic direction and confirmation:

1. *Jacob and his children* (Genesis 48:13–22; 49:1–28). The old man laid his hands on them and gave prophetic guidance concerning their futures.
2. *Moses' ordination of Joshua* (Deuteronomy 34:9). Joshua received wisdom by impartation through Moses' hands.
3. *Elisha and the king's bow* (2 Kings 13:14–19). Elisha placed his hands on the king's arms and prophesied about the future of his people.
4. *Isaiah and Hezekiah* (Isaiah 38:1–8). The prophet brought God's direction to the king.
5. *Haggai and Zechariah* (Ezra 5:1–2; 6:14). This dynamic prophetic team enabled the people to build God's house because of their prophesying.

Scriptural Background, New Testament

Here are another five examples of prophetic encounter and ministry, this time from the New Testament.

1. *Simeon and Anna* (Luke 2:25–38). These two elderly saints came as a prophetic team to confirm the Christ Child and strengthen the parents.
2. *The Antioch presbytery* (Acts 13:1–4). The Holy Spirit spoke prophetically, saying the time had come for thrusting out Paul and Barnabas on the first missionary journey.
3. *The apostolic team* (Acts 15:22, 25, 27, 32). Two apostles (14:14) and two prophets traveled together, visiting and strengthening the churches.
4. *The Timothy triad* (1 Timothy 1:18; 4:14; 2 Timothy 1:6). These three references, mentioned frequently in this study, indicate the importance of prophetic guidance and impartation to Paul.
5. *Don't despise, do examine* (1 Thessalonians 5:19–21; 1 Corinthians 14:29). It was common practice to test and examine the prophetic guidance that came to the early New Testament churches.[5]

Public Ministry to Individuals

In addition to congregational prophecy done on a regular basis, and prophetic presbytery ministry performed at more selected times, we can experience the ministry of church members inspired with insights that are shared with other individuals.

Public Statements

In the atmosphere of meetings like the presbytery meetings just described, it is not unusual during worship or another appropriate time for a visiting prophet to receive a prophetic word for an individual or for the whole church.

Apart from the presbytery meeting, ministry to an individual is usually given by a visiting prophet or recognized ministry in the local church family. In the local church setting, it is always important that permission be acquired from the pastor or the person addressed before making any such public declaration.

It is possible in a local church setting for a church member to receive a revelation about another person in the same church. My wife and I received such a word approximately eight years ago from a man in our own church. He prophesied that Joy and I would be known as "the galloping grandparents." A few years passed and we found ourselves in a traveling ministry. We have since "galloped" all over the country and to a number of foreign nations as well! We wondered at the time about the

361

accuracy of the prophecy, but it has proven true and we have since verified it to the church.

Futuristic prophecies should be noted, and later confirmed or rejected.

Personal Statements

Since Christians generally pray for one another, it should not seem strange that God might give one Christian a prophetic insight about a friend. Such a thought can be edifying, helpful and encouraging. Without using God's name, I think we can talk sincerely with our friends and share whatever we are feeling for their welfare.

It is detrimental, in contrast, to go around delivering judgmental impressions about people. Anything of that nature should be directed to the church leadership for review.

REFLECTIONS

We can only teach you what to do with the words. Nobody can teach you how to receive words from God. Those things are the activity of the Holy Spirit in our human experience. We can only teach you how to cooperate with the activity of the Spirit, not how to produce the activity of the Spirit.[6]

Paul Cain

God, who is divinely unique, has also made us unique. Therefore, it is difficult to teach others how to hear from a God who is diverse in expression. Depending on the circumstances God speaks in many different forms, ranging from an audible voice to an inner voice, from dreams to visions, and mental pictures to inner impressions. Yet, in spite of how we hear from God, we can become more receptive to His voice and attentive to His ways through prayer, fasting, meditation, worship and intense scrutiny of the Scripture.[7]

Larry Randolph

The order Paul urged was never to rule out prophecy. He intended that all the gifts of the Spirit should be exercised and tested under authority. Those who rightly insist upon decency and order should be equally pressing about the place prophecy should have in the coming together of God's people for worship (1 Corinthians 14:40).[8]

David Pytches

23

INSIGHTS ON HOW
TO PROPHESY

Let all things be done for edification.

1 Corinthians 14:26

I SAT IN THE MEETING dumbfounded!

I was in an old camp meeting tabernacle at White Rock, British Columbia, just outside Vancouver. The year was 1950 and Joy and I were two of the visitors at the annual summer camp meeting—the one we almost left because it was so rustic—sponsored by Glad Tidings Temple of Vancouver. People had been drawn to this meeting from all over, since word had gotten out that God was moving again. I had heard that the prayer, worship, ministry of the Word and operation of spiritual gifts at this gathering were outstanding. (The reports were correct.) Several prophets were laying hands on candidates and prophesying over them. I had seen nothing like this in Pentecostal services and was amazed to observe the power of it. In my circles hands were customarily laid on ministerial candidates and prayers offered, but never with prophecy.

For several years afterward, Joy and I returned for this annual meeting. It was like spiritual post-graduate work. But I was not prepared for the strange phenomenon that began happening to me. As a candidate would receive prophetic ministry on the platform, a clear, mental image would suddenly come to my mind. At first I did not realize I was seeing a kind of vision; all I knew was that I was not thinking these things up!

363

That was the beginning of my seeing visions in my ministry. The nature of these visions was remarkable. Although I had never had much interest in botany, I saw every candidate's situation pictured as some form of plant life, such as a coconut tree, a vine, an oak or a flower. This went on at the White Rock camp meeting for two years. I never knew there were so many plants!

After several years of observing from my place in the congregation, I cautiously approached Pastor Reg Layzell, the minister in charge, for some direction about the use of this unique gift. He graciously invited me to participate with them, thereby allowing them to better evaluate and mentor the budding ministry. Until then very few prophetic ministers had seen this type of vision.

The Lord began to unfold insights about people that could be likened to various aspects of plant life. Later He graduated me from the botanical kingdom into all avenues of life. I was surprised when Pastor Myrtle D. Beall, pastor of the well-known Bethesda Missionary Temple in Detroit, told me I was a "seer." Regardless of the title, I have been thrilled time and again by the operation of this prophetic gift all over the world.

If you were to ask me how to make it happen, I could not tell you. All I know is that a person must walk in the Spirit, be expectant in faith and open to God's opportunities—and then the gifting functions at appropriate times and places. It is impossible to teach someone how to hear the voice of God. The most someone can do is provide practical suggestions that will enhance the reception and delivery of God's message. The best I can propose in this chapter, therefore, are ways you can cooperate with the Holy Spirit in your life. I can also give suggestions of what you can do with the thoughts the Spirit brings so that the communication is most edifying to the church.

True prophecy is the voice of the Lord opening a door of opportunity for His people. Through it God's heart desire—what He longs to do for us—is expressed, and new insight given on how to live and serve Him. If a person responds in faith and walks through that door of opportunity, he or she will see dramatic events take place. What a privilege for any of us to be used by God, through prophecy, in sharing God's intentions for His people! We can work with God to bless His people.

Ways That Prophecy Comes

In chapter 5 I mentioned that prophecy during Old Testament times came in one of four ways: an audible voice, a mental picture (vision), an immediate unction or an ecstatic experience. This prophetic illumination found expression in manifold ways (Hebrews 1:1). It is much the same in the Church, except that the Old Testament prophet was usually given a dramatic experience to verify the Lord's presence, whereas today's Christian has the Holy Spirit abiding within.

Local church prophecy springs from the same anointing and inspiration that causes a person to speak in tongues. Fluency in personal, devotional "spiritual language" greatly facilitates the ability to experience inspiration and speak with prophetic unction. Tongues and prophecy are closely allied and have an overlapping effect, since both are inspired utterance.

Here are some ways prophecy comes and how we can cooperate with God and each other to see the best possible results:

A strong, undeniable mental impression. In its simplest form, New Testament prophecy consists of receiving a "revelation" from God *(apokalupsis)* and then reporting that revelation publicly under the impetus of the Holy Spirit. Usually there is a strong, persistent, unshakable thought that one perceives to be from God. God makes "a direct, divine impression" spoken in the inner spirit of the prophet.[1] This is similar—and can even be identical—to the Old Testament experience of hearing the audible voice of God. Jack Hayford describes prophecy like this: ". . . When a Christian either hears, sees, or senses a prompting from the Holy Spirit and speaks what he or she has received . . . to someone needing the ministry that gift will supply."[2]

If a person actually hears an audible voice or receives a mental impulse from the Holy Spirit, it may mean that he or she is to retell what God has spoken. The empowerment of the Spirit may come on the person and he or she will be saying it exactly as it was given.

A vision. In this case a person relates a word or picture that is seen, as John did (Revelation 1:11). These mental pictures are God's prophetic visual effects, and they sometimes make a clearer statement than words can. Usually the person receiving the vision simply tells it as it has been (or is) unfolding in his or her mind. A divine vision is attended by the special presence and anointing of the Holy Spirit. Often such a vivid visualization of a spiritual truth is better retained in human memory than words would be. I have met people with whom I shared such a vision years before, and the picture was still fresh in their minds.

A revelation from God has a unique touch on it. There is such clarity of picture, logic of sequence, forcefulness of meaning and power of expression that it can clearly be attributed to God. It is best to wait for the meaning of a vision before giving it.

A spontaneous burst of words. This is generally a more dynamic, Pentecostal style of prophecy. In chapter 5 I called this "an immediate unction." Old Testament prophets and prophetesses would sometimes prophesy like this. Although powerful, such unpremeditated manifestation can still be held in check in the local church setting until the right opportunity presents itself. Sometimes a person feels so excited and empowered that it seems the message must explode forth, like a tissue popping out of its box. This is the way I was in my first prophecy; but I have gradually learned better how to work with the word that is given me. A wise pastor once told me concerning spiritual gifts, "The locomotive will not have much power if it releases it all out in steam."

Inspired song and music. An example of this is found in 1 Chronicles 25:1–3. The prophet sometimes played a musical instrument to facilitate his spiritual sensitivity and cut through mental unbelief and emotional disturbance. Elisha found it hard to prophesy until the psalmist began to sing Davidic odes (2 Kings 3:15). The same thoughts apply to the musician as to the person prophesying. At times the musician's music is more than mere accompaniment; it is actually prophetic ministry capable of affecting people powerfully.

General Principles to Guide

Here are fourteen concepts to keep in mind for maintaining a smooth, orderly flow in a public worship service. This section will be followed by another one listing helps for the person *before* going to the microphone, and another on the person's decorum while *at* the microphone.

My objective: to suggest a reasonable prophetic protocol. These guidelines are not meant to be applied harshly. Church leadership should never have as its primary role the discouragement of oddball prophecies. We are not policemen but shepherds and must encourage the development and maturity of this wonderful gift in as many of God's people as possible. We must "[speak] the truth in love" (Ephesians 4:15).

Shaming. If a church member ventures out in prophecy but makes a mistake, our biggest error would be to publicly rebuke and harshly criticize. Any hint of shaming should be avoided. This is a time for the leadership to show great love and concern. A constructive approach will not discourage but encourage that person (as well as the rest of the church) to maintain interest in prophesying.

Imperfection. In all these things we admit that no one has a corner on God, and nothing is yet perfect. People are still learning, and there is great variety in all our gifts and ministries. All this requires patience and tolerance.

Edification. It is important for us to search out personal motives when considering whether to prophesy. Those coming to the mike should feel they have something worthwhile for the entire congregation. For the Sunday service the tendency should be to select prophetic contributions that are stronger and more edifying for the whole body of Christians. A word for the congregation will be in the realm of comfort, edification and exhortation. It will not focus on personal needs or state of mind but will help all the people.

Timing. Timing is of utmost importance. No one should break into the high praises and worship of God with something that could go unsaid or wait until later. Hasty prophecies do not inspire.

Clarity. If a person has only bits and pieces of thoughts, yet feels these are from the Lord, the lack of clarity suggests that it is premature to speak the thoughts forth publicly. A public prophecy must make sense to the people; we cannot rely on the leadership to clarify something that confuses even us.

Confirmation. Sometimes you may not be sure about a thought. Don't become agitated but consider it an opportunity to seek the Lord. He is not so anxious to see His will accomplished that He must rely on confused messengers. Cindy Jacobs says, "A good thing to remember is this: *God never minds confirming His word to us.* Matthew 18:16 says, 'By the mouth of two or three witnesses every word may be established.' If you are unsure whether something is from God, ask Him for further confirmation. I have had Him graciously confirm prophecies to me again and again until I was sure they were from Him. He will confirm the word in many ways for you. . . . It rarely hurts to wait."[3]

Direction. There are two types of directive prophecy—one positive, the other negative. A prophecy that gives direction and flows with the mood and frame of mind of the congregation and leadership will be received in a positive way, and even acted on in faith. In contrast, a directive prophecy that asserts itself to lead the congregation or an individual to do or say something strange, bizarre or in obvious conflict with the policies of the church is inappropriate and should be adjusted by the pastoral leadership.

Kindness. The privilege of prophetic ministry must not be abused through negative statements or personal concerns. Let the message declare good news. Glenn Foster advises, "Wash out the negatives." Then he adds, "All prophecies should be washed through the faith of Jesus until they reflect only God's grace."[4] Avoid bringing a rebuke or harsh word. This is extremely rare and should be reserved for the proven ministry of the prophet or pastoral leadership. A word can be strong and challenging without being destructively critical. Larry Randolph says, "The main purpose of the prophetic is positive affirmation, not correction and rebuke."[5]

Patience. On occasion time does not permit a prophetic word, or else the leadership feels compelled to move the service in another direction.

In such cases the people of the church should not take personal offense when they are not asked to share. All this requires patience and tolerance. We are still learning.

Humility. Be willing to have your words tested. Never insist you are right or try to prove that you are. Simply give the message and leave the results to God and His people (Ecclesiastes 11:1; Isaiah 55:11). Learn from your mistakes.[6] Remember, no one is infallible. Let others vindicate you. Pride goes before a fall (Proverbs 16:18). Guard against highmindedness and keep from coming across as super-spiritual.

Faith. Never fear failure. If you aim for nothing, you will achieve nothing. You are not a failure, however, if you try. Faith must be exercised to come forward and speak. A perfectly good prophetic insight does not qualify as prophecy unless it is proclaimed audibly to the assembled church. Prophesy "according to the proportion of [your] faith" (Romans 12:6) and the level of your maturity. But avoid prophesying *beyond* your proportion of faith. Having someone screen candidates, listen and judge helps us all perfect our skills in this.

Announcements. Visitors and new people should be informed of the church's procedures through the bulletin and platform announcements. Generally it is best if a new person who comes to the mike is instructed to return to his or her seat and be talked to after the service. Testimonies should not be given during this time but shared with the whole church at a scheduled time. (Such testimonies can be gleaned from the church's home groups, where people are sharing regularly, and the more impressive ones brought to the entire church.) Every church moving in the prophetic needs to have its teaching on prophecy available to the local church body. As Bickle says: "The prophetic ministry in the local church functions in an 'orderly freedom' only when both the pastors and the congregation have a common understanding of how things should work."[7]

Titles. Usually the more secure a person is in a ministry, the less necessary for him or her to have recognition or a title. When a person is called a prophet, even if this is true, attention is drawn to the verification of the person while the message is subordinated. Take the humble approach and do not boast of your gifting or insist that you have any gift. Never manipulate to prove you are right. Keep a teachable outlook.[8] Larry Randolph suggests: "It's not what you say but what you are that makes the difference. . . . By simply being what God has called you to be, the Church will recognize your prophetic office and respond to it. . . . If you have to convince people that you are a prophet, you have most likely demonstrated that you are not a prophet."[9]

Judgment. The possibility of a margin of error is always present. I agree with Pytches when he says, "We have met a number who have been greatly used of God in prophecy, but we do not know of one who has not been wrong about a prophecy at one time or another."[10] The Church does not have infallible, canonical prophets. We do have sincere, Spirit-filled people trying seriously to do the will of God. We can contend for one hundred percent accurate prophecy, but part of our contention must be the willingness to submit our revelations to the church.

Before Going to the Monitor

Before going to the microphone monitor to obtain permission to minister to the church, it might be well to consider these suggestions:

Be yourself. Remember there is a difference between those who prophesy, those with the gift of prophecy and prophets. Do not compare yourself with others; simply seek to minister from your heart in the power of the Holy Spirit. Acting in a weird manner does not make a person more anointed. Jack Deere comments that "spiritual gifts occur with varying degrees of intensity or strength."[11] Yet our most intense prophetic actions must not make our message so strange to the people that the meaning is lost.

Be healthy. It is best to avoid prophesying when you are upset or ill.[12] Speak from a heart filled with faith, not from a heart that is discouraged, doubting or bitter. Do not prophesy if you are wrought up over world conditions or a bad dream. And never deal with personal problems by prophesying to the church! There should be no threats made or the sins of any of the people revealed. Be sensitive and loving and see the people as Jesus sees them. A healthy prophecy brings life to the church.

Be worshipful. It is not necessary to be in an emotional frenzy or trance when you start. Be worshipful and "in the Spirit" and you will be an open channel if God wants to use you.

Go with the flow. The flow of the Spirit is tremendously important. Sometimes people ministering prophetically are so caught up with their own needs and spiritual dealings that they are not really tuned in to the direction and flow of all that is taking place in the service. This produces an unfortunate message that cuts across the theme being brought by the Holy Spirit to the congregation.

Be alert. It is good to be attuned to all that is happening, particularly in the flow of worship and prophetic manifestation. Since we prophesy according to our faith, a person who expects to prophesy should be in a state of confidence and trust. You need not feel hyperspiritual, but when the anointing or unction of God comes on you, you will experience spiritual exhilaration and excitement.

Listen. A theme or keynote usually emerges out of worship. Listen carefully to the previous prophecies in the service. What was the subject matter? Will your word augment, just repeat or completely change the prophetic theme of the service? Avoid crosscurrents—strange words contrary to what the Spirit is speaking.

Be sensitive. Timing and sensitivity are critical. Be mature enough to decide if your word corresponds with the flow or theme of the service.

Evaluate. Ask yourself, Is this impression really the Lord or is it just me? Prophecy sometimes comes through listening for a key word that will ignite in your spirit. Sometimes it can be a single word, a phrase, or occasionally an entire message, but it must be more than just your own idea. A good thought may still not be prophecy. We must perceive that the thought is not of our own making and that its clarity and persistence in our mind persuade us of its divine origin. As Howells has said: "No one can speak for the Lord if the Lord has not first spoken to him."[13] Bickle adds, "Remain silent when God is silent."[14]

Determine. Is it scriptural? It may not quote Scripture, but it must not violate the tenor of the Bible. Is it biblical?

Consider. Is this for the entire congregation or just for you personally? Public prophecy should be of general interest to the whole church.

Distinguish. Distinguish between what is a true or good statement and what is "prophetic." Example: "I love you, My children" is a true and good statement but it might not necessarily be prophetic. Graham Cooke suggests that "if we move out solely on the basis of something we feel, or because we have a few phrases or a picture, we may end up in front of a microphone with precious little to say. To cover our embarrassment, we may turn to volume or repetition to pad out our 'word' and make it more acceptable."[15]

Wait. Remember, the monitor has a very responsible job. While waiting to be called on, spend your time worshiping with the congregation, and do nothing to distract from what others might say or from the worship taking place.

Microphone Procedure

The following suggestions are given to enhance the worship experience and make microphone delivery more effective:

Combination. Remember, the most successful and helpful prophecies combine revelation, anointing and wise, appropriate delivery.

Stance. Stand normally (1 Corinthians 14:30) and avoid any distracting, nervous movements or disruptive mannerisms. Be animated, excited and anointed without being so emotional that it detracts from the message. Do not wrestle with or "pop" the microphone. Act like an ambassador of Jesus Christ.

Opener. Avoid prefixing a prophecy with "Thus saith the Lord!" Take a more humble route, letting the message speak for itself, realizing that others will judge the prophecy. Let's not give the impression that church members are canonical prophets[16] but remember that we "do not consider the word that comes to us through the gift of prophecy equal to the Bible."[17] People respond more readily to an unpretentious approach. A more modest preface such as "I believe the Lord is impressing me to say" will accomplish the purpose while exemplifying gracious humility.

Content. Speak *only* what God gives (1 Kings 22:13–14). Do not attempt to ad lib or embellish the message for personal enhancement. The message can be filled with Scripture quotations or have none at all; both approaches are acceptable. Do not simply repeat someone else.

Delivery. Speak strongly and clearly. Use normal speech without strange voice sounds or religious twangs. Speak into the microphone. Remember, screaming or being loud does not mean a person is anointed.

Language. Avoid Shakespearean English. Try to use contemporary language or terminology. *Thees* and *thous* are not necessary. King James English is confusing today, and the use of *eth* on the end of verbs is inconsistently used and consistently misunderstood.

Brevity. Be specific, brief and to the point. If the message fails to reach a peak or if your mind goes blank, it is time to stop. The microphone ministry is not for extended periods. A basic thought can be presented in a minute or two. Both visitors and regulars get nervous when valuable time is taken away from the ministry of worship and the Word. No one should monopolize a meeting. Do not begin in the Spirit, get nervous and continue in the flesh.

Suggestions about the Song of the Lord

These suggestions can enhance prophetic expression through music:

Source. Is the song a prophetic statement to the people or an expression of personal feelings? Sometimes a person translates his own private devotions into a prophetic song when the thoughts are for him alone. It is important to differentiate between a devotional song (such as a testimony) and a prophetic song. Both have their place.

Quality. Generally if a person is not at least an average singer, he or she should not attempt to sing out a prophecy. It would be better simply to say it or chant it than to have people focus on the poor presentation

371

and miss the message entirely. The mind cannot receive what the ear cannot endure.

Continuity. Sometimes the Lord inspires a series of prophetic songs. Such a wonderful manifestation should not be broken up by some irrelevant exhortation or word. Maintain the continuity of expression, for a beautiful thing is happening.

Feeling. The song of the Lord is primarily to soothe, comfort and inspire. More feeling is involved than with spoken prophecy, and this is an important tool of the Holy Spirit. Sometimes, however, the song of the Lord takes on a militant tone and is like a call to war. This can be a powerful experience for the church.

Mood. A musician may be inspired to play an instrument prophetically without accompanying words. The message is carried through the sounds produced on the instrument. This is an elementary type of prophecy geared for mood setting and emotional change.

Prophecies to Avoid

Use wisdom and common sense. Don't seek to be spectacular. Love the people and seek to bless them. Let the prophet decrease; let Jesus increase. The following areas should be avoided in church prophecies:

Obvious troubled areas. These include resolving church disputes, ministry to the sick or dying, a romance or marriage in which you are involved emotionally, or any situation about which you have natural knowledge, emotional investment or strong opinions.

Date-setting. Do not date the Second Coming of Christ or predict the end of the world (Matthew 24:36). Beware of setting dates for earthquakes unless you are a prophet, and even then there should be confirmation from reliable sources.

Discipline. Let the leadership handle disciplinary problems. If you truly feel something is revealed to you, discuss it only with the church leaders and leave it with them.

Fantasy. "Beware of any words, dreams, visions about oneself where it involves something like finding a treasure, marrying 'a film star', taking a leadership role in the church, giving up a job which has become frustrating."[18]

Sin. Do not dig up past sins.[19] This approach does not edify anyone and is taking the prerogative in a matter for God alone to handle.

Marriage and divorce. No one should marry or divorce because of prophecy. These are very personal matters and best handled through pastoral counseling.[20]

Money. Beware the glowing promises of prophetic words bought with money! One of the key characteristics of the false prophet is obsession with taking people's money for himself.

Sacrifice. Do not order others to give up all earthly possessions.[21] Although people need to be challenged, they must not be robbed of their personal direction from God. Leave the amount of sacrifice in God's hands. A wrong statement in this area can boomerang easily.

Qualifications for Those Who Prophesy in the Church

We can prepare ourselves to prophesy in church by keeping in mind the following qualifications for the person who prophesies. He or she should be:

A Spirit-filled believer. If we walk in the Spirit, being sensitive to His guidance in our daily lives, it will not be difficult for God to use us for prophecy at appropriate times.

A committed worshiper. Worship shifts attention from bankrupt self to glorious Lord. Prophecy functions best, as we have seen, in an atmosphere of worship.

A faith-filled person. God delights in finding people with an expectant frame of mind. People of faith please God. They are like ready servants, anxious to do the Master's bidding.

A person of active prayer. A person who talks frequently to God—and receives responses from God—has opened a channel of communication vital in prophecy.

A church family member. Prophecy is received more easily if the person is a member in good standing of the local church. A good person will be respected and believed.

A student of the Word of God. Meditation on the thoughts of God prepares a person to be a conduit for God's thinking. The more one can think as God thinks, the more acceptable that person is as a channel for prophecy.

A cooperative participant. Those who prophesy in the Church today are not like the thundering prophets of the Old Testament. Instead we are team members, graciously accepting one another's ministry. The team will succeed if every member is cooperative and gracious.

An exemplary person. We expect our leaders to live lives above reproach. Surely this standard can be expected of those who prophesy.

A person with a clear conscience. Unresolved problems and sins cause spiritual and emotional upheaval counterproductive for those who wish to prophesy. We must know the joy of sin forgiven and be walking in this state of gratitude and appreciation.

Five Basic Bible Safeguards

As prophets and prophecy are emphasized more in conferences, seminars and writings, we must maintain balance in our churches by practicing five basic Bible safeguards:[22]

1. We must elevate the written Word above all gifts, including prophecy.
2. We must elevate Jesus above all personalities, including charismatic ministers with dynamic prophetic gifts.
3. We must respect the local church under the leadership of pastors and elders as the primary place for ministering prophecy, not conferences or seminars where prophecies can be given without proper oversight. We should train our people not to run to get prophecies, and to examine them if they are given.
4. We must elevate the use of wisdom and basic Bible principles as means for church problem-solving above the gift of prophecy or the word of a prophet.
5. We must practice the principle that "in the multitude of counselors there is safety" (Proverbs 11:14, KJV), and not allow a *single* prophecy or prophet to guide our lives. We need two or three witnesses, not two or three prophecies, for confirmation. Confirmation obtained from counseling with wise leadership and from the written Word of God, as well as the confirmation of our own personal spiritual peace, must be considered.

My prayer is that Holy Spirit renewal will invigorate our churches and that the gifts of the Spirit, particularly prophecy, will again become common among us. May God use this book to help accomplish this purpose.

Selected Reading: Practical Advice for Church Prophecy

This page replaces my usual "Reflections." These authors present insightful help in developing a balanced prophetic ministry in the local church. They represent various streams of renewal, so they will not see eye to eye with each other or with me on every issue. For publication information refer to the Bibliography on p. 410.

Mike Bickle, *Growing in the Prophetic,* chapters 11–12.

David Blomgren, *Prophetic Gatherings in the Church,* sections 2–3.

Alex Buchanan, *Prophecy,* chapters 5–6.

Graham Cooke, *Developing Your Prophetic Gifting.*

Glen Foster, *The Purpose and Use of Prophecy,* chapters 10–16.

Wayne Grudem, *The Gift of Prophecy in the New Testament and Today,* chapter 13.

Bill Hamon, *Prophets and Personal Prophecy,* chapter 19.

Jack Hayford, *The Beauty of Spiritual Language,* chapter 7.

I. Howells, *Prophecy in Doctrine and Practice,* lesson 8.

Cindy Jacobs, *The Voice of God,* chapters 7–9.

David Pytches, *Prophecy in the Local Church,* chapters 4–13.

Larry Randolph, *User Friendly Prophecy,* chapters 10–13.

Bruce Yocum, *Prophecy,* chapters 5–8.

APPENDIX 1

A Roster of Old Testament Prophets and Those Who Prophesied

Code: **Bold print** = prophets; **BOLD CAPS** = canonized prophets

Name or Description	Reference	Situation
Aaron	Ex. 7:1	Moses' spokesman or prophet
Abiathar the priest	1 Sam. 23:9–12	Connected to ephod revelation
	1 Sam. 30:7–8	Connected to ephod revelation
Abraham	Gen. 20:7	A prophet, according to God
Adam	Gen. 2:20–25	First words were prophetic
Agur, son of Jakeh	Prov. 30:1	Gave an oracle or prophecy to 2 men
Ahijah the Shilonite	1 Kings 11:29–39	Confronted Jeroboam; 10 tribes given
	1 Kings 12:15	Turn of events established his word
	1 Kings 14:1–18	Jeroboam sends wife but child dies
	1 Kings 15:29	House judged according to his word
	2 Chron. 9:29	Acts of Solomon written in his prophecy
	2 Chron. 10:15	Word spoken to Jeroboam fulfilled
Amasai	1 Chron. 12:18	Short ode of dedication to David
AMOS	Amos 1:1; 7:10, 12, 14–15	Prophet and seer
Asaph	1 Chron. 25:1–3	Prophesied with musical instruments
	2 Chron. 29:30 (35:15)	A seer
	Matt. 13:35 (Ps. 78:2); Ps. 50; 73–83 (12 psalms)	Psalms quoted as prophecy

Name or Description	Reference	Situation
Azariah, son of Oded	2 Chron. 15:1, 8	Spoke to Asa
Azzur from Gibeon	Jer. 28:1; Ezek. 11:1; Neh. 10:17	2 misguided sons (Ezek. 11:1)
Balaam, Gentile soothsayer	Num. 22–24; Mic. 6:4, 5	Acquired by Balak to curse Israel; could not but gave evil counsel
	2 Pet. 2:15–16	Peter's criticism
	Rev. 2:14	Influenced Pergamum
DANIEL	Dan. 10:11	Addressed by Man in vision
	Matt. 24:15; Mark 13:14	Daniel the prophet
David	1 Chron. 14:10	God gave him battle directions
	1 Chron. 16:22	"Do My prophets no harm"
	1 Chron. 28:19	Revelation of Temple plan
	Acts 2:29–30	"He was a prophet"
Deborah, prophetess & judge	Judg. 4:4	Defeat of Sisera
Eldad	Num. 11:26–27	One of Moses' elders who prophesied
Eliezer, son of Dodavahu	2 Chron. 20:37	Prophesied against Jehoshaphat
Elijah the Tishbite	1 Kings 17:1–2, 8, 16, 24; 18:1	Word of the Lord came to him
	1 Kings 18:22, 36	The prophet Elijah
	1 Kings 18:30–46	Prophet, God's servant on Mt. Carmel
	1 Kings 19:15–16	Commissioned to anoint 3 men
	1 Kings 21:17, 28	Word of the Lord came to him
	2 Kings 1:3	Sent to Ahab's messengers
	2 Kings 1:10, 12	Called down fire on soldiers
	2 Kings 1:17	Ahaziah died
	2 Kings 9:36	"His servant Elijah the Tishbite"
	2 Kings 15:12	Jehu's sons to reign until 4th generation
	2 Chron. 21:12–15	Sent letter of judgment to Jehoram
	Mal. 4:5	To come again
Elisha, son of Shaphat	1 Kings 19:16– 2 Kings 13:21	Anointed to replace Elijah
	2 Kings 3:11	"Is there not a prophet of the Lord here?"
	2 Kings 5:8; 6:12	"He shall know there is a prophet in Israel"
	2 Kings 9:1–6	His servant anointed Jehu king
	Luke 4:26	Sent to widow
Miracles of Elisha	2 Kings 2:19–22	Purified waters
	2 Kings 2:23–24	Cursed the 42 lads
	2 Kings 3:11–15	Consulted by Jehoshaphat
	2 Kings 3:16–27	Defeated Moab with trenches
	2 Kings 4:1–7	Multiplied widow's oil

Name or Description	Reference	Situation
	2 Kings 4:14–17	Woman conceives a son
	2 Kings 4:32–37	Son raised from dead
	2 Kings 4:38–41	Healed stew of poison
	2 Kings 4:42–44	Multiplied bread
	2 Kings 5:8–14; Luke 4:27	Healed Naaman
	2 Kings 5:25–27	Cursed Gehazi with leprosy
	2 Kings 6:6	Made the iron axehead float
	2 Kings 6:8–14	King's secrets revealed
	2 Kings 6:18	Army struck blind
	2 Kings 7:1–2, 16–17	Abundance, death of officer predicted
	2 Kings 13:17	Arrow of deliverance with Joash
	2 Kings 13:21	Dead man revived when bones touched
Titles of Elisha	2 Kings 5:3, 8, 13; 6:12	Prophet
	2 Kings 5:8, 14–15, 20; 6:6, 9–10; 7:2	Man of God
Enoch, 7th from Adam	Jude 14	His book quoted
Ethan the Ezrahite	Ps. 89	Wrote psalm
EZEKIEL	Ezek. 4:7; 6:2; 11:4; 13:2; 20:46; 21:2, 9, 14, 28	Prophesied; did signs
EZRA	Ezra, Neh.	Recorded in those books
Gad, David's seer	1 Sam. 22:5	Told David to go to Judah
	2 Sam. 24:18	Told David to erect an altar
	2 Sam. 24:11–19; 1 Chron. 21:9	His seer gave him 3 choices
	1 Chron. 29:29	"Chronicles of Gad the seer"
	2 Chron. 29:25	The king's seer
HABAKKUK	Habakkuk 1:1; 3:1	Saw oracle
HAGGAI	Haggai 1:1, 3, 12; 2:1, 10; Ezra 5:1–2; 6:14	Word of the Lord came
Hanani the seer	2 Chron. 16:7, 10; 19:2	Spoke to Asa
	1 Kings 16:1, 7; 2 Chron. 19:2; 20:34	4 times called father of Jehu
Hannah	1 Sam 2:1–10	Prayed and exulted in God
Heman, the king's seer	1 Chron. 25:1, 5; 2 Chron. 35:15	12 chapters in Psalms (e.g., Ps. 88) with sons; "Korah"?
HOSEA	Hosea 1:1; Rom. 9:25	The word of the Lord came to him
Huldah the prophetess	2 Kings 22:14–20; 2 Chron. 34:22–28	Spoke judgment on Jerusalem, encouraging word to Josiah
Iddo the seer	2 Chron. 9:29	"In the visions of Iddo the seer"

Name or Description	Reference	Situation
	2 Chron. 12:15	Shemaiah and Iddo the seer
	2 Chron. 13:22	Chronicled Ahija's reign
Isaac, son of Abraham	Gen. 27:27–29; Heb. 11:20	Blessed Jacob prophetically
	Gen. 27:39–40	Blessed Esau prophetically
ISAIAH	2 Kings 19:2, 6–7	Predicted Rabshakeh's retreat
	2 Kings 19:20–28	Demise of Sennacherib's army
	2 Kings 20:1–11	Hezekiah & sundial miracle
	2 Kings 20:17–20	Predicted Babylonian captivity
	2 Chron. 26:22	Isaiah the prophet
	2 Chron. 32:20	Prayed with Hezekiah
	2 Chron. 32:32; Is. 1:1	"Vision of Isaiah the prophet"
	Isa. 20:3	"My servant Isaiah"
	Isa. 37:2; 38:1; 39:3	Isaiah the prophet
	Matt. 3:3; 4:14; 8:17; 12:17; 13:14; 15:7; Mark 7:6; Luke 3:4; 4:17; John 1:23; 12:38; Acts 8:28–34; 28:25	Quoted as prophet
Jacob, son of Isaac	Gen. 31:10	Addressed by angel in dream
	Gen. 48:14–21; Heb. 11:21	Blessed Ephraim and Manasseh
	Gen. 49	Blessed his sons
Jahaziel, son of Zechariah	2 Chron. 20:14–17	Word to Jehoshaphat
Jeduthun the king's seer	2 Chron. 35:15	King's seer
Jehu the son of Hanani the seer	1 Kings 16:1–4, 7, 12	Judged Baasha's house
	2 Kings 10:30	"The LORD said to Jehu"
	2 Kings 15:12	Word of the Lord to Jehu
	2 Chron. 19:2–3	Went out to meet Jehoshaphat
JEREMIAH	2 Chron. 35:25	Chanted lament for Josiah
	2 Chron. 36:12, 21–22	Challenged Zedekiah
	Ezra 1:1	The word of the Lord by his mouth
	Jer. 1:5	Prophet to the nations
	Jer. 20:2; 25:2; 32:2; 34:6; 36:8, 26	Jeremiah the prophet
	Jer. 28:1–17	Challenged Hanani
	Matt. 2:17; 27:9	Prophecies quoted in NT
	Matt. 16:14	Cited by Jesus' disciples
JOB	James 5:10–11	"The endurance of Job"
JOEL	Joel 1:1	Word of the Lord came
	Acts 2:16	Quoted on Pentecost
JONAH, son of Amittai	Jonah 1:1	Word of the Lord came
	2 Kings 13:5	Was he "a deliverer"?

Name or Description	Reference	Situation
	2 Kings 14:25	Predicted restoration of Israel's border
	Matt. 12:39; 16:4; Luke 11:29	Cited in NT
Joseph, son of Jacob	Gen. 37:5; 40:8; 41:15	Dreamer and interpreter of dreams
	Gen. 50:24; Heb. 11:22	Predicted the Exodus
Joshua, son of Nun	Josh. 6:26; 1 Kings 16:34	Cursed Jericho by word of Lord
Laban	Gen. 31:10	God came to Jacob in a dream
MALACHI	Mal. 1:1	Word of the Lord came
Medad	Num. 11:26–27	One of Moses' elders
MICAH of Moresheth	Mic. 1:1; Jer. 26:18	Word of the Lord came
Micaiah, son of Imlah	1 Kings 22:8, 13–28	Declared defeat of king of Israel
	2 Chron. 18:6–27	Judgment on Ahab's efforts
	Jer. 36:11–13	"Declared all the words"
Miriam the prophetess	Ex. 15:20–21	Led singing, dancing
Moses	Deut. 18:15, 18; 34:10; Hos. 12:13	Raised up by God
NAHUM	Nah. 1:1	Recorded vision
Nathan the prophet	2 Sam. 7:2, 5–17	Told David he wouldn't build Temple
	2 Sam. 12:1–25	Rebuked David for taking Bathsheba
	2 Sam. 12:25	Named Solomon "Jedidiah"
	1 Kings 1:8, 10, 22, 23, 32, 34, 38, 44–45	Nathan the prophet
	1 Chron. 17:1, 3	David spoke to him, then God spoke
	1 Chron. 29:29	"Chronicles of Nathan the prophet"
	2 Chron. 9:29	Wrote the acts of Solomon in records
	2 Chron. 29:25	Command given from the Lord through prophets
Noah	2 Pet. 2:5	Herald of righteousness
OBADIAH	Obad. 1	Recorded vision
Oded the prophet	2 Chron. 15:8	Father of Azariah
	2 Chron. 28:9–11	Challenged returning army about capturing their brethren
SAMUEL the seer/ prophet	1 Sam. 3:11–21 (esp. 20)	God spoke to him as child; established before Israel
	1 Sam. 7:3	Promised deliverance
	1 Sam. 8:10–18	Warnings about a king
	1 Sam. 9:15, 19	God revealed Saul's coming
	1 Sam. 9:27	Proclaimed word of Lord to Saul

Name or Description	Reference	Situation
	1 Sam. 12:17	Called down thunder and rain
	1 Sam. 15:2, 10, 28	To Saul: "Smite Amalek"; God's displeasure
	1 Sam. 16:3, 12–13	Went to Jesse; anointed David
	1 Sam. 28:15–19	Called up from the dead
	1 Chron. 9:22	Appointed gatekeepers
	1 Chron. 11:3, 10	His word anointed David king
	1 Chron. 12:23	Kingdom given from Saul to David
	1 Chron. 26:28; 29:29	Seer
	2 Chron. 35:18	Prophet
	Acts 3:24; 13:20	Cited in NT
Saul	1 Sam. 10:11–12; 18:10; 19:20–24	"Is Saul also among the prophets?"
Shemaiah	1 Kings 12:22–24	Told Rehoboam to return, not fight
	2 Chron. 11:2–4	Man of God warned Rehoboam
	2 Chron. 12:5, 7	Warned leaders of Judah
	2 Chron. 12:15	Records of Shemaiah & Iddo the prophet
SOLOMON	1 Kings 3:5	Lord appeared to him in dream
	Prov., Song of Sol.	Recorded God's Word
Uriah, son of Shemaiah	Jer. 26:20–23	Slain by sword at Jehoiakim's order
Zadok the seer	2 Sam. 15:27	David called him a seer
Zechariah, son of Jehoiada	2 Chron. 24:20–21	Stoned for stand against Joash
Zechariah	2 Chron. 26:5	Had understanding through visions
ZECHARIAH	Zech., Ezra 5:1; 6:14	Word of Lord came
ZEPHANIAH	Zeph. 1:1	Word of Lord came

APPENDIX 2

Descriptive Terms of the Old Testament Prophets and Others Who Prophesied

Name or Description	Reference	Situation
Elders	Num. 11:25–26	Prophesied with Spirit on them
A prophet	Judg. 6:8	Sent to sons of Israel
A man of God	1 Sam. 2:27	Came to Eli
The man of God	1 Sam. 9:6, 8	Formerly called a seer (vv. 9, 11)
The seer (Samuel)	1 Sam. 9:11–14	Went to bless sacrifice
A group of prophets (*company,* KJV)	1 Sam. 10:5–6, 10	Met Saul; his heart changed
They (who inquired)	1 Sam. 10:22	Located Saul
A company of the prophets	1 Sam. 19:20	Prophesied under Samuel's leadership
Three groups of Saul's messengers	1 Sam. 19:20–21	Prophesied by God's Spirit
David (inquiring of the Lord)	2 Sam. 2:1; 5:19	Sent to Hebron against Philistines
A man of God from Judah	1 Kings 13:1–32	Rebuked Jeroboam & his altar
An old prophet	1 Kings 13:11–32	Lied, then prophesied, then buried man of God
Prophets of the Lord	1 Kings 18:4	Destroyed by Jezebel
100 prophets	1 Kings 18:4, 13	Hidden for protection
"Thy prophets"	1 Kings 19:14	Killed by sons of Israel
A prophet, a man of God	1 Kings 20:13, 22, 28	Sent to Ahab for defeat of Syrians
A certain man of the sons of the prophets	1 Kings 20:35, 38, 41–42	Cried judgment on Ahab
A prophet of the Lord	1 Kings 22:7–28	Summoned by Jehoshaphat
Sons of the prophets at Bethel	2 Kings 2:3	Challenged Elisha

383

Name or Description	Reference	Situation
Sons of the prophets at Jericho	2 Kings 2:5; 2 Kings 2:15–18	Challenged Elisha
50 men of the sons of the prophets	2 Kings 2:7	Watched Elijah & Elisha from distance
A woman of the wives of the sons of the prophets	2 Kings 4:1	Cried out to Elijah
A holy man of God	2 Kings 4:9, 16, 22, 25, 27, 40, 42	Restored Shunammite's son; provided for sons of prophets
Sons of the prophets	2 Kings 4:38	Starving; provided for
Sons of the prophets	2 Kings 6:1–2	Relocated at Jordan
The man of God	2 Kings 6:5–6, 9–10	Restored axehead; warned king
One of the sons of the prophets	2 Kings 9:1, 4	Served the prophet Elisha
My servants the prophets	2 Kings 9:7; Ezra 9:11; Jer. 7:25	Were commanded, sent, avenged
His prophets & every seer	2 Kings 17:13	Used for warning
All His servants the prophets	2 Kings 17:23	Spoke God's word
His servants the prophets	2 Kings 21:10–15	Prophesied against Manasseh
The prophets	2 Kings 23:2	Went to Jerusalem to hear word read
The man of God	2 Kings 23:16	Proclaimed defilement of graves
His servants the prophets	2 Kings 24:2	Spoke judgment on Jerusalem
His prophets	2 Chron. 20:20	To be trusted
Prophets	2 Chron. 24:19	Sent to bring people back to the Lord
Many oracles	2 Chron. 24:27	Against Joash
A man of God	2 Chron. 25:7	Warned Amaziah
A prophet	2 Chron. 25:15–16	Angered Amaziah
Manasseh	2 Chron. 33:10	Ignored voice of the Lord
The seers	2 Chron. 33:18	Spoke in God's name
Hozai (seers)	2 Chron. 33:19	Wrote records
His messengers and prophets	2 Chron. 36:15–16	Sent by God, mocked
Sons of Korah	Pss. 42–50, 84, 85, 87	Inspired to write 12 psalms
The oracle	Prov. 31:1–31	Given by Lemuel's mother
The prophetess	Isa. 8:3	Bore a son to Isaiah
The prophets in exile	Jer. 29:1	Taken to Babylon
My servants the prophets	Jer. 29:19; 35:15; 44:4	Sent by God
Two olive trees	Zech. 4:11–14	Possibly Zechariah & Haggai?

APPENDIX 3

New Testament Prophets and Those Who Prophesied

Code: **Bold print** = prophets; **BOLD CAPS** = canonized prophets

Name or Description	Reference	Situation
Agabus	Acts 11:28; 21:10	Predicted famine & Paul's imprisonment
Ananias	Acts 9:10–17	Vision and conveyed message
Anna	Luke 2:36	Prophesied over baby Jesus
Caiaphas	John 11:51	High priest unwittingly prophesied
Disciples at Tyre	Acts 21:4	Warned Paul about imprisonment
Elizabeth	Luke 1:41–45	Prophesied while greeting Mary
Ephesian Baptists	Acts 19:6	Spoke in tongues and prophesied
JESUS	Luke 7:16; 13:33; 24:19; John 4:19; 6:14; 7:40; 9:17; Acts 3:22–23; 7:37	A great prophet
	Matt. 7:15; 10:41; 23:34; 24:24	What Jesus said
Jezebel	Rev. 2:20	Called herself a prophetess
JOHN	Rev. 1:1–3; 10:11; 22:7, 10,18,19	Recorded the book of Revelation
John the Baptist	Matt. 21:26, 46; Mark 11:32; Luke 1:76; 7:26–28; 20:6	A prophet
Joseph, Mary's fiancé	Matt. 1:20–25; 2:13, 19	Dreams and visions
Judas	Acts 15:32	Prophet sent with Paul
Mary	Luke 1:46–55	Magnificat
PAUL	Acts 13:9; 20:23; 27:10, 23, 24, 31	At Antioch & on journey to Rome

Name or Description	Reference	Situation
PETER	Matt. 16:17	2 epistles, revelation from God
Philip's four daughters	Acts 21:9	Prophesied on regular basis
Presbytery	1 Tim. 4:14	Prophesied over Timothy
Prophets	Acts 2:17; 11:27; 13:1–4; 1 Cor. 12:28–29; Eph. 4:11	Given by God
Prophets over last-day Babylon	Rev. 18:20–24	Rejoicing
Silas	Acts 15:32	Prophet sent with Paul
Sons and daughters	Acts 2:17–18	Peter quoting from Joel 2
Stephen, first martyr	Acts 7:55–56	Vision
Thessalonica, church at	1 Thess. 5:20–21	Don't despise, but test
Two witnesses	Rev. 11:3, 6	Won't rain in the days of their prophecy
Women in Corinthian church	1 Cor. 11:5	Rebuked for not covering heads
Zacharias	Luke 1:67	Father of John the Baptist

NOTES

Chapter 1: God's Thoughts toward Us

1. David Watson, *I Believe in the Church* (Grand Rapids: Eerdmans, 1978), p. 258. Admittedly Watson is discussing prophecy in the Church, but this general idea also applies to Old Testament prophecy. (Although definitions of prophecy appear throughout this book, chapter 10, "Christian Prophecy," features the largest concentration of definitions by various authors.)

2. Cindy Jacobs, *The Voice of God* (Ventura, Calif.: Regal, 1995), p. 90.

3. This is the first occurrence of *angel* in the Scripture (see Genesis 16:7), so it has special relevance. Abraham is the only person called a prophet during this time (see Genesis 20:7, the first use in Scripture of *prophet),* but obviously he was not yet a prophet or else he was too involved emotionally in the situation to make a proper messenger for God.

4. Charles H. Spurgeon, *The Treasury of David* (Byron Center, Mich.: Associated Publishers and Authors, 1970), Vol. II (of unabridged two-volume edition), comments on Psalm 139:17, p. 227.

5. Bruce Yocum, *Prophecy: Exercising the Prophetic Gifts of the Spirit in the Church Today* (Ann Arbor, Mich.: Servant, 1976), p. 11.

6. Dick Stark, "A Call to Prophetic Expression," Sunday bulletin of Faith Temple Church in Alexander City, Alabama, August 18, 1996.

7. Glenn Foster, *The Purpose and Use of Prophecy* (Glendale, Ariz.: Sweetwater, 1988), p. 36.

8. Kim Clement, *The Sound of His Voice* (Orlando: Creation House, 1993), pp. 90–91.

Chapter 2: Increased Interest in Prophecy

1. Michael G. Maudlin, "Seers in the Heartland," *Christianity Today* 35 (January 14, 1991), pp. 18–22.

2. Three examples: Wayne A. Grudem, "Why Christians Can Still Prophesy: Scripture Encourages Us to Seek the Gift Yet Today," *Christianity Today* 32/13 (September 16, 1988), pp. 29–35; C. Peter Wagner, "The Gift of Prophecy Is for Today," *Church Growth* (autumn 1994); Jamie Buckingham, "The Prophet's Calling," *Ministries Today* (January/February 1992), pp. 55-63.

3. Mark J. Cartledge, "Charismatic Prophecy and New Testament Prophecy," *Themelios* 17 (October-November 1991), pp. 17–19. He also gives a good summary of recent thought.

4. See David Hill, *New Testament Prophecy* (Atlanta: John Knox, 1979); Graham Houston, *Prophecy: A Gift for Today?* (Downers Grove, Ill.: InterVarsity, 1989); Jacobs, *Voice.*

5. See, for instance, Bill Hamon, *Prophets and the Prophetic Movement: God's Prophetic Move Today* (Shippensburg, Pa.: Destiny Image, 1990), Vol. 2.

6. A comment made by F. F. Bruce in his foreword for Clifford Hill, *Prophecy Past and Present* (Crowborough, East Sussex: Highland, 1989), p. xii. This excellent, scholarly book argues persuasively for modern-day prophecy.

7. See David E. Aune's fourteen-page survey of five significant treatments, *Prophecy in Early Christianity and the Ancient Mediterranean World* (Grand Rapids: Eerdmans, 1983), pp. 1–14.

8. The specific articles used are listed in the bibliography.

9. John W. Hilber, "Diversity of Old Testament Prophetic Phenomena and New Testament

Prophecy," *Westminster Theological Journal* 56 (1994), p. 243.

10. Stanley M. Burgess deals with the tension between prophecy and form in a fine study of the Church from the end of the first century A.D. to the end of the fifth century. *The Spirit and the Church: Antiquity* (Peabody, Mass.: Hendrickson, 1984). Also see chapter 15 in this book.

11. See M. Eugene Boring, *The Continuing Voice of Jesus: Christian Prophecy & the Gospel Tradition* (Louisville: Westminster/John Knox, 1991), chapter 1. Also see Aune, *Prophecy in Early Christianity*, chapter 9, and "Christian Prophecy and the Sayings of Jesus," *New Testament Studies* 29 (1982), pp. 104–112.

12. See Clifford Hill, *Prophecy*, pp. 160–185. Also his journal article "On the Evidence for the Creative Role of Christian Prophets," *New Testament Studies* 20 (1973–1974), pp. 262–274.

13. Boring, *Continuing Voice*, p. 20.

14. See the challenging testimonial critique of the historical-critical method by Eta Linnemann, a reputable scholar who studied under Bultmann and other German scholars: *Historical Criticism of the Bible: Methodology or Ideology?* (Grand Rapids: Baker, 1990).

15. F. David Farnell, "When Will the Gift of Prophecy Cease?" *Bibliotheca Sacra* 150 (April–June 1993), p. 171.

16. Refer to chapter 14 where I give my basic refutation of the five major arguments for the cessation of prophecy and the interpretation of the five major Bible passages used for the support of cessationism.

17. C. F. D. Moule comments that Revelation 19:10 "seems . . . to identify the testimony borne by Jesus himself as 'the concern or burden of the Spirit who inspired prophecy.' . . . There is strong evidence for taking 'of Jesus' as a subjective genitive: it is not 'witness to Jesus' but 'the witness borne by Jesus.'" *The Holy Spirit* (Grand Rapids: Eerdmans, 1979), p. 63.

18. Rick Joyner, *The Prophetic Ministry* (Charlotte, N.C.: MorningStar, 1997), p. 49.

19. Wayne A. Grudem, *The Gift of Prophecy in the New Testament and Today* (Wheaton: Crossway, 1988). The book represents a popularized and expanded edition of Grudem's earlier work, *The Gift of Prophecy in 1 Corinthians* (Lanham, Md.: University Press, 1982), which in turn is a publishable edition of his doctoral dissertation of the same title (Cambridge: Cambridge University, 1978).

20. F. David Farnell, "Is the Gift of Prophecy for Today?" (given in 4 parts), *Bibliotheca Sacra* 149 (1992), July–September, pp. 277–303; 149 (1992), October-December, pp. 387–410; 150 (1993), January–March, pp. 62–88; 150 (1993), April–June, pp. 171–202. This is probably the most detailed critique of Grudem given by a cessationist.

21. Ibid., 149 (1992), July–September, p. 277.

22. Grudem, *Gift of Prophecy in the New Testament*, p. 14.

23. That is, the desire to protect the prophetic integrity of the Bible by acknowledging only the validity of prophecy in the Church that produced Scripture.

24. Gordon D. Fee, *God's Empowering Presence: The Holy Spirit in the Letters of Paul* (Peabody, Mass.: Hendrickson, 1994), p. 892.

25. Perhaps we should contend at the same time for one hundred percent accuracy in preaching!

26. Joyner, *Prophetic Ministry*, pp. 117–118.

27. Scripture itself seems to take in stride certain prophecy that was not fulfilled verbatim and could be classified as inspired or Spirit-quickened but not God-breathed or inscripturated. Agabus' "thus saith the Spirit" prophecy was fulfilled in meaning but not in minute detail of actual words used (see Acts 21:11, 33).

28. Some interesting references are Bruce Yocum's chapter 1, "A Brief History of Christian Prophecy," *Prophecy;* Jack Deere's chapter 5, "Presbyterian Prophets" (examples from A.D. 1500s and 1600s), *Surprised by the Voice of God* (Grand Rapids: Zondervan, 1996); David Pytches' chapter 15, "Prophecy during the Dark Ages," and his chapters 16–19, which talk about the French prophets (A.D. 1500–1600), the German prophets (1500s), the Ranters (1500–1700) and the Quakers (1600s), *Prophecy in the Local Church: A Practical Handbook and Historical Overview* (London: Hodder & Stoughton, 1993).

29. For the Hebrew prophets see Edward J. Young, *My Servants the Prophets* (Grand Rapids: Eerdmans, 1952), chapter 1 and appendix. See also Christopher Forbes' impressive work *Prophecy and Inspired Speech: In Early Christianity and Its Hellenistic Environment* (Peabody, Mass.: Hendrickson, 1997 reprint), an excellent, scholarly examination of the Hellenistic evidence that clearly shows there are "no compelling parallels" between Christian glossolalia or prophecy and Hellenistic ecstatic religion.

30. Ronald A. N. Kydd, *Charismatic Gifts in the Early Church: An Exploration into the*

Gifts of the Spirit during the First Three Centuries of the Christian Church (Peabody, Mass.: Hendrickson, 1984). Also see Burgess, *Spirit and the Church*.

31. C. Peter Wagner, *Praying with Power* (Ventura: Regal, 1997), p. 43.

32. Joyner, *Prophetic Ministry*, pp. 13–14.

33. Grudem, *Gift of Prophecy in the New Testament*, p. 132.

34. Buckingham, "The Prophet's Calling," p. 55.

Chapter 3: Mission: What Was a Prophet?

1. Alfred Edersheim, *Bible History: Old Testament* (Peabody, Mass.: Hendrickson, 1995, a reproduction of the 1890 seven-volume ed.), p. 712.

2. Cecil M. Robeck Jr., "Gift of Prophecy," p. 730. Taken from *Dictionary of Pentecostal and Charismatic Movements* by Stanley M. Burgess, Gary B. McGee and Patrick H. Alexander. Copyright © 1988 by Stanley M. Burgess, Gary B. McGee and Patrick H. Alexander. Used by permission of Zondervan Publishing House.

3. Charles A. Briggs, *Messianic Prophecy* (Peabody, Mass.: Hendrickson, 1988 reprint of an 1886 edition), p. 2.

4. Jacob M. Myers and Edwin D. Freed, "Is Paul Also among the Prophets?" *Interpretation* 20 (1966), p. 48. Original thought from H. Wheeler Robinson, "The Council of Yahweh," *Journal of Theological Studies* 45 (1944), pp. 151–157.

5. Ibid., p. 49.

6. Leon J. Wood, *The Prophets of Israel* (Grand Rapids: Baker, 1979), p. 63.

7. Daniel Powell Williams, *The Prophetical Ministry in the Church* (Penygroes, Wales: Apostolic Church, 1931), p. 11.

8. Or *gazer,* as suggested by David J. Zucker, *Israel's Prophets* (New York: Paulist, 1994), p. 16.

9. Walter C. Kaiser, *Back toward the Future: Hints for Interpreting Prophecy* (Grand Rapids: Baker, 1989), p. 74.

10. *Gad* in 1 Samuel 22:5; 2 Samuel 24:11; 1 Chronicles 21:9; 2 Chronicles 29:25. *Iddo* in 2 Chronicles 9:29; 12:15; 13:22. *Amos,* one of the great writing prophets, in Amos 7:12.

11. See Isaiah 30:9–10, where the term *nabi* is not used, but rather *roeh* is translated "seer" and the term *hozeh* is translated "prophet." Thus *nabi* had no exclusive claim on speaking forth for God.

12. Since a person could be a *nabi* and a *roeh* (see 1 Samuel 7:7), and three men are called both a *hozeh* and a *nabi,* it appears that the three terms present the same ministry. The term itself suggests either a messenger making an announcement, or that the message has come to the messenger in visionary form. Also note that seers were sometimes spokespersons (see Isaiah 30:9–10, where both *roeh* and *hozeh* are used). For an excellent discussion of the subject, see Young, *My Servants,* "The Seer," pp. 61–66.

13. G. Friedrich, *Theological Dictionary of the New Testament,* Vol. VI, p. 796.

14. Robert D. Culver, "Nabi," R. Laird Harris, ed., *Theological Wordbook of the Old Testament* (Chicago: Moody, 1980), Vol. 2, p. 544.

15. Hobart E. Freeman gives one of the best explanations, and I follow his outline in *An Introduction to the Old Testament Prophets* (Chicago: Moody, 1968), pp. 37–39. His basic outline is also copied in the *Theological Wordbook of the Old Testament,* p. 544. The scholars supporting each view are listed in those places.

16. See Kaiser, *Future,* p. 73.

17. Samuel Prideaux Tregelles, tr., *Gesenius' Hebrew and Chaldee Lexicon to the Old Testament Scriptures* (Grand Rapids: Eerdmans, 1949), p. 528.

18. W. Sibley Towner, "On Calling People Prophets in 1970," *Interpretation* 24 (October 1970), p. 495.

19. Culver, "Nabi," p. 544.

20. Samuel W. Barnum, ed., "Prophet," *Smith's Comprehensive Dictionary of the Bible* (New York: Appleton, 1867), p. 887.

21. This seven-point framework is used again in chapter 9, where it is expanded to eleven points and comparison is made between prophecy in the Old and New Testament eras.

22. C. Douglas Weaver, *The Healer-Prophet, William Marrion Branham: A Study of the Prophetic in American Pentecostalism* (Macon, Ga.: Mercer University, 1987), p. xiii.

23. Clarence E. Macartney, from the foreword of *The Unity of Isaiah* by Oswald T. Allis (Presbyterian and Reformed Publishing, 1974). This excellent book by a renowned scholar argues persuasively for the supernatural in the prophets' ministries.

24. J. Barton Payne, *Encyclopedia of Biblical Prophecy* (Grand Rapids: Baker, 1980), p. 681.

25. See also Allis, *Unity,* chapter 1, for his 21 illustrations of predictive prophecy and how

it is most feasible to accept the supernatural element in these prophecies.

26. David du Plessis as told to Bob Slosser, *A Man Called Mr. Pentecost* (Plainfield, N.J.: Logos, 1977), pp. 1–2.

27. Ibid., pp. 5–6.

28. Jack Hywel-Davies, *The Life of Smith Wigglesworth* (Ann Arbor, Mich.: Vine/Servant, 1988), p. 155.

29. R. P. Spittler, "Du Plessis, David Johannes," pp. 253–254. *Dictionary of Pentecostal and Charismatic Movements* by Stanley M. Burgess, Gary B. McGee and Patrick H. Alexander. Copyright © 1988 by Stanley M. Burgess, Gary B. McGee and Patrick H. Alexander. Used by permission of Zondervan Publishing House.

30. Freeman, *Old Testament Prophets,* p. 24.

31. Bernhard Duhm, *Israels Propheten,* quoted by Klaus Baltzer, *Harvard Theological Review* 61 (1968), p. 567.

32. Wood, *Prophets,* p. 9.

33. Kevin J. Conner, *The Church in the New Testament* (Portland: BT Publishing, 1989), pp. 55–56.

Chapter 4: Makeup: Traits That Characterized a Prophet

1. Young, *My Servants,* p. 205.

2. Actually, on Mount Carmel (1 Kings 18), "The quiet and dignified attitude of Elijah, the true prophet of God . . . is in vivid contrast to the orgiastic and ecstatic activities attributed to these prophets of Baal." A. A. MacRae, "Prophets and Prophecy," Merrill C. Tenney, gen. ed., *Zondervan Pictorial Encyclopedia of the Bible* (Grand Rapids: Zondervan, 1975), Vol. 4, p. 891.

3. There are ostensibly five divination passages in Scripture: Genesis 44:5, 15 (when Joseph pretended to use divination); 1 Samuel 28 (when Saul attempted to reach Samuel through a medium); 2 Samuel 5:24 (the shaking of leaves as God's hosts pass before David); Isaiah 8:19 (an exhortation *not* to consult mediums and spiritists!); and Ezekiel 21:21 (when the king of Babylon used divination). Two favorite references to show prophecy as an out-of-control ecstasy would be 1 Samuel 10:10–12 and 19:20–24; Saul is the very poorest example of Hebrew prophecy, however, and this kind of behavior is not portrayed elsewhere as normative for Israel.

4. See Wood, *Prophets,* chapter 2; Cecil M. Robeck Jr., "I. Prophetic Speech in the Ancient World," pp. 728–730, *Dictionary of Pentecostal and Charismatic Movements* by Stanley M. Burgess, Gary B. McGee and Patrick H. Alexander. Copyright © 1988 by Stanley M. Burgess, Gary B. McGee and Patrick H. Alexander. Used by permission of Zondervan Publishing House. Also see Young, *My Servants,* chapter 1 and appendix: "Extra-Biblical 'Prophecy' in the Ancient World."

5. Those who speak contrary to Scripture remain in the darkness of deep spiritual night. When they turn from their own ways to the Word of God, spiritual morning will break.

6. Edward J. Young, who was a leading Hebrew expert, says in his classic book *My Servants the Prophets* (p. 21): "Nine superstitions are enumerated, practices which for one reason or another the Canaanites employed. At the head of the list stands februation, or the custom of passing one's son and daughter through the fire." After looking at several commentaries on this (I have found the word *februation* nowhere else), it appears that most feel it refers to child sacrifice through burning. But an interesting comment from *The Torah: A Modern Commentary* (Jewish) says: "The Talmud offers two explanations. One is that the children were made to walk between two fires as a symbol of their dedication to the god." Hence it could be "sons *and* daughters," as in Deuteronomy 12:31, and imply that they would come out the other side. The other explanation, according to *The Torah,* "is that the children were tossed back and forth over a fire till they were burned" (p. 883). 2 Kings 23:10 says "that no man might make his son *or* his daughter pass through the fire for Molech" (emphasis added). *The Torah* concludes its discussion of Molech worship in Leviticus with this statement: "All we can say with certainty is that these laws forbid the devotion of children to a pagan cult. How barbarous the form of devotion was is uncertain" (p. 884). Gunther Plaut, *The Torah* (New York: Jewish Publication Society, 1981). Most evangelical commentators would probably say that it was child sacrifice by fire, although I find *The Torah*'s explanation a good one.

7. Various scholars believe this, but perhaps Young gives the best explanation (*My Servants,* pp. 20–35).

8. Joyner, *Prophetic Ministry,* p. 23.

9. Theodore H. Robinson, *Prophecy and the Prophets in Ancient Israel* (London: Duckworth, 1936), p. 29.

10. For an interesting discussion of "The Role of the Watchman," especially among today's intercessors, see Jacobs, *Voice,* pp. 46–53.

11. John Skinner, *Prophecy and Religion: Studies in the Life of Jeremiah* (London: Cambridge University, 1951), p. 31.

12. *Theological Wordbook of the Old Testament,* Vol. 1, p. 479.

13. James Hastings, ed., *A Dictionary of the Bible* (New York: Charles Scribner's Sons, 1902), Vol. IV, p. 113.

14. See Kaiser, *Future,* p. 76. Also, Wood, *Prophets,* p. 13.

15. H. L. Ellison, *Men Spake from God* (Grand Rapids: Eerdmans, first U.S. printing 1958), p. 14.

16. I. Howells says: "The central place given to the Prophets in the Massoretic [sic] text can be supported by the fact that in one sense the whole of the Old Testament is a prophetic book and the phrase: 'saith the Lord' is cited some 3,500 times in its pages. The impact made by the prophets on the history of Israel cannot be over-estimated. . . ." *Prophecy in Doctrine and Practice* (Penygroes, Dyfed, Wales: Apostolic Church Training School, 1991), Section II, p. 1.

17. Young, *My Servants,* p. 50.

18. 1 Kings 20:35–43; 2 Kings 2:5, 7, 15; 4:1, 38; 5:22; 6:1; 9:1.

19. This terminology is a misnomer. Actually no Scripture uses this terminology. There is nothing to substantiate the existence of a school as we know it.

20. Patrick Fairbairn, *Prophecy* (Grand Rapids: Baker, 1976 reprint from the edition issued in 1865 by T. & T. Clark), p. 23.

21. Edersheim, *Bible History,* p. 416.

22. Jay P. Green Sr., gen. ed. and trans., *The Interlinear Bible* (Grand Rapids: Baker, 2nd ed. 1986), p. 240.

23. It appears that there were "schools" or gatherings of these prophets in at least four places: Ramah (see 1 Samuel 19:18-24); Bethel (see 2 Kings 2:3); Jericho (see 2 Kings 2:5, 15); and Gilgal (see 2 Kings 2:1; 4:38).

24. See James G. Williams, "The Prophetic 'Father': A Brief Explanation of the Term 'Sons of the Prophets,'" *Journal of Biblical Literature* 85:1966 (Part 3, September 1966), pp. 344–348.

25. Edersheim, *Bible History,* p. 710.

26. Demos Shakarian, *The Happiest People on Earth* (Old Tappan, N.J.: Revell, 1975), pp. 16–19.

27. See, for instance, *Stories from the Front Lines* by Jane Rumph (Grand Rapids: Chosen Books, 1996).

28. Wood, *Prophets,* p. 16.

29. Freeman, *Old Testament Prophets,* pp. 12–13.

30. Clifford Hill, *Prophecy,* p. 45.

31. D. P. Williams, *Prophetical Ministry,* p. 14.

32. Seeley D. Kinney, "Restoration in the Church," *The Banner* 27(3) spring 1995, p. 7.

Chapter 5: Mind: How Did Prophecy Come to a Prophet?

1. H. Wheeler Robinson comments: "The cardinal fact of the prophetic consciousness, as it is displayed in Amos and his great successors, is the absolute conviction of a divine call, mission, and message." *The Religious Ideas of the Old Testament* (London: Duckworth, 1913), p. 113.

2. Pytches, *Prophecy,* p. 51.

3. The more modern expression (as in the NLT), "The Lord gave these messages to —," is understandable but lacks the dynamic, forceful simplicity of God's original intent in the Hebrew.

4. Such an experience was no everyday occurrence! In contrast the New Testament Christian has the Holy Spirit abiding constantly within, giving impressions and assurances and sometimes speaking a clearly defined word. This is one of the main differences between prophecy in the Old and New Testaments, as we will see in chapter 9. God oversaw the accuracy of the *logos* word of the Old Testament, whereas the Church oversees the accuracy of the *rhema* word for current events in the New Testament.

5. This terminology *internal* and *external* is used by A. A. MacRae in his article "Prophets and Prophecy," p. 880.

6. Lit. Heb., *"the* cave" (1 Kings 19:9). The Hebrew has the definite article, which some scholars feel indicates a special, well-known cave—perhaps the cleft of the rock where Moses met with God (Exodus 33:22; 34:6)?

7. These forms of hearing from God are explained by Jack Deere, *Surprised by the Voice of God,* chapters 9 and 10.

8. Wagner has given some insight on this. *Praying with Power,* chapter 2, "Two-Way Prayer: Hearing God," gives good illustrations and a positive testimony for this approach.

9. Twelve in the Old Testament: Abram, Balaam, Samuel, Nathan, Iddo, Zechariah, Isaiah, Ezekiel, Daniel, Obadiah, Nahum and Habakkuk; and five in the New Testament: Zacharias, Peter, James, John and Paul.

10. Charles H. Spurgeon, *Lectures to My Students* (Grand Rapids: Baker, 1977 reprint), p. 49.

11. Story by Pytches, *Does God Speak*, pp. 48–49. Taken from *The Early Years*, the first volume of Spurgeon's autobiography.

12. Robert L. Alden, "Ecstasy and the Prophets," *Bulletin of the Evangelical Theological Society*, 9 (1966), p. 155. This article gives a good summary of the various interpretations available.

13. See MacRae's article "Prophets and Prophecy," Section H, "Ecstasy and the Prophet," p. 891ff, where he answers the arguments for the seven most-quoted Old Testament references used to argue that the prophets had abnormal psychological conditions or behavior.

14. Theodore Robinson, *Prophecy and the Prophets*, p. 50. I picked up this book in England at an old bookstore, expecting a more positive approach by one of the most notable exponents of Hebrew prophecy in England.

15. David E. Aune, "Ecstasy," Geoffrey W. Bromiley, gen. ed., *The International Standard Bible Encyclopedia*, Vol. 2, p. 14.

16. Cecil M. Robeck Jr., *Prophecy in Carthage* (Cleveland: Pilgrim, 1992), p. 102.

17. Usually Sunday school classes picture Samuel as younger, say six years of age, probably because of the use of the word *boy* (1 Samuel 2:11, 18, 21, 26; 3:1, 8). A. M. Renwick in his commentary on 1 Samuel in *The New Bible Commentary* (Grand Rapids: Zondervan, 1953), p. 265, suggests that Samuel was "now about twelve years old," which seems reasonable to me.

18. This was the evaluation of Jesus (Matthew 11:11).

19. For a more thorough explanation, see F. F. Bruce, *The New Testament Documents: Are They Reliable?* (Grand Rapids: Eerdmans, 5th ed., 1959), chapter 3, "The Canon of the New Testament." Also, Josh McDowell, *Evidence that Demands a Verdict, Vol. 1* (San Bernardino: Here's Life, 25th printing, 1986), chapter 3, "The Canon."

20. Michael Harper, *Prophecy: A Gift for the Body of Christ* (London: Fountain Trust, 1964), p. 11.

21. See Ned B. Stonehouse, "Special Revelation as Scriptural," Carl F. H. Henry, ed., *Revelation and the Bible* (Grand Rapids: Baker, 1958), chapter 5.

22. Henry Barclay Swete, *The Holy Spirit in the New Testament* (Grand Rapids: Baker, 1976 reprint of the original 1910 edition), p. 388.

23. Charles Hodge, *Systematic Theology* (Grand Rapids: Eerdmans, 1989 reprint), Vol. 1, p. 154.

24. Ralph Earle, "2 Timothy," Frank E. Gaebelein, gen. ed., *The Expositors Bible Commentary* (Grand Rapids: Zondervan, 1978), Vol. 11, p. 409.

25. Alan M. Stibbs, "Witness of Scripture to Its Inspiration," *Revelation and Bible*, p. 109.

26. Harold Lindsell, *The Battle for the Bible* (Grand Rapids: Zondervan, 1976), p. 34.

27. Ibid, pp. 50–51. Quoted from Edward J. Young, *Thy Word Is Truth*, pp. 20–22.

28. Simon J. Kistemaker, *Peter and Jude, New Testament Commentary* (Grand Rapids: Baker, 1993), p. 273.

29. Stibbs, "Witness of Scripture," p. 110. He also has an excellent page and a half dealing with the right of Scripture to vindicate itself: "Place of Self-Authentication," pp. 108–109.

30. As of Hosea in Romans 9:25; of David in 1 Corinthians 15:27; and of Isaiah in 2 Corinthians 6:2,17.

31. Hebrews 1:6–8; 2:12; 3:7; 4:3–4; 5:5; 7:21; 8:8; 9:8; 10:5, 15–16; 12:26; 13:5.

32. Acts 1:16; 4:25; 13:47; 28:25–27.

33. Matthew 1:22; 4:14; 8:17; 12:18.

34. Matthew 2:17.

35. Matthew 21:5.

36. Romans 2:16; 1 Corinthians 2:9, 13; 14:37–38; 2 Corinthians 13:3; Galatians 1:6–12; 1 Thessalonians 2:13; 4:8, 15; 5:27; 2 Thessalonians 3:6, 14; 2 Peter 3:2, 15–16; Revelation 1:3; 22:18ff. Paul treats his own writings as sacred documents, urging the churches to read and circulate them (Colossians 4:16; 1 Thessalonians 5:27).

37. I believe that the Bible is the Word of God given in the words of men in history, so I am not offended by an honest evangelical attempt to evaluate the historical context or to research the text studiously. We do not have the original manuscripts, nor do we speak the original languages as they did, so we need a total trust in the original Word God gave, as well as sincere efforts to bring that Word into meaningful contemporary expression. For a helpful outlook, see George Eldon Ladd's *New*

Testament and Criticism (Grand Rapids: Eerdmans, 1967).

38. Shakarian, *Happiest People*, pp. 19–22. Those of us who live in California have a constant, living reminder of how this prophecy came to pass. The descendants of those pilgrims still worship in their Armenian Pentecostal churches in central and southern California.

39. Samuel W. Barnum, ed., "Prophet," *Smith's Comprehensive Dictionary of the Bible* (London: D. Appellation, 1884), p. 889.

40. G. Friedrich, *Theological Dictionary of the New Testament*, Vol. VI, p. 851.

41. Paul Cain, "Hearing God," *MorningStar Journal* 4 (No. 1), 1994, p. 54.

42. Joseph Bryant Rotherham, *The Emphasized Bible* (Grand Rapids: Kregel, 1959 reprint), p. 608.

43. Quoted by J. Sidlow Baxter, *Explore the Book* (Grand Rapids: Zondervan, 1966), p. 44.

Chapter 6: Message: Various Ways of Prophetic Expression

1. Gene M. Tucker, "Prophetic Speech," *Interpretation* 32 (January 1978), p. 31.

2. Wood, *Prophets*, p. 63.

3. Tucker says: "An essential step in the analysis of the [prophetic] literature is the separation of these materials according to units. In this respect the most useful clues are the introductory and concluding formulas such as the call to hear ('Hear this word. . .') or the prophetic word formula ('The word of Yahweh came to. . .'), and the typical structures of the different genres which suggest where they began and ended." "Prophetic Speech," p. 32.

4. Edersheim, *Bible History*, p. 637–638.

5. Tucker, "Prophetic Speech," p. 35.

6. G. H. Livingston, "Burden," *Zondervan Pictorial Encyclopedia of the Bible*, Vol. 1, p. 671.

7. J. Millar, "Burden," *Dictionary of the Bible*, Vol. 1, p. 331.

8. Isaiah uses this burden form for his messages against the foreign nations. It occurs at 13:1 (Babylon); 14:29 (Philistia); 15:1 (Moab); 17:1 (Damascus); 19:1 (Egypt); 21:1 (Babylon); 21:11 (Dumah); 21:13 (Arabia); 22:1 (Valley of Vision); and 23:1 (Tyre). "These messages are all minatory in nature, although occasionally there is subjoined a rose-tinted promise such as the one in Isa 19:16-25." W. C. Kaiser, *"Massa," Theological Wordbook of the Old Testament*, Vol. II, p. 602.

9. Clifford Hill, for instance, discusses five categories: declaration, pronouncement, communication, announcement and apocalyptic literature. *Prophecy,* pp. 278–280.

10. Theodore Robinson, *Prophecy and the Prophets*, p. 47.

11. Towner, "Calling People Prophets," p. 505.

12. Edersheim, *Bible History*, p. 437.

13. Kaiser, *Future*, p. 76.

14. Ellison, *Men Spake*, p. 16.

15. See the "Foretelling" section in chapter 3.

16. Clifford Hill, *Prophecy,* pp. 98–100.

17. Kaiser says, "These two texts with their alternative prospects for obedience and disobedience were directly quoted or alluded to by the sixteen writing prophets literally hundreds of times." *Future,* p. 36.

18. Published by the B. B. Kirkbride Bible Co., Indianapolis.

19. Published by Thomas Nelson Publishers, Nashville.

20. Tucker, "Prophetic Speech," p. 36.

21. This story, taken from the NLT, which agrees with the NKJV and NASB, is more logical than that presented in the KJV.

22. H. McKeating, "The Prophet Jesus—II," *The Expository Times* 73 (1961–1962), p. 52.

23. Myers and Freed, "Among the Prophets," p. 49.

24. For a modern evangelistic application of this concept, see Dutch Sheets, *Intercessory Prayer* (Ventura: Regal, 1995), chapter 13, "Actions that Speak and Words that Perform." Throughout the world Christians are prayer-walking their neighborhoods, marching through the streets and literally anointing and praying for oppressive walls, etc., as a modern-day adaptation of this ancient concept.

25. Arthur Blessitt, *Arthur, a Pilgrim* (Hollywood: Blessitt Publishing, 1985).

26. Houston, *Prophecy*, p. 43.

27. D. P. Williams, *Prophetical Ministry*, p. 59.

28. Theodore Robinson, *Prophecy and the Prophets*, p. 48.

29. Fairbairn, *Prophecy*, p. 5.

30. Ellison, *Men Spake*, p. 14.

Chapter 7: Madness: What Compelled the False Prophet?

1. Or, "He that is" or "He is being." "I AM THE ONE WHO ALWAYS IS" (NLT) or "I AM WHO I

AM" or "I WILL BE WHAT I WILL BE." The CEV says, "I am the eternal God," and in the margin suggests, "I am the one who brings into being." Note how Revelation 4:8 (Message) capsulates this thought: "THE WAS, THE IS, THE COMING."

2. The Hebrew name is generally referred to as *Yahweh*, rather than the awkward English *I AM*. Appearing 6,823 times in the Hebrew Old Testament, the name is usually translated in our English versions by the capitalized LORD or GOD. The original Hebrew form was considered so sacred that it could not be spoken or read, so the Jews took the vowel points of the Hebrew word *Adonai* (English, *Lord*) and placed them on the sacred Tetragrammaton to remind them always to speak the substituted name *Adonai* rather than the original name.

The old English *Jehovah* was a misguided attempt of the translators in A.D. 1520 to translate the vowel points of Adonai (*e, o* and *a*) with the four consonants *J, H, V, H,* thus obtaining a pronounceable *JeHoVaH* for the unpronounceable name. Jewish encyclopedias, however, identify the name *Jehovah* as a hybrid word and unacceptable as an authentic rendition of God's name. Naturally Jesus and the early Church did not use this word because it did not even exist at the time.

3. Other than Jesus, Moses was the agent of more stupendous manifestations of divine power than any other person. It was a momentous time in history, for God was founding the Hebrew nation as the medium for producing the Messiah, through whom all nations would be blessed.

4. Henry H. Halley, *Halley's Bible Handbook* (Grand Rapids: Zondervan, 1965, 24th ed.), p. 282.

5. Plaut, *Torah*, p. 1182ff.

6. That such statements should come first from a heathen soothsayer indicates God's desire for all nations to be reached with His message—an amazing sign that God would in the end make every knee bow and every tongue confess (including every false spirit and prophet).

7. The New Testament commentators had nothing good to say of Balaam; see 2 Peter 2:15, Jude 11 and Revelation 2:14.

8. G. V. Smith, "Prophecy, False," *The International Standard Bible Encyclopedia*, Vol. 4, p. 984.

9. Hananiah, for instance, prophesied that the yoke of the king of Babylon would be broken (Jeremiah 28); Noadiah the prophetess tried to frighten Nehemiah (Nehemiah 6:14); and Zedekiah made horns of iron and declared the consummation of the Arameans (1 Kings 22:11).

10. C. F. Keil, "Jeremiah," *Keil and Delitzsch Commentary,* Vol. VIII, p. 357.

11. Ibid., p. 358.

12. Also note the following confirmations: 1 Kings 22:18–22; 2 Chronicles 18:22; Psalm 81:11–12; 109:17–18; Isaiah 29:9–10; 44:20; 66:3–4; Ezekiel 14:9; John 12:39–40; Romans 1:21, 25, 28.

13. H. A. Baker, *Visions beyond the Veil* (Springdale, Pa.: Whitaker, 1973), pp. 5–6. More than 125,000 copies of this remarkable story are in print. I am pleased that Whitaker House has republished the account. I have a dilapidated, fifty-year-old copy that I first read as a teenager; it had a remarkable effect on my life. Other page numbers from this volume follow in the text.

14. Plaut, *Torah*, p. 1428.

15. Joyner, *Prophetic*, p. 98.

16. D. P. Williams, *Prophetical Ministry*, p. 26.

17. Edersheim, *Bible History*, pp. 287–288.

Chapter 8: The Reappearance of Prophecy

1. "The seventy men who are chosen become not merely deputized administrators but also purveyors of prophecy. While a jealous Joshua urges his master to restrict such competition, Moses rejects a narrow interpretation of prophetic privilege." Plaut, *Torah*, p. 1088.

2. Clifford Hill comments: "'Being filled with the Spirit' would, in Jewish usage, be tantamount to saying 'becoming prophets'. . . ." *New Testament Prophecy*, p. 96.

3. Frederick E. Greenspahn, "Why Prophecy Ceased," *Journal of Biblical Literature* 108/1 (1989), pp. 37–49.

4. MacRae, "Prophets and Prophecy," p. 884.

5. Greenspahn, "Prophecy," p. 45.

6. See David Hill, "2. The Intertestamental Literature," *New Testament Prophecy*, pp. 21–25. For a history of this time see Charles F. Pfeiffer, *Between the Testaments* (Grand Rapids: Baker, 1961).

7. Aune, *Prophecy*, p. 103.

8. Pytches, *Prophecy*, pp. 17–22.

9. Ernest Best, "Prophets and Preachers," *Scottish Journal of Theology* 12 (1959), p. 140.

10. Freeman, *Old Testament Prophets*, p. 130.

11. James D. G. Dunn, "New Wine in Old Wine-Skins: VI. Prophet," *The Expository Times* 85 (1973), p. 6.

12. I like "The Chronometrical Principle" of Kevin J. Conner and Ken Malmin, *Interpreting the Scriptures* (Portland: BT Publishing, 1976), pp. 153–162. They feel that God has divided and arranged time into a series of successive ages, times and seasons. Our interpretation of a given Bible text, therefore, should take into consideration the given time frame.

13. Freeman says: "John is designated by Christ as the greatest of the prophets inasmuch as he forms the connecting link between the Old Testament prophets who foretold the Messiah and the appearance of the Messiah Himself." *Old Testament Prophets*, p. 131.

14. T. W. Manson, *The Sayings of Jesus* (Grand Rapids: Eerdmans, 1979 reprint), p. 70.

15. F. F. Bruce, *The Hard Sayings of Jesus* (Downers Grove, Ill: InterVarsity, 1983), p. 114.

16. W. Harold Mare says, "That this miracle working function was thought to be important in a prophet and, particularly, of Christ as prophet is evidenced in Luke 24:19 where the two traveling to Emmaus speak of Christ as a 'prophet mighty in *deed* and *word.*'" *Bulletin of the Evangelical Theological Society* 9:3 (1966), p. 144.

17. The last three thoughts suggested by H. A. Guy, *New Testament Prophecy: Its Origin and Significance* (London: Epworth, 1947), one of the early pioneer scholars in this subject. He concludes: "In his words and his works, as portrayed in the Gospels, Jesus appears as a true prophet. He shared many of the characteristics of the Old Testament prophets and seers, but transcended them all" (p. 143).

18. F. F. Bruce, *The Gospel of John* (Grand Rapids: Eerdmans, 1983), p. 72.

19. Dunn, "New Wine," p. 6.

20. See Kevin J. Conner's detailed comparison between Moses and Christ, *Church in the New Testament*, p. 160ff.

21. George Eldon Ladd, *A Theology of the New Testament* (Grand Rapids: Eerdmans, 1974), p. 343.

22. Dunn, "New Wine," p. 5.

23. George T. Montague, *The Holy Spirit: Growth of a Biblical Tradition* (New York: Paulist, 1976), p. 399ff.

24. Fairbairn, *Prophecy*, p. 11.

Chapter 9: Comparing Prophecy in Both Testaments

1. "In the LXX [Septuagint] *nabi* is always translated *prophetes;* there is not a single instance of any other word." *Theological Dictionary of the New Testament*, VI, p. 812.

2. Clifford Hill, *Prophecy*, p. 242.

3. For instance, this opinion: "The Old Testament makes no obvious attempt to distinguish the activities of the early prophets from those of the writing prophets, and in fact the same titles are given to both groups." R. R. Wilson, "Early Israelite Prophecy," *Interpretation* 32 (1978), p. 7. This can also be said in evaluating Old versus New Testament prophets.

4. See David Hill's insights, *New Testament Prophecy*, chapter 1.

5. See Buckingham, "The Prophet's Calling," pp. 55–63. Three leaders of today's "prophetic movement" give their views on the office of a prophet.

6. Glenn Foster, *The Purpose and Use of Prophecy*, p. 42. The illustration of the scaffolding also comes from his book, p. 44.

7. Fairbairn, *Prophecy*, p. 30.

8. Edersheim, *Bible History*, p. 438.

9. Clement, *The Sound of His Voice*, p. 57.

10. Michael Green develops this thought admirably in chapter 2, "The Spirit in the Old Testament," of *I Believe in the Holy Spirit* (Grand Rapids: Eerdmans, 1980 reprint).

11. Yocum, *Prophecy*, pp. 34–35.

12. David Hill, "Christian Prophets as Teachers or Instructors in the Church," J. Panagopoulos, ed., *Prophetic Vocation in the New Testament and Today* (Leiden, The Netherlands: E. J. Brill, 1977), p. 128.

13. Emil Brunner, *The Misunderstanding of the Church* (Philadelphia: Westminster, 1953), p. 20.

14. Howells, *Prophecy*, chapter 2, p. 5.

15. Graham Cooke, *Developing Your Prophetic Gifting* (Kent, Sussex, U.K.: Sovereign World, 1994), p. 141.

16. Kaiser, *Future*, pp. 77–78. He adds: "And there are Amos 1–2, the entire prophecies of Jonah, Nahum, Obadiah, and many other sections in the prophets."

17. Cooke, *Prophetic Gifting*, p. 141.

18. *Theological Dictionary of the New Testament*, Vol. VI, p. 849.

19. Joyner, *Prophetic*, pp. 55–56.

20. Alex Buchanan, *Explaining Prophecy* (Chichester, West Sussex: Sovereign World, 1991), p. 38.

21. Isaiah 61:6; 1 Corinthians 14:1, 31, 39; 1 Peter 2:5, 9; Revelation 1:6; 5:10; 20:6.

22. Harold Horton, *The Gifts of the Spirit* (Burbank: World MAP, 1979 reprint), p. 161. Horton believes there is also a "prophetic office" in the New Testament Church.

23. Grudem, *Gift of Prophecy in the New Testament*, p. 32.

24. Mike Bickle, *Growing in the Prophetic* (Orlando: Creation House, 1996), p. 95.

25. Young, *My Servants*, p. 101.

26. Such as Paul and Silas (Acts 14:14; 15:32, 40).

27. E. Earl Ellis says "the term 'son of *paraklesis*,' applied to Barnabas in Acts 4, 36, possibly represents, 'son of prophecy.'" *Prophecy and Hermeneutic in Early Christianity* (Grand Rapids: Eerdmans, 1978), p. 131.

28. Carl F. H. Henry, "Divine Revelation and the Bible," John F. Walvoord, ed., *Inspiration and Interpretation* (Grand Rapids: Eerdmans, 1957), p. 257.

29. See Young, *My Servants*, chapter 1.

30. Ellison, *Men Spake*, p. 17.

31. Clifford Hill, *Prophecy*, pp. 296–297.

32. David Blomgren, *Prophetic Gatherings in the Church* (Portland: Bible Temple Publications, 1979), p. 41.

33. Brunner, *Misunderstanding*, p. 19.

34. Roxanne Brant, *How to Test Prophecy, Preaching, and Guidance* (O'Brien, Fla.: Roxanne Brant Ministries, 1981), p. 184.

35. Gordon D. Fee, *Paul, the Spirit, and the People of God* (Peabody, Mass.: Hendrickson, 1996), p. 172.

36. Ted J. Hanson, *The New Testament Prophet* (Bellingham, Wash.: House of Bread, 1996), p. 69.

Chapter 10: Definition of Christian Prophecy

1. Matthew 7:15, 22; 24:11; Luke 1:67; John 11:51; Acts 2:17; 11:27; 13:1–2; 15:28, 32; 16:6; 19:6; 20:23; 21:4, 9–11; Romans 12:6; 1 Corinthians 11:4–5; 12:10, 28–31; 13:2, 8–9; 14:3, 4–6, 22, 24, 29, 31–32, 39; Ephesians 2:20; 3:5; 4:11; 1 Thessalonians 5:20; 1 Timothy 1:18; 4:1, 14; 1 Peter 1:10; 1 John 4:1; Revelation 1:3; 10:7, 11; 11:3, 6, 10, 18; 16:6, 13; 18:20, 24; 19:10; 22:6–7, 9–10, 18–19.

2. See Aune, *Prophecy in Early Christianity*, p. 190.

3. Houston, *Prophecy*, p. 97. See also the following discussions: Grudem, *Gift of Prophecy in*

the New Testament, pp. 93, 143; David Hill, *New Testament Prophecy*, pp. 2–9; Jack Hayford, *The Beauty of Spiritual Language: Unveiling the Mystery of Speaking in Tongues* (Nashville: Thomas Nelson, 1996), chapter 7.

4. As, Acts 13:2; 19:6; 21:11; 1 Corinthians 14:3, 29–31. This, of course, is the ideal; faulty prophecy and the problems of people errors will be dealt with later.

5. Hayford, *Spiritual Language*, p. 121.

6. James D. G. Dunn, *Jesus and the Spirit* (Philadelphia: Westminster, 1975), p. 228.

7. Fairbairn, *Prophecy*, p. 14 (emphasis added).

8. Forbes says, "There is virtually no evidence to suggest that Christian prophecy was practiced outside the gathering together of Christian groups." *Prophecy and Inspired Speech*, p. 246.

9. 2 Corinthians 1:21; 1 John 2:20, 27. Any ministry can be "anointed" in the sense that the Holy Spirit is empowering its function, but there is an anointing of the Spirit unique to each gifting. Thus a preacher can be preaching under the impetus of the Holy Spirit, yet this is not the same as a prophecy.

10. William Barclay, *The Letters to the Corinthians* (Philadelphia: Westminster, 1975 revision), pp. 127–128.

11. See Forbes, *Prophecy and Inspired Speech*, chapter 8, for an excellent discussion.

12. Dunn, *Jesus*, p. xx. Also, Gordon D. Fee, *The First Epistle to the Corinthians, The New International Commentary* (Grand Rapids: Eerdmans, 1987), p. 595. Also, Grudem, *Gift of Prophecy in the New Testament*, chapter 6.

13. Houston, *Prophecy*, p. 96.

14. I. Howells, *Prophecy*, 3, p. 2.

15. J. Rodman Williams, *The Era of the Spirit* (Plainfield, N.J.: Logos, 1971), p. 28.

16. Romans 12:6-7; 1 Corinthians 12:28; 14:6; Ephesians 4:11. See also Acts 13:1 and 2 Peter 2:1.

17. Best, "Prophets and Preachers," p. 142.

18. Cooke, *Prophetic Gifting*, p. 18. This is not an ironclad rule. Preaching can impart the express purpose of God in a current situation, and prophecy, God's principles for life, growth and service. But prophecy usually speaks to a more specific and immediate situation.

19. David Schoch, *The Prophetic Ministry* (Long Beach, Calif.: Bethany, 1970), p. 22.

20. One criticism of prophecy by non-charismatics concerns the practice of writing down an orally delivered prophecy and treat-

ing that written word as inspired (although not on a par with the Bible). Noncharismatics tend to see this practice as undermining biblical revelation. I see no problem with maintaining a personal file of significant prophecies. Whether for future or immediate reference, however, any prophecy should be subject to the biblical criteria for judging a prophecy (see chapters 20–21). Cecil M. Robeck Jr. gives excellent insight on why circulating prophecies can become a dangerous practice. "The Gift of Prophecy and the All-Sufficiency of Scripture," *Paraclete* 13:1 (winter 1979), pp. 27–31.

21. I also feel a prophecy can be given on occasion to an individual, as Ananias to Saul (Acts 9:10–19). The text itself does not call this prophecy, but it seems to me to be so.

22. Some churches operate as if preaching/teaching is the most significant gift. I could not verify such a claim with Scripture but do feel that the public worship of God and the presentation of His Word should be given primary position in our church services.

23. I refer to 1 Corinthians 14.

24. Foster, *Purpose and Use,* p. 33.

25. J. R. Williams, *Era,* pp. 26–27.

26. Bill Hamon, *Prophets and Personal Prophecy* (Shippensburg, Pa.: Destiny Image, 1987), p. 57.

27. Harper, *Prophecy,* p. 19.

28. Grudem, *Gift of Prophecy in the New Testament,* p. 153.

29. See chapter 2, pp. 30–32, for more on this point.

30. This subject has already received some attention in chapters 2, 3 and 5. Also see chapter 20.

31. See the practical discussion by Yocum, *Prophecy,* chapter 7. He focuses from a Catholic charismatic viewpoint on the role of the Christian community in testing and forming prophets who can be trusted to speak the word of God.

32. Robeck, "Gift of Prophecy and the All-Sufficiency," p. 30.

33. Houston, *Prophecy,* p. 38.

34. Pytches, *Prophecy,* p. 13.

35. Everett F. Harrison, "Romans," *Expositors Bible Commentary,* Vol. 10, p. 130.

36. C. K. Barrett, *The Epistle to the Romans* (New York: Harper & Row, 1957), p. 238; Also, A. T. Robertson, *Word Studies in the New Testament* (Nashville: Broadman, 1931), Vol. IV, p. 403.

37. Ellison, *Men Spake,* p. 18. Nineveh was not destroyed, and we understand why because of the book of Jonah. Ellison also points out that the judgment of Tyre, Egypt and Babylon were all "suspended."

38. F. F. Bruce, in his foreword for Clifford Hill, *Prophecy,* p. xii.

39. Cecil M. Robeck Jr., "The Gift of Prophecy in Acts and Paul, Part II," *Studia Biblica et Theologica* 2 (October 1975), p. 54.

40. Stephen Clark, *Spiritual Gifts* (Pecos, N.M.: Dove, 1969), pp. 18–19.

41. Green, *Holy Spirit,* p. 170.

42. J. R. Williams, *Era,* pp. 27–28.

43. Boring, *Continuing Voice,* p. 38.

44. David Hill, *New Testament Prophecy,* pp. 8–9.

Chapter 11: Channels of Prophetic Expression in the Church

1. Two scholarly, well-done yet contrasting books about the Holy Spirit and initiation into the early Church are James D. G. Dunn's *Baptism in the Holy Spirit* (Philadelphia: Westminster, 1970), and a strong but cordial "Pentecostal" critique of Dunn's book by Howard M. Ervin, *Conversion-Initiation and the Baptism in the Holy Spirit* (Peabody: Hendrickson, 1984).

2. See Ernest Gentile, *Worship God! Exploring the Dynamics of Psalmic Worship* (Portland: BT Publishing, 1994), chapter 33, "Gathering the Called-Out Ones."

3. Charismatic authors use various terms and categories (not always arranged the same) to describe prophetic events: "realms" (Schoch, Damazio); "channels" (Hamon); "functions" (C. Hill); "degrees of prophetic inspiration" (Conner); "levels" (Blomgren, Bickle, Cooke, Joyner); "manifestations" (Howells).

4. Gentile, *Worship God!,* pp. 154–155; Jack Hayford, *Worship His Majesty* (Waco: Word, 1987), p. 150.

5. Green, *I Believe,* p. 170.

6. Through the years I have appreciated the insights of a book (now unfortunately out of print) by Seeley D. Kinne, *The Prophetic State,* republished by Wings of Healing, 1950.

7. Aune, *Prophecy in Early Christianity,* p. 190. Also see Ralph P. Martin's comments on 1 Thessalonians 5, which support the thesis that prophecy was a gift exercised within the context of congregational worship. *Worship in*

the Early Church (Grand Rapids: Eerdmans, 1964), pp. 135–136.

8. This passage is applied to the Church in Hebrews 8:8–12 and 10:16.

9. Forbes, *Prophecy and Inspired Speech,* pp. 241–242. Forbes gives a good summary of scholarly opinion on the subject.

10. See Rumph, *Stories.*

11. See Howells, *Prophecy,* lesson 6; also, Schoch, *Prophetic Ministry,* pp. 25–35. Also note Hamon's "Five Channels" in *Prophets and Personal Prophecy,* chapter 5, and Bickle's "Four Levels" in *Growing in the Prophetic,* chapter 9.

12. Schoch, *Prophetic Ministry,* p. 25.

13. See Blomgren, *Prophetic Gatherings,* p. 36. Also, Frank Damazio, *Developing the Prophetic Ministry* (Portland: Trilogy, 1983), p. 8; Howells, *Prophecy,* section 6, p. 1; Hamon, *Prophets and Personal Prophecy,* pp. 58–60.

14. Some argue that since all now have the Spirit, all may prophesy and be considered prophets. Anyone can on occasion prophesy, I feel, and some will have a resident gift of prophecy, but comparatively few will be prophets. Unless this is true the term *prophet* becomes meaningless in light of its specific usage in Acts and the Pauline epistles.

15. Jane Rumph, in her interesting chapter 3 about stories of prophetic messages, suggests that in this one-on-one ministry, "words of knowledge are best shared tentatively, even if the intercessor senses them with great clarity. Asking questions and letting the person being prayed for confirm them (or not) may trigger fewer defense mechanisms. . . ." *Stories,* p. 9.

16. Any significant correctional or directional word should be referred first to church leadership for appraisal. This safeguard protects and ensures the continuance of this ministry in the local church. See Pytches, *Prophecy,* pp. 103–104.

17. See Michael Griffiths, *Grace-Gifts* (Grand Rapids: Eerdmans, 1979), pp. 28–37. Also, Clifford Hill, *Prophecy,* p. 121.

18. Howells speaks of this gift as "deposited permanently." *Prophecy,* section 6, p. 3.

19. Schoch, *Prophetic Ministry,* p. 26.

20. Bickle, *Growing,* p. 121.

21. Dunn, *Jesus,* p. 403, footnote 62.

22. Aune, *Prophecy in Early Christianity,* p. 195.

23. Howells, *Prophecy,* Section 6, p. 6.

24. Blomgren, *Prophetic Gatherings,* p. 37.

25. Interesting references on this subject: Don Williams, *The Apostle Paul and Women in the Church* (Van Nuys, Calif.: BIM, 1977); Ben Witherington, *Women and the Genesis of Christianity* (Cambridge: Cambridge University, 1990); Antoinette Wire, *The Corinthian Women Prophets* (Minneapolis: Fortress, 1990); Paul K. Jewett, *The Ordination of Women* (Grand Rapids: Eerdmans, 1980); Cindy Jacobs, *Women of Destiny* (Ventura, Calif.: Regal, 1998).

26. Robeck, "Gift of Prophecy in Acts and Paul," p. 39.

27. Bryn Jones, "Apostles and Prophets: The Vital Role of these Foundational Ministry Gifts," *Issachar Journal* 1, No. 2 (summer 1995), pp. 13, 15–16.

28. David Hill contends that Barnabas "best represents the figure of the 'prophet' in the earliest decades of the church." Luke's intention in the Acts record, Hill argues, is to present Barnabas as "son of prophecy" (i.e., "one who is a prophet") on the assumption that *paraklesis* means "exhortation" (*New Testament Prophecy,* p. 101).

29. Wayne Grudem argues persuasively in his first book, *The Gift of Prophecy in 1 Corinthians,* p. 97, that Ephesians 4:11 should be translated "the apostles who are also prophets."

30. Aune lists four strong arguments for John's status as a prophet in *Prophecy in Early Christianity,* pp. 206–208.

31. Forbes, *Prophecy and Inspired Speech,* pp. 242–243.

32. Hanson, *New Testament Prophet,* p. 41.

33. Pytches, *Does God Speak,* p. 56.

34. Watson, *I Believe,* pp. 43–44.

35. Donald Gee, "Messages through the Gifts," *Pentecost* 60 (June–August 1962), last page.

36. Yocum, *Prophecy,* p. 24.

37. Bickle, *Growing,* pp. 169–170.

38. Fee, *Empowering Presence,* p. 170.

39. Donald Bridge, *Signs and Wonders Today* (Downers Grove, Ill.: InterVarsity, 1985), pp. 202–204.

Chapter 12: Prophets and Prophecy in the Book of Acts

1. Like most Christians I am persuaded that St. Luke was the writer of both the gospel of Luke and the Acts of the Apostles. For a thorough discussion see *The Expositor's Greek Testament,* "The Acts of the Apostles," R. J. Knowl-

ing, W. Robertson Nicoll, ed. (Grand Rapids: Eerdmans, 1951), pp. 3–48.

2. William Barclay, *Commentary on Acts* (Philadelphia: Westminster, 1975 revision).

3. George T. Montague suggests the possibility that this phenomenon was a miracle of hearing—that is, an interpretation of tongues in the minds of the hearers. *Holy Spirit*, p. 281. I believe each hearer heard his own language.

4. The clear pattern in Acts and the testimony of millions of people who have accepted this plan, acted on it and received the same phenomenal results is so striking that it is hard to ignore.

5. E. Earl Ellis confirms my conclusion: "Probably the equation of the proclamation in tongues with prophecy arises because the various tongues are, in fact, the native, understood languages of the respective hearers." *Prophecy and Hermeneutic*, p. 129.

6. W. E. Warner, "Tom Hezmalhalch," p. 389. *Dictionary of Pentecostal and Charismatic Movements* by Stanley M. Burgess, Gary B. McGee and Patrick H. Alexander. Copyright © 1988 by Stanley M. Burgess, Gary B. McGee and Patrick H. Alexander. Used by permission of Zondervan Publishing House.

7. This is the story as related by David E. Schoch, who knew Tom personally.

8. This kind of experience is debated a great deal, but I can testify of its beneficial effect on my life. See John L. Sherrill's bestseller *They Speak with Other Tongues* (Old Tappan, N.J.: Spire, 1964) and H. Newton Malony's article "Debunking Some of the Myths About Glossolalia" in *Charismatic Experiences in History*, Cecil M. Robeck Jr., ed. (Peabody: Hendrickson, 1985), chapter 6.

9. B. H. Streeter, *The Primitive Church* (New York: Macmillan, 1929), p. 73. He refers to "that outburst of prophetism which was a conspicuous feature in early Christianity" (p. 203).

10. David Hill comments that "'being filled with the Spirit' would, in Jewish usage, be tantamount to saying 'becoming prophets'. . . ." *New Testament Prophecy*, p. 96.

11. Additional Old Testament Scriptures traditionally associated with Joel 2 are Isaiah 2:2–4; Jeremiah 31:31–34; Ezekiel 36:26–28.

12. Deuteronomy 18:15; John 5:46; Acts 3:22; 7:37.

13. For example, Acts 10:19; 11:12; 16:6–7.

14. Aune, *Prophecy in Early Christianity*, p. 215.

15. For *semaino* compare John 12:33; 18:32; 21:19; Revelation 1:1. These references all indicate prophecy.

16. F. F. Bruce, *The Acts of the Apostles* (Grand Rapids: Eerdmans, 1970 reprint), p. 239.

17. Gleason L. Archer, *Encyclopedia of Bible Difficulties* (Grand Rapids: Zondervan, 1982), p. 384.

18. Bruce, *Acts*, p. 387.

19. McKeating, "The Prophet Jesus—II," p. 51.

20. David Hill, *New Testament Prophecy*, p. 108.

21. Grudem, *Gift of Prophecy in the New Testament*, p. 96–102. Although Grudem is an advocate of prophecy in the Church, he does seem to allow his belief in secondary prophecy (which is susceptible to mistakes) to make more of this episode than Luke or the early Church apparently did.

22. Robeck, "The Gift of Prophecy in Acts and Paul, Part I," *Studia Biblica et Theologica* 1 (March 1975), pp. 27–28.

23. Apparently God was not confused about the prophecy! Note Acts 23:11: "That night the Lord appeared to Paul and said, 'Be encouraged, Paul. Just as you have told the people about me here in Jerusalem, you must preach the Good News in Rome'" (NLT).

24. K. S. Latourette, *A History of the Expansion of Christianity: The First Five Centuries* (Eyre & Spottiswoode, 1939), p. 61.

25. Yocum, *Prophecy*, p. 58.

26. Jacobs, *Voice*, p. 103.

27. Bickle, *Growing*, p. 118.

Chapter 13: The Prophetic Confusion at Corinth

1. Sholem Asch, trans. by Maurice Samuel, *The Apostle* (New York: Putnam's Sons, 1943 reprint), pp. 439–440.

2. An excellent in-depth commentary on 1 Corinthians 14, in both content and sympathetic treatment, is that of Gordon D. Fee, *First Epistle to the Corinthians, The New International Commentary on the New Testament* (Grand Rapids: Eerdmans, 1987), pp. 653–713. I also suggest C. K. Barrett, *A Commentary on the First Epistle to the Corinthians* (New York and Evanston, Ill.: Harper & Row, 1968), pp. 312–334.

3. W. Harold Mare, "1 Corinthians," *Expositors Bible Commentary*, Vol. 10, p. 271.

4. Joseph Henry Thayer, *A Greek-English Lexicon of the New Testament* (New York: American Book, 1886), p. 153.

5. Fee, *The First Epistle*, p. 655.

6. F. W. Grosheide, *Commentary on the First Epistle to the Corinthians* (Grand Rapids: Eerdmans, 1953), p. 316.

7. Martin, *Spirit and Congregation* (Grand Rapids: Eerdmans, 1984), p. 61.

8. Jack Hayford's book *The Beauty of Spiritual Language* is the best on tongues that I know of.

9. 1 Corinthians 13:1 intimates that there are tongues "of angels," suggesting the possibility that the early Church considered some prayer languages to be angelic languages.

10. Forbes suggests the five main options: 1) the miraculous ability to speak unlearned human languages; 2) the miraculous ability to speak heavenly or angelic languages; 3) some combination of 1 and 2; 4) a kind of sub- or prelinguistic form of speech or a kind of coded utterance; or 5) an archaic or idiosyncratic language. *Prophecy and Inspired Speech*, pp. 56–65.

11. Marion Meloon, *Ivan Spencer: Willow in the Wind* (Plainfield, N.J.: Logos, 1974), p. 210.

12. Dennis J. Bennett, "The Gifts of the Holy Spirit," Michael P. Hamilton, ed., *The Charismatic Movement* (Grand Rapids: Eerdmans, 1975), p. 27.

13. For documented accounts of utterances by the Spirit, see Ralph W. Harris, *Spoken by the Spirit* (Springfield, Mo.: Gospel Publishing, 1973).

14. Hayford, *Spiritual Language*, p. 138.

15. The theme of 1 Corinthians 14 is *edification*, mentioned seven times; the Greek verb three times: 14:4a, 4b, 17b; and the noun four times: 14:3, 5d, 12b, 26c.

16. Usually to a special-language audience or person, so the tongue given acts as a supernatural sign.

17. David Hill calls this verse "the nearest approach in Paul's letters to a definition of prophetic function. . . ." (*New Testament Prophecy*, p. 123). Jannes Reiling says, "There is no other statement in the New Testament which comes closer to a definition than this." "Prophecy, the Spirit and the Church," *Prophetic Vocation*, p. 69.

18. Theodore M. Crone, *Early Christian Prophecy: A Study of Its Origin and Function* (Baltimore: St. Mary's University, 1973), p. 213.

19. Clifford Hill, *Prophecy*, p. 212.

20. Edouard Cothenet, "Les prophètes Chrétiens comme Exégètes Charismatiques de L'Écriture," *Prophetic Vocation*, p. 79.

21. Kistemaker, *I Corinthians*, p. 478.

22. Barrett says: "Not 'the church', for *ekklesian* does not have the article; literally *an assembly,* but the sense is *the assembly of which he is one member; ekklesia* in the sense of *assembly* is frequent in this chapter." *First Epistle to the Corinthians*, p. 316.

23. Clifford Hill, *Prophecy*, p. 213.

24. Thomas W. Gillespie, *The First Theologians* (Grand Rapids: Eerdmans, 1994), p. 148.

25. Fee, *The First Epistle*, p. 659.

26. Grosheide, *First Epistle to the Corinthians*, p. 319.

27. Kistemaker, *I Corinthians*, p. 485.

28. Unprovable, but a point that seems justified in terms of 12:1, 3 and the entire context.

29. Kistemaker comments: "In this passage . . . the inability to understand a spoken language, not an inability to understand the Christian faith, is at issue." *I Corinthians*, p. 493.

30. Fee, *The First Epistle*, p. 672. Note these references: Deuteronomy 27:26; 1 Chronicles 16:36; Nehemiah 5:13; 8:6; Psalm 106:48; Revelation 5:14; 7:12; 19:4. Justin, *Apology* I. 65:3; 67:5.

31. Some commentators suggest that these people would be catechumens or candidates to be accepted into the Church. I find nothing credible to substantiate this.

32. Translated variously as "uninformed" (NKJV), "ungifted" (NASB), "ordinary man" (TEV), "those who don't understand" (LB), "uninstructed man" (Phillips), "outsider" (RSV), "the plain man" (NEB), "the uninitiated" (Knox), "the simple learner" or "listener" (C. K. Barrett).

33. Bauer, Walter, trans., W. F. Arndt and F. W. Gingrich, eds., *A Greek-English Lexicon of the New Testament and Other Early Christian Literature* (Chicago: University of Chicago, 1957), p. 371.

34. "The law," *nomos*, to which Paul was appealing, applies here to the Old Testament generally, as in John 10:34; 12:34; 15:25; Romans 3:19.

35. Barrett, *First Epistle to the Corinthians*, pp. 322–323.

36. The unbelievers in Corinth, for instance, did not reject the Gospel in the same way the Jews (in Isaiah 28:11) rejected their Hebrew prophets.

37. Wayne A. Grudem, "1 Corinthians 14:20–25: Prophecy and Tongues as Signs of

Notes

God's Attitude," *Westminster Theological Journal* 41:2 (spring 1979), pp. 387, 391.

38. Ibid., p. 390.

39. Forbes, *Prophecy and Inspired Speech,* p. 181.

40. J. Rodman Williams, *Renewal Theology: Systematic Theology from a Charismatic Perspective* (Grand Rapids: Zondervan, 1990), Vol. 2, p. 381.

41. Forbes, *Prophecy and Inspired Speech,* p. 179.

42. See Gentile, *Worship God!,* chapter 33, "Gathering the Called-Out Ones."

43. One reason many of the older Pentecostal groups had such long public utterances of tongues, followed by long interpretations, was to keep from violating the supposed principle that a speaker could not speak out in tongues more than a few times.

44. Fee, *Empowering Presence,* p. 251.

45. Montague, *Holy Spirit,* p. 181.

46. Fee, *The First Epistle,* pp. 694–695. Also note the confirmation by Trevor Chandler, *The Functioning Church* (Brisbane, Australia: C. L. Publishing, 1984), pp. 91–92. Wayne Grudem says: "Paul calls anyone who prophesies a *prophetes* in 14:32." *Gift of Prophecy in 1 Corinthians,* p. 232.

47. Williams, *Renewal Theology,* p. 381.

48. I am convinced that Paul was a happy man, boisterous in his praise of God. He did have ecstatic experiences, such as recorded in 2 Corinthians 12:1–10, yet maintains the importance of controlled prophetic presentations in the church service. In regard to renewal manifestations, scholars and mainline church members come from traditions of more subdued worship forms and denominational parameters. In contrast, today's amoral college graduates, biblically void youth and TV generation addicts search desperately for something that will satisfy. Youth go to rock concerts and scream out their most urgent longings and needs. When such ones come into God's house, they, like the Corinthians of old, must encounter God. These acute needs must be met head-on, and when this happens there are bound to be manifestations—some exteme—that might upset the sensitivities of today's mainline church members.

49. Hayford, *Spiritual Language,* p. 74.

50. Bennett, "Gifts of the Holy Spirit," pp. 28–29.

51. Dunn, "New Wine," p. 7.

52. Fee, *The First Epistle,* p. 676.

Chapter 14: Did Prophecy Cease—or Does It Continue?

1. The best article I have seen refuting cessationism is by Jack Deere, "Anatomy of a Deception," *MorningStar Journal* 4:2 (1994), pp. 39–49. He is a former associate professor of Old Testament at Dallas Theological Seminary. Also see the article by Jon Ruthven, "A Place for Prophecy?", *Paraclete* 6:2 (spring 1972), pp. 8–14.

2. Charles C. Ryrie, *The Holy Spirit* (Chicago: Moody, 1965), p. 86.

3. Such as 1 Corinthians 12–14; Romans 12; Ephesians 4.

4. The best statement I have seen by a cessationist is the four-part series of articles in *Bibliotheca Sacra* (a journal published by Dallas Theological Seminary) by F. David Farnell. See my footnote 20, chapter 2.

5. Deere, "Anatomy," p. 42.

6. *To teleion* is translated variously "that which is perfect" (KJV, NKJV), "perfection" (Williams, NIV, JB), "wholeness" (NEB), "the complete" (Phillips). F. David Farnell prefers "mature" or "complete." "Gift of Prophecy," 150 (April–June 1993), p. 192.

7. Those of us who believe this are in good scholarly company—e.g., F. F. Bruce, C. K. Barrett, Gordon D. Fee, H. Conzelman and Michael Harper, to name a few.

8. See the interesting article by R. Fowler White, "Richard Gaffin and Wayne Grudem on 1 Cor 13:10: A Comparison of Cessationist and Noncessationist Argumentation," *Journal of the Evangelical Theological Society* 35/2 (June 1992), pp. 173–181.

9. See, for example, Merrill F. Unger, *The Baptism and Gifts of the Holy Spirit* (Chicago: Moody, 1974), pp. 141–142.

10. Farnell, "Gift of Prophecy," 150 (April–June 1993), p. 192.

11. Ibid., p. 193.

12. Deere, "Anatomy," pp. 42–43.

13. Farnell, "Gift of Prophecy," p. 190.

14. Ibid., p. 171.

15. Robert L. Thomas, "Prophecy Rediscovered? A Review of the Gift of Prophecy in the New Testament and Today," *Bibliotheca Sacra* 149 (January–March 1992), p. 95.

16. Cecil M. Robeck Jr., "Ecclesiastical Authority and the Power of the Spirit," *Paraclete* (summer 1978), p. 17.

17. Harper, *Prophecy,* p. 7.

18. Three recent books should prove helpful: Jack Deere, *Surprised by the Power of the Spirit* (Grand Rapids: Zondervan, 1993); William DeArteaga, *Quenching the Spirit* (Lake Mary, Fla.: Creation House, 1992); and Jane Rumph's compilation of forty true, dramatic accounts of worldwide conversions resulting from "power evangelism" (which includes prophecy), *Stories from the Front Lines*.

19. Deere, "Anatomy," p. 55.

20. See the fascinating book *Doomsday* by Russell Chandler (Ann Arbor, Mich.: Servant, 1993), which chronicles colorful tales of individuals and groups throughout history who have believed the end was near.

21. Joseph Hogan, "Charisms of the Holy Spirit," *Restoration* (March 1972), p. 8.

22. See, for instance, *Does God Speak Today?* by Bishop David Pytches, one of the leading charismatic ministers in England. He gives 47 fascinating stories of God's revelations to individuals, followed by fifteen counterfeit revelations. An interesting balance!

23. Fee, *Empowering Presence*, p. 59.

24. Barclay, *Letters to the Corinthians,* p. 127.

25. Cartledge, "Charismatic Prophecy," p. 19.

26. Pytches, *Does God Speak*, p. 83.

27. J. B. Phillips, *New Testament Christianity* (London: Hodder & Stoughton, 1956), p. 15.

28. Fee, *Empowering Presence*, p. 902.

29. Joyner, *Prophetic Ministry*, p. 17.

30. Ruthven, "A Place for Prophecy?", p. 14.

Chapter 15: When Bishops Replace Prophets

1. Best, "Prophets and Preachers," p. 150.

2. Larry Christenson, *A Message to the Charismatic Movement* (Minneapolis: Bethany, 1972), back cover.

3. Derek Tidball, *The Social Context of the New Testament* (U.K: Paternoster, 1983), p. 124.

4. Clifford Hill, *Prophecy*, p. 273.

5. Forbes, *Prophecy and Inspired Speech,* p. 250.

6. Robeck, "Ecclesiastical Authority," p. 18.

7. David O. Moberg, *The Church as a Social Institution* (Englewood Cliffs, N.J.: Prentice-Hall, 1962), pp. 118–124. My chart was based on his insights and those of Derek Tidball.

8. Tidball, *Social Context*, p. 124.

9. In *The Social Teaching of the Christian Churches*, Olive Wyan, trans. (London: Allen & Unwin, 1931), 2 vols. An outstanding analysis of the factors that cause deterioration in churches.

10. Elmer L. Towns, "Sociological Background of Postdenominational Church," a paper presented at the National Symposium on the Postdenominational Church, Fuller Theological Seminary, May 22, 1996.

11. C. Peter Wagner, *The New Apostolic Churches* (Ventura: Regal, 1998). He points out nine *new* distinctives of these churches: name, authority structure, leadership training, ministry focus, worship style, prayer forms, financing, outreach and power. Chapter 1.

12. Towns, "Sociological Background," pp. 4–5.

13. Wagner, *New Apostolic*, pp. 18–19.

14. Towns, "Sociological Background," p. 2.

15. Ibid.

16. Watson, *I Believe*, pp. 73–74.

17. *Called-out ones* is a term appropriated by both Jesus and Paul to describe the new people of God. *Ecclesia* referred to the citizens, the qualified voters, of a city-state. Jesus and Paul were describing the Church as a spiritual community within a secular community (Matthew 16:18; 18:17; 1 Corinthians 1:2; 12:28; 14:23).

18. See Brunner, *Misunderstanding*.

19. Scripture for "gathering together": Matthew 18:20; Acts 2:42; 11:26; 14:27; 15:6, 22, 30; 20:7–8; 1 Corinthians 5:4; 14:23, 26, 28, 34; 1 Timothy 3:15; James 2:2.

20. Gentile, *Worship God!*, chapter 33. Also, C. K. Barrett suggests that "the word means not simply the people of God, but the people of God assembled." *Commentary on the First Epistle to the Corinthians*, p. 261.

21. Burgess, *Spirit and the Church*, p. 12.

22. Kydd, *Charismatic Gifts*, p. 87. See Burgess, *Spirit and the Church*.

23. Aune, *Prophecy in Early Christianity*, p. 313.

24. Von Campenhausen, *Ecclesiastical Authority*, p. 181.

25. Hippolytus, *Refutation of All Heresies* 8.12; Epiphanius, *Panarion* 48.1; Jerome, *Epistle* 41.3.

26. Phillip Schaff, *History of the Christian Church* (Grand Rapids: Eerdmans, 1950), Vol. II, p. 417.

27. For discussions and illustrations of the sixteen recorded prophecies, see Aune, *Prophecy*

in Early Christianity, pp. 314–316; Burgess, *Spirit and the Church,* p. 50; Robeck, "Origen," pp. 19–23.

28. Geoffrey W. Bromiley, "The Charismata in Christian History," *Theology, News & Notes* (March 1974), p. 3.

29. Henry Wace and William C. Percy, eds., *A Dictionary of Christian Biography* (Peabody: Hendrickson, 1994 reprint), p. 739.

30. Clifford Hill, *Prophecy,* p. 262.

31. Paul Tillich, *A History of Christian Thought* (New York: Harper & Row, 1968), p. 41.

32. Kenneth Scott Latourette, *A History of Christianity, Vol. I* (New York: Harper & Row, 1953), p. 134.

33. James L. Ash, for instance, argues persuasively against Harnack's position. "The Decline of Ecstatic Prophecy in the Early Church," *Theological Studies* 36:2 (June 1976), pp. 227–252.

34. Actually the teachers could also have taught on the nature and use of spiritual gifts (as well as other subjects), and this would have brought balance.

35. Brunner, *Misunderstanding,* p. 59.

36. Pytches, *Prophecy,* p. 149.

37. Brunner, *Misunderstanding,* p. 81.

38. Ash, "Decline of Ecstatic Prophecy," pp. 227, 249.

39. See endnote 11. I was surprised, reading Wagner's book, how closely my own suggestions parallel his characteristics of "The New Apostolic Churches."

40. See Gentile, *Worship God!*

41. J. E. C. Welldon, *The Revelation of the Holy Spirit* (London: Macmillan, 1902), p. 296.

42. Deere, *Surprised by the Power of the Spirit,* p. 73. His footnote says that both David Hill and David Aune, in their recent scholarly studies of New Testament prophecy, "conclude that it was the leadership of the church that abandoned the gift of prophecy rather than God withdrawing the gift" (p. 273, #16).

43. Wilson, "Early Israelite Prophecy," p. 8.

44. Clifford Hill, *Prophecy,* p. 262.

45. James D. G. Dunn, *Unity and Diversity in the New Testament* (Philadelphia: Trinity, 1990, 2nd ed.), p. 351.

46. Bruce, *Spreading Flame,* p. 217.

Chapter 16: Edward Irving, Morning Star of Renewal

1. Other interesting prophetic groups keep appearing, such as the Kansas City Fellowship Prophets, 1983 (see David Pytches, *Some Said It Thundered* [Nashville: Thomas Nelson, 1991] and Bickle, *Growing);* the Network of Prophetic Ministries founded by Bill Hamon in 1988 (*Prophetic Ministries News,* Santa Rosa Beach, Fla.); the Toronto Airport Christian Fellowship "Blessing," 1993 (see Guy Chevreau, *Catch the Fire* [London: Marshall Pickering, 1994] and John Arnott, *The Father's Blessing* [Orlando: Creation House, 1995]); MorningStar Publications, Charlotte, N.C., Rick Joyner, ed.

2. Arnold Dallimore, *The Life of Edward Irving* (Edinburgh: Banner of Truth, 1983), p. ix.

3. H. C. Whitley, *Blinded Eagle* (London: SCM, 1955), p. 17.

4. Ibid., p. 20.

5. Christenson, *Message,* p. 33.

6. George H. Williams and Edith Waldvogel, "A History of Speaking in Tongues and Related Gifts," Hamilton, ed., *Charismatic Movement,* p. 85.

7. D. D. Bundy, "Irving, Edward," p. 471. *Dictionary of Pentecostal and Charismatic Movements* by Stanley M. Burgess, Gary B. McGee and Patrick H. Alexander. Copyright © 1988 by Stanley M. Burgess, Gary B. McGee and Patrick H. Alexander. Used by permission of Zondervan Publishing House.

8. For a most interesting account of why there was such spiritual receptivity at this time, see Gordon Strachan, "Theological and Cultural Origins of the Nineteenth Century Pentecostal Movement," Paul Elbert, ed., *Essays on Apostolic Themes: Studies in Honor of Howard M. Ervin* (Peabody: Hendrickson, 1985), p. 144ff. Apparently the strong "double Calvinism" doctrine that had robbed the people of expectant faith had been replaced by a fresh understanding of the "free grace and love" of God in Christ.

9. Bundy, "Irving, Edward," p. 471.

10. Time does not permit me to investigate this subject here, tempting as it is. Suffice it to say that the average minister today would find himself hard pressed to refute Irving's position that Christ assumed our human nature as the Son of Man and yet lived a sinless life through the empowerment of the Holy Spirit. Perhaps the most helpful book on the subject is Gordon Strachan's *The Pentecostal Theology of Edward*

Irving (Peabody, Mass.: Hendrickson, 1988 reprint), especially Part I, pp. 25–52.

11. G. H. Williams, "History," p. 86.

12. Whitley, *Eagle*, p. 30. This moving, compassionate account of Irving was written by a man who was an early part of the Catholic Apostolic Church.

13. Christenson, *Message*, p. 36.

14. Strachan, *Pentecostal Theology*, p. 182. His account of this time relies on a number of sources and is probably one of the most accurate and sympathetic.

15. Christenson, *Message*, p. 37.

16. Dallimore, *Edward Irving*, p. 161.

17. Christenson, *Message*, pp. 39–40.

18. Strachan, *Pentecostal Theology*, p. 55.

19. Christenson, *Message*, p. 74.

20. Whitley, *Eagle*, p. 76.

21. G. H. Williams, "History," p. 86.

22. See chapter 20, "Guidelines for Testing Prophetic Utterances."

23. A negative review of the Irving meetings is given by Monsignor Ronald A. Knox, focusing in particular on some of the prophetic utterances that lacked structure and clarity. These are things that pastoral direction can correct. *Enthusiasm* (Westminster, Md.: Christian Classics, 1983), pp. 550–558.

24. Christenson, *Message*, p. 53.

25. Ibid., p. 57.

26. Bundy, "Irving, Edward," p. 471.

27. Quoted by Strachan, *Pentecostal Theology*, p. 82.

28. Whitley, *Eagle*, p. 105.

29. Note from the same panel: The promise of the gifts was seen as "valid for all times, and to the end of time."

30. Christenson, *Message*, p. 32.

Chapter 17: The Apostolic Church of Great Britain

1. Sometimes called "The Apostolic Church of Wales," although this title seems to be a misnomer. Although the beginning came about because of Welsh action, the Apostolic Church became involved from its inception throughout other parts of the United Kingdom and soon sent missionaries across the nations. John W. J. Hewitt, for fourteen years superintendent of the Apostolic Church in Australia, told me that from these early days of expansion "it has been officially known as the 'Apostolic Church.'"

2. For a very informative book, based on much research, see James E. Worsfold, *The Origins of the Apostolic Church in Great Britain*

(Julian Literature Trust, P.O. Box 12-555, Thorndon, Wellington, New Zealand, 1991).

3. D. W. Cartwright, "Apostolic Church," *Dictionary of Pentecostal and Charismatic Movements* by Stanley M. Burgess, Gary B. McGee and Patrick H. Alexander. Copyright © 1988 by Stanley M. Burgess, Gary B. McGee and Patrick H. Alexander. Used by permission of Zondervan Publishing House.

4. Worsfold, *Origins*, pp. 31–32.

5. Ibid., p. 152ff.

6. For a three-page summary of the movement and a statement of faith, see Walter J. Hollenweger, *The Pentecostals* (Peabody: Hendrickson, 1988 reprint), pp. 191–193, p. 518.

7. Worsfold, *Origins*, p. 37. Prophecies were published in *Showers of Blessing* and the later *Riches of Grace*.

8. Information supplied by John W. J. Hewitt.

9. D. P. Williams, *Prophetical Ministry*, p. 100.

10. Howells, *Prophecy*, p. 9. This most recent publication on prophecy in the Apostolic Church shows great care and concern.

11. Worsfold, *Origins*, p. 183.

12. Ibid., p. 122.

13. Ibid., p. 51.

14. Ibid., p. 120.

15. Howells, *Prophecy*, p. 5.

16. See David Hill, *New Testament Prophecy*, p. 135. Also Grudem, *Gift of Prophecy*, chapter 3, and Robeck, "Gift of Prophecy and the All-Sufficiency," pp. 27–31.

17. Cecil M. Robeck Jr., "Prophetic Authority in the Charismatic Setting: The Need to Test," *Theological Renewal* 234 (July 1983), p. 7.

18. W. A. C. Rowe, *One Lord, One Faith* (Bradford, England: Puritan, 1960), preface.

19. Ibid., p. 184.

20. Ibid., p. 272.

21. Worsfold, *Origins*, p. 173.

22. Ibid., p. 60.

23. Ibid., p. 67.

24. Ibid., p. 71.

25. Ibid., p. 112.

26. Acts 13:2–3; 14:23; 1 Timothy 4:14.

27. Acts 6:3.

28. 1 Timothy 3; Titus 1:5–9.

29. Note the comments of David Blomgren on confirmation in *Prophetic Gatherings*, p. 67.

30. Worsfold, *Origins*, p. 302.

31. Ibid., p. 286.

32. William Henry Lewis, *And He Gave Some Apostles* (Bradford: Puritan, 1954), p. 101.

33. Worsfold, *Origins,* pp. 86, 112, 281, 284, 306.

34. Ibid., p. 184. John Hewitt commented to me: "Over the past two decades, the AC in Australia and New Zealand has moved forward with a great awareness of the spontaneity of the prophetic ministry in the Church. This has caused growth in the number of churches and size of congregations. This refreshing release of the prophetic linked with the apostolic is having a beneficial influence on the AC in other nations, including Wales."

35. D. P. Williams, *Prophetical Ministry,* p. 97.

36. Worsfold, *Origins,* pp. 307–308.

37. Gerhard Friedrich,*Theological Dictionary of the New Testament,* Vol. 6, p. 849.

38. George Mallone, *Those Controversial Gifts* (Downers Grove, Ill.: InterVarsity, 1983), p. 37.

39. C. Peter Wagner, *Your Spiritual Gifts Can Help Your Church Grow* (Ventura, Calif.: Regal, 1979), p. 229.

40. Donald Gee, *Spiritual Gifts in the Work of the Ministry Today* (Springfield, Mo.: Gospel Publishing, 1963), p. 10.

Chapter 18: The Latter Rain Movement

1. The best study I have seen on Branham—remarkably candid, forthright and well-researched—is by C. Douglas Weaver, a book made from his Ph.D. dissertation at Southern Baptist Theological Seminary: *The Healer-Prophet, William Marrion Branham: A Study of the Prophetic in American Pentecostalism* (Macon, Ga.: Mercer University, 1987).

2. Richard M. Riss, *A Survey of 20th-Century Revival Movements in North America* (Peabody: Hendrickson, 1988), p. 1.

3. See Frank Bartleman, *What Really Happened at Azusa Street?* (Northridge, Calif.: Voice Christian Publications, 1962). Also, Carl Brumbach, *Suddenly . . . from Heaven* (Springfield, Mo.: Gospel Publishing, 1961).

4. Riss, *A Survey,* p. 1.

5. Also, the revival at Wheaton College (February 5–12, 1950) received national publicity. More than twenty other college revivals occurred during this period. J. Edwin Orr, *Campus Aflame* (Glendale, Calif.: Gospel Light, 1971), pp. 165–182.

6. David Harrell, *All Things Are Possible: The Healing and Charismatic Revivals in Modern America* (Bloomington, Ind.: Indiana University, 1975), p. 162.

7. Richard M. Riss, *Latter Rain: The Latter Rain Movement of 1948 and the Mid-Twentieth Century Evangelical Awakening* (Mississauga, Ont.: Honeycomb, 1987), p. 57.

8. A source of great influence on the North Battleford brothers was a book published by Franklin Hall in 1946 called *Atomic Power with God thru Fasting and Prayer.* The cover pictures the great arm of the Lord holding the gifts of the Spirit behind a locked door. The key that unlocks the door and releases the gifts of the Spirit is prayer and fasting. All the major healing evangelists, according to Harrell, "began following his fasting regime and miracles erupted everywhere." *All Things,* p. 244.

9. Riss, *A Survey,* p. 112.

10. Ernest Hawtin, "How This Revival Began," p. 3, as quoted by Riss, *Latter Rain,* pp. 62–63.

11. George R. Hawtin, "Revival at Sharon," *Sharon Star* (1 August 1949), p. 2. Quoted from Riss, *A Survey,* p. 66.

12. Riss, *Latter Rain,* p. 63.

13. Read the firsthand account of Pastor Reg Layzell of Vancouver, B.C., who was present. *The Pastor's Pen* compiled by B. M. Gaglardi (Vancouver, B.C.: Mission, 1965), pp. 52–63.

14. *Presbytery* is the plural form of *presbyter.* A presbyter is an elder (*presbuteros,* one who is older, more experienced) or bishop (*episcopos,* an overseer, director, shepherd)—both terms referring to the same individual's respective status and function. See Acts 20:17, 28; Titus 1:5, 7.

15. Richard Riss, *A/G Heritage* (fall 1987), p. 17.

16. Reg Layzell, "My Testimony," *The Sharon Star* (1 February 1949), pp. 1–2. From Riss, *Latter Rain,* pp. 88–89.

17. The dedication and outbreak of revival followed seven years of regular fasting and prayer on the part of the members of the church.

18. By 1949 a number of centers for revival had arisen in North America: in Memphis (Paul N. Grubb); St. Louis (Omar Johnson); Portland (Thomas Wyatt); Los Angeles (A. Earl Lee); Cleveland (L. O. McKinney); Port Arthur, Texas (Charles Green); and other places.

19. Time and space does not allow for a fuller treatment. See Riss, *Latter Rain,* p. 90ff.

20. Gaglardi, *Pastor's Pen,* pp. 8–9.

21. Dick Iverson, foreword in Kevin J. Conner, *Today's Prophets: New Testament Teaching on Today's Prophets* (Portland: BT Publishing, 1989), pp. 2–3.

22. Told to me by David Schoch on June 25, 1994.

23. Gaglardi, *Pastor's Pen*, p. 16.

24. Ivan Q. Spencer, "Who are the Custodians of Latter Rain?" *The Elim Pentecostal Herald* 20, 211 (January 1950), p. 9. See Riss, *Latter Rain*, p. 110.

25. P. G. Chappell, "Healing Movements," p. 372. *Dictionary of Pentecostal and Charismatic Movements* by Stanley M. Burgess, Gary B. McGee and Patrick H. Alexander. Copyright © 1988 by Stanley M. Burgess, Gary B. McGee and Patrick H. Alexander. Used by permission of Zondervan Publishing House.

26. Ibid.

27. Ibid.

28. Bickle, *Growing*, pp. 63–64.

29. The ending of an address by David du Plessis at the opening of the First World Pentecostal Conference in Zurich, Switzerland, in 1947. Riss comments: "Within a few months after these words were spoken, the 'Latter Rain Movement' exploded upon the Pentecostal scene, bringing about the very conditions foreseen by du Plessis, including disapproval from most established denominational Pentecostal organizations." *Latter Rain*, p. 15.

30. Marion Meloon, *Ivan Spencer, Willow in the Wind* (Plainfield, N.J.: Logos, 1974), p. 157.

31. Bill Hamon, *The Eternal Church* (Phoenix: Christian International, c. 1981), p. 249.

32. Hollenweger, *Pentecostals*, p. 355.

Chapter 19: Denominational Response to Prophecy in the Charismatic Renewal

1. For a detailed account see the 31-page article "Charismatic Movement" by P. D. Hocken in *Dictionary of Pentecostal and Charismatic Movements*, pp. 130–160.

2. At the 18th Pentecostal World conference in Seoul, South Korea (in 1998)—as reported by Stephen Strang in "Pentecostals at a Crossroads" in *Charisma* Magazine (November 1998), p. 130—"the conference press office distributed a news release showing that of the 6 billion people on earth, almost 2 billion are Christians, and of these, 540 million are Pentecostals or charismatics." The article also says, "The size of the Pentecostal movement is stag-

gering. Vinson Synan of Regent University says that of the world's 540 million Pentecostals, 52 million are from China, and 92 million are charismatic Catholics. Another 71 million are Protestant charismatics, and 215 million belong to classical Pentecostal denominations. . . ."

3. Lyle E. Schaller, ed., *Creative Leadership Series, Church Growth Strategies that Work* (Nashville: Abingdon, 1980), p. 7.

4. For an interesting, succinct treatment see Riss' *Survey of 20th Century Revival Movements*.

5. Hocken, "Charismatic Movement," p. 156, *Dictionary of Pentecostal and Charismatic Movements* by Stanley M. Burgess, Gary B. McGee and Patrick H. Alexander. Copyright © 1988 by Stanley M. Burgess, Gary B. McGee and Patrick H. Alexander. Used by permission of Zondervan Publishing House.

6. Kilian McDonnell, ed., *Presence, Power, Praise: Documents on the Charismatic Renewal* (Collegeville, Minn.: Liturgical Press, 1980), Vol. I, pp. xix–xx.

7. This conference embraced the West Indies and some adjacent coastal areas.

8. This document was issued by two groups within the same Church: the Church of England Evangelical Council and the Fountain Trust.

9. For ten essays reflecting diverse reactions see Hamilton, *Charismatic Movement*.

10. McDonnell, *Presence*, Vol. 1, Introduction, p. xxii.

11. Ibid., p. xxxvii.

12. Green, *I Believe*, p. 209. After a very fine study on the Holy Spirit, Green closes his book with the 22-page chapter "What To Make of the Charismatic Movement?" He clearly identifies both the positives and the negatives, although I have quoted only the positives.

13. Hocken, "Charismatic Movement," p. 158, *Dictionary of Pentecostal and Charismatic Movements* by Stanley M. Burgess, Gary B. McGee and Patrick H. Alexander. Copyright © 1988 by Stanley M. Burgess, Gary B. McGee and Patrick H. Alexander. Used by permission of Zondervan Publishing House.

Chapter 20: Guidelines for Testing Prophetic Utterances

1. Clifford Hill, *Prophecy*, p. 5.

2. Cooke, *Prophetic Gifting*, p. 145.

3. Dunn, *Unity and Diversity*, p. 178.

4. From the Malines Document I, a statement on the Catholic charismatic renewal (see chapter 19), from the Roman Catholic Church

in 1974 as quoted in McDonnell, *Presence,* Vol. III, p. 59.

5. The church people were apparently wrong in the way they were interpreting the prophetic messages about Paul's imprisonment, and the apostle had to set them straight. He continued on to Jerusalem, feeling that the prophecy gave general information and was not directive in nature. Acts 21:11–14.

6. J. R. Williams, *Era,* p. 29.

7. Cecil M. Robeck Jr., "How Do You Judge a Prophetic Utterance?" *Paraclete* 11:2 (spring 1977), p. 13.

8. Fee, *Empowering Presence,* p. 62.

9. Cooke, *Prophetic Gifting,* p. 151.

10. Pytches, *Prophecy,* pp. 107–108.

11. Bishop Pytches says: "It would be so satisfying and so satisfactory at this stage to be able to set out a fool-proof biblical check-list for anyone to apply at any time. Unfortunately it does not work like that. It is never so simple." *Thundered,* p. 84.

12. Dunn, "New Wine," p. 7.

13. Pytches, *Thundered,* p. xiv.

14. Robeck, "Prophetic Utterance," p. 12.

15. Three helpful sources, for instance, are: Conner, *Today's Prophets,* pp. 26-29; Clifford Hill, *Prophecy,* chapter 13; and "Introducing Prophetic Ministry," *Equipping the Saints* (fall 1989, Vol. 3, No. 4), John Wimber, pub., Kevin Springer, ed.

16. I appreciate in particular two articles by Cecil M. Robeck Jr. In the first, "Prophetic Utterance" (pp. 12–16), he suggests that prophetic problems can be related to three areas. From his good suggestions, I enlarged to six areas. Also, note "Prophetic Authority," pp. 4–10.

17. This is common teaching in charismatic and Pentecostal circles. See, for instance, Roxanne Brant, *How to Test: Prophecy, Preaching, Guidance* (O'Brien, Fla.: Roxanne Brant Ministries, 1981), p. 26ff. Conner, *Church in the New Testament,* p. 167.

18. Rowe, *One Lord,* p. 173.

19. David Aune makes this interesting comment: "The most appropriate English translation for both the noun in 1 Cor. 12:10 and the verb in 1 Cor. 14:29 is 'evaluation' and 'evaluate' respectively, since the term combines the notions of discrimination, interpretation, and examination in a suitably ambiguous way." *Prophecy in Early Christianity,* p. 221.

20. Fee feels that *spirits* refers "to the prophetic utterances that need to be 'differentiated' by the others in the community. . . ." *The First Epistle,* p. 597. James D. G. Dunn feels that our passage "is best understood as an evaluation, an investigating, a testing, a weighing of the prophetic utterance by the rest (of the assembly or of the prophets) to determine both its source as to inspiration and its significance for the assembly. . . ." *Jesus,* p. 234.

21. Dunn, *Jesus,* p. 233; Aune, *Prophecy in Early Christianity,* p. 223; Rowe, *One Lord,* p. 173.

22. It is appropriate to use basic judging criteria from the Old and New Testaments since the general principles apply to prophecy in general and are constant through both Testaments.

23. Ruthven, "A Place for Prophecy?", p. 14.

24. David Hill, "Reports of the Work Groups," *Prophetic Vocation,* p. 232.

25. John Blattner, "Pitfalls of Prophecy and How to Avoid Them," *Equipping the Saints* 3:4 (fall 1989), p. 19.

26. Houston, *Prophecy,* p. 201.

27. Ulf Ekman, *The Prophetic Ministry* (Minneapolis: Word of Life, 1990), p. 210.

28. Alex Buchanan, *Explaining Prophecy* (Chichester, West Sussex: Sovereign World, 1991), p. 43.

29. Barrett, *First Epistle to the Corinthians,* p. 281.

30. Robeck, "Gift of Prophecy," p. 733. *Dictionary of Pentecostal and Charismatic Movements* by Stanley M. Burgess, Gary B. McGee and Patrick H. Alexander. Copyright © 1988 by Stanley M. Burgess, Gary B. McGee and Patrick H. Alexander. Used by permission of Zondervan Publishing House.

31. Eusebius' *Ecclesiastical History* (Grand Rapids: Baker, 1981), p. 86.

32. A question asked by David Watson and quoted by Green, *I Believe,* p. 189.

33. Kydd, *Charismatic Gifts,* p. 2.

34. Ibid., pp. 6–11; *The Didache* 11:4-6, 12.

35. Yocum, *Prophecy,* p. 63.

36. Mallone, *Controversial Gifts,* p. 44.

37. Cecil M. Robeck Jr. in an interview, "David Watson on Spiritual Gifts," *Theology, News & Notes* (June 1987), pp. 16, 29.

38. Brant, *How to Test,* p. 142.

39. James Ryle, *Hippo in the Garden* (Orlando: Creation House, 1993), p. 254.

40. See chapter 22 of this book.

41. Much has been said about the so-called ecstatic state of a biblical prophet. See chapter 5 for my thoughts on the subject. Neither Old nor New Testament prophets were out of con-

trol in their public ministries. See Hayford, *Spiritual Language*, chapter 7.

42. Cooke, *Prophetic Gifting*, pp. 156–168.

43. Russell Chandler, *Doomsday* (Ann Arbor, Mich.: Servant, 1993), p. 293.

44. Bruce Yocum also uses this illustration, and I notice other authors, too, have picked up on the "resonance test." *Prophecy*, p. 115.

45. Schoch, *Prophetic Ministry*, p. 17.

46. Donald Gee, "Missions and Prophets," *Pentecost* 10 (December 1949), p. 17.

47. Robeck, *Prophetic Authority*, p. 8.

48. E. Earl Ellis, "Prophecy in the New Testament Church—and Today," *Prophetic Vocation*, p. 57.

49. Cooke, *Prophetic Gifting*, p. 145.

Chapter 21: Who Judges the Prophecies?

1. Pytches, *Prophecy*, pp. 108–109.

2. Jacobs, *Voice*, p. 57.

3. As quoted by Bruce, *Spreading Flame*, p. 217.

4. Fee, *The First Epistle*, p. 660.

5. Harper, *Prophecy*, p. 27.

6. Weaver, *Healer-Prophet*, p. 8.

7. This list is a rewording and restructuring of "How to Hear and Receive Prophecy" by John Robert Stevens, *Studies on Prophetic Utterance* (Burbank, Calif.: self-published, 1967), p. 24.

8. Unfortunately the KJV has *other* in the singular; the NKJV correctly translates it in the plural.

9. Such as Aune, *Prophecy in Early Christianity*, p. 402 (#36); Arnold Bittlinger, *Gifts and Graces* (Grand Rapids: Eerdmans, 1967), pp. 110–112; Friedrich, "*Prophetes*," *Theological Dictionary of the New Testament*, 6:855; David Hill, *New Testament Prophecy*, p. 133. James D. G. Dunn, a leading scholar in this kind of study, is somewhat evasive, but feels that "in the immediate context" of 14:29, this would be the meaning. *Jesus*, p. 434 (#113).

10. Fee points out that *hoi alloi* ("the others") "basically means 'others different from the subject.' Whereas it could mean 'the rest,' had Paul intended that idea the more correct term would have been *hoi loipoi* . . . [which] would almost certainly have meant 'the rest of the same class,' i.e., prophets. Paul's word could mean. . . in the plural, 'the others that make up the larger group.'" *The First Epistle*, p. 694.

11. See Dunn's discussion, *Jesus*, p. 233ff. Also, Grudem, *Gift of Prophecy*, pp. 70–72.

12. Grudem strongly contends that "'the others' refers to the entire congregation." Ibid., pp. 73–74.

13. Robeck, "Gift of Prophecy," p. 733. Taken from *Dictionary of Pentecostal and Charismatic Movements* by Stanley M. Burgess, Gary B. McGee and Patrick H. Alexander. Copyright © 1988 by Stanley M. Burgess, Gary B. McGee and Patrick H. Alexander. Used by permission of Zondervan Publishing House.

14. Rowe, *One Lord*, p. 272.

15. Ibid., p. 272.

16. Yocum, *Prophecy*, p. 69.

17. The two terms are synonymous as seen in two texts where they are used interchangably to describe the same ministry: Acts 20:17, 28; Titus 1:5, 7.

18. Fee, *The First Epistle*, pp. 694–695. Also, note the confirmation by Chandler, *Functioning Church*, pp. 91–92.

19. Everyone, of course, does not agree. Ralph Martin, for example: "We may dismiss the idea of a church hierarchy deputed to act as arbiters in this matter." *Spirit and Congregation*, p. 81.

20. Jack Hayford, "Despise Not Prophesying," *Ministries Today* (July–August 1989), p. 24.

21. This does not quench the Spirit but enhances the spiritual flow through proper management. A person can be inspired to prophesy and also patient and controlled until an appropiate moment.

22. Yocum, *Prophecy*, p. 63.

23. Rowe, *One Lord*, p. 187.

24. Hayford, "Despise Not Prophesying," p. 24.

25. Jack Hayford, *The Church on the Way* (Lincoln, Va.: Chosen, 1982), p. 105.

26. Hayford, *Spiritual Language*, p. 126.

27. See Clifford Hill's illustration of a Church of England gathering and what might have been. *Prophecy*, p. 285.

28. Suggestions gleaned from Pytches, *Prophecy*, chapters 11–12.

29. Bickle, *Growing*, p. 153.

30. Ibid., p. 156.

31. Ibid.

32. Derek Prince, "How to Judge Prophecy" (Part I), *New Wine* 9:1 (January 1977), p. 15.

33. Donald Gee, *Concerning Spiritual Gifts* (Springfield: Gospel Publishing, 1972 revision), p. 53.

34. Blomgren, *Prophetic Gatherings*, p. 54.

35. Houston, *Prophecy*, p. 170.

36. Robeck, "Gift of Prophecy," p. 738. Taken from *Dictionary of Pentecostal and Charismatic Movements* by Stanley M. Burgess, Gary B. McGee and Patrick H. Alexander. Copyright © 1988 by Stanley M. Burgess, Gary B. McGee and Patrick H. Alexander. Used by permission of Zondervan Publishing House.

Chapter 22: Suggestions for Public Services

1. It is amazing how worshiping people often equate sound with the anointing of the Spirit. This whole experience was an education for us. We learned to worship in spite of sound and sun and architectural differences, and to realize that the Holy Spirit is present in spite of bad acoustics. Near the time we left that building three years later, we had overcome our problems and visitors commented on the beautiful praise and worship that filled the sanctuary! Incidentally, we got to like the Lutheran prayer altar so much that we put the same style into our new sanctuary.

2. *Presbytery* is the plural of *presbyter,* the term used of an elder in the early Church. Every local church should have its regular presbytery team of leaders who sometimes function prophetically. But in our use, the presbyters are guest ministers who do not know the people, thereby enhancing the prophetic dimension.

3. I am aware that there has been much abuse of prophecy. Some years ago in southern California, a church group went overboard in prophecy, holding presbytery-type meetings each week and using their own in-house prophets. The approach became so focused and inclusive that people were told not to make simple decisions of life without prophetic confirmation. I abhor this approach. This particular group got to the point of laying hands on people's heads and publicly declaring so-called revelations based on the bumps they felt on their heads! Delusion unchecked only becomes more confusing. Glenn Foster has said that this indicates people have surrendered "the leadership of the Holy Spirit in their lives to the prophet." *Purpose and Use,* p. 152.

4. Ibid., p. 93.

5. For further information on prophetic presbytery, see my 25-page booklet, *The Prophetic Presbytery in the Local Church* (Portland: BT Publishing, 1990). Also, David Blomgren, *Prophetic Gatherings.*

6. Paul Cain as quoted by Mike Bickle, *Growing,* p. 124.

7. Larry Randolph, *User Friendly Prophecy* (Century City, Calif.: Cherith, 1995), p. 205.

8. David Pytches, *Prophecy,* p. 126.

Chapter 23: Insights on How to Prophesy

1. Blomgren, *Prophetic Gatherings,* p. 43. Also, note these words of W. A. C. Rowe: "It should be realized that at no time is the 'gifted' person deprived of his consciousness and forced to act in a manner generally understood of spiritualist mediums. At no point does the person lose control of himself and he must not consider himself immune from direction, instruction and discipline as to his activity and demeanour." *One Lord,* p. 181.

2. Hayford, *Spiritual Language,* p. 121.

3. Jacobs, *Voice,* p. 86.

4. Foster, *Purpose and Use,* p. 117.

5. Randolph, *Prophecy,* p. 87.

6. Foster, *Purpose and Use,* p. 136.

7. Bickle, *Growing,* p. 134.

8. Foster, *Purpose and Use,* p. 135.

9. Randolph, *Prophecy,* p. 181.

10. Pytches, *Prophecy,* p. 1.

11. Deere, *Surprised by the Power of the Spirit,* p. 65.

12. Foster, *Purpose and Use,* p. 125.

13. Howells, *Prophecy,* lesson 4, p. 4.

14. Bickle, *Growing,* p. 105.

15. Cooke, *Prophetic Gifting,* p. 188.

16. Graham Houston comments, "If prophetic claims appear to be couched in absolutely authoritative terms, as the first-person terminology tends to suggest, there seems to be no room for weighing what is said . . . which is simply not compatible with what Paul taught the Corinthians." *Prophecy,* p. 174.

17. Foster, *Purpose and Use,* p. 15.

18. George Mallone, *Arming for Spiritual Warfare* (Leicester, U.K.: IVP, 1991), chapter 9, quoted by Pytches, *Prophecy,* p. 94.

19. Foster, *Purpose and Use,* p. 82.

20. Bill Hamon says, "I have found that romance, love, and marriage are the most dangerous areas for receiving personal prophecies from others." *Prophets and Personal Prophecy,* p. 78.

21. Foster, *Purpose and Use,* p. 80.

22. This section taken from Ernest B. Gentile, *Position Paper on the Prophetic Ministry* (Portland: Ministers Fellowship International, 1995), p. 14.

BIBLIOGRAPHY

Alden, Robert L. "Ecstasy and the Prophets." *Bulletin of the Evangelical Theological Society* 9 (1966), pp. 149–156.

Allis, Oswald T. *The Unity of Isaiah: A Study of Prophecy.* Presbyterian and Reformed Publishing, 1974.

Archer, Gleason L. *Encyclopedia of Bible Difficulties.* Grand Rapids: Zondervan, 1982.

Armerding, Carl E. and W. Ward Gasque, eds. *A Guide to Biblical Prophecy.* Peabody, Mass.: Hendrickson, 1989.

Arnott, John. *The Father's Blessing.* Orlando: Creation House, 1995.

Ash, James L. "The Decline of Ecstatic Prophecy in the Early Church." *Theological Studies* 36:2 (June 1976), pp. 227–252.

Asch, Sholem, trans. by Maurice Samuel. *The Apostle.* New York: G. P. Putnam's Sons, 1943 reprint.

Aune, David E. "Ecstasy." Geoffrey W. Bromiley, ed. *The International Standard Bible Encyclopedia.* Grand Rapids: Eerdmans, 1982, pp. 4–16.

———. *Prophecy in Early Christianity and the Ancient Mediterranean World.* Grand Rapids: Eerdmans, 1983.

Baker, H. A. *Visions beyond the Veil.* Springdale, Pa.: Whitaker House, 1973.

Barclay, William. *The Letters to the Corinthians.* Philadelphia: Westminster, 1975, rev. ed.

———. *Commentary on Acts.* Philadelphia: Westminster, 1975, rev. ed.

Barnum, Samuel W., ed. "Prophet." *Smith's Comprehensive Dictionary of the Bible.* New York: D. Appleton, 1867, pp. 887–890.

Barrett, C. K. *The First Epistle to the Corinthians.* New York: Harper & Row, 1968.

Bartleman, Frank. *What Really Happened at Azusa Street?* Northridge, Calif.: Voice Christian Publications, 1962.

Bauer, Walter, trans., W. F. Arndt and F. W. Gingrich, eds. *A Greek-English Lexicon of the New Testament and Other Early Christian Literature.* Chicago: University of Chicago, 1957.

Baxter, J. Sidlow. *Explore the Book.* Grand Rapids: Zondervan, 1960.

Bennett, Dennis J. "The Gifts of the Holy Spirit." Michael P. Hamilton, ed. *The Charismatic Movement.* Grand Rapids: Eerdmans, 1975.

Best, Ernest. "Prophets and Preachers." *Scottish Journal of Theology* 12 (1959), pp. 129–150.

Bickle, Mike. *Growing in the Prophetic.* Orlando: Creation House, 1996.

Bittlinger, Arnold. *Gifts and Graces.* Grand Rapids: Eerdmans, 1968.

Blattner, John. "Pitfalls of Prophecy and How to Avoid Them." John Wimber, pub. *Equipping the Saints* 3:4 (fall 1989), p. 19.

Blessitt, Arthur. *Arthur, a Pilgrim.* Hollywood: Blessitt Publishing, 1985.

Blomgren, David K. *Prophetic Gatherings in the Church.* Portland: BT Publishing, 1979.

Bibliography

Boring, M. Eugene. *The Continuing Voice of Jesus: Christian Prophecy in the Gospel Tradition.* Louisville: Westminster/John Knox, 1991.

Brant, Roxanne. *How to Test Prophecy, Preaching, and Guidance.* O'Brien, Fla.: Roxanne Brant Ministries (P.O. Box 1000), 1981.

Bridge, Donald. *Signs and Wonders Today.* Downers Grove, Ill.: InterVarsity, 1985.

Briggs, Charles A. *Messianic Prophecy.* Peabody, Mass.: Hendrickson, 1988 reprint of 1883 ed.

Bromiley, Geoffrey W. "The Charismata in Christian History." *Theology, News & Notes* (March 1974), p. 3.

Bruce, F. F. *The Spreading Flame.* Grand Rapids: Zondervan, 1973 reprint.

———. *The Hard Sayings of Jesus.* Downers Grove, Ill.: InterVarsity, 1983.

———. *The New Testament Documents: Are They Reliable?* Grand Rapids: Eerdmans, 5th ed. 1959.

———. *The Acts of the Apostles.* Grand Rapids: Eerdmans, 1951.

Brumbach, Carl. *Suddenly . . . from Heaven.* Springfield, Mo.: Gospel Publishing, 1961.

Brunner, Emil. *The Misunderstanding of the Church.* Philadelphia: Westminster, 1953.

Buchanan, Alex. *Explaining Prophecy.* Chichester, West Sussex, U.K.: Sovereign World, 1991.

Buckingham, Jamie. "The Prophet's Calling," *Ministries Today* (January/February 1992), pp. 55–63.

Bundy, D. D. "Irving, Edward." Stanley M. Burgess, Gary B. McGee and Patrick H. Alexander, eds., *Dictionary of Pentecostal and Charismatic Movements.* Grand Rapids: Zondervan, 1988.

Burgess, Stanley M. *The Spirit and the Church: Antiquity.* Peabody, Mass.: Hendrickson, 1984.

———, Gary B. McGee and Patrick H. Alexander, eds. *Dictionary of Pentecostal and Charismatic Movements.* Grand Rapids: Zondervan, 1988.

von Campenhausen, Hans. *Ecclesiastical Authority and Spiritual Power in the Church of the First Three Centuries.* Peabody, Mass.: Hendrickson, 1997 reprint of 1969 translation by J. A. Baker.

Cain, Paul. "Hearing God." *MorningStar Journal* 4:1 (1994): 54.

Cartledge, Mark J. "Charismatic Prophecy and New Testament Prophecy." *Themelios* 17:1 (October-November 1991), pp. 17–19.

Cartwright, D. W. "Apostolic Church." Stanley M. Burgess, Gary B. McGee and Patrick H. Alexander, eds., *Dictionary of Pentecostal and Charismatic Movements.* Grand Rapids: Zondervan, 1988.

Chandler, Russell. *Doomsday.* Ann Arbor, Mich.: Servant, 1993.

Chandler, Trevor. *The Functioning Church.* Brisbane, Australia: C. L. Publishing, 1984.

Chappell, P. G. "Healing Movements." Stanley M. Burgess, Gary B. McGee and Patrick H. Alexander, eds. *Dictionary of Pentecostal and Charismatic Movements.* Grand Rapids: Zondervan, 1988.

Chevreau, Guy. *Catch the Fire.* London: Marshall Pickering, 1994.

Christenson, Larry. *A Message to the Charismatic Movement.* Minneapolis: Bethany, 1972.

Clark, Stephen, *Spiritual Gifts*, Pecos, N.M.: Dove, 1969.

Clement, Kim. *The Sound of His Voice.* Orlando: Creation House, 1993.

Conner, Kevin J. *Today's Prophets.* Portland: BT Publishing, 1989.

———. *The Church in the New Testament.* Portland: BT Publishing, 1989.

Cooke, Graham. *Developing Your Prophetic Gifting.* Kent, Sussex, U.K.: Sovereign World, 1994.

Crone, Theodore M. *Early Christian Prophecy: A Study of Its Origin and Function.* Baltimore: St. Mary's University, 1973.

Culver, Robert D. "Nabi." R. Laird Harris, ed. *Theological Wordbook of the Old Testament.* Chicago: Moody, 1980.

Dallimore, Arnold. *The Life of Edward Irving: The Forerunner of the Charismatic Movement.* Carlisle, Pa.: Banner of Truth Trust, 1983.

Damazio, Frank. *Developing the Prophetic Ministry.* Portland: Trilogy Productions, 1983.

Davidson, A. B. "Prophecy and Prophets." James Hastings, ed., *A Dictionary of the Bible.* New York: Charles Scribner's Sons, 1903, pp. 106–127.

DeArteaga, William. *Quenching the Spirit: Examining Centuries of Opposition to the Moving of the Holy Spirit.* Lake Mary, Fla.: Creation House, 1992.

Deere, Jack. *Surprised by the Power of the Spirit.* Grand Rapids: Zondervan, 1993.

———. "Anatomy of a Deception." *The MorningStar Journal* 4:2 (1994), pp. 39–49.

———. *Surprised by the Voice of God.* Grand Rapids: Zondervan, 1996.

Dunn, James D. G. *Baptism in the Holy Spirit.* Philadelphia: Westminster, 1970.

———. "New Wine in Old Wine-Skins: VI. Prophet." *The Expository Times* 85 (1973), pp. 4–8.

———. *Jesus and the Spirit.* Philadelphia: Westminster, 1975.

———. *Unity and Diversity in the New Testament.* Philadelphia: Trinity, 2nd ed., 1990.

Earl, Ralph. "2 Timothy." Frank E. Gaebelein, gen. ed. *The Expositors Bible Commentary.* Grand Rapids: Zondervan, 1978, Vol. 11, p. 409.

Eckman, Ulf. *The Prophetic Ministry.* Minneapolis: Word of Life, 1990.

Edersheim, Alfred. *Bible History: Old Testament.* Peabody, Mass.: Hendrickson, 1995 reprint of 1890 ed.

Elbert, Paul, ed. *Essays on Apostolic Themes: Studies in Honor of Howard M. Ervin.* Peabody, Mass.: Hendrickson, 1985.

Ellis, E. Earle. "Prophecy in the New Testament Church—and Today." J. Panagopoulous, ed. *Prophetic Vocation in the New Testament and Today.* Leiden, The Netherlands: Brill, 1977.

———. *Prophecy and Hermeneutic in Early Christianity.* Grand Rapids: Eerdmans, 1978.

Ellison, H. L. *Men Spake from God.* Grand Rapids: Eerdmans, 1958.

Ervin, Howard M. *Conversion-Initiation and the Baptism in the Holy Spirit.* Peabody, Mass.: Hendrickson, 1984.

Eusebius. *Eusebius' Ecclesiastical History.* Grand Rapids: Baker, 1981.

Fairbairn, Patrick. *Prophecy: Viewed in Respect to Its Distinctive Nature, Its Special Function, and Proper Interpretation.* Grand Rapids: Baker, 1976 reprint from 1865 edition by T. & T. Clark.

Farnell, David F. "Is the Gift of Prophecy for Today?" *Bibliotheca Sacra* (in 4 parts). 149 (1992) July-September, pp. 277–303; 149 (1992) October-December, pp. 387–410; 150 (1993) January–March, pp. 62–88; 150 (1993) April-June, pp. 171–202.

Fee, Gordon D. *The First Epistle to the Corinthians, The New International Commentary on the New Testament.* Grand Rapids: Eerdmans, 1987.

———. *God's Empowering Presence.* Peabody, Mass.: Hendrickson, 1994.

———. *Paul, the Spirit, and the People of God.* Peabody, Mass.: Hendrickson, 1996.

Forbes, Christopher. *Prophecy and Inspired Speech: In Early Christianity and its Hellenistic Environment.* Peabody, Mass.: Hendrickson, 1997 reprint.

Foster, Glenn. *The Purpose and Use of Prophecy.* Glendale, Ariz.: Sweetwater, 1988.

Freeman, Hobart E. *An Introduction to the Old Testament Prophets.* Chicago: Moody, 1968.

Gaglardi, B. M. *The Pastor's Pen.* Vancouver, B.C.: Mission, 1965.

Gee, Donald. *Spiritual Gifts in the Work of the Ministry Today.* Springfield, Mo.: Gospel Publishing, 1936.

———. "Missions and Prophets." *Pentecost* 10 (December 1949), p. 17.

———. "Messages through the Gifts." *Pentecost* 60 (June–August 1962), last page.

———. *Concerning Spiritual Gifts.* Springfield, Mo.: Gospel Publishing, 1972.

Gentile, Ernest B. *The Prophetic Presbytery in the Local Church.* Portland: BT Publishing, 1990.

Bibliography

———. *Worship God! Exploring the Dynamics of Psalmic Worship.* Portland: BT Publishing, 1994.

———. *Position Paper on the Prophetic Ministry.* Portland: Ministers Fellowship International, 1995.

Gillespie, Thomas W. *The First Theologians: A Study in Early Christian Prophecy.* Grand Rapids: Eerdmans, 1994.

Greenspahn, Frederick E. "Why Prophecy Ceased." *Journal of Biblical Literature* 1 (1989), pp. 37–49.

Griffiths, Michael. *Grace-Gifts: Developing What God Has Given the Church.* Grand Rapids: Eerdmans, 1979 reprint.

Grudem, Wayne A. "1 Corinthians 14:20–25: Prophecy and Tongues as Signs of God's Attitude." *Westminster Theological Journal* 41:2 (spring 1979), pp. 381–396.

———. *The Gift of Prophecy in 1 Corinthians.* Lanham, Md.: University Press of America, 1982.

———. *The Gift of Prophecy in the New Testament and Today.* Wheaton, Ill.: Crossway, 1988.

Guy, H. A. *New Testament Prophecy: Its Origin and Significance.* London: Epworth, 1947.

Hall, Franklin. *Atomic Power with God thru Fasting and Prayer.* Franklin Hall, 1946.

Halley, Henry H. *Halley's Bible Handbook.* Grand Rapids: Zondervan, 1965, 24th ed.

Hamilton, Michael P., ed. *The Charismatic Movement.* Grand Rapids: Eerdmans, 1975.

Hamon, Bill. *The Eternal Church.* Phoenix: Christian International Publishers, c. 1981.

———. *Prophets and Personal Prophecy: God's Prophetic Voice Today.* Shippensburg, Pa.: Destiny Image, 1987, Vol. 1.

———. *Prophets and the Prophetic Movement: God's Prophetic Move Today.* Shippensburg, Pa.: Destiny Image, 1990, Vol. 2.

———. *Prophets, Pitfalls and Principles.* Shippensburg, Pa.: Destiny Image, 1991, Vol. 3.

Hanson, Ted J. *The New Testament Prophet.* Bellingham, Wash.: House of Bread, 1996.

Harper, Michael. *Prophecy: A Gift for the Body of Christ.* London: Fountain Trust, 1964.

Harrell, David. *All Things Are Possible: The Healing and Charismatic Revivals in Modern America.* Bloomington, Ind.: Indiana University, 1975.

Harrison, Everett F. "Romans." *Expositor's Bible Commentary.* Grand Rapids: Zondervan, 1976. Vol. 10.

Hayford, Jack W. *The Church on the Way.* Lincoln, Va.: Chosen, 1982.

———. "Despise Not Prophesying." *Ministries Today* (July/August 1989), p. 24.

——— with Gary Matsdorf. *People of the Spirit.* Nashville: Thomas Nelson, 1993.

———. *The Beauty of Spiritual Language.* Nashville: Thomas Nelson, 1996.

Hengstenberg, E. W. *Christology of the Old Testament,* trans. 1854. MacDonald Pub. Co. MacDill AFB, Florida: reprint.

Henry, Carl F. H. "Divine Revelation and the Bible." John F. Walvoord, ed. *Inspiration and Interpretation.* Grand Rapids: Eerdmans, 1957.

Hilber, John W. "Diversity of OT Prophetic Phenomena and NT Prophecy." *Westminster Theological Journal* 56 (1994), pp. 243–258.

Hill, Andrew E. and John H. Walton. *A Survey of the Old Testament.* Grand Rapids: Zondervan, 1991.

Hill, Clifford. *Prophecy Past and Present.* Crowborough, East Sussex: Highland, 1989.

Hill, David. *New Testament Prophecy.* Atlanta: John Knox, 1979.

Hocken, P. D. "Charismatic Movement." Stanley M. Burgess, Gary B. McGee and Patrick H. Alexander, eds. *Dictionary of Pentecostal and Charismatic Movements.* Grand Rapids: Zondervan, 1988, pp. 130–160.

Hodge, Charles. *Systematic Theology.* Grand Rapids: Eerdmans, 1989 reprint, Vol. 1, p. 154.

Hogan, Joseph. "Charisms of the Holy Spirit." *Restoration* (March 1997), p. 8.

Hollenweger, Walter J. *The Pentecostals.* Peabody, Mass.: Hendrickson, 1988 reprint.

Horton, Harold. *The Gifts of the Spirit.* Burbank, Calif.: World MAP, 1979 reprint.

Houston, Graham. *Prophecy: A Gift for Today?* Downers Grove, Ill.: InterVarsity, 1989.

Howells, I. *Prophecy in Doctrine and Practice.* Penygroes, Dyfed, Wales: Apostolic Church Training School, 1931.

Hywel-Davies, Jack. *The Life of Smith Wigglesworth.* Ann Arbor, Mich.: Vine/Servant, 1988.

Jacobs, Cindy. *The Voice of God.* Ventura, Calif.: Regal, 1995.

———. *Women of Destiny.* Ventura, Calif.: Regal, 1995.

Jewett, Paul K. *The Ordination of Women.* Grand Rapids: Eerdmans, 1980.

Jones, Bryn. "Apostles and Prophets: The Vital Role of These Foundational Ministry Gifts." *Issachar Journal* 1:2 (summer 1995), pp. 13, 15–16.

Joyner, Rick. *The Prophetic Ministry.* Charlotte, N.C.: MorningStar, 1997.

Kaiser, Walter C. "*Massa.*" R. Laird Harris, ed. *Theological Wordbook of the Old Testament.* Chicago: Moody, 1980, Vol. II, p. 602.

———. *Back Toward the Future: Hints for Interpreting Prophecy.* Grand Rapids: Baker, 1989.

Kinney, Seeley D. *The Prophetic State.* Portland: Wings of Healing, c. 1950 reprint. Vols. 1 and 2.

———. "Restoration in the Church." *The Banner* 27 (3) (spring 1995):7.

Kistemaker, Simon J. *I Corinthians (New Testament Commentary).* Grand Rapids: Baker, 1993.

———. *Peter and Jude (New Testament Commentary).* Grand Rapids: Baker, 1993.

Knowling, R. J., and W. Robertson Nicoll, eds. *The Expositor's Greek New Testament.* Grand Rapids: Eerdmans, 1951.

Knox, Ronald A. *Enthusiasm.* Westminster, Md.: Christian Classics, 1983.

Kydd, Ronald A. N. *Charismatic Gifts in the Early Church.* Peabody, Mass.: Hendrickson, 1984.

Ladd, George Eldon. *The New Testament and Criticism.* Grand Rapids: Eerdmans, 1967.

Latourette, K. S. *A History of Christianity.* New York: Harper & Row, 1953, Vol. I.

Lindblom, J. *Prophecy in Ancient Israel.* Philadelphia: Muhlenberg, 1973.

Lindsell, Harold. *The Battle for the Bible.* Grand Rapids: Zondervan, 1976.

Linnemann, Eta. *Historical Criticism of the Bible.* Grand Rapids: Baker, 1990.

Livingston, G. H. "Burden." Merrill C. Tenney, gen. ed. *The Zondervan Pictorial Encyclopedia of the Bible.* Grand Rapids: Zondervan, 1975, Vol. 1, p. 671.

Macartney, Clarence E. from the foreword of Oswald T. Allis. *The Unity of Isaiah.* Presbyterian and Reformed Publishing, 1974.

MacRae, A. A. "Prophets and Prophecy." Merrill C. Tenney, gen. ed. *The Zondervan Pictorial Encyclopedia of the Bible.* Grand Rapids: Zondervan, 1975, Vol. 4, p. 875ff.

Malony, H. Newton. "Debunking Some of the Myths about Glossolalia." Cecil M. Robeck Jr., ed. *Charismatic Experiences in History.* Peabody, Mass.: Hendrickson, 1985.

Manson, T. W. *The Sayings of Jesus.* Grand Rapids: Eerdmans, 1979 reprint.

Mare, W. Harold. "Prophet and Teacher in the New Testament Period." *Bulletin of the Evangelical Society* 9:3 (1966), pp. 139–148.

Martin, Ralph P. *Worship in the Early Church.* Grand Rapids: Eerdmans, 1964.

———. *The Spirit and the Congregation.* Grand Rapids: Eerdmans, 1984.

Maudlin, Michael G. "Seers in the Heartland." *Christianity Today* 35 (January 14, 1991), pp. 18–22.

McDonnell, Kilian, ed. *Presence, Power, Praise: Documents of the Charismatic Renewal.* Collegeville, Minn.: Liturgical, 1980. Vols. I, II, III.

McDowell, Josh. *Evidence that Demands a Verdict.* San Bernadino: Here's Life, 25th printing, 1986.

McKeating, H. "The Prophet Jesus—I" and "The Prophet Jesus—II." *The Expository Times* 73 (1961/1962), pp. 4–7; 50–53.

 414

Bibliography

Meloon, Marion. *Ivan Spencer: Willow in the Wind.* Plainfield, N.J.: Logos, 1974.

Millar, J. "Burden." James Hastings, ed. *A Dictionary of the Bible.* New York: Charles Scribner's Sons, 1902, Vol. 1, p. 331.

Moberg, David O. *The Church as a Social Institution.* Englewood Cliffs, N.J.: Prentice-Hall, 1962.

Montague, George T. *The Holy Spirit: Growth of a Biblical Tradition.* New York: Paulist, 1976.

Moule, C. F. D. *The Holy Spirit.* Grand Rapids: Eerdmans, 1979.

Myers, Jacob M. and Freed, Edwin D. "Is Paul Also among the Prophets?" *Interpretation* 20 (1966), pp. 40–53.

Neff, David. "Inside CT: Late Night with John Wimber." *Christianity Today* (January 14, 1991).

Newman, Barclay M. Jr. *A Concise Greek-English Dictionary of the New Testament.* London: United Bible Societies, 1971.

Orr, J. Edwin. *Campus Aflame.* Glendale, Calif.: Gospel Light, 1971.

Panagopoulos, J., ed. *Prophetic Vocation in the New Testament and Today.* Leiden, The Netherlands: Brill, 1977.

Pfeiffer, Charles F. *Between the Testaments.* Grand Rapids: Baker, 1961.

Plaut, Gunther, ed. *The Torah.* New York: Union of American Hebrew Congregations, 1981.

Prince, Derek. "How to Judge Prophecy" (Part I). *New Wine* 9:1 (January 1977), p. 15.

Pusey, E. B. *The Minor Prophets: A Commentary.* Grand Rapids: Baker, 1950, Vol. II.

Pytches, David. *Does God Speak Today?* Minneapolis: Bethany, 1989.

———. *Some Said It Thundered: A Personal Encounter with the Kansas City Prophets.* Nashville: Thomas Nelson, 1991.

———. *Prophecy in the Local Church: A Practical Handbook and Historical Overview.* London: Hodder & Stoughton, 1993.

Randolph, Larry. *User Friendly Prophecy.* Century City, Calif.: Cherith, 1995.

Reiling, Jannes. "Prophecy, the Spirit and the Church." J. Panagopoulous, ed. *Prophetic Vocation in the New Testament and Today.* Leiden, The Netherlands: Brill, 1977: p. 71.

Renwick, A. M. "1 Samuel." *The New Bible Commentary.* Grand Rapids: Zondervan, 1953, p. 265.

Riss, Richard M. *Latter Rain.* Mississauga, Ont.: Honeycomb, 1988.

———. *A Survey of 20th Century Revival Movements in North America.* Peabody, Mass.: Hendrickson, 1988.

Robeck, Cecil M. Jr. "The Gifts of Prophecy in Acts and Paul, Part I." *Studia Biblica et Theologica* Vol. 1 (March 1975), pp. 15–38. Also, Part II, Vol. 2 (October 1975), pp. 37–54.

———. "How Do You Judge Prophetic Utterance?" *Paraclete* 11:2 (spring 1977), pp. 12–15.

———. "Ecclesiastical Authority and the Power of the Spirit." *Paraclete* (summer 1978), pp. 17–23.

———. "The Gift of Prophecy and the All-Sufficiency of Scripture." *Paraclete* 13:1 (winter 1979), pp. 27–31.

———. "Written Prophecies: A Question of Authority." *Pneuma: The Journal of the Society for Pentecostal Studies* 2:2 (fall 1980), pp. 26–45.

———. "Montanism: A Problematic Spirit Movement." *Paraclete* 15:3 (summer 1981), pp. 24–29.

———. "Visions and Prophecy in the Writings of Cyprian." *Paraclete* 16:3 (summer 1982), pp. 21–25.

———. "Prophetic Authority in the Charismatic Setting: The Need to Test." *Theological Renewal* 24 (July 1983), pp. 4–10.

———. "Hippolytus on the Gift of Prophecy." *Paraclete* 17:3 (summer 1983), pp. 22–27.

———. "The Prophet in the Didache." *Paraclete* 18:1 (winter 1984), pp. 16–19.

———. "Prophecy in The Shepherd of Hermas." *Paraclete* 18:2 (spring 1984), pp. 12–17.

————, ed. *Charismatic Experiences in History.* Peabody, Mass.: Hendrickson, 1985.

————. "Canon, Regulae Fidei, and Continuing Revelation in the Early Church." James E. Bradley and Richard A. Muller, eds. *Church, Word, and Spirit: Historical and Theological Essay in Honor of Geoffrey W. Bromiley.* Grand Rapids: Eerdmans,1987, pp. 65–91.

————. "David Watson on Spiritual Gifts" (an interview). *Theology, News & Notes* (June 1987), pp. 11–16.

————. "Prophecy, Gift of." Stanley M. Burgess, Gary B. McGee and Patrick H. Alexander, eds., *Dictionary of Pentecostal and Charismatic Movements.* Grand Rapids: Zondervan, 1988, p. 13.

————. *Prophecy in Carthage: Perpetua, Tertullian, and Cyprian.* Cleveland: Pilgrim, 1992.

Robertson, A. T. *Word Studies in the New Testament.* Nashville: Broadman, 1931. Vol. IV.

Robinson, H. Wheeler. *The Religious Ideas of the Old Testament.* London: Duckworth, 1913.

————. "The Council of Yahweh." *Journal of the Evangelical Theological Society* 45 (1944), pp. 151–157.

Robinson, Theodore H. *Prophecy and the Prophets.* London: Duckworth, 1923.

Rotherham, Joseph Bryant. *The Emphasized Bible.* Grand Rapids: Kregel, 1959 reprint.

Rowe. W. A. C. *One Lord, One Faith.* Bradford, Yorkshire: Puritan, 1960.

Rowley, H. H. *The Servant of the Lord.* Oxford: Basil Blackwell, 1965, 2nd ed.

Rumph, Jane. *Stories from the Front Lines.* Grand Rapids: Chosen, 1996.

Ruthven, Jon. "A Place for Prophecy?" *Paraclete* 6:2 (spring 1972), pp. 8–14.

Ryle, James. *Hippo in the Garden.* Orlando: Creation House, 1993.

Ryrie, Charles C. *The Holy Spirit.* Chicago: Moody, 1965.

Schaff, Philip. *History of the Christian Church.* Grand Rapids: Eerdmans, 1950, Vol. II.

Schaller, Lyle E. *Creative Leadership Series: Church Growth Strategies that Work.* Nashville: Abingdon, 1980.

Schoch, David E. *The Prophetic Ministry.* Long Beach, Calif.: Bethany, 1970.

Shakarian, Demos. *The Happiest People on Earth.* Old Tappan, N.J.: Fleming H. Revell, 1975 reprint.

Sheets, Dutch. *Intercessory Prayer.* Ventura: Regal, 1995.

Skinner, John. *Prophecies and Religion: Studies in the Life of Jeremiah.* London: Cambridge University, 1951 reprint.

Smith, G. V. "Prophecy, False." Geoffrey W. Bromiley, gen. ed. *The International Standard Bible Encyclopedia.* Grand Rapids: Eerdmans, 1982, p. 984.

Smith, William. "Prophet." Samuel W. Barnum, ed. *Smith's Comprehensive Dictionary of the Bible.* London: D. Appleton, 1884, p. 889.

Spittler, R. P. "du Plessis, David Johannes." Stanley M. Burgess, Gary B. McGee and Patrick H. Alexander , eds. *Dictionary of Pentecostal and Charismatic Movements.* Grand Rapids: Zondervan, 1988, pp. 253–254.

Spurgeon, Charles H. *The Treasury of David.* Byron Center, Mich.: Associated Publishers and Authors, 1970 reprint. Vol. II.

————. *Lectures to My Students.* Grand Rapids: Baker Book House, 1977 reprint.

Stevens, John Robert. *Studies on Prophetic Utterance.* Burbank, Calif.: John Robert Stevens, 1960.

Stibbs, Alan M. "The Witness of Scripture to Its Inspiration" (chapter 7). Carl F. H. Henry, ed. *Revelation and the Bible.* Grand Rapids: Baker, 1958.

Stonehouse, Ned B. "Special Revelation as Scriptural" (chapter 5). Carl F. H. Henry, ed. *Revelation and the Bible.* Grand Rapids: Baker, 1958.

Strachan, Gordon. *The Pentecostal Theology of Edward Irving.* Peabody, Mass.: Hendrickson, 1988 reprint of 1973 copyright.

Strang, Stephen. "Pentecostals at a Crossroads." *Charisma* (November 1998): p. 130.

Streeter, B. H. *The Primitive Church.* London: Macmillan, 1930.

Swete, Henry Barclay. *The Holy Spirit in the New Testament.* Grand Rapids: Baker, 1976 reprint.

Bibliography

Thayer, John Henry. *A Greek-English Lexicon of the New Testament.* New York: American Book, 1886.

Thomas, Robert L. "Prophecy Rediscovered? A Review of *The Gift of Prophecy in the New Testament and Today.*" *Bibliotheca Sacra* 149 (January-March 1992), pp. 83–96.

Tidball, Derek. *The Social Context of the New Testament.* UK: Paternoster, 1983.

Tillich, Paul. *A History of Christian Thought.* New York: Harper & Row, 1968.

Towner, W. Sibley. "On Calling People Prophets in 1970." *Interpretation* 24 (October 1970), pp. 495–509.

Towns, Elmer L. "Sociological Background of Postdenominational Church." Pasadena: National Symposium on the Postdenominational Church, Fuller Seminary, May 22, 1996.

Tucker, Gene M. "Prophetic Speech." *Interpretation* 32 (January 1978), pp. 31–39.

Unger, Merrill F. *The Baptism and Gifts of the Holy Spirit.* Chicago: Moody, 1974.

Wace, Henry and William C. Percy, eds. *A Dictionary of Christian Biography.* Peabody, Mass.: Hendrickson, 1994 reprint.

Wagner, C. Peter. "The Gift of Prophecy Is for Today." *Church Growth* (autumn 1994).

———. *Praying with Power: How to Pray Effectively and Hear from God.* Ventura, Calif.: Regal, 1997.

———. *The New Apostolic Churches.* Ventura, Calif.: Regal, 1998.

Watson, David. *I Believe in the Church.* Grand Rapids: Eerdmans, 1978.

Weaver, C. Douglas. *The Healer-Prophet, William Marrion Branham: A Study of the Prophetic in American Pentecostalism.* Macon, Ga.: Mercer University, 1987.

Welldon, J. E. C. *The Revelation of the Holy Spirit.* London: Macmillan, 1902.

White, R. Fowler. "Richard Gaffin and Wayne Grudem on 1 Cor. 13:10: A Comparison of Cessationist and Noncessationist Argumentation." *Journal of the Evangelical Theological Society* 35:2 (June 1992), pp. 173–181.

Whitley, H. C. *Blinded Eagle.* London: SCM Press, 1955.

Williams, Daniel Powell. *The Prophetical Ministry in the Church.* Penygroes, Dyfed, Wales: Apostolic Church Training School, 1931.

Williams, Don. *The Apostle Paul and Women in the Church.* Van Nuys, Calif.: BIM, 1977.

Williams, George H. and Edith Waldvogel. "A History of Speaking in Tongues and Related Gifts." Hamilton, Michael P., ed. *The Charismatic Movement.* Grand Rapids: Eerdmans, 1975.

Williams, J. Rodman. *The Era of the Spirit.* Plainfield, N.J.: Logos, 1971.

———. *Renewal Theology: Salvation, the Holy Spirit, and Christian Living.* Grand Rapids: Zondervan, 1990, Vol. 2.

Williams, James G. "The Prophetic Father." *Journal of Biblical Literature* 85:3 (September 1966), pp. 344–348.

Wilson, R. R. "Early Israelite Prophecy." *Interpretation* 32 (1978), pp. 3, 7.

Wimber, John, pub. "Introducing Prophetic Ministry." *Equipping the Saints* 3:4 (fall 1989).

Wire, Antoinette Clark. *The Corinthian Women Prophets: A Reconstruction through Paul's Rhetoric.* Minneapolis: Fortress, 1990.

Witherington, Ben. *Women and the Genesis of Christianity.* Cambridge: Cambridge University, 1990.

Wood, Leon J. *The Prophets of Israel.* Grand Rapids: Baker, 1979.

Worsfold, James E. *The Origins of the Apostolic Church in Great Britain.* The Julian Literature Trust, P.O. Box 12-555, Thorndon, Wellington, New Zealand, 1991.

Yocum, Bruce. *Prophecy: Exercising the Prophetic Gifts of the Spirit in the Church Today.* Ann Arbor, Mich.: Servant, 1976.

Young, Edward J. *My Servants the Prophets.* Grand Rapids: Eerdmans, 1952.

Zucker, David J. *Israel's Prophets: An Introduction for Christians and Jews.* New York/Mahwah, N.J.: Paulist, 1994.

SUBJECT INDEX

Subject Index

423

NAME INDEX

Name Index

SCRIPTURE INDEX

Scripture Index

Ordained at the age of seventeen, Ernest B. Gentile has been in active ministry for the past 52 years, including pastoring for 41 years. He speaks frequently at ministers' conferences, camp meetings and churches in the U.S. and has ministered in twenty foreign countries. He is noted for his prophetic ministry, unique biblical insights and transparent approach to today's practical problems. In addition to his pastoral ministry, Ernest has been active for the past 36 years in prophetic presbytery ministry in numerous churches across the country. He serves on the Leadership Team of MFI (Ministers Fellowship International), which has ministers in more than thirty nations of the world.

After founding and then pastoring Christian Community Church in San Jose, California, for 33 years, he and his wife, Joy, turned the pastorate over to their son-in-law and daughter. Since then, for the past six years, Ernest and Joy have been active in an extensive traveling ministry.

Ernest has been married 49 years, has four children and four grandchildren, all of whom are serving the Lord. He has a diploma from Bethel Temple Bible School (Seattle), a B.A. from Whitworth College (Spokane) and an M.A. in Biblical Theology from Fuller Theological Seminary (Pasadena). He is the author of Charismatic Catechism (New Leaf Press), Awaken the Dawn! (City Bible Publishing) and Worship God! (City Bible Publishing).

In addition to preaching and teaching, Ernest has a special involvement in prophetic ministry. He travels extensively at home and abroad, mainly with church and ministerial groups that believe in and exercise prophecy. In these circles he is well known for his participation and teaching on the subject. He has done extensive seminary-level research on the subject and consulted with leaders in the field.